INTERNATIONAL BUSINESS CASE STUDIES

THE MCD SERIES
MANAGING CULTURAL DIFFERENCES

Series Editors: Philip R. Harris, Ph.D., and Robert T. Moran, Ph.D.

INTERNATIONAL BUSINESS CASE STUDIES

FOR THE MULTICULTURAL MARKETPLACE

ROBERT T. MORAN, DAVID O. BRAATEN,
AND JOHN E. WALSH, JR., EDITORS

Gulf Publishing Company
Houston, London, Paris, Zurich, Tokyo

International Business Case Studies for the Multicultural Marketplace

Gulf Publishing Company
Book Division
P.O. Box 2608, Houston, Texas 77252-2608

10   9   8   7   6   5   4   3   2

Library of Congress Cataloging-in-Publication Data

Moran, Robert T., 1938–
    International business case studies for the multicultural market-place / Robert T. Moran, David O. Braaten, John E. Walsh, Jr.
      p. cm. — (Managing cultural differences series)
    Includes bibliographical references and index.
    ISBN 0-88415-193-X
    1. International business enterprises—Management—Case studies. 2. Industrial management—Social aspects—Case studies. 3. Intercultural communication—Case studies.   I. Braaten, David O.
II. Walsh, John Edward, 1927– . III. Title. IV. Series.
HD62.4.M665   1994
658′.049—dc20
                                      93-45859
                                      CIP

Printed in the United States of America.

To individuals, working to make their organizations better by studying and benefitting from the approaches of others.

—*Eds.*

To Arlene Braaten, whose encouragement, support and passion make much of what I do possible and to our new son, Joshua.

—*D. B.*

Contents

Global Strategic Alliances

Globalization

International Business Negotiations

International Marketing

International Management

Managing a Culturally Diverse Work Force

International Service Excellence

Acknowledgments

There are many people who made important contributions to this volume of cases:

The individual most responsible for bringing the case study manuscripts, which were submitted in varying stages of readiness, to the publisher is Judith Soccorsy. She worked skillfully and persistently with the editors, their assistants, and many authors.

From the American Graduate School of International Management (Thunderbird) President Roy Herberger, Vice-President David Ricks, and International Studies Department Chairman Lew Howell, who provided support in a number of important ways, including funds to hire several research assistants.

Randy Schilling, Associate Vice-President for Development at Thunderbird, was also supportive.

We are grateful to the Kearny Foundation for its financial support and to Merle A. Hinrichs its chairman for his continuing encouragement of case research.

Dr. Joseph DiStefano as a colleague and friend made many suggestions for improving two of the cases.

We also wish to acknowledge Christine Wilkins who conducted major editorial surgery on first submissions of several cases and Pamela Unternaehrer who made major improvements to earlier drafts of two cases.

Edward M. Luttwak provided all of the primary research material for the Nissan case.

Charles W. Cook, Jr., for his contribution to the Motorola case.

Catherine Gillot for her contribution to the Anheuser Busch case (Great Britain).

Tina Marti, Jane D'Amico, Tina Raynes, and Karen Busch of the Washington University staff who typed the first drafts of many of the cases.

Joe Lombardo who served as an effective editorial assistant on seven cases and as a thoughtful sounding board.

Maria De Lourdes Ballira, a great translator and note taker.

And Wendy Connelly for her hours at the computer.

Series Preface

To thrive and, in many cases, to survive in the 1990s, it is necessary for organizations to globalize in strategy, structure, and people. Companies have realized that developing strategies or managing people as if the internal and external environments of the organization had not changed is a major mistake. "Bashing" others rather than taking the inward journey and becoming a revolutionary learning organization is dysfunctional and counterproductive to corporate survival. As expected, many organizations in various countries have taken the inward journey and are effectively managing this challenge. Some are not.

The *Managing Cultural Differences Series* is intended to stimulate and support the effort of globalization in all of its dimensions. The books have been widely accepted in academic circles and by practicing internationalists.

As series editors, we are pleased that Gulf Publishing Company has risen to the challenge of addressing questions of people, cultures, organizations, and strategy in a rapidly changing, highly interdependent community.

Philip R. Harris, Ph.D.
Robert T. Moran, Ph.D.

Foreword

To understand the complexities of the changing global environment, executives, managers, and graduate students must use a variety of approaches. The case study method is one of a number of effective teaching strategies used in more and more graduate schools including Thunderbird.

This book of cases is unique in several ways. First, the thirty-six cases are all interactive illustrating the cultural diversity of people, products, and issues as they come together—and can be taught cross-functionally. Second, there are no "arm chair" cases. All are based on actual business experiences. Third, there is a geographical balance in the selection of countries such as Japan, Mexico, South Africa, Yugoslavia, United States, Korea, Singapore, and Germany among others. In most instances, the perspective of each side (country, culture, and organization) is presented.

The thirty-six cases are divided into seven sections, Global Strategic Alliances (12 cases), Globalization (3 cases), International Business Negotiations (3 cases), International Marketing (6 cases), International Management (6 cases), Managing a Culturally Diverse Work Force (4 cases), and International Service Excellence (2 cases).

A careful study of the cases on these topics will provide professors, business students, and persons working in the international area with some of the additional tools required to understand and implement their business strategies in the 1990s.

Professors Moran, Braaten, and Walsh are to be complimented for further developing the *Managing Cultural Differences Series* with their book of cases. *Managing Cultural Differences* has been enormously successful over the past 13 years. I anticipate that *International Business Case Studies* will add to this success, but more importantly contribute to the further education of persons working in the global arena.

David A. Ricks
Vice-President, Academic Affairs
Thunderbird—The American
Graduate School of
International Management

INTERNATIONAL BUSINESS CASE STUDIES

Chapter 1
The New China Hotel in Beijing

Yuen Ching Karen Lee
and
Su-ging Wang

The New China Hotel

Spring 1987 in Beijing, China was unusually cold, ironically appropriate considering the icy state of relations between Peter Morris and his company, the Asian Development Corporation (ADC), and its Chinese joint venture partner, the Yellow River Tourist Service (YRTS) for the New China Hotel (NCH) project. After years of futile attempts to salvage the alliance, Morris, vice-chairman of the board of directors of the New China Hotel in Beijing, had just settled an agreement with his Chinese counterparts to withdraw ADC's equity investment in the hotel.

Close to a decade later, he still vividly recalled the day the Foreign Investment Commission in the People's Republic of China broke the news of the venture to the *Asian Wall Street Journal*. In December of 1979, the commission announced its informal approval of the New China Hotel alliance between ADC and YRTS. Ecstatic upon receiving permission to pursue the project, Morris considered this a major success, because it was one of a rare handful of large joint ventures allowed in the early days of China's "open-door policy." By 1985, however, soon after the hotel unofficially opened, ADC reluctantly opted to relinquish its interest in the project. Two years later in 1987, the company finally ended a series of long, bitter negotiations with YRTS and reduced its investment to a mere 10% from its original share of 51%.

This case was written by Yuen Ching Karen Lee and Su-ging Wang under the supervision of Professor Robert T. Moran, as a vehicle for discussion rather than to illustrate either the effective or ineffective handling of business situations. Although this case includes factual information, based on actual situations, the real names of the company have been changed.

Stealing a last glance at the glittering glass wall facade of the hotel before departing for Los Angeles, Morris remained convinced that the joint venture had been a sound strategic decision for ADC, one in line with the company's desire to enter the Chinese market. He was at present, however, reevaluating the decision-making and negotiation process to identify any miscalculations and false expectations that may have contributed to the grave problems ADC encountered, particularly those related to the deeply implanted Chinese bureaucracy.

China's Open Door Policy

The end of the 1970s marked a significant change in China's economic strategy with the government's implementation of a new "open-door" policy. Prior to this, the nation adhered to a strict program of import-substitution. Few goods and services were imported, and international trade was severely curtailed, except limited trade activity with Western Europe. Trade between the U.S. and China was, for the most part, non-existent. Foreign investment was discouraged, the economy was centrally-planned, and little, if any, private ownership was allowed.

In the late 1970s, China announced a new open-door policy that welcomed and actively sought foreign capital to finance modernization projects. Foreign investments were evaluated and approved based upon their ability to attract the foreign currency, Western technology, and management skills the Chinese needed to revamp the economy.

In the early stages of this relatively liberal policy, joint ventures emerged as the most common structure of foreign investment projects, because this form allowed Chinese partners to gain management skills and access to new technology. However, the Chinese government severely restricted long-term and permanent foreign ownership. Generally, joint venture agreements ranged in duration from ten to twenty-five years, and foreign investors were prohibited from holding a majority interest.

Hotel Industry in China

Tourism ranked as an important sector of the open door policy due to its ability to generate foreign currency earnings to finance development of other industries. Existing hotel and tourism facilities, however, were underdeveloped and incapable of meeting the demands of growing numbers of tourists and business people. In response to the need for more and better hotels, several hotel chains rushed to China to propose projects.

New China Hotel

The New China Hotel, among the first world-class hotels in Beijing, the Chinese capital, opened in 1984. Prior to this, many guest houses and inns were available to local travelers; however, relatively few were equipped with facilities capable of accommodating foreign visitors according to Chinese government standards. Beijing Hotel, despite its poor amenities and limited services, was the best available. The Diaoyutai Hotel, which surpassed the level of comfort and service offered by other lodges, was reserved for government and foreign officials.

To be jointly constructed and managed by ADC and YRTS, the NCH project was designed as a 1,000-room luxury hotel with seven restaurants and delicatessens. Located within a ten-minute drive to the city center and situated on the road to the airport, the hotel was built to attract both tourists and business travelers.

The Asian Development Company

The Asian Development Company (ADC) was owned by the Asian Investment Corporation (AIC) and Webb International Corporation, both U.S.-based companies. AIC, formed in April 1979 and owned by the Bergel Group of Companies and Eastern Construction Company, specialized in consortium joint ventures and compensation deals in China. The Bergel Group, a pioneer with more than thirty years of experience in project development in the former Soviet Union and Eastern Europe, extended its business into China in 1978. When the deal with YRTS to construct the New China Hotel came to fruition in 1979, AIC engineered a consortium to establish ADC, the entity that eventually entered into the 49% equity joint venture with YRTS for the New China Hotel.

Peter Morris, executive vice-chairman and general manager of ADC, participated as a member of the negotiation team involved in the initial meetings with YRTS. Reflecting later upon ADC's enthusiasm in the early stages, Morris noted the company's expectations of an excellent return on its investment due to considerably lower construction costs, cheaper labor, and forecasted inflows of hard currency immediately upon the hotel's opening.

The company was confident that it could draw on its previous success in similar hotel projects in such socialist countries as Hungary, Rumania, Cuba, and the former Soviet Union. In fact, its experience, acquired through years of dealing with the business practices and mentalities ingrained in planned economies, constituted the company's greatest competitive advantage in the bidding process.

Project Negotiations

The Bergel Group, neither large nor an international hotel chain, won the right to pursue the project amid strong competition from several competitors, including Hilton and Inter-Continental. According to the Foreign Investment Commission, which approved the YRTS-ADC joint venture, size factored only nominally in the decision; instead, the terms a foreign partner set forth were crucial.

Project Team

In late 1978, ADC assembled a project team comprising several members with expertise in diverse areas related to the venture. The crew consisted of Peter Morris, several experienced negotiators, a project manager, a construction manager, several design experts, a project finance expert, and, most importantly, two China experts. Most team members possessed extensive experience in project management in Eastern Europe, and many spoke Chinese and were familiar with Chinese culture. Of the two experts, both overseas Chinese-Americans, K.C. Tung, chairman of the Eastern Construction Company, was born in China and educated in the U.S. The other, David Chen, born and educated in the U.S., lived in China for several years prior to liberation.

Morris later commented on Tung's and Chen's negotiating skills: "We understood that the Chinese regard modesty as a virtue, and that many Americans are often arrogant when conducting international business. They don't realize that aggressive salesmanship does not work in China and, therefore, seem unable to comprehend why negotiations invariably stall. Be a Roman when in Rome; that's why we tried our best to adapt to Chinese customs, regulations, methods and requirements."

The China experts, through excellent connections in the government, soon found themselves acquainted with officials of YRTS, a state organization charged with promoting and regulating travel nationwide. Because of China's dire need for additional, modern hotel facilities to develop its tourism sector, YRTS and the Beijing municipal government aggressively sought foreign investment and participation in hotel construction projects.

By February 1979, a few months after the ADC team initiated preliminary attempts to enter the Chinese hotel market, the company succeeded in securing letters of intent from both YRTS and the municipal government. According to these documents, ADC retained responsibility for administration of the financing, design, construction management, and foreign procurement activities. The Chinese partners agreed to provide the site, necessary Chinese government approvals, certain project materials, and hotel construction and operations labor.

Morris was thrilled about the letters of intent, until discovering that YRTS and the municipal government had signed similar documents with other hotel groups. In the U.S., these agreements constituted a commitment that both parties would work together until a deal was consummated or abandoned. To ADC's dismay, in China, letters of intent were neither binding nor exclusive. A Chinese ministry might, as it appeared that YRTS and the local government had done, sign a similar letter with several companies.

Slow progress in moving forward to the next stage of the negotiations after the signing of the agreement spurred ADC's realization that both YRTS and the municipal government were continuing to discuss proposals with other prospective partners. At this point, the importance of negotiating directly with the key decision-maker and of structuring an extremely appealing offer struck the team. Tung and

Chen immediately began delving into the layers of the Chinese bureaucracy and ultimately succeeded in identifying the general secretary of the YRTS as the official who held the true decision-making power.

Keys to Success

Acknowledging that a principal weakness in China's attempts at modernization stemmed from an acute shortage of foreign currency, the ADC team focused on its ability to circumvent this problem. By designing its offer to successfully address this issue, ADC believed it would greatly enhance the probability of securing approval of the project.

In most centrally-planned economies, the central bank acts as the prime guarantor for repayment of loans to foreign lenders. However, as elsewhere in the socialist world, China's hard currency reserves were quite limited. Thus, the Bank of China had proven unwilling to offer financial guarantees for joint ventures. In fact, numerous foreign companies had expended significant amounts of capital to develop, bid for, and secure projects in China, only to ultimately fail because they were incapable of gaining approval for foreign loans due to the bank's refusal to act as guarantor.

Morris knew that the key to the project's success involved ensuring ADC's ability to secure financing, a lesson learned through the team's collective experience in the former Soviet Union and Eastern Europe. Based upon previous joint venture proposals accepted by East European governments, the team's initial plan emphasized the point that financing for the project would not involve guarantees from the Bank of China. Under the company's plan, lenders would be assured that the partners would be held jointly liable for repayment of loans and that a steady stream of hard foreign currency earnings would be immediately directed toward debt service upon the hotel's opening. These earnings would be received by customers who would be required to pay in foreign currency or "foreign exchange certificates," a special form of exchange in China.

Furthermore, during an April meeting with the secretary of YRTS, the ADC team presented a unique proposal concerning interest rates to its prospective Chinese partner. To counter YRTS assertions that the prevailing world commercial prime lending rate was too high to attain governmental approval, ADC offered YRTS a lower fixed interest rate than the prevailing 8–8½%. The difference between this fixed rate and the variable global rate would be paid by ADC.

A crucial final decision remained at this point: selecting a partner for the project. In a centrally-planned economy, an influential and powerful partner offers significant advantages to a venture, including facilitating procurement and government approvals. After extensive consideration, ADC selected YRTS based upon the belief that, as a nationwide ministry charged with promoting and regulating travel in China, it would offer greater benefits than the municipal government. This view was later substantiated; YRTS swiftly obtained the required approvals from more than 25 various government departments, bureaus, and ministries.

The Joint Venture Contract

ADC's efforts were rewarded in May 1979, at which time it signed a formal joint venture agreement with YRTS. Although binding, the document was subject to the terms of a final contract to be negotiated within five months. The size, class, and site of the hotel, as well as the method of cooperation, division of profits and losses and period of joint operation, were outlined in the agreement. The duration of the project was set at ten years; at the end of this period, ADC would be required to relinquish all rights of ownership to YRTS. The contract also described promises made by YRTS concerning certain guarantees related to the repayment of loans and the repatriation of profits.

In the early stages of the open door policy, China had not yet developed a comprehensive commercial law. Thus, a procedure to be followed in the case of a dispute between the two parties was also set forth in the joint venture agreement. The Chinese partner insisted, and ADC acquiesced, on the exercise of the principle of "mutual discussion and agreement" to resolve future conflicts. This meant that all disagreements would be settled in China under Chinese law.

The absence of an established commercial law fueled foreign skepticism concerning the methods that the Chinese would use to enforce "mutual discussion or agreement." However, ADC, enthusiastic about concluding negotiations and beginning the project, dismissed its reservations about the clause and proceeded to finalize the contract. At the time, Morris never dreamed that one day he would be haunted by the Chinese principle of "mutual discussion" to which he so easily agreed.

In October 1979, the final joint venture contract was signed. YRTS and ADC drafted contracts in both Chinese and English, both of which were binding. ADC employed its own lawyers and translators to ensure that the English contract was identical to the Chinese one. Achieving perfect translations, however, proved nearly impossible, because the two languages differ greatly in syntax and concept. Poor translation quality further complicated the task and resulted in numerous discrepancies between the two versions. Though the ADC team was assisted by its two China experts, they could not be held responsible for flawless translation and a failure to detect subtle errors. Thus, the team relied heavily upon its lawyers, who in turn counted upon their translators. In the end, although each party certified that the agreements carried the same content, numerous discrepancies still existed at the time the contracts were signed.

Financing of the Project

From the outset, ADC intended to avoid contributing its corporate capital to the project. Rather, the company planned to fully finance the project costs, estimated at $72 million, through bank loans. To accomplish this goal, ADC created a financial plan based on two assumptions. First, ADC was confident that the hotel would immediately generate substantial hard currency cash flows upon opening, given expectations of high occupancy and low labor costs. Second, the company predicted that the total debt incurred would be self-liquidating within six to ten years. Some time later, Peter Morris revealed that ADC initially anticipated earning a $40 to $50 million profit from its 49% share over the project's duration.

To allay the prospective lenders' fears of default, ADC secured the YRTS's commitment to joint liability for 100% of the outstanding debt. Initially, however, YRTS agreed to undertake responsibility for only 51% of the loan in accordance with its share of the hotel. Lacking extensive exposure to, and understanding of, international financing, YRTS failed to comprehend the common international lending practice that required all parties of a joint venture to be jointly and severally liable for the full sum of the debt incurred. After several weeks, ADC eventually convinced its Chinese partners of the necessity of agreeing to the joint liability clause.

Describing the resolution of this conflict, Tung remarked, "At first, they were adamant that they retain responsibility for only 51% of the debt. Later, YRTS realized that it's an international practice and that stubbornness on its part would only hurt the joint venture. But, because the Chinese are proud of their history and culture and hate losing face, we had to take care not to upset our partners. So, we acted as if we, too, were learning about the process, and we worked together to determine the best solution."

Because the bank loan was to be repaid from operating profits, the joint venture established a moratorium on debt service during the construction period. After operations commenced, all revenues would be deposited into a loan amortization account, from which funds would be transferred to another account for operations.

By the fall of 1980, the joint venture secured a $72 million syndicated loan to finance construction. The syndicate was headed by the Nordic Bank Limited of Norway, and, not surprisingly, the Bank of China participated in the financing coalition. Under the terms of the contract, YRTS would pay a fixed interest rate lower than the 8% prime lending rate. ADC assumed responsibility for payment of the difference between the fixed and market rates, a stipulation that proved devastating when the prime lending rate skyrocketed to 20% in 1983.

The Construction Process

In May 1980, the Foreign Investment Commission formally approved the New China Hotel, Ltd. ADC, though contractually responsible for the structure's design, was required to obtain approval by YRTS. The design, a modern structure with a glass wall curtain facade submitted by an American architectural firm hired to provide design and construction expertise, delighted the Chinese.

However, although YRTS quickly agreed to the project's design, several misunderstandings concerning the construction of the hotel occurred. The most serious transpired at a mid-1980 meeting during which the Chinese admitted their lack of expertise in construction management. Interpreting this confession to mean that the Chinese wished for the hotel to be built on a turnkey basis, the American directors arranged to hire a foreign contractor to undertake the entire construction project. To the Americans' surprise during the next directors' meeting, the proposal to invite bids for the job from foreign construction firms was met by an icy response from the Chinese.

At this point, the ADC team realized that a serious communication gap concerning the construction process existed. The Chinese did not want to hire a foreign firm to complete the project entirely; YRTS hoped to absorb the advanced building technology and skills by working on the project together with a foreign firm. Eventually, the architectural company in Los Angeles was assigned responsibility for design and construction management activities, while Beijing's Construction Company would undertake the actual construction work. This misunderstanding concerning management of the construction process constituted the first in a series of obstacles that culminated in the current bitter situation between YRTS and ADC.

Construction of the hotel began at the end of 1980. At that time, the Los Angeles architectural firm provided a set of designs to Beijing's Construction Company. The latter, however, complained that the drawings did not include detailed shop drawings, another problem originating from conflicting cultural norms. In China, architects supply both work and shop drawings, while architects in the U.S. provide work drawings only. The Beijing Construction Company's resentment grew upon discovering that the American engineers on the construction management team could not produce the expected shop drawings, a fact subsequently reported to the Chinese directors.

Unease on the part of the American team was evident as well, especially related to concerns about delays in the construction schedule. At the outset, the project was planned to be completed within 24 to 26 months. Remaining optimistic about its ability to meet the target completion date in January 1983, ADC believed that its Chinese partner was equally committed to finishing the hotel on time. It was also confident of the ability of the Chinese labor to quickly learn to use new construction techniques and advanced equipment. To ADC's disappointment, however, the construction process was poorly managed, and labor was exceptionally unskilled. Thus, progress was slow, and the quality was sub-standard.

These factors, and several others, resulted in numerous construction delays. First, the Chinese construction workers, mostly farmers from the rural areas, experienced great difficulty in delivering an acceptable standard of building quality and learning the new technology. Furthermore, the government-owned Beijing's Construction Company was completely unfamiliar with Western building technology and construction management practices. Though assisted by the American engineers, the company lacked the experience and expertise to ensure adherence to the construction time line. Moreover, the BCC's slow and bureaucratic decision-making style hindered the company's ability to make the quick decisions and handle crisis situations necessary to avoid project setbacks. Furthermore, the Construction Management Team, composed of both American engineers and several YRTS-appointed members, was less effective than expected. The inexperience of the Chinese members in managing large construction projects especially impeded progress.

Financial Crisis

Near the end of 1981, the $72 million construction fund reached the point of exhaustion. ADC proposed borrowing more to continue construction, but YRTS refused, knowing that the Chinese government would deny requests for additional funding. A deadlock resulted, and construction halted. Though resolution of the impasse in accordance with the principle of "mutual agreement" clearly failed at this stage, YRTS, fearful of losing face, continued to attempt to solve the problem according to Chinese law. ADC requested, but was not provided with, a copy of the Chinese commercial law to consult in hopes of ending the standstill. In fact, no comprehensive commercial law existed at the time.

YRTS sensed the pressure increasing daily. Failure of the joint venture would lead not only to serious financial losses, but also to a loss of face and negative publicity that would profoundly dampen investors' confidence in China.

In early 1982, YRTS resumed negotiations with ADC in search of a solution. An agreement was finally reached under which YRTS agreed to finance all subsequent costs required to complete the remaining construction work. For its part, ADC agreed to delay the hotel completion date until the end of 1984, two years after the original deadline. Moreover, according to the settlement, if YRTS failed to meet the new project deadline, it would be held responsible and would be required to compensate ADC for losses resulting from the delay.

In December 1984, YRTS unofficially opened the New China Hotel to avoid incurring the damages that it was liable for to ADC as specified in the newest agreement. At the time, only 300 of the 1,000 rooms and one of the seven planned restaurants were ready. Six months later, the hotel was completed and officially began operations in June 1985.

The Break-Up

At this point, dissolution of the partnership between YRTS and ADC appeared imminent. The bitterness, initiated during the construction period and never completely overcome, intensified as a result of numerous problems arising from disparate management styles and the ambiguity and discrepancies inherent in the Chinese and English versions of the joint venture contract. A final blow to the relationship occurred in 1986 when ADC was denied the right to repatriate profits to the U.S. as a result of a serious shortage of capital experienced by YRTS. Soon after, ADC demanded to be allowed to extract itself from the partnership, and YRTS contracted with another international hotel group to manage the hotel.

Final Settlement

In 1987, Morris reached an agreement with his Chinese counterparts to end the two-year-long negotiation process. ADC reduced its equity interest in the hotel to 10% and received some financial compensation, leaving YRTS with a controlling share of 90%.

Disappointed and disillusioned, Morris continued to reflect upon the situation during his final drive from the hotel to the airport. As he reviewed the past several years, he wondered if the problems that ultimately caused the project to fail to meet ADC's expectations could have been avoided, and, if so, how. While he still believed that entering the joint venture to develop the New China Hotel had been a sound decision for ADC, he realized that the risks inherent in conducting business in China may not have been outweighed by the potential returns in the case of the New China Hotel.

2
Tentative Withdrawal from a Joint Venture: Shalimar Laboratories, Ltd.

John E. Walsh, Jr.

Shalimar Laboratories, Limited

Henry Chesterfield, executive vice-president of the Thorndike Pharmaceutical Company, called Harrington Stuart, the recently promoted general manager of the Aspirin Division, to his office.

When Stuart appeared, Chesterfield said, "I want you to go to Bombay, India, the day after tomorrow. As you know, we have a piqued and alienated partner, Dr. Dara Rau, president of Shalimar Laboratories, who deeply resents our tentative decision to withdraw from our joint venture in the production of aspirin and salicylic acid. He has reacted with bitterness and vengeance by denouncing us to Indian businessmen and government officials. He has even erroneously proclaimed that we are pulling out of India entirely.

"In an effort to spare himself embarrassment, John Coleman, our area director in New Delhi, told Dr. Rau that the tentative decision to withdraw had been initiated in the United States, which of course isn't quite true. Our president, George Thorndike, does believe that India is politically unstable. Two political leaders have been assassinated, and the country suffers from deep seated strife between Hindus and Muslims. And, in my priorities, India does not rate very high. But, the decision to divest was based largely on Coleman's recommendations.

"The aspirin division is your responsibility now, so I would like you to fax Dr. Rau to inform him of your visit. I'll want to hear your evaluation of him when you return."

The flight to Bombay was long, providing Harrington Stuart with ample time to thoroughly review the project files he had brought with him. The first page of the first file explained how the joint venture had originated. Almost ten years ago, Dr. Rau had sent a letter to George Thorndike, requesting technical assistance in the processing of aspirin. Thorndike considered India a high-risk country plagued with bureaucratic red tape and, in his reply, had expressed only mild interest in Dr. Rau's proposal. Several months later, however, his feelings changed. Apparently, several executives in the company managed to convince him of the wisdom of making a small investment in India to learn about doing business there, to develop a market for salicylates, and to use a joint-venture company as a manufacturing vehicle for other products. A background investigation of Dr. Rau conducted by reliable informants indicated that he was a responsible person and that his laboratory had sound equipment, but inadequate technology.

Thus, the decision to establish the joint venture company was made. Thorndike Pharmaceutical Company: (1) purchased 42% of the equity of Shalimar Laboratories for $35,000 in cash and used aspirin processing equipment valued at $53,500; (2) was designated the sole selling agent of aspirin and salicylates; (3) was allowed to appoint a member to the board of Shalimar Laboratories; and (4) was to provide, for one year, the services of a technical advisor who was to improve the process of producing salicylic acid.

Because of a lack of proper equipment and competitive pressures, the joint venture company lost money during the first year. To improve the situation, a new agreement was negotiated with the government of India and with Shalimar Laboratories, whereby Thorndike Pharmaceutical Company would obtain 50% of the equity capital of Shalimar Laboratories and undertake the technical management of the company. More equity was sought, but the government, at that time, limited equity participation to a maximum of 50%. Administrative control of Thorndike Pharmaceutical Company was arrived at by appointing an equal number of directors from Shalimar Laboratories and Thorndike Pharmaceuticals.

Thorndike Pharmaceutical Company invested an additional $95,000 in Shalimar Laboratories and extended to the company a loan of $220,000, which could be converted into equity in five years if Dr. Rau or other Indian nationals invested a similar amount. Both the equity contribution and the loan, with the exception of $8,750 cash for the purchase of shares from Dr. Rau, were provided to Shalimar Laboratories in the form of used processing equipment or equipment to be purchased in convertible currencies outside India.

Also, under the terms of the agreement, Glenn Prescott, a Thorndike Pharmaceutical Company engineer, was appointed technical manager of Shalimar Laboratories and assigned to India for a five-year tenure. Thorndike Pharmaceutical Company, as the sole selling agent, was guaranteed receipt of a 3% royalty for ten years on Shalimar Laboratories' net sales and a 10% commission on sales.

Additional loans of $52,500 were advanced to Shalimar Laboratories during the next two years according to the same conditions as the original loan. Thorndike

Pharmaceutical Company's equity capital on December 31 last year was $183,500, and its convertible loans were $325,000. Total gross investment in Shalimar Laboratories reached approximately $1,000,000, including total equity capital of $300,000.

As Stuart's flight was nearing its end, enough time remained to read the next report in the file concerning Glenn Prescott's end-of-assignment account. Highlights of the report are shown in Appendix A at the end of this chapter.

Harrington Stuart in Bombay

On the morning after his arrival in Bombay, Stuart was sitting in the lobby of the Taj Mahal Hotel when he heard a man say in rapid but understandable English, "I beg your pardon, but are you Mr. Harrington Stuart?"

Looking up, he saw a short, slim, neatly dressed Indian in his late forties with a dark face, sharp features, and sleek black hair. He could not help but notice the man's brown, lustrous eyes observing him intently. "Yes, I am," he replied, "and are you Dr. Rau?" "That's correct," the man said crisply and promptly handed him a card. It read:

Shalimar Laboratories Private Limited

Khardi, India

Dr. Dara Rau, B.A., B.S., M.D.

President

Harrington Stuart glanced at it quickly and put it in his pocket.

"Shall we visit the plant?" Dr. Rau asked. "You should see it. I have an automobile, and it is less than 70 miles from here."

Then, he paused for a moment, as if to make his next statement more dramatic and effective. "I've been greatly distressed by the decision of your company to end our joint venture. I can't understand why. After you've seen the plant, perhaps we can have some time together to discuss this matter."

"Why, of course we can discuss it, Dr. Rau," Harrington Stuart replied, "and I can appreciate your concern."

The drive to Shalimar Laboratories presented a kaleidoscopic view of life in India. First, they drove through the industrial suburbs of the city, with their oil refineries, steel mills, and rectangular housing estates. Beyond the suburbs, they passed ubiquitous villages and Hindu temples, people of all ages riding on oxcarts and camels or walking.

During most of the trip Dr. Rau was silent and intense, which made him seem furtive and suspicious. He failed to respond to Stuart's humor and wit and displayed none of his own. To Stuart he appeared completely devoid of the energetic, dynamic, confident personality that might be expected of an entrepreneur.

They reached the plant in less than two hours, and Stuart was immediately introduced to Mr. Patel, the plant manager, and Mr. Gor, the plant engineer. The plant was considerably larger than he had expected. It comprised an office building, two large warehouses, three processing buildings, a boiler room, and a machine shop.

The plant site spanned almost thirty acres and the processing equipment was modern and operational.

All shipping was completed by truck, but perhaps a railway spur line not far away could be brought into the plant. Because there was only one telephone line into the plant, he suspected that telephone service was poor.

At the outset Stuart asked Dr. Rau a succession of questions and in return received several ambiguous answers. He concluded that Dr. Rau tried to give the appearance of knowing more than he did. He then turned to Mr. Patel and Mr. Gor and asked them questions about wages, employee housing, plant capacity and sources of raw materials, and costs of power and fuel oil.

The questioning stopped abruptly when Dr. Rau mentioned that it was time for lunch. After lunch, Stuart probed deeper to gain a complete understanding of the plant's operation. The hours passed quickly. Sometime later, Dr. Rau, a glitter of moisture on his brow, winced, wrung his hands, and said, "It's getting late, and we must return to Bombay. If we don't return before the work day ends, we will find ourselves completely snarled in traffic."

Dr. Rau's Concern for the Joint Venture

It was during the return trip that Dr. Rau returned to the question that was paramount in his mind. "Why is Thorndike Pharmaceutical Company ending the joint venture? Is it because you are pulling out of India?"

"We are not pulling out of India entirely, and the final decision concerning divestment in our joint venture hasn't been made," Harrington Stuart answered. "Many points remain to be considered. One reason I am here is to take another long and appraising look at our joint venture. A good deal of our senior executives' time and energy has been spent on this project. In relation to our total investments, though, the project is exceedingly small. Several of our top executives feel that this operation should be your domain, not ours. As you know, most of the technical problems have been solved, and you could well become one of the leading Indian entrepreneurs in the pharmaceutical field."

"But how am I to obtain funds without your backing and increased sales without your prestige?" Dr. Rau asked gravely.

"Regarding your first question, I think we have enough contacts in India to enable us to assist you in obtaining loans," Stuart replied. "As for the second, Shalimar Laboratories possesses a fine reputation with or without us."

This statement seemed to please him, at least for the moment. Shortly before they reached the suburbs of Bombay, he invited Stuart to his home for dinner, and the invitation was accepted.

That evening, Stuart, who believed himself a connoisseur of good food and drink, ate what he considered a good curry, but was offered a poor brand of Scotch to wash it down. Dr. Rau seemed a little more relaxed, although at one point during their conversation he did mention that Thorndike Pharmaceutical Company had not shared their best technical knowledge with him. Later, he added that, while he was pleased with Glenn Prescott, the cost of his services was much too high. "Why, his apartment in Bombay alone costs us more than we pay ten workers," he said to substantiate his view.

After more curry and more conversation, Stuart thanked his host and hostess, said good-by and returned to his hotel. He planned to catch a late morning flight to New Delhi and Dr. Rau would see him off at the Bombay airport.

The comments of Stuart the night before must have left their mark on Dr. Rau because the following morning his mood was perceptibly brighter. If Thorndike Pharmaceutical Company divested, he would gain a growing, profitable business and increased freedom as the controlling stockholder, which was exactly in line with the objectives of the Indian government. Moreover, he could then expand into new products that currently placed low on Thorndike Pharmaceutical Company's list of investment priorities.

When Stuart met Dr. Rau at the airport, he noticed that the Indian's eyes had lost their look of melancholy interrogation. After exchanging greetings, Dr. Rau said, "You know, relations between Thorndike Pharmaceutical and Shalimar Laboratories have met some rough weather, but I'm happy to say that the storm over the tea-cup has now died and an amicable settlement may be around the corner."

"An amicable agreement may be difficult as long as it is rumored that Thorndike Pharmaceutical Company is pulling out of India and squeezing you out of Shalimar Laboratories. We don't like these rumors, and if you have misinterpreted our intentions, you may be seriously embarrassed by our increased activities in other projects in the pharmaceutical field," Harrington Stuart interposed somewhat candidly.

"No, no my dear Harrington, neither I nor any of my associates has consciously given these impressions to anyone."

"Perhaps. But I know of no one else from whom they could have come. What is important now is that these impressions should be corrected without delay."

"I thoroughly agree with you. We have had a nice time and healthy discussions. And, I can truly appreciate your understanding and gesture of a helping hand. Have a pleasant journey."

Meetings in New Delhi

Harrington Stuart was met at the airport by John Coleman and Prakash Dube, the Indian manager of the company's New Delhi office. The automobile ride to the Ashoka Hotel made him feel at home, for the tree-lined streets were broad, and Western Indian architecture dominated the numerous government buildings.

After arriving at the hotel, the men talked briefly in Stuart's room. John Coleman asked, "What was the outcome of your talks with Dr. Rau?"

"I asked him to correct the impressions he had given to Indian government officials and businessmen. But, I suspect that he won't put his heart in it. The rumors will continue to spread, and many Indians are all too ready to put their interpretations on our actions," answered Stuart.

Prakash Dube added, "You're quite right, Harrington. He has approached a number of people who have talked to others. At least four have checked with me. Our salespeople are constantly hearing rumors in the bazaars. I've tried to give Thorndike Pharmaceutical Company's side of the story to members of the staff here. The managers, at least, seem to understand."

"At a meeting with government officials in New Delhi several weeks ago," John Coleman interjected, "we were told in Dr. Rau's presence that if Thorndike Pharmaceutical Company was backing out of Shalimar Laboratories, we would have a hard time getting a favorable position in any future projects. We have made arrangements for you to meet tomorrow with Mr. R. Kanna Dastoor, a powerful bureau chief in the Ministry of Finance who has considerable influence with the minister. You'll get from him a good idea of the reaction of high government officials."

After an exchange of formalities, Stuart discussed his point of view with R. Kanna Dastoor regarding the tentative withdrawal of Thorndike Pharmaceutical Company from the Shalimar Laboratories joint venture.

"Your actions are understandable," Dastoor replied, "but remember that the government of India must approve the price of your stock, and the Reserve Bank of India would have to find the exchange. As to price, I suspect that the break-up value would be appropriate."

"Not quite," Stuart interjected, "because the company is not breaking up. We are turning over to Dr. Rau a profitable, growing concern."

"Then why is Thorndike Pharmaceutical Company backing out?" Dastoor asked.

The question remained unanswered.

"By the time the Indian government clearances are obtained, your company might wish to keep the money in India to finance your other investment programs," Dastoor continued.

"I doubt it," Stuart replied. "Nothing would hurt the prospects for future investment in this country more than protracted approvals for the repatriation of funds related to this one."

"If you really want to get your money out, then perhaps you truly are withdrawing from India," Dastoor said, with a questioning look.

"Quite to the contrary," Stuart answered. "We've nurtured Shalimar Laboratories through a difficult period and now are simply considering the possibility of "Indianizing" the producer of a key pharmaceutical. Can you see anything wrong with this?"

"No," countered Dastoor emphatically, "but we want to "Indianize" the Thorndike Pharmaceutical Company. Each day India moves closer to being an active member of the global economy. We have and will continue to liberalize industrial and foreign investment policies. Foreigners can now invest directly in Indian stocks. We have a large pool of scientists, engineers, and managers, an established industrial base, and adequate natural resources in iron and coal. We also produce two-thirds of our petroleum consumption. We have over 200 million upper and middle class consumers, and our economists estimate a growth rate of about 5% over the next several years. Furthermore, we have sent missions to major industrial companies to explain the dramatic changes in India's economic policies and business practices and to seek joint ventures and trade opportunities."

Economic Conditions in India

The day after his meeting with Dastoor, Stuart held discussions with several American businessmen in India and then spent several hours talking with John Coleman. What he learned from these conversations might be summed up as follows.

Economic conditions in India were visibly improving. The attitude of the Indian government toward private capital investment was becoming increasingly liberal. Ownership arrangements could now be negotiated, sometimes resulting in equity participation exceeding 50%. In fact, during the previous week, a large American company, bullish on money-making possibilities in India, had obtained 60% of the equity in a fertilizer joint venture with the Indian government. Moreover, several American competitors of Thorndike Pharmaceutical Company, despite their complaints about conducting business in India, were investigating joint venture possibilities.

Observations on Shalimar

On Saturday, Stuart returned to the United States. On Monday, he met with Henry Chesterfield.

"Dr. Rau seems like a nice guy, and he was in a good mood when I left him in Bombay. He seems confident that with our assistance he will be able to borrow the money he needs to acquire our equity stake in Shalimar Laboratories. He assures me that there will be no other partner. He plans to run the show alone. At times, he almost seemed to be glad to be rid of us.

"Regretfully, I would rate him rather low as a manager and entrepreneur, which is not really surprising considering that his training and experience are in medicine. He says specifically that he wants to take over our marketing activities as soon as a definite divestment decision is reached and subsequent negotiations are completed. He plans to create new products, but he is disturbingly vague about how he plans to market them. He has expressed interest in several of our employees, but has apparently given no real thought to how many he would need and where he would place them. He likes the Indian manager who has been handling the Shalimar Laboratories account for us, but his only specific comment was that he was too expensive. He has talked, but only in the vaguest terms, about establishing an office in New Delhi to cover the northern and eastern part of India."

"What was your impression of the plant?" Henry Chesterfield asked.

"It appears to me that most of the technical problems have been solved. Of course, the plant is crawling with people. I was amazed to discover 420 employees on the payroll. This seems excessive, especially when sales for this year will be only slightly more than one and a half million dollars. Granted, at least 100 employees were temporary, but the extensive use of hand labor is quite obvious."

"You might be interested in knowing, Harrington, that during your brief absence Gordon Potter was appointed vice president of our processing division. He understands that we are considering divesting in Shalimar Laboratories and has requested current financial reports, historical sales, and profit data to gain a perspective. He has also been reviewing our long-range plans for our international operations. Let me suggest that you send a memo to him and to Ward Crowell, vice-president of our international division, and give them the benefit of your observations. During January and February, Potter, Crowell, and I will be extremely busy working with George Thorndike in reorganizing our future European operation. I have, therefore, planned a meeting early in March during which all of us can discuss Shalimar Laboratories and try to reach an agreement on the preferred course of action for our company."

Final Action on Divestiture

Within one month after Stuart's return, Chesterfield called a meeting to determine final action on the divestiture decision. Henry Chesterfield began the discussion by asking, "The decision to consider divestiture in Shalimar Laboratories was initiated almost a year ago. At that time, no objections were raised by the divisions directly involved. What are your feelings now?"

Ward Crowell was the first to answer. "Historically, our operations in India have been made difficult and complicated by pressure from the Indian government to increase our investment base and by certain conflicts of interests with our partner resulting from his desire to expand the scope of the enterprise in directions in which we preferred not to move. When the possibility of divestiture was considered last year, we contacted each interested division to gauge interest in continuing the joint venture with Shalimar Laboratories and evaluate possible adverse effects from the disposal of our equity interest on future business planning in India. As Henry pointed out, negative replies were received in every instance. The international division supports divestiture for several reasons: (1) the present relationship fails to provide an attractive base for our future interests in India; (2) Indian government controls will continue to inhibit profitability; and (3) divestiture will enable us to better structure and control our marketing activities in our primary areas."

Crowell continued, "Furthermore, since we entered the joint venture, Shalimar Laboratories' operating performance has been erratic. The acquisition of a salicylic sublimer and the ban on purified salicylic imports enabled Shalimar Laboratories, the sole supplier, to turn a significant profit last year. However, the questionable ability of the Indian government to control inflation makes Shalimar Laboratories' future profit potential most uncertain, particularly in view of India's exhibited tendency to rigorously control prices in the drug and pharmaceutical fields. The combination of poor government investment climate, financial scandals, excessive management time, partner problems, and uncertain profit potential contributes to my recommendation that the investment in Shalimar Laboratories be sold without further delay."

"I agree with most of the things you have said, Ward," Gordon Potter added. "Still, I oppose the sale for several reasons. Thorndike Pharmaceutical Company is a major world producer of aspirin and the related salicylic acid family of products. The market for these products is growing, and we expect it to continue to grow worldwide. Operations in the United States, the United Kingdom, and Australia have traditionally been profitable and will remain so. Therefore, we should not knowingly put in business an independent producer of salicylic acid and aspirin. We should exercise leadership in this area of chemistry and expand our participation, not withdraw. Our investment in Shalimar Laboratories has already been made. The worst is behind us, and Shalimar Laboratories, with 70% of the market, is the dominant producer in India. It's true, management of Shalimar Laboratories is difficult, but the firm should continue to grow slowly and generate profits in the years ahead. Why sell out now and settle for a short-term, one-time-only profit when we have already committed so much time and effort and have survived the initial bad years?"

Potter continued, "The profit records mentioned are correct, but they ignore payment to us of a technical fee of 3% of sales, which will cease upon divestiture. In addition, our sales company has profited as a result of handling Shalimar Laboratories' product line, in addition, to Thorndike Pharmaceutical's products. Overall, we have made money from Shalimar Laboratories."

"Moreover," concluded Potter, "I understand that the Indian government, which is becoming more global minded and business oriented, has recently granted Shalimar Laboratories a further price increase on aspirin, a significant factor in their future profit picture. Therefore, although we have no expansion plans for Shalimar Laboratories, and we recognize its limitations and problems, I would prefer to retain our participation. If negotiations have gone too far to pull back now, the loss of Shalimar Laboratories will not, of course, be critical. In principle, however, I remain opposed to divestiture and believe that it is not in our interest long term."

"As you know, I was not party to the decision to consider the sale of our interest in Shalimar Laboratories," said Harrington Stuart. "During my short stay in India, I did not see the possibility of building, with Dr. Rau as a full partner, the kind of hard-hitting, efficient, direct-dealing organization we would like to have there. Difficult as it is to divorce ourselves from him to address the rampant rumors in India, I would rather cope with these issues than with the public relations problems we would expose ourselves to should we try to force Dr. Rau to a minority position."

"Gentlemen, I see it is almost noon," interjected Henry Chesterfield. "Let's stop for lunch. I hope we can come to a decision on Shalimar Laboratories this afternoon."

Appendix: Highlights of End-of-Assignment Report

The first problems encountered in my assignment as technical manager were ineffi-ciencies in processing, a surplus of workers, and sub-standard quality. We were obtain-ing less than the proper yield of crude sodium salicylate and a greater yield of by-prod-ucts. After correcting the situation, I was surprised to find Dr. Rau disappointed by, as he told me, the reduced yield of by-products. After working with him for only a short time, I concluded that he knew very little about production of salicylic acid.

It was evident from the start that we had too many workers in the plant, so I quickly replaced eight women materials-handlers with a conveyor, justifying its cost by the eight salaries that were eliminated. One day, I noted these same women tending the lawn, flowers, and plants surrounding the buildings. Later, Dr. Rau told me it was impossible to lay them off, so they had simply been reassigned to gardening jobs.

Shalimar Laboratories is far enough from Bombay to miss the rapidly increasing wage raises, and good labor is available in Kahrdi. However, new employee buildings are needed. It is located near a hydro-electric generating station that borders on water. This presents an environmental hazard because of the potential poisonous or offensive effluents.

Purified salicylic acid requires processing through a vacuum sublimer. Until two years ago, we shipped our crude salicylic acid from India to London for refining in a sublimer and then shipped it back to India. A new, U.S. model sublimer was recently purchased and is now operational.

For the past two years the plant operated at 33%–40% of capacity. Now that the sub-limer is operational, the Indian government will cut off importation of salicylic acid. At which time the plant should operate at 60% capacity or more.

The price of aspirin was frozen by the Indian government two years ago under the Drug-Industry Price Control Act. The frozen price is below the Shalimar cost of produc-ing aspirin. An application for a price increase has been filed with the Indian government.

The approval of the Shalimar price increase application is being vigorously expedit-ed by management. Approval is expected within a few weeks. The new price coupled with the monopoly position on salicylic acid will permit Shalimar to become a reason-ably profitable company.

3
Confronting Globalization: Atencio Plasticos' Search for a Strategic Alliance

C. Roe Goddard

Introduction

Early in the afternoon on November 3, 1992, Cesar Atencio, president and chief executive officer of Atencio Plasticos, a division of Atencio, S.A., arrived at the Westin Peachtree Plaza Hotel in Atlanta, Georgia. Later that afternoon, he and Juan Rivera, president of Atencio, S.A., would sign contracts allying Atencio Plasticos with Denning Corporation in a joint venture. Cesar Atencio and Rivera were pleased with the formation of this strategic alliance. Three years earlier, both companies had decided to seek a strategic alliance in response to changes in the international and national business operating environment. Mexican President Salinas' abandonment of Import Substitution Industrialization policies, and his commitment to opening the protected Mexican market and negotiating a North American Free Trade Agreement meant that Atencio Plasticos would have to compete with highly-competitive global firms. If Atencio Plasticos was to survive in this changed environment, it would have to become a global firm. However, Atencio Plasticos lacked the necessary capital to finance a major expansion of its operations. Counseled by Rivera, Cesar began the search for an alliance to help Atencio Plasticos accomplish its strategic goals. The new international environment, the search for an appropriate ally, and the ensuing negotiations, are the subjects of this case study.

Changes in the International Environment

Since the end of World War II, revolutionary changes in the nature of international business competition have occurred. An increase in the number of competitors and the global reach of many of these firms, explain the increased competition.

In the immediate post World War II era, U.S. corporations dominated many of the world's major markets and major industries. In 1966, the heyday of American corporate power and influence abroad, U.S. firms accounted for 79% of worldwide foreign direct investment. However, by the early 1970s, U.S. domination began to erode. Firms, primarily from Western Europe and Asia appeared. Although Japan was a relative latecomer to international investing, its total aggregate foreign direct investment skyrocketed in the 1980s.

In this new more highly-charged competitive environment, firms that have traditionally serviced only their national markets found it increasingly difficult to compete in a world where large multinationals were penetrating all corners of the world marketplace. The global purview and economies of scale advantages of truly globalized firms provided competitive advantages lacking in a firm serving strictly a local or national market. For a firm to prosper today, it must be able to compete internationally. This means becoming a global firm.

Demise of Centrally-Planned and Protected Economies

The disintegration of the Soviet Union and the collapse of other centrally-planned economies, most notably in Central and Eastern Europe, has added new impetus to the single global market movement. Marxist economic doctrine, always critical of capitalism, supported the notion of independent development, and, therefore, provided the basis for resisting the openness inherent in an international capitalist economy. Structuralists argued that the international capitalist economy was exploitative by nature and that it contained an anti-development bias. As evidence, they cited what they deemed to be the exploitative relationship between the developing and developed world. For them, true economic growth could only be attained through autonomous development. Countries that embraced structuralism often adopted Import Substitution Industrialization (ISI) policies that called for high tariff levels to prevent the penetration of foreign products into the domestic market, and prohibitive restrictions on foreign direct investment.

However, with the disintegration of the Soviet Union brought on largely by the failure of their centrally-planned economy, and an increasing awareness of the productive power of capitalism among the world's nations, support for a highly protective autonomous development strategy waned. Many countries started to actively participate in the capitalist economy by freeing their markets and welcoming foreign direct investment. For the industries previously protected by high tariff walls and restrictions on foreign direct investment, it meant confronting international competition for the first time.

The Opening of Mexico

Of the many countries that have abandoned Import Substitution Industrialization policies, Mexico is one of the more notable. Since the beginning of the Cardenas administration in 1934, Mexico has pursued a policy designed to protect its domestic industries by isolating itself from the influences of the international economy. Mexico, historically, has maintained a particularly strong isolationist stance in its dealings with the U.S.

A tremendous international debt burden and the need to attract foreign capital to resume economic growth, however, forced President Salinas to radically reverse traditionally insular development policies to more open and outward-looking ones. His economic growth strategy, outlined early in his administration, had four primary components: (1) permanent stabilization of the economy; (2) improvement of social conditions; (3) enlargement of resources available for investment; and (4) modernization of the economy. Salinas removed restrictions on foreign direct investment in a broad range of industrial sectors to raise the necessary capital for his program. To create a macroeconomic environment attractive to foreign investors, he negotiated and carried out a tough macroeconomic stabilization program intended to quell inflation and reduce currency volatility. Salinas believed that his new open economic policies would lead to improved social conditions, modernization of the economy, and increased growth. This new openness to participation in the international economy has led Salinas to actively participate in free trade negotiations with the U.S. and Canada.

The Rise of Regionalism

The fashionability of unrestricted markets and limited restrictions on foreign direct investment has not meant that governments have allowed their domestic economies to rise or fall upon the vagaries of the global marketplace. Government intervention continues; what has changed is the strategy of intervention. Instead of adopting defensive strategies, such as higher tariff levels and outright restrictions on foreign direct investment that can contribute to bloated public sectors and inefficient enterprises, governments have sought to advance their domestic firms' interests in more offensive ways.

Nations who have pursued more aggressive policies have found comfort in the movement toward regionalization and economic integration during the 1980s and 1990s on the premise that the creation of larger unobstructed markets and the subsequent gains in economies will enhance the competitiveness of domestic firms. It is believed that larger markets are essential to a firm's chances of competing with multinationals that already operate in the global marketplace.

In Europe, for example, the need for firms to be able to compete with U.S. multi-nationals guarantees national support for the European Community's (EC) drive toward greater integration. Recent negotiations among the twelve member-states have focused on moving the EC beyond a single market, as realized on January 1, 1993, toward full monetary integration as envisioned under the Maastricht Treaty. Regardless of whether Maastricht is or is not realized, the Europeans have taken a big step toward monetary integration by creating a single market that has a "domestic" customer base comparable to the U.S.

NAFTA and Beyond: A Western Hemisphere Free Trade Area?

In response to regionalism in Europe, and ever mindful of the competitive strength of Japanese firms, the U.S., formerly under President George Bush and now under President Bill Clinton, has sought to create its own enlarged marketplace under the guise of a western hemisphere free trade area. U.S. goals have centered on eliminating nontariff barriers on goods and services, eliminating barriers to investment, reducing tariffs to zero, ensuring an open investment climate, and full protection of intellectual property rights.

The proposed North American Free Trade Agreement (NAFTA), currently being negotiated between Canada, Mexico and the U.S., grew out of the Enterprise for the Americas Initiative (EAI), as announced by President Bush on June 27, 1991. Cloaked in goodwill toward Latin America, the EAI's apparent goal was to bolster U.S. leadership in the hemisphere and to inject growth into the fledgling economies of Latin America's nascent democracies. The EAI was designed to bring prosperity and peace to the hemisphere through trade, investment, and debt relief.

Closer examination of the EAI, however, reveals that although it may bring improved economic conditions to Latin American countries, the overriding aims of the initiative, as envisioned by the U.S. government, were to enhance the competitiveness of U.S. multinational corporations by increasing their access to hemispheric markets for both investment and sales. More specifically, the investment component of the initiative called for a new investment sector lending program under the Inter-American Development Bank (IDB) to promote privatization and the liberalization of investment regimes.

The cornerstone of Bush's EAI, the trade component, called for the creation of a hemispheric free trade area and the immediate beginning of negotiations to bring Mexico into the existing free trade agreement between Canada and the U.S. The inclusion of Mexico was only the first step. "Framework agreements," or bilateral agreements, that in the past have been precursors to full-blown free trade agreements similar to the one being negotiated with Mexico, were signed in October 1991 with Bolivia, Colombia, Costa Rica, Chile, Ecuador, El Salvador, Guatemala, Honduras, Panama, Peru, Nicaragua, Venezuela, the thirteen Caribbean communities (CARI-

COM) countries, and the Southern Cone group of Argentina, Brazil, Uruguay, and Paraguay. Excluding the listed framework agreement countries, a North American free trade zone composed of Canada, Mexico, and the U.S. alone would create the world's largest market with almost 370 million customers and with an annual production of more than $6 trillion.

The Corporate Response: Global Changes Force Atencio's Reevaluation

Increased foreign competition in domestic markets and the likely completion of NAFTA led Atencio, S.A., Mexico's largest maker of plastic kitchenware, to reevaluate its position in the industry and to consider new strategies to guarantee its future survival. On August 11, 1991, Cesar Atencio, president and chief executive officer of Atencio Plasticos, S.A., a division of Atencio, S. A.; Juan Rivera, president of Atencio, S.A.; and Javier Ceballos, vice-president for planning and administration of Atencio Plasticos, S.A., met in the thirty-fifth floor office of Cesar Atencio in Atencio Plasticos headquarters in Guadalajara, Jalisco, Mexico.

Two months earlier, President Bush, with the backing of President Salinas, had announced his intent to negotiate a free trade agreement with Mexico. Although Cesar Atencio had limited contacts within the Salinas administration, because he had supported the opposition party (PAN) in the presidential elections, he was aware that members of President Salinas' inner circle of Harvard-educated technocrats had participated in discussions that preceded Bush's announcement. He knew that plastic kitchenware was an industrial sector in which U.S. firms were competitive and well represented in Washington. No doubt the gradual elimination of tariff restrictions on plastic kitchenware products would probably be discussed.

Although Atencio Plasticos dominated the protected Mexican kitchenware market, with more than a 95% market share, it had little prospect of maintaining its position when Mexico opened its economy. Foreign competition was now a major concern for the company. Javier Ceballos remarked that, "We in Mexico learn to ride the bicycle with two training wheels and we never give them up. Now, with our government no longer protecting us, some businesses will fall, some will learn to ride, but either way it's shaky."

Adding to the sense of urgency, Rivera further commented that, "The movement to a homogeneous unified global marketplace is coming very fast with modern travel and communication; we must look at the world as a whole in terms of our competition. It is not just the Americans that are a threat."

During this important meeting, Cesar Atencio, Rivera, and Ceballos agreed that change was approaching fast and discussed what they were going to do next. Several questions were raised: How do we characterize the global marketplace? Who are our competitors? To what degree are our competitors specialized? What are the strengths of Atencio Plasticos, as well as the strengths of our competitors? What market niche could we fill? What is the anticipated demand for our products in the future? What new strategies should we adopt in meeting the new challenge? Their inability to answer these fundamental questions meant they had to seek outside help. At the conclusion of the meeting, Ceballos was given the responsibility of hiring a well known and reputable international consulting firm to research the plastic kitchenware industry and to provide recommendations for competing in the global marketplace.

Ceballos met with representatives from international consulting firms headquartered in New York, San Francisco, Princeton, Paris, and Tokyo. After reviewing their work and accepting bids, Ceballos selected the Strategic Research Institute (SRI) of Princeton, New Jersey. SRI's industry analysis and strategic recommendations were to be completed and submitted three months after the contract signing. The entire project would cost $70,000.

Macroeconomic Conditions and the Industry

On Monday, December 3, 1991, Cesar Atencio, Rivera, and Ceballos met a team of representatives from SRI Consulting Group at the Plaza Hotel in New York. Following a cordial business lunch, SRI representative, David Bernhardt, gave the presentation. SRI was confident in its conclusions.

Bernhardt began with an overview of the industry. First, profit margins have been historically slim for all producers of plastic kitchenware, averaging 2–3%. Second, growth in annual sales volume will continue to be weak. The major industrial economies, including Western Europe, Japan, and the U.S., which account for 80% of global demand for plastic kitchenware, are in recession and an upturn is not anticipated for 1992-3. He also noted that the Clinton Administration wants to raise taxes to reduce the budget deficit, the German Bundesbank is maintaining a tight monetary policy to control inflation and to finance reunification that is suppressing growth throughout all of Europe, and that the Japanese stock market is depressed. With all of the industrial economies in recession, there is not a single major economic power to propel the world economy toward sustained growth. Even with GNP growth rates in the industrial world averaging 3¼% the growth in sales of plastic kitchenware would only be 1½%. In the United States, a primary market for kitchenware, most of the would-be customers are beyond the kitchenware purchasing age. "The demographics are not favorable," Bernhardt remarked.

SRI's Analysis

Next, the SRI team presented information on the competition. There are five major industrial producers of plastic kitchenware that compete globally: Lemont (France), Denning (U.S.), Georgia Plastics (U.S.), Panalache (Turkey), and Senuki (Japan). Bernhardt commented that there were several smaller producers, but they only served national markets and could not be considered global. SRI classified Atencio Plasticos as a non-global firm. Moreover, given anticipated changes in the macroeconomic environment, SRI concluded that unless Atencio Plasticos began thinking globally and acted quickly, it would not survive in a global market. Atencio Plasticos had to become global.

It was time for Atencio Plasticos to make some decisions. Cesar Atencio's long-term objective for the division was to penetrate other countries' markets and to make Atencio a truly global firm. He approached Rivera about corporate financial support for his division's international expansion. Specifically, Cesar Atencio's ambitious plans included broadening the product line, establishing sales forces in the American, European, and Asian markets as well as in numerous less developed countries that showed potential for fast growth, while simultaneously expanding the capacity of Mexican plants.

Rivera was less than enthusiastic. Citing slow growth, weak profit margins, and overcapacity in the plastic kitchenware industry, Rivera observed, "Your division generates the least ROI of all our divisions, and now you want me to transfer capital that could be invested in the other more profitable divisions. It does not make sense." Rivera though knew that the trend in plastics, as well as other industries, was toward globalization and he wanted Cesar Atencio's division to survive the intensified competition. Rivera commented, "Although we lack the capital base to go alone, I recognize the threat. Our next best option may be to explore a strategic relationship with one of our competitors."

Search for a Strategic Alliance Begins

Cesar Atencio's decision to pursue a joint venture was primarily based on hard data and conclusions provided by SRI. Many Mexican firms with their low labor costs had already formed alliances with U.S. firms; however, many of these alliances, referred to collectively as "maquiladoras" in Mexico, are not true partnerships. Maquiladoras mainly serve as assembly plants for finished products that are then shipped across the border into the U.S. The maquiladoras add little value to the finished product and pay minimum wage. Cesar Atencio wanted Atencio Plasticos to be more than a maquiladora. In the first strategic planning meeting with his staff since his conversation with Rivera, Cesar Atencio said: "We want to be full participants in the industry, not a maquila for a U.S. firm."

This is not to say that Cesar Atencio opposed strategic alliances with foreign firms. He had given the potential benefits of a "sound" alliance considerable thought. Several years earlier, he had written an article in a Mexican business journal extolling the virtues of joint ventureships. He had argued that there are five primary motivations for a joint venture: (1) to gain access to new technology; (2) to overcome barriers in national or international markets; (3) to apply existing technology; (4) to leap downstream by going into partnership with a firm that manufactures the subsystem or system for which your product is a component; and (5) to enter markets that are difficult to penetrate. These objectives Cesar Atencio sought to fulfill in the forming of an alliance.

Cesar Atencio quickly eliminated several potential alliance partners. He felt that cultural and linguistic barriers would be too costly to overcome with a Japanese or Turkish partner and Atencio Plasticos had had no significant experience in cross-cultural strategic relationships. This eliminated both Panalache and Senuki from consideration.

Lemont of France had a product mix similar to Atencio Plasticos. Furthermore, Lemont had broad market penetration in many smaller markets, but it had not been successful in penetrating the large German and U.S. markets. The production of competing as opposed to complementary products, as well as the limited market shares in the larger markets, made Lemont a less attractive option.

With the elimination of these three firms, only two remained, Denning and Georgia Plastics. The strategic planning group at Atencio Plasticos agreed that having a U.S. partner, given geographical proximity, would simplify conferencing and training, and ease the movement of workers and their families in worker exchanges. Cultural and language barriers were deemed to be manageable. Ceballos noted that "in Monterrey, we are exposed to American magazines and TV, and are geographically so close to the U.S. that we sometimes feel culturally closer to the Americans than our own fellow citizens from Mexico City." Denning might be the more logical choice because it had joint ventures in several countries with different cultures, spanning both the developed and developing world.

Atencio, S.A. had experience in joint ventures with U.S. firms. Ironically, Cesar Atencio's division itself, had entered into a joint venture with Denning in the latter 1970s. It ultimately failed and both Atencio Plasticos and Denning parted company. This did not, however, affect Cesar Atencio's desire to pursue a joint venture with its former partner. In fact, Humberto Ortega, vice-president of operations for Atencio Plasticos, and formerly chief negotiator during the aforementioned joint venture commented that "if two partners experience a failure together and they depart as friends, this can provide a solid basis for building a future relationship."

Marketing

Jorge Martinez was vice-president of marketing at Atencio Plasticos at the time the search for an alliance began. He knew Denning well. Both Denning and Atencio, S.A. have a long history in the plastics business. This allowed both firms to develop extensive product lines and marketing expertise. Of critical importance to both firms was whether their product lines were complementary or competing, and their respective penetration of the various markets of the world. In terms of both the complementarity of product lines and market penetration the firms were compatible. Denning's product line complemented Atencio's line. Denning specialized in heavy high-end items, Atencio specialized in light low-end items. Atencio was particularly successful in the industrial market. Denning was dominant in the consumer-household market. Denning had also penetrated the gift and retail chain market whereas Atencio had not. Although Atencio Plasticos was an important player in the U.S. market, Denning was clearly dominant in both breadth of product line and market share. Given that plastics had been a protected sector under previous Mexican administrations, Atencio controlled and knew the Mexican market. Atencio's knowledge and domination of the Mexican market made it very attractive as a strategic partner. Particularly to Denning officials. They had long sought access to the Mexican market, and a joint venture in which Atencio would agree to market Denning's products in the Mexican market provided tremendous appeal.

Denning's appeal as an alliance partner went beyond a complementary product mix. Particularly attractive was its marketing skills. For Atencio, this was important. As Martinez commented, "With a protected market where you are the only producer, marketing tends to take a back seat to production. We can be globally competitive in terms of production, but not in marketing." Denning was well known for its expertise in market research, program selling, and customer relations.

The strategic planning group, led by Cesar Atencio, also had to consider the compatibility of each firms' sales force. Along with its in-house marketing skills, Denning was known for having an extensive network of sales personnel, as evident by the firm's presence in all of Western Europe, Central America, Japan, Australia, New Zealand, and in some countries in South America, the Caribbean, Eastern Europe, Africa, the Middle East and southeast Asia. Atencio only had sales forces in their primary markets, Mexico and the U.S. In other countries, Atencio relied on distributors and marketing representatives. It was apparent to the planning group that in combining sales forces redundancies could be eliminated, market coverage could be broadened, and in-house sales personnel could replace less committed distributors and marketing representatives.

Marinez also felt that "in addition to marketing there were purchasing synergies." Boxes, for shipping purposes, account for approximately 20% of the total cost of production. By combining the purchase of boxes and negotiating quantity discounts, the planning group projected that the total cost of shipping boxes could be reduced by 6–8%. This would represent a significant potential saving for both Denning and Atencio. There were other purchasing synergies to be exploited. Combined purchasing power would also reduce petrochemical costs by a projected 2–4%.

Technology

Enrique Mercado, an engineer and graduate of the prestigious Monterrey Tech, had risen through the ranks of the plant management to vice-president of operations and technology. He was well versed in plastics production technology. As a technology liaison with Denning during the previous joint venture, he was familiar with the firm's technology, production processes, and research/laboratory capabilities.

There was no doubt in his mind that Denning was the industry leader in basic research and plastic production. Mercado respected the quality of basic research conducted by Denning. Whereas Atencio possessed less than one hundred patented formulas for plastics, Denning had over one thousand different patents and was particularly strong in specialty plastics formulas. The formula for plastic is the most important and expensive part of the production process. While Enrique did not expect Denning to share all of its patents with Atencio in the event of an alliance, possession of such technology was, in Mercado's opinion, a minimal requirement for any partner. He was well aware of Atencio's vulnerability in this area.

Other areas where Mercado felt improvements could be made included pollution control, energy conservation, and tank design. U.S. concerns over the laxity of Mexican efforts to control pollution had spilled over into the NAFTA negotiations. Mercado anticipated that Mexico City would soon be forced to adopt more stringent restrictions on pollution. Denning had operated for several years under the Environmental Protection Agency's (EPA) strict anti-pollution laws. In meeting these legal restrictions, Denning had successfully developed advanced technology for pollution control and energy conservation. Not much attention had been given to energy conservation in Mexico because the country's sizeable oil reserves kept energy costs low.

A more critical aspect of plastic production is tank design. Raw materials are combined and heated in a tank to form molten plastic, which is then processed and shaped into a finished product. This is a critical stage in the production process. Temperatures in the molten plastic must be kept balanced. According to Mercado, Atencio's tank technology was fairly good and did maintain balanced temperatures within narrow parameters, but "our tank design could still be improved. Combining our engineering talents with those of Denning could lead to other improvements in our production process."

Negotiating the Joint Venture

Two months after SRI's presentation in New York and after many meetings with his top executives in the strategic planning group, Cesar Atencio decided to approach the Denning Corporation regarding a possible strategic alliance. The week before, he had received full support from Juan Rivera and the board of directors of Atencio, S.A. Like Atencio, S.A., Denning was composed of several divisions.

On February 26, 1992, Cesar Atencio contacted Jim Crutcher, his counterpart at Denning. Jim Crutcher was the vice-president and general manager of the plastic products division of Denning. Cesar Atencio and Crutcher had known each other for a while and often saw each other at professional association meetings. The idea of collaboration between the two firms often surfaced at these association meetings, so the call from Cesar Atencio and its purpose did not come as much of a surprise to Crutcher. Crutcher was confident that he could secure approval from his corporate headquarters to explore the possibility of a joint venture. His division had been the least profitable of Denning's five divisions and Crutcher had earlier been directed to improve the bottom line. Crutcher and Cesar Atencio agreed to arrange several meetings among their departmental heads to explore a potential alliance.

During March, April, and May of 1992, departmental heads of both firms from marketing, research, personnel, finance, and technology and production met bimonthly. The meeting sites rotated between Monterrey, Mexico, and Pittsburgh, Pennsylvania, the headquarter city for Denning. During these meetings, side-trips were also taken to visit and inspect various plants that were being considered for inclusion in the joint venture. By the end of May, executives from Atencio Plasticos and Denning's plastic products division felt that they had a clear understanding of the issues at hand. Both groups believed that a joint venture could be profitable and it was agreed to enter into negotiations.

Although Cesar Atencio and Crutcher had final approval authority, both appointed lead negotiators. Cesar Atencio appointed Carlos Miranda, vice-president of finance, to represent Atencio Plasticos and Jim Crutcher appointed David Seligman, the newly appointed chief of finance in the division. David Seligman had previously been a part of negotiating teams for several other Denning joint ventures.

Miranda and Seligman held their first meeting on Monday, June 15, 1992, in the Westin Peachtree Plaza Hotel, in Atlanta. They had instructions not to return until they had a deal. Both entered the negotiation from different perspectives. This led to some conflict. Seligman, after many years' experience in negotiating joint ventures with Denning, approached the session with confidence. He was very methodical in his approach to negotiating. Carlos Miranda commented, "I was impressed with David's thoroughness. I had to keep in mind that Denning was experienced in these matters and we were at the beginning of the learning curve. I was willing to learn."

Miranda also felt, though, that the early tenor of the negotiations was a function of more than Seligman's personal professionalism or Denning's greater experience in negotiating joint ventures. He felt that there were also cultural factors at work. He remembered that, in his past relationships with Denning staff, as an organization, Denning was very focused; more focused than Atencio Plasticos. He perceived, during preliminary meetings, that Denning's employees were strongly committed to the organization itself. Miranda remarked, "They were very focused on the organization's needs, not on the boss's. Personal relationships play a more important role in Mexican business." At Atencio Plasticos, "decisions are made to support the boss. At Denning, decisions are made to support the organization."

Miranda also noted that he was not being treated as an equal in the negotiations, and this was unacceptable. The root of the inequality, as evidenced by Seligman's demeanor, rested in the historical relationship between the U.S. and Mexico. Miranda was not willing to negotiate from a position of imposed inferiority. He commented, "Frankly, at the beginning of the negotiations, the Americans could not forget colonialism. This I could not accept. I resisted David's heavy handedness. I said put the rule on the table and let's discuss it. At the end of the negotiations, we had respect."

For the next several days, Miranda and Seligman exchanged financial information and discussed the types of plants and lines that were to be combined. This part of the negotiation process went smoothly, primarily because of the obvious marketing and production synergies. By Thursday, Miranda and Seligman could both sense that things were beginning to take shape.

A more difficult issue—assigning a monetary value to each firm's respective contribution—had not been addressed. After considerable haggling over the methods of valuation, a compromise was accepted. They agreed to value their contributions in three ways: (1) value of equity on a GAAP basis, (2) cash flow generation, and, (3) return on equity (ROE). The total value of their respective contributions would be based upon the average of all three methods. After calculating the average of their respective contributions, Denning's contribution was $73 million more than that of Atencio Plasticos. They agreed that this sum would be paid to Denning at the close of the deal. It was Saturday afternoon, Miranda and Seligman departed the hotel pleased with the success of their negotiations.

Politicization of the Joint Venture

On August 6, a letter of intent was signed by Cesar Atencio and Crutcher and their parent corporation's CEOs. The process was going well; both boards had given their full approval to the joint venture and no major legal hurdles had yet surfaced.

Both firms needed approval for their joint venture from the U.S. Federal Trade Commission (FTC). One of the agency's major responsibilities is to monitor markets with an eye to preventing monopolies. In communications between the FTC and the two firms, the FTC was particularly concerned with two product lines. With the joint venture, Atencio Plasticos and Denning combined would control in excess of 60% of the market share for these two lines. According to the FTC, this was close to a monopoly position. Representatives from the smaller U.S. plastic producers had publicly stated that this proposed joint venture could "put them out of business." These smaller firms had supporters in Congress lobbying the FTC.

Focusing additional public attention on the proposed joint venture, simultaneous to the FTC's review, the NAFTA negotiators were discussing the degree and rapidity of tariff reductions in the plastic industries. Crutcher remarked, "We realized that, in terms of the political environment, we could not have picked a worse time to seek FTC approval of this venture. The industry was in the public eye. But Cesar Atencio and I both felt that we had to press ahead." In the end, after considerable effort by both firms' lobbyists, the FTC approved the joint venture.

Signing of the Joint Venture

By October 21, two weeks following FTC approval, legal counsel for both firms had prepared 212 different contracts for signing. On November 3, 1992, Cesar Atencio, Juan Rivera, Jim Crutcher, and Robert Jameson, chief executive officer for Denning Corporation, met at the Atlanta Westin Peachtree Plaza to sign the contracts. Jameson was handed a bank draft for $73 million. The Atencio-Denning Corporation had been formed.

4
The Potato Business

Mitja I. Tavčar

Late in the afternoon, Andrej Lesak, director of Iskra Avtomatizacija, stood at the window of one of the hotels that had recently popped up north of Hyde Park. Absorbed in his thoughts, he gazed into the stream of white and red lights running parallel along the Baywater Road down to the Marble Arch. The atmosphere was imbued with a spring fragrance, and the low, west-wind driven clouds shifted now and then to reveal the clear blue afternoon sky.

Yet, it was not the weather that burdened Andrej's meditation. He was unsuccessfully trying to uncover the reasons behind an unexpected culmination at the end of the day's long meeting with the managing staff of Process Automation, Ltd. As he and John Steel, managing director of Process Automation, discussed the usual topics, such as delivery terms and quantities, payments and complaints, deals and competition, each was well aware of the critical, unresolved issue looming on the horizon.

Iskra Avtomatizacija and Process Automation

Upon dissolution of the former Yugoslavia, Slovenia, where Iskra is situated, managed to attain its independence, but Slovenian enterprises were subsequently deprived of their traditional markets in Yugoslavia. Overnight, more than 40% of Iskra's sales vanished, leading to a considerable reduction of personnel and a drop in volume below the break-even point. Business with Process had also recently declined, a point that Lesak wanted to address during this meeting.

For understandable business and personal reasons, the identity of many individuals, companies, government institutions, and the places and times mentioned in the case were changed. All essential circumstances, however, are true, although they were not derived from a single business project. The author would like to thank the numerous Iskra managers for their valuable suggestions and improvements.

Earlier that day before the lunch break, Lesak tackled the matter with Process' managing director. "Well, John, I suppose we have more or less resolved the basic matters, so let's have a look at the business for the rest of this year. Process placed fewer orders than agreed upon in November and we, for the time being, cannot count on the large, already agreed-upon projects in the South . . ."

He continued, "Look, John, the situation is quite simple. We've lost one-third of our markets, and Slovenia is too small to compensate for this. The Russians are the only other customers to whom we still manage to sell some equipment based on the old 8-bit processors. We have no chance to expand into other markets, because you prohibit us from selling the 16-bit equipment, let alone the 32-bit equipment that you have been developing. Still, for you, doing business with us means an investment in, and future access to, markets in other republics including Croatia. Serbia and Macedonia also would have made purchases, if they had not been subjected to the international ban."

"That's true," countered Steel, "yet we are concerned with our own drop in sales, in the United Kingdom by 12% and to the continent by 14%. Given that we purchase the less sophisticated part of the equipment from you, if we do not get orders, we cannot order from you. Furthermore, the situation in the former Yugoslavia is making everyone very nervous. Andrej, you should try to speak to our trade union just once. According to them, we should immediately stop the deliveries from the risky Balkans and make all equipment by ourselves."

The discussion continued along these lines throughout the afternoon. Steel knew that Lesak's points about the importance of access to Eastern Europe were valid; in fact, Yugoslavia used to be one of its most profitable markets.

Lesak persisted in his purpose. "John, this won't take us anywhere. If you refuse to let us penetrate additional markets, we are heading straight for destruction. To do this, we will certainly require the 16-bit equipment. Maybe you could give us some of the less profitable markets, like Spain or Italy."

"Be earnest, Andrej. The managing board will fire me on the spot if I do anything like that. You have to adapt yourself to this temporary situation. You yourself tell me that Yugoslavia will open again, won't it?"

Lesak, however, refused to capitulate. He mercilessly pressed further, because he felt that there was little to lose. Just when he began to feel that his efforts had been to no avail, Steel suggested, "Andrej, let's finish it off. There's no point talking like that. I'm not quite sure, but an idea has crossed my mind. In Uralburg in Russia, we've concluded a contract for more than five million pounds for 16-bit equipment, of course."

Steel continued, saying that the prices there were good, the Russians were not demanding, and that Iskra could increase its revenues by buying equipment from Process Automation, adding value to it and delivering it to the Russians. He concluded by suggesting that Iskra review the offer and promised to submit an official offer within one week. Then he gave his Slovenian colleague an authoritarian tap on the shoulder and said, "You see, Andrej, that's how a big company behaves. Now you have to think it over."

Andrej Lesak's meditation was interrupted by a phone call from Peter Derman, an Iskra veteran and director of the Iskra's commercial firm in London, phoning from the hotel's reception desk. They drove to a nearby Italian restaurant, found a quiet corner, and ordered a light meal.

They could not help reflecting upon the day's unexpected turn of events. Steel had never given something for nothing, let alone a deal worth five million pounds. While it was true that Process Automation had announced this deal to the press during the past autumn, Iskra Avtomatizacija had yet to receive orders for the subassemblies to be built into the Russian equipment. The two concluded that something was wrong with the deal and guessed that it concerned the financing of the project.

Upon departing late that evening, Lesak advised Derman to ask his acquaintances at Process Automation about the deal. He also mentioned that he would call his associate Janez in Moscow, who had several sales contacts in Uralburg. Furthermore, he stated that he would call Derman in the next few days and would possibly ask him to come to Ljubljana to approach Iskra Commerce about further action.

A Week Later in Ljubljana

As usual on Monday morning, the members of the board of directors gathered in the office of Andrej Lesak at Iskra Avtomatizacija's headquarters, located at the center of Iskra's industrial zone on the northern outskirts of Ljubljana. Process Automation and the Russian deal was the third point on the agenda; everyone was aware of the critical nature of the matter.

"Well, gentlemen," started Managing Director Lesak, "Last week, Peter and I visited Process Automation and pressed John Steel about their orders." He continued with a short but substantial description of the discussion, and, in particular, of the unanticipated, Russian proposal.

"John hasn't called me yet, maybe he's waiting for us. Peter made inquiries about Process Automation. They did enter into a contract with the Russians, but it appears that the process has reached a standstill. He was told that the problem related to the advance payments issue. He is still investigating the matter and will let us know what else he finds. Also, I phoned Janez in Moscow on Wednesday; he has some acquaintances in the communications administration in Uralburg and he promised to feel out the deal. In fact, he booked a flight to Uralburg the day after I spoke with him."

Lesak continued with a grin. "He called me on Sunday morning, from Uralburg and told me he had a terrible headache. That's good. It means he spent the night with his friends from the communications administration and a certain Jevšenko, presumably an "eminence grise" from the Automacija Combine, who knows everything that happens in the Uralburg "vyerhooshka," the local upper echelon.

"The Russians have, somewhat unwillingly, entered into the deal with those arrogant Englishmen. Actually, they wouldn't have, but they couldn't find any other solution. They evaluated the equipment and found it to be satisfactory, though they would prefer 32-bit processors to 16-bit ones. But, they claim the English are terribly hard to deal with."

"Moreover, the Russian Combine is experiencing real difficulty obtaining funds for the required advance payments. They have, however, been guaranteed a hard currency allowance allocated from defense budget adjustments, but this may take an eternity to materialize. Also, they tried to persuade the Englishmen that at least part of the equipment should be manufactured in Uralburg, but the latter wouldn't even consider it. The managing director of Automacija is fed up with them and maintains that this deal is committed to failure. Yet, they want and need the equipment, though they would prefer to manufacture it in the combine."

"Jevšenko and Janez quickly became friends. Like Janez always says, the Slavs, forever, hold together. He managed to persuade Jevšenko that we are different from the colonial Englishmen, especially because we already have several joint ventures and cooperation agreements in Russia and manufacture products in several Russian factories. He got an even more positive response after he explained that a great deal of Iskra deliveries, as a rule, are compensated with Russian goods."

"And, you know that Janez wouldn't be Janez if he didn't offer to organize a visit of an Iskra delegation in Uralburg. He mentioned bringing along some members of the Slovenian government, to establish greater connections between Slovenia and the Uralburg District. I already called Mr. Kovač, the undersecretary in the Ministry of Industry, and he promised to have a word about it with the secretary."

The board's discussion extended far beyond the time schedule. They were all well aware of the importance of such a large order from Russia to enable Iskra Avtomatizacija to survive. From past experience, they also knew that managing the project would be a time-consuming and difficult task.

Mr. Skopuh, the finance director, was first to comment. "Process Automation," he said, "wants to carry out the deal through our company, because it trusts us more than the Russians with whom it has already encountered problems about the advance payments. With us, they are assured of at least partial coverage through our counterdeliveries. We still need access to adequate financing or at least some guarantees, but we aren't able to get them from our bank at acceptable terms now. We'd better talk to Iskra Commerce and ask them for assistance."

The technical director insisted that Iskra should by all means offer the Russians the 32-bit Process Automation technology. Before the Russian deal became operative, the 16-bit technology would be outdated.

The commercial director, Viktor, was also in favor of the deal, of course. "But the prices," he warned, "are rapidly changing in Russia. Because financing is likely to be expensive, we have to be very careful about our agreements with Process Automation. We cannot continue paying the colonial prices that we have in the past. Andrej, it's up to you to arrange it with John Steel." He closed by noting that the Russian deal would be complicated, but that it wouldn't be easy to get another project like it.

Iskra Commerce

The meeting with the managing director of Iskra Commerce, the director of the Eastern European Region, Tilen Čepe, and Ivan Alja, director of the Iskra Commerce countertrade subsidiary Ponti, was held the next afternoon and continued late into the night. They found the deal to be very interesting and decided that, if invited, Ivan and Tilen, as well as Janez from Moscow, would travel to Uralburg. Boris Lasin, the director of ISEL Stuttgart, an Iskra Commerce subsidiary in Germany, would work together with Tone Skopuh from Avtomatizacija to arrange the financing of the deal.

Visit to Uralburg

Thereafter, progress toward completion of the deal stalled. The Director of Iskra Avtomatizacija spoke with Janez from Iskra Commerce Moscow twice a day. The latter kept calling Uralburg and received various promises, but still nothing happened. This, however, was not unusual.

Soon after, however, John Steel, declared in writing that Process Automation stood ready to leave the deal, which remained stalled as a result of problems related to imprecise technical specifications and lack of advance payments, to Iskra Avtomatizacija. The offer was made on the condition that Iskra had to be able to offer identical or better conditions than the Russians.

Also, in the middle of April, Janez forwarded a letter from Ivan Ivanovič Ivanov, the president of the Uralburg district, inviting the government delegation of Slovenia to visit to establish manifold relations and to promote economic cooperation. Iskra then arranged to send a high-level economic delegation headed by the president of the Chamber of Economy of Slovenia and Mr. Kovač, the vice-secretary of the Ministry of Industry and a personal friend of Lesak.

In Uralburg at the beginning of May, Andrej Lesak thoughtfully observed the drowsy group of people descending before dawn from the old Aeroflot aircraft at the airport in Uralburg, the former Uralskogorsk. The flight took sixteen hours and included a seven-hour delay and two changes of aircraft to travel the more than 2,200 miles from Ljubljana to Uralburg. The group of seven included the technical director and Lesak from Iskra Avtomatizacija, three members of Iskra Commerce, several representatives from the Slovenian Ministry and Chamber of Economy. Lesak mused that if such an assembly had gathered at Process Automation in London, it was doubtful that they would have had enough chairs for everyone.

At the airport, they were greeted by three shiny Volgas with drivers, the president of the combine, the "eminence grise," i.e., the chief of district protocol, and several others. Then, they drove through the foggy morning to Uralburg, a big industrial center with 1.5 million inhabitants. It was the usual scene—a dusty road lined with blocks of flats, light morning traffic, few pedestrians. The factories were already lit, because the working day starts early there.

Lesak proceeded to engage the interpreter in a conversation about life in Uralburg. Though salaries are fairly low, apartments are almost free as are the two ample meals that factory workers receive. Children attend nurseries and kindergartens that are free of charge and provide all meals. Citizens have access to swimming pools and health centers. Compared to Slovenia, Lesak thought to himself, people do not live so badly. However, one must have a job; those who are unemployed find themselves on the edge of survival.

The hotel near the town center was comparatively modern, with a slow, but operative, reception desk. Upon checking in and learning that breakfast would not be served before seven, Janez, used to such problems, invited the group to his room for some vodka before resting for a few hours.

On Wednesday afternoon, Thursday, Friday, and Saturday, the group visited numerous factories, offices, and memorials, and attended many lunches and dinners with many toasts and lots of vodka. All in all, Iskra's hosts were hospitable and wholehearted, though the trip was tiring. The visit reinforced the importance of Slavic brotherhood and the great value placed on relationships and social ties shared by the two cultures.

Several reasons for the stalemate experienced by London Process Automation became evident throughout the trip. During a relaxed dinner atmosphere, the hosts described the Englishmen as strange people. Process Automation evidently had sent to Uralburg its Eastern European exports manager, Smith, a technically competent businessman who behaved like an imperial sergeant. He maintained a disdainful approach to the hotel, food, smoking in offices, documentation in the combine, and Russian international trade regulations. Furthermore, because he spoke no Russian, the combine hired two interpreters, but this, predictably, worked poorly during the evening social events. Moreover, Smith's dislike for the ample dinners followed by saunas and vodka was barely concealed, and he appeared to find the toasts extremely boring. In sum, he did his best to make the Russians feel as inferior to the English as possible.

Moreover, in business matters, he strictly observed a "take-it-or-leave-it" style. He insisted on hard currency payments or credit guaranteed by a first-class Western bank as was presumably agreed upon the ministerial level in Moscow. Further, Smith was only willing to agree to licensed production in Russia, an unreasonably expensive demand, and demanded the exclusive use of English documentation and specifications.

During the week, Director Andrej and Janez from Iskra Commerce Moscow met each morning before breakfast. Little by little, the following points emerged from the multitude of speeches and toasts, personal discussions, and meetings of working teams.

- The processing equipment from Process Automation and Iskra Avtomatizacija was technically acceptable; the chances for this deal would, however, greatly improve with the 32-bit system, which Process Automation had thus far refused to offer.

- The first equipment was designated for one of the combine factories that was under construction. The supplier was expected to deliver the "appropriate" equipment, and the combine engineers remained ready to help with the specifications but were not able to prepare them without assistance.
- The chances for the business would increase rapidly if the supplier offered the "joint-venture" cooperative alternative, one aimed at production of at least 50% of the equipment in the combine.
- While it would be unreasonable to expect payments in hard currency, the combine and district authorities were prepared to assist Iskra in the search for countertrade opportunities, which should include commodities (crude oil, ferrous metals, gold, diamonds) as well as automobiles, lumber, special chemicals, and rare metals.
- Recommendations and approvals from Moscow authorities, though welcome, were not necessary. The rich Uralburg District's distant location from Moscow lessened its reliance on the central government. Also, expanded relations with the fraternal Slovenia would, by all means, considerably encourage business relationships.
- Uralburg, like other regions of the former Soviet Union, continued to be informally dominated by the powerful "vyerhooshka," including local administrative and political leaders and managing directors of the large combines. No important business deals could reach conclusion without cultivating a favorable attitude of the "vyerhooshka."

The hosts were very obliging. Iskra's technical director spent many hours with his colleagues, and by the end of the second day, announced that he had obtained all the necessary data to prepare the specifications. He also described the combine engineers as "nice, well-educated chaps who know a lot and are eager to learn more." He noted that the combine was definitely capable of manufacturing an important part of the equipment, because it already possessed much of the required technology.

Ivan Alja from the countertrade subsidiary of Iskra Commerce also worked diligently during the trip and obtained a lengthy list of candidates for an offset program. It included two hundred Samara cars, one to two hundred tons of special chemicals, several thousand cubic meters of pine-wood, and sparse quantities of rare metals. Iskra expected to be able to sell much of these items in Slovenia and the remainder to Italy, Spain, and Germany through existing distribution channels.

On Saturday afternoon before the farewell dinner, the hosts invited their guests to their homes. According to Janez, this was an excellent sign and meant that "they like us." Andrej Lesak was invited by Jurij Andrejevič Šamonov, the managing director of the combine, to his "dacha."

Due to a misunderstanding, Lesak arrived almost an hour early at the "dacha," an unpretentious wooden summer cottage, not particularly luxurious and surrounded by a large garden. Thus, Lesak surprised his host and his wife and son who were busy planting potatoes. Jurij Andrejevič Šamonov, a large man himself and one of the most influential members of the "vyerhooshka," gave his guest a friendly reception with bread, salt, and the obligatory vodka and apologized profusely for the miscommunication.

Undaunted, Lesak quite coolly removed his jacket, rolled up his sleeves and joined his host at potato planting. The host initially opposed Lesak's participation, but finally gave in and the group spent more than an hour in nice sunny weather laying seed potatoes into the furrows. Afterwards, Jurij Andrejevič Šamonov jokingly promised to give Andrej Ivanovič (Lesak is referred to in the traditional Russian way as Ivanovič after his father's name) a share of the crop and the latter promised to return for it.

In turn, Lesak, upon departing, invited his host to Slovenia to sign the agreement, which obviously pleased Jurij Andrejevič Šamonov. He said he gladly looked forward to visiting Slovenia, preferring it to London and "those arrogant Englishmen."

From May to June, Between Stuttgart and London

Two weeks later, Finance Director Skopuh and Ivan Alja from Iskra Commerce defined the necessary terms for interim financing and for payments in kind. Boris Lasin, Iskra Commerce—ISEL, Stuttgart, effected the preliminary consulting of banks. At the same time, an expert team at Iskra Avtomatizacija prepared draft specifications of the equipment to be purchased from Process Automation, Ltd., and that to be manufactured by Avtomatizacija and subsequently produced in Uralburg. Also, the lawyers of Iskra Commerce prepared the agreements relating to deliveries and countertrade, financing and guarantees, and protection of patent rights.

Though the progress on the project is far from smooth, Lesak knows that the problems encountered are quite normal. "Nevertheless, we know our way from now on," thinks Andrej. Successful in the Balkans for many decades, he is skilled in dealing with complicated transactions and human whims. Process Automation may be capable of developing the latest hi-tech, 32-bit processors, but he was certain that they lacked the ability to manage deals like this.

At the end of June, the preparations neared the end. The key actors, Director Lesak, Ivan Alja, Tilenepe, Peter Derman from Iskra Commerce London, and Boris Lasin, convened at Iskra Commerce-ISEL Stuttgart.

Financing of the project has been secured. Iskra Avtomatizacija, failed to obtain acceptable financing terms and necessary guarantees from the Slovenian commercial banks. However, ISEL, a respectable industrial and trading company in Baden-Wuertenberg, succeeded in accessing comprehensive credit lines from its commercial banks, backed by the guarantee of a Slovenian commercial bank. ISEL offered to make this credit line available to Iskra at a slightly higher interest rate. In accordance with this arrangement, Iskra Avtomatizacija agreed to channel its deliveries to Process Automation London through ISEL Stuttgart for a moderate commission.

In addition, because the lending capacity of ISEL Stuttgart depended on the value of its commercial transactions, the parties agreed that all deliveries from Process to Iskra should be carried out through ISEL Stuttgart as well. From the English point of view, Process would then not be selling to Iskra Avtomatizacija from Slovenia, a country still subject to elevated political risk due to the circumstances in the former Yugoslavia, but to ISEL Stuttgart, a sizable German trading company with outstanding bank references. On these grounds and to compensate for the acquisition of the Russian deal, Process Automation committed to a considerable reduction in the price of its deliveries to Iskra, and ISEL Stuttgart would receive a standard commission.

During tiring negotiations with Process Automation, Peter Derman from Iskra Commerce London, requested, as a prerequisite, Process Automation's consent to supply the 32-bit technology to which John Steel strongly objects. He was primarily afraid that subsequent Russian production of the equipment would lead to increased competition in western markets.

Several sessions later, a compromise was reached; Process Automation ceded access to Iskra the latest technology and allowed the sale of the equipment to Russia. However, it demanded that exports from Russia be channeled through Iskra and that Process Automation be consulted before sales were conducted outside the former Yugoslavia. Though hesitant, Process Automation also agreed to lower its prices to ISEL Stuttgart by 8% due to the decrease in risk and by another 5% due to the increase of business.

Preliminary negotiations with the combine, started through Janez from Iskra Commerce Moscow, followed. They encompassed issues including countertrade, technology transfer, initial and subsequent sale of the equipment, terms of payments in kind, personnel training and provision of spare parts and documentation.

The project was complicated by poor business decision-making on the part of the managers and experts of the combine and the district authorities of Uralburg. This, however, was understandable given the influence of the Russian culture with its centrally-planned economic system. Recognizing this, Iskra Commerce organized a three-week managerial seminar taught by lecturers from Slovenian MBA courses. Concepts related to reliability and accuracy in business, including on-time delivery, were quite new to them, and some were less than eager to learn. Though representatives from Iskra often almost ran out of patience, they managed to restrain their feelings due to their new friendships with their colleagues in the Combine.

In Ljubljana in September

Andrej Lesak took personal responsibility for the preparations leading to the signing of the final agreement. According to the usual practice of the Russian partners, much importance was placed on adhering to proper protocol.

The Russian delegation of eleven prominent people included persons of various ranks, including Ivan Ivanovič Ivanov, the president of the district authority, and Jurij Andrejevič Šamonov, the managing director of the combine, to Jevremov, the "eminence grise" from the combine, a few middle-rank directors of the combine, the director of the export company from Moscow and two less important members of the local authority. The five-day visit was strictly governed by an official program of visits, presentations, discussions, a farewell party, and numerous social events.

From the Slovenian perspective, the visit was highly successful. The guests, who all speak only Russian, became more relaxed upon discovering that they could easily make themselves understood, without an interpreter, in the street, in shops, and in restaurants. The guests were also enchanted by the beautiful landscape of Slovenia, its people, the order and cleanliness, the settlements of small dwellings, the neat and well-kept factories, good telephone communications and cable TV, and the shops that were well-supplied with technical and fashionable products.

Finally, accompanied by due ceremony and much publicity, came the signing of the sales agreement, cooperation agreement, agreement on counter-deliveries and the agreement on collaboration among the chambers of economy and of protocol with the Ministry of Foreign Affairs of Slovenia. Concerts, speeches, an exchange of memorial presents, and a pleasant social evening and farewell concluded the event.

The Project

The business with the Uralburg Combine was nicknamed "the potato business" for two reasons. The first is semantic; in the Slovenian language, the expression "to have potato" means "good luck." The other is related to the following story often told by Iskra's director, Andrej Lesak.

When the Russian delegation from Uralburg arrived to sign the agreement with Iskra, Jurij Andrejevič Šamonov, the managing director of the combine, paid a special visit to Andrej Lesak on the first morning after his arrival. The secretary helpfully opened the door for him into the director's office and Jurij Andrejevič strode forward to firmly shake hands with Lesak and to give him a squeeze of the hand and, according to old Slavic habit, a friendly hug and kiss.

Stepping backwards, he placed his brief-case on the desk and opened it saying: "I've got a present for you, Andrej Ivanovič. It's from my home." He then reached into his case, brought out a neat, small cotton bag, untied it and poured out three large potatoes onto Lesak's desk. "There are some more of your potatoes left at my dacha. Will you come to fetch them?"

Afterwards, they ceremoniously baked the Russian potatoes at a picnic on the banks of the Sava river not far away from Ljubljana. Everyone shared a bit of the three potatoes. Since then, Director Lesak has become known for having his own patch of ground in the spacious garden surrounding the datcha of Jurij Andrejevič Šamonov, the managing director of the Uralburg Combine. Lesak later mused that, though the significance of the potatoes held great meaning for him, the full weight of their symbolism would probably be lost on the director of Process Automation.

APPENDIX: Iskra Avtomatizacija and Process Automation

Iskra Avtomatizacija is one of the medium-size companies of the Iskra group. With more than 10,000 employees and an annual turnover of approximately 1 billion USD, it is a noteworthy European manufacturer of telecommunications, automation, electronic equipment, automotive products, and component parts. Iskra was founded in Slovenia after World War II. Available experts and skillful manpower, as well as the centennial industrial tradition of the country, were the initial competitive advantages of Iskra. Beginning more than 25 years ago, the Slovenian, and subsequently the Yugoslav markets, became increasingly unable to support further growth, thus, Iskra concentrated on exports, in particular to developed countries and the countries of the third world. Gradually, Iskra built a network of more than 20 representative offices and companies abroad, and, at present, exports represent 40% of Iskra production.

The Iskra Avtomatizacija division was established by Iskra twenty years ago with the purpose of satisfying the needs of Yugoslav industry in the domain of process automation. Later, a strategic alliance was entered into with Process Automation to gain access to modern technologies necessary to penetrate additional markets. Iskra Avtomatizacija employs about 300 people, of which one-fifth are educated as engineers. Its annual turnover derived from the sale of equipment, products, services and know-how, amounts to 20 to 30 million USD.

Iskra Commerce is the central trading organization in Iskra. Consisting of a group of companies, it plays an important role as the main Iskra distribution channel (in former Yugoslavia as well as internationally). The Iskra Commerce companies include Iskra International (exports and imports, with several representations abroad), Iskra Domestic (Slovenia and the markets of former Yugoslavia), Iskra Ponti (countertrade), and several more. Iskra Commerce owns a holding company, Cranex, in Zurich, Switzerland, which is the major shareholder in all Iskra trading companies outside Slovenia and former Yugoslavia. ISEL Stuttgart, Iskra Ltd. London and Iskra Moscow, mentioned in this case, also comprise some of these companies.

Slovenia was constituted in 1991 upon the dissolution of the former Yugoslavia, of which it was the most north-western republic and shares borders with Italy, Austria, Hungary, and Croatia. It covers 20,000 km^2 (7,800 m^2) and has a population of 2 million. It is a predominantly mountainous country on the eastern range of the Alps, and its natural resources are fairly limited. Its capitol is Ljubljana.

Farming, stock-farming, and forestry support only a minor part of the population. The country is quite industrialized, and of major importance are the steel, metal-processing, electrotechnical and electronic, textile and chemical, food processing, and motor vehicle industries. In addition, Slovenia has widely developed summer and winter tourism. Slovenia has good air, road, railway and maritime connections and facilities.

The educational system is fairly good, and intellectuals constitute a powerful segment of the society. Constitutionally, Slovenia is a parliamentary democracy with several political parties and a two-chamber parliament. Slovenia has forever been a part of the European culture and civilization. Since its independence, Slovenia has undergone extensive re-privatization and economic restructuring. Because Slovenia is located at the crossroads of the Adriatic Sea, the Panonian Plain, the Central Europe, and the Balkans, it has throughout history been an agent in the economic and political currents of the area and played a mediator's role therein. Upon its loss of the traditional markets in Yugoslavia, Slovenia turned to Central Europe again, but has at the same time preserved its connections with Eastern Europe generated and cultivated during several decades.

5
Nissan United Kingdom, Ltd.

John E. Walsh, Jr.

Entering into a Business Relationship in the United Kingdom

In 1970, three thousand Datsun cars rusting on the docks of Rotterdam, abandoned by the existing U.K. concessionaire, was the catalyst for the relationship that developed between Nissan United Kingdom Limited (Nissan U.K.) and Nissan Motor Company of Japan (Nissan M.C.). Nissan Motor Company approached Octav Botnar, who arranged the transshipment and sale of the Rotterdam Datsun automobiles.

Botnar had arrived in Great Britain from West Germany in 1966 to reorganize a failing and insolvent U.K. distribution company (See Appendix A). By 1969, he had increased company sales by 300% with substantial profits, and in 1970, had established his own automobile marketing company called Moorcrest Motors.

Late in 1970, Botnar flew to Tokyo and arranged an agreement for a sustained distributorship relationship between Nissan M.C. and himself, changing the name of his company from Moorcrest Motors to Datsun U.K. Ltd.

In 1971, the Datsun name was unknown and customer resistance to Japanese products was high. If you told someone you had a Datsun, they assumed you were the owner of a small, German, sausage-shaped dog. The automobiles had questionable visual appeal, but were economical and reliable. In 1971, Datsun U.K. sold 6,900 vehicles; 30,000 vehicles in 1972; and 60,500 in 1973.

According to one Datsun U.K. executive, the phenomenal rate of growth was achieved by a totally new approach to marketing and selling automobiles. Botnar's philosophy was that the right kind of dealer is self-motivated to make money and

I would like to thank and acknowledge Edward M. Luttwak who helped in the preparation of this case.

does not need a management hierarchy. Thus, the whole operation was single-tiered with direct contact between individual dealers and the Datsun U.K. office.

Dealers were given high margins, and profits earned by Datsun U.K. were constantly reinvested to improve facilities. Reinvestment was strongly encouraged by Nissan M.C. Botnar believed staff should be kept to a minimum (20 people established Datsun U.K.), and his was the smallest headquarters staff of any sizable automobile distributor in the U.K. with the best record of sales and turnover per employee.

Datsun U.K. avoided relying on outside suppliers, preferring to develop in-house facilities where possible. The print room was a department of one, converted from the ladies' toilet, and producing all the company's publicity material.

In October 1973, the company suffered a major disaster when one of the worst fires on record in West Sussex destroyed the parts warehouse. Staff were outside watching helplessly as firemen battled the blaze. Botnar, keen to keep business running as usual, approached the parts manager. "What are you doing?" he inquired. "Watching the fire," replied the parts manager. "I'll watch the fire," said Botnar, "You order the parts."

In-house facilities continued to be a feature of Datsun U.K.'s operation and now included Datsun Finance, Datsun Insurance, and Datsun Extended Warranty. Together, they provided the customer with a total ownership package.

Datsun U.K. was so successful during its first three years of operation that Nissan M.C. amended the existing clause in their distribution agreement that would change the automatic renewal from three years to five, and renew automatically every five years, provided that Datsun U.K.'s obligations in the contract were met and agreed sales targets achieved.

By 1974, Datsun U.K. was outselling Toyota, its nearest Japanese rival by more than three to one. The U.K. was the only market in the world where Nissan outsold Toyota. The growth of Japanese automobile sales provoked British demands for import restraint. The Japan Automobile Manufacturer's Association (JAMA) agreed in 1976 to confine sales within the limits of current market shares, which left Datsun U.K. with 6% of the entire U.K. market or 60% of total Japanese automobile sales in the U.K., and also 60% of total Nissan M.C. sales in Europe. In 1977, Datsun U.K. sold 82,000 automobiles. In 1978, sales exceeded 100,000, whereas Toyota sold 28,000 and Honda only 19,500.

Octav Botnar respected Chairman Katsuji Kawamata and President Takashi Ishihara, the two senior Nissan Motor Company executives, and they in turn respected him and depended heavily on his talents and advice. He and Ishihara had an understanding that any major operational difficulties could be referred directly to Ishihara who would resolve the problems personally. This procedure was rarely needed, but when it was, Ishihara took immediate action.

Under President Ishihara, management decision-making at Nissan Motor Company was based on seniority, as typified in these statements by Paul Ingrassia and Kathryn Groven in a *Wall Street Journal* article on November 1, 1989:

For years, a strict regimen governed the staff meetings at Nissan Motor Company's technical center in Tokyo's Western suburbs.

Employees wore identification badges listing not only their names but also their date of hire. No one could voice an opinion until everybody with more seniority had spoken first, so younger employees—often the most enthusiastic and innovative—seldom spoke at all. According to Satoko Kitada, a young designer, ". . . tasks were assigned strictly on the basis of seniority. The oldest designer got to work on the dash board. The next level down did doors. If a new person got to work on part of the speedometer, that was a great deal."

Quite aside from his business interests, Botnar developed a deep interest in Japan and its history, in which he was widely read. He admired the Japanese belief in long-term relationships, the importance of mutual trust and harmony (wa).

Planning a Manufacturing Facility in the U.K.

The strength of the U.K. market motivated Octav Botnar to meet with President Takashi Ishihara in early 1980 to suggest that a base existed to support manufacturing facilities in the U.K. A new plant would not only service the U.K. but would be a source of exports that would overcome the restrictions on foreign automobiles enforced in other European markets like France, Italy, and Spain.

In July 1980, a meeting was held between key Nissan M.C. executives, Octav Botnar, and the U.K. Minister of State and Department of Labor to discuss the proposed facility. After long discussions and many meetings about employment and industrial relations, financial assistance, environmental protection, local content, and nationalism, Nissan M.C.'s first step was to consider whether to proceed with a detailed feasibility study. The Minister of State would present the possiblity of the study to the House of Commons. If the House of Commons was in agreement, an outline program for an investment would be prepared and presented to the Department of Labor for further discussion.

The project would include an assembly plant with a capacity of 5,000 units per month from one shift, which could be doubled later. A stamping plant would be operative from the start with engines, axles, suspensions, and instruments initially being imported from Japan. Depending on the U.K. and E.C. market, one or two basic models would be produced; these would be world models—front-wheel drive with good fuel economy, suitable for the fleet market and previously introduced in Japan. If a decision to go ahead was made, the aim would be to start production within 2 or 3 years.

Norman Tebbit, the Minister of State, presented the proposed feasibilty study to the House of Commons. A lengthy and spirited discussion waged, and continued sporadically throughout 1982 and 1983.

The U.K. Assembly Plant

By the end of 1986 an assembly plant in Sunderland, England began operations. The initial assembly started with minor changes to the Bluebird and Sunny models. In 1987, the plant began assembling the new Stanza (GP model). Plant capacity was approximately 200,000 cars per year of a single model. The plant consisted of a car assembly plant incorporating a paint plant, a welding plant, a stamping plant, a unit assembly plant, and a machine plant.

The new Stanza model was substantially modified to make it increasingly suitable to U.K. conditions at the manufacturing stage in early 1990. The annual capacity in 1993 was 300,000 cars and engines, with 88% of production for export.

Because the plant was wholly owned by Nissan M.C., key management positions were held by Japanese. These managers introduced employees to "the Nissan way," which stressed the proper use of people, lean car production, consensus flexibility and team work, and the social organization of control.

Sale of the Stock in Datsun U.K.

In June 1981, Botnar recognized that it was in the long term interest of Nissan M.C., Datsun U.K., and the U.K. dealership network for Nissan M.C. to acquire control of Datsun U.K. All of the shares, except those held by the Camelia Botnar Foundation, representing less than 2% of the total, would be sold. The effective transfer would occur when the U.K. plant became operational. Nissan M.C. agreed it was essential for them to have control. The price of the shares would be based on the certified balance sheet as of July 31, 1981, with adjustments for any change at date of acquisition of net asset value and real estate value.

Nissan M.C. wished only to acquire the distribution of vehicles and parts. Botnar pointed out that the subsidiary companies, Datsun Finance Ltd., Datsun Parts Transport, Ltd., Datsun Plant and Industrial Machinery, Ltd., and Datsun Fleet and Leasing, Ltd. were of a vertical integration and formed an essential part of the operation and distribution. Nissan M.C. agreed but suggested that they should be separately valued by the assessors. Botnar stated that if Nissan M.C. did not wish to acquire or operate the subsidiaries, they would be sold off in whole or in part, and thereafter, to maintain their service to Datsun U.K. if required.

In May 1985, officials of Nissan M.C., and Botnar signed a letter of intent for the sale of Nissan U.K.* The shares would be sold in two stages. In the first stage, 26% would be sold, but no later than July 31, 1986. In the second stage all of the rest of the shares available would be sold on a date fixed by mutual agreement but would be completed before July 31, 1988.

---

* The name of Datsun United Kingdom, Ltd. was changed to Nissan United Kingdom on January 2, 1984.

For determining the value of the shares of Nissan U.K., the independent professional valuer(s) would be nominated respectively by both parties from among the internationally reputed valuation firms in the U.K. The report of the valuer(s) would not be binding on either party in respect to the value of the shares, but would be the basis for negotiation of the shareholders and buyers. The final price would be decided in negotiation between the shareholders and the buyers in consideration of the valuation.

A major management reshuffle occurred in April 1985. Nissan M.C.'s market share in Japan had dropped every year since the late 1970s. To revive the company's marketing strategies and to shore up domestic sales, Yutaka Kume, 63, was made president, Takeshi Ishihara, chairman, and Katsuji Kawamata, counselor. Kume joined the company in 1946 as an engineer, with a background in manufacturing.

At the time of the reorganization, Yoshitada Uchiyama, executive vice-president in charge of overseas sales, wrote Botnar stating, "I am determined to contribute to the greater development of our overseas business, to ensure sales in the U.K. market." After a personal visit to Botnar, Uchiyama praised Botnar's energetic sales of Nissan automobiles and Botnar's excellent planning and timing in upgrading the dealership network in the U.K. At the end of 1985, Nissan U.K. sold 105,000 automobiles while Toyota sold 34,700.

Ending a Business Relationship in the United Kingdom

In March 1986, Katsuji Kawamata, the former chairman of Nissan died, signaling to Botnar a change in focus; the deference shown to foreigners. At that time, Yoshikazu Kawana, 50, a soft-spoken economist and a member of the board of directors of Nissan M.C., headed up European operations.

A Business Relations Agreement was signed on September 25, 1986. The agreement would be in effect until terminated by either party giving the other at least thirty days prior notice in writing. Any termination would be without prejudice to the rights and obligations of the parties as they relate to vehicles at the time when the termination takes effect, and the rights and obligations would continue in force and effect until such time as their agreement shall have been fully performed in relation to such vehicles. No mention was made of arbitration procedures.

In 1988, the merchant bankers retained by Botnar valued total Nissan U.K. holdings at 750 million pounds. Nissan Motor Company's merchant bankers, after specifically noting that the estimate was not to be taken as a definite offer, stated that their method of valuation had produced the figure of 330 million pounds. This figure in Botnar's eyes treated Nissan U.K.'s book value as if it were bankrupt, not a highly profitable business. Botnar countered with a memorandum to Nissan M.C. suggesting the sale of the core distribution business for 390 million pounds, while he retained the automotive financial group, the financial services, and a car removal unit. Kawana suggested tabling any negotiation about the subsidiaries until after the sale of Nissan U.K., and proposed an outside audit to determine profits and value.

Discussions with Kume and the negotiations for a sale price for Nissan U.K. led Botnar to write Kume in November 1988. He wrote:

I had an understanding with Mr. Ishihiara when he was president that any major operational difficulties could be referred to him directly when necessary. I seldom needed to use this line except in very extreme cases, but he resolved the problems personally.

I was trying to ascertain whether a similar arrangement could be established between us, because when I have addressed problems to you once or twice in the past, you have delegated them to your subordinates which was futile for us both. Nevertheless, I feel I should update you regarding the negotiations. I have never approached Nissan with a proposal to sell Nissan U.K. There was an agreement in principle in 1980 when Nissan publicly undertook a feasibility study on setting up a plant.

I agreed that it was reasonable for Nissan to aim to control the sales business in the U.K. in view of the large production volume involved and the importance of the U.K. market to the production plant. Furthermore, as Nissan M.C. did not have and still does not have staff with the experience and expertise necessary for managing a business like Nissan U.K., it was agreed that a number of selected staff would spend some time working at Nissan U.K. prior to the acquisition in order to assimilate as much knowledge and know-how as possible to enable Nissan Motor Company eventually to take control of the business successfully.

In 1985, Nissan had decided to reduce its investment and to make in phase one a small plant, producing 25,000 cars per year initially from assembly kits, rising in phase two to 100,000 per year in 1992. This made the task of managing Nissan U.K. even more complicated.

Suddenly Nissan presented itself as being ready to take over Nissan U.K. within a few months, with no training of any staff, no preparation, no knowledge of the company or the market and with no interest in the effect such a takeover would have on the management and staff of Nissan U.K. or the dealer body, and regardless of the fact that relations between Nissan U.K. staff and the dealer body had greatly deteriorated in recent years.

We were amazed at how Nissan personnel could have acquired the intricate know-how and expertise necessary for running a complex business like Nissan U.K., without having any knowledge of the business. Yet the whole problem as far as the Nissan delegates were concerned was to find out the purchase price—everything else was no problem.

We, on the contrary, consider that for Nissan to acquire the company at this time would be the worst thing which could happen to Nissan U.K., our staff, the dealer body, and for Nissan itself. The whole franchise in the U.K. would suffer considerable damage.

The Nissan delegates however were uninterested in the substantial factors which made the acquisition ill-timed, ill-advised and even absurd.

Briefly, the situation with Nissan U.K. and the dealer network is as follows:

The protracted public debate between Nissan's top management in Japan, which was widely reported in the U.K. press, coupled with five years of shipping restrictions on Japanese cars to the U.K., severely undermined dealers' confidence in the future of the franchise here. Many dealers left the network during this period, leaving the franchise greatly weakened.

From 1983, the problem of excess production in Europe heightened, and the fight for market share in the U.K. became fierce. Nissan's main competitors bought market share at any price: Ford increased its share from 25% to 30%, General Motors from 8% to 16%, the smaller manufacturers increased their share and new direct competitors to Nissan entered the market in the shape of Hyundai, Seat, and the Eastern European Marques.

Throughout this period, manufacturers have been applying a permanent policy of discounting, special terms for contract hire, leasing, and car rental companies. In order to compete in the market, Nissan U.K. has to offer the same incentives to its dealers.

The net result of this marketing policy is a huge increase in the size of the used car market in the U.K. and the sale of used cars has become crucial to the success of the dealers' new car business—the used car market is now three times as big as the new car market.

The majority of Nissan dealers had insufficient space to cope with volume used car sales and the concomitant workshop activity, so the Nissan franchise ceased to be profitable for them and they turned to low volume/high profit margins such as Toyota, Honda, Mazda, Saab, Volvo, etc.

This, coupled with the appreciation of the yen from 1983 to 1986 of c. 50%, has made the whole new Nissan car sales business unprofitable, for the dealers as well as for Nissan U.K.. Both Nissan U.K. and the dealers therefore had to engage in ancillary activities in order to survive in business.

No one in Nissan Motor Company seems to understand that even in the most profitable European franchises, Ford and General Motors, only 20% of the dealership profit comes from new car sales; used car profits are much higher and the dealers rely on their accessories, bodyshop servicing, insurance repair, car rental and financing activities to keep the business viable.

The Nissan delegates were very interested in Nissan U.K.'s reported overall profitability, but although we tried to explain the business to them, they were not interested and seemed not to understand that the profit shown on the balance sheet is not generated only from new car sales, but mainly from returns on retained dividends, the finance business, transport, accessories, property rental and retail activities, etc.

The delegates were not aware and/or interested in the dealer network and how much had to be done to enable Nissan U.K. to maintain its market share in the wake of the shipping restrictions, the erosion of the price competitiveness of Nissan cars, not to mention the increased sales in line with the extra production available from the U.K. plant.

This was strongly reminiscent of my short experience with Nissan when I gave up the Nissan franchise in Switzerland in order to concentrate on the greater task of developing the U.K. market in view of the production plant. When I handed over Nissan Suisse to Nissan (without asking any consideration for goodwill), its market share had been increased threefold in five years; we were ready to overtake Toyota and we were making 10 million Swiss francs profit per year.

Now, three years later, Nissan has doubled the headcount, lost market share to the extent of being overtaken even by Subaru and Mitsubishi, experienced a drop in sales to one third of Toyota's, and shows annual losses of several million Swiss francs.

It is ironic that at the time of Nissan's acquisition of Nissan Suisse, the general manager, a German gentleman, had the impertinence to announce several times in the press and in the presence of the new chairman of Nissan Suisse, that some "order" would be returned to the franchise now that Nissan was running the company.

Such a level of crass and mindless behavior is really unbelievable in a company of purported international standing, even if the top management were unaware of it—like the fact that before discussions about Nissan U.K. had seriously started, the delegates were asking Nissan U.K. staff to help them to find a replacement for me, as chairman of Nissan U.K.

In view of this, I could not permit the same fate to fall upon my loyal staff and dealers in the U.K. In fact, we honestly and openly believe that now the absurd saga of discussions with Nissan's delegates about the acquisition of Nissan U.K. is over, Nissan has been dealt a great service.

Since 1985, we have been buying and building 150 new dealerships, of a high enough standard for Rolls Royce and Mercedes. The showrooms are first class, they have ample facilities for volume new and used car retailing, bodyshops for used car repair, and profitable insurance work and government testing facilities for used cars; an investment so far of £250 million.

We have created our own separate retailing network, which trades exclusively new Nissan cars, operating under the name of AFG Limited, an independent commercial enterprise. It has the capacity to retail 100,000 used cars. It is the largest motor retailing company in the U.K. and probably the largest in Europe.

We are convinced that it has turned out to Nissan's advantage not to have invested in Nissan U.K.; the investment would have been wasted because we do not think Nissan could ever have done a similar job.

In relieving Nissan from this burden, we consider that Nissan M.C. will be in a position to use all its know-how and competence in other major markets in Europe such as Germany, France, the Netherlands, Spain, and Italy, where Nissan cars are sold through back street garages with no investment or facilities, leaving Nissan obliged to underprice and discount the cars in order to sell them; in Europe, Nissan retail prices are on average 25% under the local competition, which must have a significant bearing on Nissan's profitability, whereas in the U.K. we sell at the same price as Ford and General Motors, the market leaders.

As far as the U.K. is concerned, we would ask you not to worry. We are doing everything necessary and possible to develop the business in view of the expansion of the U.K. plant. We are also ready to repeat that we are not considering selling the company. Should the situation ever change in the future, Nissan would have first refusal.

I appreciate your confidence in Kawana, and I am sure that with these things clear between us, there will be cooperation on day-to-day problems between Nissan U.K. and Nissan.

I trust that this letter will not offend you or anyone else at Nissan. Although some issues may be unpleasant to face, my only intention in writing is to try to explain a very complex situation and series of events with the objective of being of help to Nissan.

Kume's reply was short, reserving comments and rebuttals. Because Nissan U.K. would not be sold, all understandings and intent premised on its purchase would cease. Nissan M.C. would need to reexamine its relationship with Nissan U.K. in the future.

At the end of 1988, Kawana met with Botnar to discuss how to reestablish the formerly good relationship between the two companies, and explain the new Nissan Europe structure that he would head. Kawana wanted both parties to cooperate and would send Nissan people to learn the U.K. market and develop some expertise. He added there were no perpetual agreements and restated Botnar's position; Botnar would not accept 12 months of termination in a new distributor agreement if it was proposed.

During the next six months, Nissan M.C. reduced Nissan U.K.'s profitability by denying supplies of models more easily saleable with higher profit margins, and exacting high transfer prices for autos that were supplied. Furthermore, Nissan U.K. was charged more for autos than its counterparts in other countries in Europe. The price differential between Germany, the Netherlands, and the U.K. averaged 19–24%.

Botnar wrote Kume complaining that Nissan's export department behaved irresponsibly in allocating in favor of Germany and the Netherlands by preferential pricing and supply. The tactics were meant to illicit a commitment from him for higher volume. A manager representing Kawana attempted to negotiate a price increase of 10–12%. After prolonged negotiations, Kawana interceded and agreed to a 3–4% increase.

In October 1989, Botnar and Nissan U.K. executives came to Tokyo with factual information to resolve pricing and model allocations through face-to-face negotiations. During the discussions, Nissan M.C. deduced that Nissan U.K. was trapped, and in Botnar's view, proposals from Nissan M.C. were insulting.

In November, Kume summarized the meeting, stressing the importance of trust and confidence for building stable and sound business relationships. He believed that all Nissan people carried out their jobs in a fair, equitable, and responsible manner under his direction. The U.K. operations were no exception, assuring Botnar that every transaction was not done to force him out of business, or to undermine him. Kume hoped that Botnar would understand Nissan's situation in respect to profitability and R & D. Nissan's export business to the U.K was not profitable, which restricted Nissan M.C.'s support.

Botnar wrote Kume and said he lacked trust in Nissan M.C. because of Nissan's unfair pricing and supply policies, and the procrastinating tactics used by Nissan in pricing negotiations over the last three years. Botnar felt that all of the tactics were designed to make trading conditions with Nissan unacceptable and the franchise unprofitable so that he would be coerced into relinquishing the Nissan franchise altogether.

In 1989, Kawana investigated the sale of 70% of the Automatic Financial Group (AFG) by Botnar. Botnar explained that this group was owned by him and was not part of Nissan U.K. Therefore, management of AFG would remain with him.Botnar expressed the hope of cooperating with Nissan M.C. honestly and fairly, but at the end of the year Nissan U.K. was notified it would be denied supplies of two highly salable high margin models.

On November 15 1990, *Automotive Magazine* published the following article:

> The war of nerves between Octav Botnar's Nissan U.K. and Nissan Europe has taken a new twist with the announcement that Nissan Europe is to set up a London office.
>
> Former Ford fleet supremo David Hurst, the Nissan Europe director responsible for the UK and Eire, will move from Amsterdam to head up a new office, in Arlington Street SW1, which opens on November 19. The move pointedly makes no reference to Nissan U.K.

The move will increase pressure on Nissan U.K., which has been locked in bitter disputes with Nissan Europe over pricing of the new Primera, and will fuel speculations that the wrangle will escalate into a full-scale power struggle over the UK concession.

The importer's retail affiliate, AFG, meanwhile, has put "for sale" signs up over the doors of yet more dealerships; currently 27 are up for grabs. Sales will continue to fall next year, the company claims.

Nissan U.K. has had to negotiate with Nissan Europe over the Primera price, and claims the margin it receives does not allow it to market the car aggressively to the fleet market. Nissan U.K. revealed that only 1,500 Primeras have been sold since the car was launched in September.

Nissan M.C. has in the past made no secret of the fact that it would like to reclaim the U.K. concession, which Mr. Botnar established in 1968 and holds "for life." But negotiations have continually faltered.

In November 1990, Botnar suggested that he and his team meet Kume and the top Nissan M.C. leadership in Tokyo to jointly develop principles for pricing and the model mix. He stated again that if Nissan M.C. desired to buy Nissan U.K. he would be ready to negotiate a sale. His letter was sent to Kawana. A meeting was held in Amsterdam, but both Kawana and Botnar sent subordinates to represent them.

Kawana accused Botnar of being responsible for the deterioration of the relationship between Nissan U.K. and Nissan M.C., and suggested that Botnar behaved irrationally and rejected the renewal of talks on the purchase of Nissan U.K. by Nissan M.C.

On December 31, 1990 Kawana formally wrote to Botnar stating that Nissan U.K.'s distribution franchise would be canceled as of December 31, 1991. He stated, "The Distribution Agreement will terminate in one year from this date. This notice does not void Nissan U.K.'s responsibilities regarding vehicles already ordered, and Nissan M.C. is ready to provide its products until the termination of the Agreement under the existing terms."

Press releases were given concurrently with the dispatch to Botnar who was questioned about the cancellation before he received the letter. Nissan U.K. filed suit against Nissan M.C. and its British manufacturing and European distribution subsidiaries, to enjoin the defendants to maintain the Distribution Agreement first signed in 1971 and the Business Relations Agreement of 25 September 1986; demanding a retraction of the cancellation of that agreement; and damages for the breach of the two agreements.

In March 1991, Botnar was approached on behalf of Nissan M.C. with offers to buy out his holdings, or at least the AFG dealerships. This time the intent was serious, but Botnar refused to negotiate because the amount offered was a distressed sale price.

In May 1991, Nissan M.C. and two of its European-based affiliates, Nissan Motor Manufacturing U.K. and Nissan Europe, petitioned the Japan Commercial Arbitration Association for arbitration, seeking to confirm the cancellation of Nissan U.K.'s distribution rights, to prohibit Nissan U.K. from using Nissan trade names, trademarks, etc., and to have Nissan U.K. pay the cost of the arbitration. The opening section suggested that Botnar had a shadowy, perhaps Nazi past, (actually,

Botnar was a resistance fighter against the Nazis, see Appendix A), and he engaged in tax evasion. Coming as it did from the foreign supplier of a U.K. importer, this accusation naturally triggered a massive tax raid (extensively covered on television). It included a search of Botnar's own home, and was followed by the false rumor that he had been arrested.

Nissan M.C. claimed that the prices it charged to Nissan U.K. over the years were especially discounted to assist its growth, and that Nissan U.K. chose to regard those prices as normal, rather than as an exceptional favor.

In the petition, Nissan M.C. further made a whole series of charges:

1. That the splitting off of Automotive Financial Group from Nissan U.K. and the subsequent transfer of a sizeable portion of its shares to the Union Bank of Switzerland violated Article 21 of the Memorandum of Distribution Agreement (see Appendix B).
2. That an attempt by Union Bank of Switzerland to sell its Automotive Financial Group holding to Nissan M.C. was blocked by Botnar.
3. That efforts by units of the Botnar group to acquire sale franchises from other car manufacturers (albeit after the cancellation notice) violated Articles of the original Distribution Agreement (Appendix B, Article 16).
4. That its cars have been sold at higher prices in Britain than on the Continent because Nissan U.K. exacts abnormally high profit margins.
5. That the publicity given to the over-pricing accusations against itself by Nissan U.K. violate Articles 18 and 28 of the Distribution Agreement.

In late 1991, Nissan U.K. answered Nissan M.C.'s petition, and also presented a counterclaim to stop attempt to have arbitration in Japan. In seeking the dismissal of all Nissan M.C.'s claims and the payment of all arbitration costs, Nissan U.K. pointed out that:

1. Nissan U.K. never signed any agreements with two of the petitioners (Nissan Motor Manufacturing U.K. and Nissan Europe) that called for disagreements with them to be handled by arbitration in Japan.
2. The current contractual arrangements between Nissan U.K. and Nissan M.C. based on the 1985 Agreement, which did not call for arbitration in Japan, whereas the 1971 Agreement arbitration clause only comes into effect if questions arise in connection with that agreement.
3. Nissan U.K. was successful because of its own widely-recognized marketing abilities, not because of any special pricing concessions from Nissan M.C.
4. The Automotive Finance Group (AFG) was separated from Nissan U.K. to accommodate Nissan M.C.'s limited funds for the purchase of Nissan U.K., and that the establishment of AFG did not constitute a transfer of the core import and distribution business. Further, when the Automotive Finance Group was established as a separate entity, Nissan M.C. raised no objection.

5. Nissan U.K. also denied further Nissan M.C. charges that it failed to submit order and sales forecasts. The latter were duly provided as requested, when Nissan M.C.'s own pricing schedules allowed such forecasts to be made on a sound basis. One cannot forecast how many cars can be sold without knowing their prices.

6. That it never failed to make payments or accept the delivery of vehicles on due dates to "any unreasonable extent."

Appendix A
Biographical Note: Octav Botnar

Ever since he became widely known in Britain as an innovative and very successful businessman, attempts by the British press to profile his life story collided with Botnar's refusal to give out any information.

Octav Botnar was born on October 21, 1913 in Czernowitz, the German-speaking cultural center of Bukovina, then part of the Hapsburg empire, annexed by Romania in 1919, annexed again by the Soviet Union in 1940, and now part of the Western Ukraine. His name at birth was Oswald Bundorf; he adopted the name Octav Botnar while in the French resistance against the German occupation.

A left-wing political activist while still a schoolboy, he was arrested at the age of sixteen and imprisoned for three years by the Romanian authorities. After the outbreak of the Spanish Civil War in 1936, he volunteered for the Republican cause, but was detained while in transit through France. When World War II began in 1939, he joined the elite *22me Regiment de Marche* of foreign volunteers. After the Armistice of June 1940, he became a prisoner of war. Escaping in November 1940, he immediately joined a resistance network of German speakers who specialized in penetrating the German occupation forces to carry out anti-Nazi propaganda.

After the arrest of the original leaders, he organized his own resistance network, which at one point edited, printed, and distributed a German-language anti-Nazi newspaper at the rate of 100,000 copies per issue. From 1943, he led escaped Russian prisoners of war in ambushes and raids against the German occupation forces. He survived numerous firefights.

Following the Allied liberation, he remained in France until his return to Romania in late 1945. Recognized as an outstanding organizer, he was first given the task of reconstructing the war-damaged transport network of the capital, Bucharest, and subsequently spearheaded the emergency relief effort during the famine of 1946. After the full Communist takeover, he continued to be given important positions, but in 1960 he was arrested and tried as a "capitalist spy."

In 1964, weighing 40 kilograms, Botnar was released from the forced-labor barges of the Danube delta where many died of hunger. In 1965, he emigrated to West Germany where he obtained immediate citizenship as a former Hapsburg citizen. Already 52 years old, he could only find work as a car salesman. He was so successful in reorganizing a dealership of NSU (the small German auto manufacturer absorbed by Volkswagen in 1969) that in 1966 he was sent to Britain to rescue NSU's failing British distribution company.

Appendix B
Articles from Memorandum of Distribution Agreement

Article 8: Term of this Agreement

This Agreement shall continue in force and govern all relations and transactions between the parties hereto for a first period of three (3) years as from the date of signing, unless this Agreement is terminated as provided for hereinafter.

Article 16: Prohibition on Dealing in Other Motor Vehicles

Without NISSAN's prior written consent, the Importer shall not buy, sell or otherwise deal in motor vehicles of any kind manufactured in Japan except the Motor Vehicles or any motor vehicles manufactured elsewhere the price, size and performance of which are similar to those of any Motor Vehicles or which are sold in competition with the Motor Vehicles. The Importer shall also strive to make its dealers agree that they will not buy, sell or deal in motor vehicles of any kind manufactured elsewhere the price, size and performance of which are similar to those of the Motor Vehicles.

Article 18: Advertising

The Importer undertakes to make the Products known in the Territory in order to achieve the maximum possible sales of such Products. NISSAN may at its own expense advertise and defray costs of public relations work to the extent NISSAN may consider advisable.

Article 21: Right of Termination

This Agreement shall continue in force and govern all relations and transactions between the parties hereto until the termination thereof or same is canceled on the grounds hereinafter mentioned.

In the event of non-performance, unsatisfactory performance and/or violation by the Importer of the provisions of this Agreement then NISSAN shall give to the Importer sixty (60) days written notice requiring the Importer to remedy such non-performance and unsatisfactory performance and/or violation as be specified in the notice.

i) An Assignment has been made by the Importer of the whole or an important part of its business without the written consent thereto first having been obtained from NISSAN which written consent shall not be unreasonably withheld.

ii) A Court Order for the liquidation of the Importer has been granted or a resolution to the effect has been adopted by the Importer to liquidate its business.

iii) A Petition in Bankruptcy has been filed against the Importer.

iv) The Importer has failed to comply with NISSAN's request to rectify any non-performance, unsatisfactory performance and/or violation specified in NISSAN's notice sent to the Importer, NISSAN shall have the right to cancel this Agreement on an additional thirty (30) days notice to the Importer.

All the outstanding orders, debits and/or credits affected prior to the termination of this Agreement under Article 8, 16, 21, and/or clause 1 (2) of this Article shall be valid even after such termination of this Agreement.

Article 28: Increase of Sales

The Importer undertakes to use its best efforts to increase the demand and enlarge the outlet of Products of NISSAN and undertakes further to do everything in its power to improve the sales from year to year and also to improve as a result thereof the reputation and the good name of NISSAN and its Products.

6

Strategic Alliance in India: Sage Publications

Victoria R. Whiting
and
Kathleen K. Reardon

Sara and George McCune, founders of Sage Publications, Inc. (SPI) wanted to close their eyes on the flight to California. However, a meeting with the board of directors for SPI was scheduled in two days. This meeting would be critical to their earning board approval for a move into India; a move they both believed would prove profitable despite the challenges of doing business in India. Unfortunately, they were not convinced that all of the SPI board members shared their enthusiasm.

The social science segment of the publishing market in India held great potential. Most academic journals and books for social scientists published in India suffered from poorly edited content, little or no proofreading, slow production, and inadequate dissemination. Foreign-produced publications, while much higher in production quality (and prestige), were also priced prohibitively high. In addition, no publisher had devised a marketing distribution system to adequately penetrate the widely dispersed population in the second most populous country in the world. The anticipated increase in literacy rates in India bode well. The demand for social science journals and books would likely increase. Sara and George saw this as a promising time to establish themselves in the Indian market.

Several board members had already questioned the feasibility of a move into India. Their perception of India was one of poverty, disease, and hunger. They knew that bureaucratic red tape had been the demise of more than one cross-cultural venture in India. Even if SPI was successful at breaking through the red tape in India, the specter of future currency devaluations made establishing trading terms a risky and tedious task.

Knowing these perceptions were in the minds of board members, Sara and George set about developing a strategy for the negotiation. They would need to consider different options for entering the Indian market that would minimize the cultural challenges while still taking advantage of the social science academic market.

History of Sage Publications, Inc.

Upon start-up of her publishing company in 1965, Sara Miller had a vision of disseminating social science knowledge around the globe. She wanted to publish and distribute information that would be used by social scientists. She envisioned a two-way flow between academics and her publishing business partners in trying to uncover and discover knowledge. Now with publishing companies in California and London, Sara believed that the time was right to branch into another foreign country.

Upon graduation from Queens College in New York with a political science major and minors in English and history, Sara sought the help of an employment agency to locate a job. Her extracurricular activities in college included feature editor for her college newspaper and editor-in-chief of the yearbook. These activities, together with Sara's course of study, prompted the recruiter at the agency to comment "Sara was made for publishing." The recruiter sent Sara on two interviews, one with the Macmillan Publishing Company, the other with *Esquire* magazine. When Macmillan offered Sara a position during her first interview, she canceled the interview with *Esquire* and joined Macmillan. Sara's position as assistant to the vice-president of sales provided her a bird's eye view of the publishing company. According to Sara, Macmillan is where she fell in love with publishing.

After two years, Sara made a move to Pergamon Press, Ltd., and at Pergamon realized she did not want to work for big companies. As Macmillan had grown, it had lost its focus on publishing. It had become a conglomerate. When Sara saw the same approach at Pergamon, she considered leaving the industry all together. A vice-president at Macmillan, George McCune, suggested that Sara start her own publishing company. Sara's father and his brothers were all in business for themselves and this exposure provided Sara an entrepreneurial inclination. "It never occurred to me that there could be any problems that were unsolvable, but then I see now that I could have been foolishly overconfident."

Sara left Pergamon Press at the age of 24 and in 1965 opened SPI with $500. Sara had saved $250. The remaining $250 needed to get her business going was attained by valuing her air conditioner as the "other half" of her working capital. Sara's plan was to serve as a consultant to publishers while shopping for publishing opportunities. George, who had suggested that Sara start SPI, admitted that he thought SPI might have problems due to Sara's age. He believed that a young woman might have trouble persuading academics to sign book contracts. Instead they learned that a bigger problem to be faced was getting and maintaining employees due to the labor intensity and low wages of the industry.

Not long after incorporating her business, Sara was having drinks with a former political science professor. The professor was lamenting the fate of a journal to be called *Urban Affairs Quarterly.* City University, where the professor taught, had no university press. The journal needed a home. Having just received her business charter that morning, Sara knew exactly how to solve the problem, and by the end of the evening, SPI had its first journal to publish. Sara sold advance subscriptions, so she had some money to work with. Still she admits that, "I enslaved myself and every penny I had in order to publish this journal."

Two months after the first publication of *Urban Affairs Quarterly,* the *American Behavioral Scientist* ran into financial difficulties. Sara had been consulting with the journal, so with some financial assistance from her reluctant family, Sara purchased the second journal for $30,000.00 (most of it in assumed debt) and, with some books in development, was on her way to joining the ranks of the publishing industry.

These journals turned out to be wise investments. Journals were a great calling card; they opened doors at universities. They provided cash flow because subscriptions were sold in advance. Journals provided a network opportunity around which SPI could build its book list.

The Early Years

The first year in business, Sara was the sole SPI employee. She was responsible for contacting authors for potential book contracts and looking for new journal opportunities. She edited and proofread copy, ensuring it was ready for the printer. A great deal of Sara's time was devoted to building up a mailing list. The mailing list was of critical importance to the future of SPI. Specialized publishing companies in the United States used mailing lists as their primary marketing source. Access to the offices of scholars is gained by direct mail marketing. This access attracted customers for journals and books and gave the publishing houses access to potential authors.

Late in her second year of business, Sara married George McCune, her lone supporter when she first conceived of the idea for starting a publishing company. George left his position as vice-president at Macmillan to join Sara in the management of SPI, which by 1966 had expanded to three employees, and was producing $100,000 in annual turnover. Earlier that year SPI added books to the product mix that, until then, had consisted solely of journals.

As SPI continued a slow and steady growth pattern, the company re-incorporated in Beverly Hills, California, and three years later took on a $100,000 debenture from outside investors. This provided seed money for Sara and George to achieve their vision of "amplifying the voices of academics and having them heard around the world." SPI's first step into the global business environment was a 1971 move to London.

Going Global—London

In 1971, American-British publishing joint ventures usually involved American firms buying the rights to British books (and vice versa) one book at a time. Sara and George saw this process as an inefficient way to do business. They were also concerned that this method would not afford them access to the European social science market. Their intention was to find unmet needs in the social science community for high quality, moderately priced information. Critical to success in this niche was the acknowledgement that the producers were also consumers, where "to serve is to succeed." Another critical success factor was an ability to disseminate material quickly and to market it widely. Because buying British books one at a time would not serve the needs of SPI, Sara and George looked for alternative entry points into the British market.

Sage, London was a strategic move based on three premises. First, London provided a door into the European marketplace. Second, London shared English as a primary language with the United States. Finally, the sooner the move into London took place, the less SPI would be giving up in the transaction. Had SPI delayed the move to a time when foreign sales were a larger portion of SPI's turnover, the task of peeling off the business to establish a joint venture would have been more difficult. When considering the move into London, approximately 10% of SPI's business was in the U.K. and continental Europe. Given SPI's annual turnover of $1 million, the founders of Sage determined they would be handing over $100,000 of the parent company's business to another entity. As Sage grew, the proportion of business that would be handed over to the London venture would grow proportionately.

While considering a move into England, Sara and George were approached by a group of energetic and experienced book distributors who owned a company named Eurospan, Ltd. This company was set up solely for book distribution, and was interested in establishing a conventional distribution contract with SPI. SPI, however, was not interested in such a limited relationship. Consequently, a joint venture agreement was made that Eurospan, Ltd. would assist SPI establish a U.K.-based publishing company to market SPI books and journals, and keep an eye open for indigenous book opportunities.

As an alternative to a conventional book distribution contract, Sara and George proposed launching Sage Publications, Ltd. as a joint venture arrangement with SPI maintaining 60% ownership in the venture, and the partners of Eurospan, Ltd. acquiring the remaining 40% of the organization. Eurospan, Ltd had not previously been involved in the actual publishing of books, let alone journals. SPI had knowledge in this area, and Eurospan had established distribution channels in London. The partnership would create synergy between the two companies.

The move into England went smoothly for a number of reasons. The economics of doing business in England were similar to business economics in the United States. No language barriers existed between the two countries. Trade arrangements between the United States and the United Kingdom were flexible. Similar political,

legal, and religious foundations in both countries allowed both cross-cultural partners to better understand each other.

Still, the partnership was separated by an ocean, and this created challenges.
While English was a common tongue, words took on different meanings on opposite sides of the ocean. When the British asked if something was "agreeable in principle" to their American partners, a "yes" was interpreted as approval to act. The
Americans thought they were merely communicating willingness to consider a
detailed proposal. On the surface the countries seemed alike, yet subtle communication differences caused cross-cultural challenges, as evidenced in the different interpretations of phrases such as "in principle."

A year after they had developed a joint venture agreement with Eurospan, Ltd.,
Sara and George learned from one of their advisory board members of an opportunity to acquire five journals from Weidenfild and Nicholson, Ltd. (the *Journal of
Contemporary History* was the flagship of the group). The British publisher was getting out of academic journal publishing and a deal to transfer ownership of these
journals to another publisher in the United States had just fallen through in the
eleventh hour. Moreover, all of the editors of these journals were located in the
United Kingdom. Sensing an opportunity to expand their publishing presence into
the United Kingdom, Sara and George suggested to their joint venture partners that
these journals be acquired immediately in England where they had originally been
started. The joint venture partners agreed. The first Sage, London employee was
hired and in early 1972 Sage, London began publishing in the United Kingdom.

The Move to India

With business in London running smoothly, Sara and George turned their thoughts
to India in the late-1970s. Sara had never been to India. She did have friends there
from her days at Pergamon Press. George had developed a fascination for the country while stationed there with the Army Air Corp in World War Two.

Why India?

Prior to focusing on India, numerous countries were considered as Sara and
George contemplated foreign expansion alternatives. The founders had no romantic
attachment to India, but were fascinated by the potential and the challenges they perceived there based on personal, cultural, and historical knowledge about the country
and its people.

In addition to this knowledge, several business conditions encouraged them to
consider expanding business to India. First, India had a huge population. It was the
second most populous country in the world, with approximately 700 million citizens. Second, India had minimal language barriers. Although there were 13 major
Indian languages, English was widely used in commerce and education. The existence of industries was also a draw. While the developing economy was based on

agriculture, a wide spectrum of industries were in existence breaking ground for further industrialization. Finally, and most important for the publishing niche SPI focused on, was the matter of education. Literacy rates in India were climbing at unprecedented rates. The number of graduates and postgraduates in the country would be 9 million by 1985, with 39 million undergraduate students enrolled in universities and colleges throughout the country. India had 150 universities, over 6,000 colleges and 100 social science research institutes. All of these educational institutions fostered demand for the products to be provided by SPI.

Cultural Challenges

As Sara and George soon learned, there were also a host of challenges to doing business in India. The relationship between India and the United States in the mid-seventies was strained. Perceptions of India, carried by mass media in the United States, portrayed India as a country riddled with poverty, hunger, and disease. Such depictions cast doubt on the feasibility of developing a market in India. Moreover, relatively few American firms operating in India gained respect from the Indians. American publishing firms had long used India as a market for their out-of-circulation textbooks. American political and economic opportunism elicited distrust on the part of Indian nationals and political relations between the two countries were strained. Americans also distrusted the business environment, which insisted on local majority ownership and was heavily encumbered by bureaucratic red tape.

The primary concern for Sara and George as they considered a move into India was the relationship between the United States and India. In geopolitical terms, India was seen as favoring Russia and the United States was perceived as favoring Pakistan. An undercurrent of tension existed between the two countries. For two decades the United States had not approved of India's decision to remain non-aligned with either the United States or Russia during the height of the Cold War. This lack of acceptance by the United States resulted in India adopting a pro-Russia leaning. The relationship between the United States and India was further strained in 1971 when India signed a friendship treaty with Russia designed to allow exchange of Indian consumer goods for Russian oil and weapons. According to some Indian nationals, as India developed further ties with Russia, American firms operating in India lost the respect of Indian nationals. Indian nationals believed that capitalism was bad. Because the United States was the bastion of capitalism, an attitude of distrust encumbered dealings between Indian and American firms.

Another consideration Sara and George could not overlook when considering foreign expansion, particularly with a developing country, was the stability of the country's currency. The value of the Indian rupee was falling at a rate of 10% a year. If Sara and George failed to consider what their exposure would be to further or more rapid devaluation of the rupee, the escalated devaluation of foreign currency could spell potential disaster for SPI in India.

One additional challenge existed that had historically deterred Americans from establishing joint ventures in India was government bureaucracy. Sara noted that, "The Indian bureaucracy is all pervasive. Bureaucratic rules govern every aspect of industry in India. The 20-page questionnaires required by the U.S. Bureau of Census, the lectures required by the Occupational Safety and Health Administration including follow-up paperwork, and the car pooling and non-smoking requirements of the American federal and local government are nothing compared to Indian bureaucracy."

The Indian government had also developed an environment hostile to foreign investment. The country feared that the flow of money from outside investors would lead to foreign control of the Indian economy and perhaps culture as well. They were also afraid of an outflow of dividends and an inflow of foreign equipment that might inhibit the growth of Indian industries. This was particularly true for multinational organizations where, at the time Sara and George were considering entry into the Indian market, foreign investment was restricted to less than a 40% ownership stake. The Indian government kept strict control over all aspects of business including expansion, automation, capital imports, and how to raise capital.

To enforce governmental control, government personnel were posted in all plants to ensure that duties were paid on every invoice. If the company neglected to pay duty on even one invoice, government personnel had the authority to shut down the entire plant. The threat of shutdown was of greater concern to multinational companies than locally owned companies because multinational companies were often bound by home office rules that prohibited the use of bribes in business dealings. Indian companies avoided paying taxes by not reporting many transactions to the government. When government personnel detected such transactions, the Indian firm would respond by offering "black money," a bribe, to the government official. Indian nationals, as well as Americans doing business in India noted that the existence of this underground economy accomplished everything from speeding up telephone installation to saving a company thousands of dollars in excise taxes.

Governmental regulation was perhaps most apparent in the area of personnel management. Once operations were established, laws governed personnel working hours and holidays. Office workers typically were restricted to 40 hours of work a week. Companies were required to provide 18 holidays, three to four weeks of vacation, one to two weeks of casual leave and two weeks of sick leave to every employee. In total, this meant a total of nine to eleven weeks of paid leave annually for each employee.

Unions also played a role in personnel management issues in India. Unions were protected by the Indian government. Forming a union in India was simply a matter of having at least seven people willing to band together. Multiple unions often operated within a single company. These unions often tried to outdo each other with regard to demands.

The Indian government was also heavily involved in the retention of employees. Hiring an employee in India needed to be very carefully considered, as Indian regulations made firing an employee extremely difficult. Establishments of 50 or more employees could not layoff any employees, or shut down a plant without prior permission from the Labor Minister in the appropriate operating state. State offices would not grant permission for layoffs or plant closures—to do so would be political suicide. Unions were affiliated with different political parties. These unions exerted pressure as necessary to ensure their members would come to no harm.

Dismissing an employee in India was nearly impossible unless there was proof of theft or assault. The process of dismissal could easily take one year, during which time the employee maintained at least 75% of his or her salary paid by the company.

As business grew, Sage Publications in India would face additional challenges unique to doing business in a developing country. Publishing was not a developed industry in India. There were numerous publishing companies, but most had a different conception of what it took to publish a journal or book. This meant that Sage Publications in India would be unable to hire experienced editors away from other publishers. Instead, they would have to look for individuals with master's degrees in journalism, then train them in the techniques, craft, and business of publishing.

Sara and George recognized the impact that understanding and working within Indian traditions and customs would have on their success. For instance, machines were prohibitively expensive due to Indian import taxes. In California, computers were critical to the publishing process. Books and journals were edited on-line. Mailing lists and order processing were also computerized. This computer-based technology that kept SPI operating smoothly in California could not be used in India. Instead, the structure of Sage Publications in India would be labor intensive.

Verbal communication was another key area requiring cultural sensitivity. Many differences showed up in simple conversations. Noted Sara, "Shaking one's head side to side signifies agreement in most parts of India and disagreement in the United States." Other aspects of verbal communication varied between the two cultures as well. Formal names were very important in India. Until an Indian suggested that his first name be used, his formal name should be used. Communication with women was vastly different between the two cultures. Few women are in management positions in India. Women's roles are generally confined to the home. This cultural norm affects business, because Indian men often will not listen to a woman in a business meeting.

Non-verbal communication could be problematic as well. Indians do not shrug their shoulders to communicate "I don't know." They raise the palm of their right hand to the ceiling and twist the hand from side to side. Acceptable physical distance when carrying on a conversation also had to be considered. Sara and George tried to be respectful by keeping a distance from Indians, thereby allowing for the Indian's private space. In greeting Indian natives, they learned the importance of not reaching out to shake the hand of an Indian. Instead, Sara and George learned to touch their own palms together and raise them slightly in the form of a welcome to the Indian.

Business Analysis

Sara and George believed that the cross-cultural issues could be overcome. They also believed that the board could be convinced. The following were their primary reasons for optimism: In the twenty years SPI had been in business, they had managed to place themselves among the top social science publishers. Authors often believed they had "made it" when they were successful at signing on with Sage. SPI had made an impact on social science fields. It had become recognized as a source of critical information within fields as diverse as communications, research methodology, criminology, and family issues. They had been selective, had achieved greater presence, and had provided higher quality than their competitors in the United States.

SPI's success had evolved from critical business decisions made early in its existence. First, they had identified several lucrative niches in the publishing world. Second, Sage had used a well-developed direct mail distribution network to reach geographically dispersed customers. Finally, SPI had made it their business to have a thorough knowledge of the market for a product before signing a contract with an author or a journal.

These three factors, in addition to the attention the company paid personally to authors resulted in authors wanting to do business with SPI. SPI courted top authors in the social science field. Once they signed these authors, they worked hard to keep them by paying careful attention to quality, by watching out for the mutual best interests of the authors and Sage, and by bringing these authors into a type of "Sage family." Because Sage books were marketed effectively and edited well, SPI was able to exert a significant positive impact on their authors' careers.

In their niche, the competitive market for SPI in India held promise. The only real competitor in the Indian social science publication market at the time was Oxford University Press (OUP). Oxford's publishing was high priced and failed to explore emerging trends. Oxford focused on the large profitable dictionary and school textbook business. It was not unusual for OUP to take up to two years to decide whether to publish a book. SPI saw both the long time required to publish as well as OUP's conservative approach to topics as leaving openings for SPI's move into India. In addition, OUP-India's publications were not well-marketed outside the subcontinent.

It was believed that the mail order business SPI had developed in the United States would transfer relatively easily into the Indian market. As an industry, academic publishers in the United States knew that the only cost effective way to bring in business was through the mail. SPI had successfully dedicated resources in an effort to perfect this marketing technique. In India, specialized retail outlets did not exist. There were only 250–300 broadly-stocked bookstores in the entire country. Additionally, the 700 million Indian citizens were spread out over 2,000 square miles. No other publishing houses were using a direct mail marketing technique to reach the Indian market. Given SPI's expertise in direct marketing, the lack of retail outlets, the widely dispersed population and the fact that no one else was taking this approach to marketing books and journals in India, direct mail appeared to offer a significant competitive advantage to SPI's entrance into India. Further support for using direct mail marketing came from the availability of free mailing lists. The secretary general of Indian Social Science Research Council promised to provide a newly complied directory to SPI if they entered the Indian market. This directory mailing list contained the names and addresses of 8,000 social scientists pursuing research which paralleled Sage's business focus.

While relationships with the Indian authors would need to be tailored to account for cultural differences, the respect and attention SPI bestowed upon each author would still benefit their mission in India. One Indian publisher related a story to Sara and George that highlighted the differences Sara and George would need to be aware of in dealing with Indian scholars. Tejeshwar Singh, a publisher with over twenty years of experience in India, told of the time early in his career when he had gotten friendly with a scholar. The two proceeded to enter into a discussion along with another scholar. Tejeshwar interjected his opinions on a book they were discussing. Later, Tejeshwar attempted to obtain a contract for a book from the scholar, but was flatly refused. The scholar had taken offense at Tejeshwar's comfort in expressing his opinions. In India, publishers do not have the stature of academics.

One segment of the SPI market virtually untouched in India was the journal market. Very few journals existed in India. Those journals that did exist were produced by universities or institutions with in-house editors. Unlike their Western equivalents, the Indian journals did not use peer reviews. Most journals were running three years behind schedule. Sage Publications in India would have difficulty establishing reasonable subscription rates. Subscribers were currently paying .70 rupee for an annual subscription of two editions of 500 pages each. With such low subscription rates, Sage Publications in India could not compete on price.

If they were to move into journal production, however, Sage Publications in India could bring numerous benefits to the journal business that would justify higher subscription rates. As in the United States, Sage Publications in India would institute peer reviews for all the journals they published, thereby enhancing the caliber of articles that were published. Journals would be produced in a timely manner. These journals would be free of errors, with professional quality desk editing (all by hand because computers were not widely used in India.)

Sage Publications in India—Alternatives

Given that the competitive climate seemed right for a move into India, Sara and George contemplated the various forms a move into India could take.

One option for entering the Indian market suggested by the managing director of Sage, London was to team up with Macmillan, India. Macmillan, India was established and had been successful in working through the Indian bureaucracy. SPI could begin exporting books and journals into the Indian market through an established reseller using a standard conventional distribution contract. This option held certain advantages for SPI. By entering into a distribution contract with Macmillan, SPI could avoid cross-cultural issues altogether. Macmillan, operating out of London, would take responsibility for the Indian bureaucracy and distribute product throughout the country using their current distribution channels. These advantages would enable SPI to quickly move into the Indian market. No up-front costs would be incurred, and no risk taken. In exchange for this service, Macmillan would take a portion of profit from each sale. Unfortunately, they would not be directly targeting the social science academics for whom SPI's products were specifically designed. Also, SPI would not have an opportunity to move into the Indian market and publish books and journals specifically for the Indian market.

Still, Sara and George traveled to India to investigate this option. Once in India, Sara and George met with the highly regarded Macmillan, India vice-president, Tejeshwar Singh. Together they looked at the possibility of SPI linking up with Macmillan, India. During the conversation, Tejeshwar found he and George had much more to talk about than an arrangement between two organizations. Tejeshwar described the initial meeting as, "a meeting of the minds." This positive interaction with Tejeshwar led George and Sara to consider the possibility of entering into a joint venture arrangement with Tejeshwar. Over the years, Tejeshwar had developed an impressive resume. He had graduated from Oxford University with a Politics, Philosophy, and Economics (PPE) degree. After his return to India, Tejeshwar became somewhat of a celebrity when he was selected to read national news on Indian television. Tejeshwar had accrued over 10 years of publishing experience. The most recent eight years had been spent with Macmillan, India, a branch of Macmillan, U.K. Having started as an editor, Tejeshwar had worked his way up to become vice-president in charge of a sales region.

A joint venture agreement with Tejeshwar offered SPI numerous opportunities. A joint venture would allow SPI to establish a direct marketing campaign in India designed to target the type of customers Sage wanted to reach. Working with an Indian native such as Tejeshwar would give George and Sara an edge when dealing with the Indian bureaucracy. However, this plan was not without concerns. Questions existed as to whether a relationship between George, Sara, and an individual such as Tejeshwar would work over the long run. This type of joint venture would require that George and Sara sacrifice a significant portion of any profits they stood to earn in India, as well as requiring a significant capital outlay to establish the business. Finally, there was an issue of control. With George and Sara working out of the United States and the joint venture partner located in India, the Indian partner would be responsible for carrying out the Sage vision in India.

This type of arrangement could certainly be beneficial to an individual such as Tejeshwar. To start a business with the name Sage was a great advantage as Indian scholars were already familiar with the Sage name and the Sage reputation for quality.

George and Sara also considered establishing a wholly owned subsidiary with Tejeshwar as managing director. A wholly owned subsidiary would afford SPI a name recognition advantage. Tejeshwar could deal with the Indian bureaucracy. If they could get the Indian government to agree to this type of an arrangement, George and Sara could maintain control over the Indian venture, and reap all the financial gains. Of course, an outlay of start-up capital would be required, and all of the risks for the move into India would rest on the shoulders of SPI. George and Sara wondered about the level of dedication that could be expected of a manager that had no ownership stake in the venture, and owners thousands of miles away. Still, if the right person could be found, and approval granted by the Indian government, this could be a lucrative way to establish Sage Publications in India. The biggest hurdle with this option would be the obtaining the approval of the Indian government. Presently, the Indian government limited foreign investment ownership to 40%.

Sara and George reminded themselves that they were getting carried away considering how they would structure a business in India. The first step was to make the board understand that the cultural challenges of entering business with India were manageable, and that a move into India would be a wise strategic business decision. It was entirely possible that even after Sara and George presented the benefits of starting a business in India, the board of directors might determine that the cross-cultural challenges outweighed the potential financial reward.

Conclusion

With the major issues outlined, Sara and George prepared their presentation to the board of directors. They were determined to convince the board members that a move into India made sense, and that to delay this decision would not be wise. With two days remaining until the meeting, Sara and George knew that they had their work cut out for them.

7
Westel (A): Start-Up of a Joint Venture

C. Thomas Howard
and
Robert P. McGowan

Briefly distracted by the sight of a spring thunderstorm that was moving in from the western Rocky Mountains, Bob Gras, chief financial officer for US West Diversified, reflected on some of the critical reasons for engaging in international diversification. It was critical that US West invest in businesses in the international arena, so it was important to find partners that shared similar values and also had some degree of clout. "We look at ourselves as being more than simply an investor," stated Bob Gras. "It is important that we find a relationship in which we can make a contribution. In addition, such relationships must have a common theme or link."

Another concern of Gras' was the degree to which they expanded internationally. "While others may prefer to work in several regions or locations," added Gras, "our philosophy from the outset was to be in fewer places but deeper in each." This meant several things. Leg extensions were important, i.e., assist in modernizing the basic telecommunications and grow geographically from there. For this reason, while Western Europe was a lucrative market, it was extremely tough to enter. Eastern Europe, due to tremendous amounts of political and social change, proved to be a better candidate.

Aside from the obvious cultural differences, currency risk was also a major concern. United States telecommunication regulators were reluctant to allow a company such as US West to guarantee non-regulated businesses for fear of placing the regulated businesses at risk.

This case was written as a basis for class discussion and not as an example of either effective or ineffective handling of an administrative situation.

As always, the problem of timing was a concern. There was a continual pull and tug between expanding the business and developing a solid base. Could US West operate in a foreign company? While it had its share of successes, US West also had made some mistakes as it sought to run different businesses, and there was still some anxiety at the board level. The next few years would be a critical test for the company.

The Worldwide Cellular Industry

In the early 1980s, the first mobile cellular communications system was installed in Sweden and cellular communications had compiled a notable success record. By the late 1980s, over 500 separate cellular systems were either in operation or being built in more than 50 countries throughout North America, Europe, and the Far East. The mobile cellular communications industry was still embryonic, and the growth potential for this technology was tremendous.

As of December 1988, cellular telephones had 2 million subscribers in the United States and 1.2 million in Europe. Installations had been growing at a rate of 4% per month in the United States and at 6% per month in Europe. Equipment sales had reached $1.8 billion per year in the United States and $1.3 billion per year in Europe, with annual service revenues in both markets at approximately $1 billion.

Forecasters had consistently underestimated the demand for mobile communications since the market began. Swedish Telecom, for example, revised its 1979 market projections upward in 1982 and again in 1983, yet the recast figures still did not approach actual demand. In another example, during the late 1970s British Telecom predicted that mobile cellular communications would have about 50,000 subscribers in the United Kingdom in 1990. When the company went private in 1980, it revised this projection to 100,000 subscribers. In 1983, when licenses were awarded to Cellnet (a joint venture between British Telecom and Securicor) and Racal Vodaphone (a competing consortium), both groups agreed that 500,000 subscribers by 1990 was more accurate. Two of BT's suppliers expected approximately 1–1.2 million subscribers by 1990.

In Scandinavia and the United Kingdom, as in the United States, the market was supply-limited, not demand-limited. This meant that if equipment could be installed more quickly, the market would grow even faster. Already congestion problems existed in major cities such as London, Los Angeles, and Oslo because the cells could not be installed fast enough. For this reason, it was not possible to make accurate straight-line projections for mobile cellular communications.

Mobile cellular communications were not merely mobile, they were personal and flexible. Surveys showed that people, particularly in the United States, wanted mobile communications for personal as well as business use. Firms with 20 or fewer employees (typically in fields like plumbing or construction) had been the primary market for mobile communications. That pattern was changing in the United Kingdom, Scandinavia, and even in the United States, as larger firms with major fleets of vehicles began to install mobile cellular communications. Some *Fortune*

"1000" corporations had installed hundreds of thousands of terminals at a time. These firms would be the major growth area for cellular over the next three years.

In addition, two new trends would help create a consumer market for mobile communications in the next few years. First, equipment costs would continue to drop. By the 1990s, mobile communications would actually be cheaper than fixed telephone for the telecommunications operator to install in most locales. Second, a wide variety of products and services for mobile cellular communications would be available, including the pan-European digital cellular mobile telephone service, the digital European cordless telephone (DECT), short-range and private mobile radio, voice messaging and other options, rental equipment, and private network use of mobile, and value-added networks. This rapidly growing variety would stimulate new applications and even faster growth.

Because mobile cellular communications was flexible, it would inevitably move into the office—an entirely separate market. A variety of new products were being developed, and in some cases tested, to serve this constituency, such as cordless PABXs (trials were under way in Scandinavia and the United Kingdom), and wireless local area networks (LANs) that integrate communications within a single location and wide-area networks (WANs) with on-demand bandwidth (so terminals could be moved from office to office) that can integrate communications within a geographical region. With these innovations it would be possible to have a video conference using the bandwidth one minute and several intersections between computers the next, making cellular telephony a natural extension of the fixed private network.

Large users of cellular in the United Kingdom had already expressed a desire to link directly into the public mobile switch as well as a need for a 2-megabyte link into the mobile telephone switch that can transmit 2 million bits of data. Essentially, these users wanted the same service with cellular that they received on extended private networks. From all indications, the office environment would be a vigorous growth business in the next few years as these capabilities became available.

The coming mobile cellular communications boom offered opportunities for equipment suppliers, capital investors, and telecommunications service providers or operators, but not equal opportunities. The opportunities for terminal equipment suppliers were not as promising as those for the other players because too many suppliers would be competing—more than 30 in Europe alone and 15 in the United States. Suppliers were being hurt by a price war that undoubtedly would continue.

The infrastructure equipment business, where European suppliers had done well, would continue to prosper. The cellular coverage a country could afford was directly proportional to two variables: population density and gross national product (GNP) per capita. Scandinavia, which had low population density (13–19 people/km^2) but high GNP per capita, could afford to cover virtually the entire area with cellular. Countries with low GNP per capita and high population densities were likewise good candidates for wide coverage. Importantly, because the terminal plus infrastructure cost was below the cost of building local loops, cellular might well be the most economical way to provide rural telephone and telecommunications services to developing countries.

The Westel Venture

Westel was a planned joint venture between US West International (USWI) and Magyar Posta, the Hungarian PTT (Postal, Telephone, and Telegraph) Company. Westel was to be formed in late 1989 to provide cellular phone service to the Budapest region.

US West, one of the regional telephone companies created from the breakup of the U.S. phone system, was a Fortune 500 company with 1990 assets exceeding $26 billion, revenues of nearly $10 billion, and net income of $1.2 billion. Like the other regional telephone companies, US West began to explore diversification opportunities that would complement its core telecommunications business as well as fit within the legal restrictions imposed by the Modified Final Judgment. Essentially, the regional telephone companies were restricted from such activities as manufacturing telecommunications equipment, as well as selling information services. The concern was also expressed that the Baby Bells might use the guaranteed profits from their regulated phone businesses to subsidize their entry into new markets.

With such concerns continually looming in the background, one of the areas of particular interest to US West and others was the international area. USWI began to explore cellular opportunities in Eastern Europe in early 1989. A number of countries seemed to represent strong opportunities—Germany, Poland, Hungary, and Czechoslovakia. Each of these countries was explored extensively and as the result of careful cultivation and fortunate timing, Hungary emerged as the leading candidate for the first cellular telephone operation in Eastern Europe. By September 1989, a letter of intent had been signed by USWI and Magyar Posta, the Hungarian PTT.

The Business Climate in Hungary

One of the central issues that needed to be addressed was the complexity of doing business in a region undergoing rapid change. Hungary was an independent state based on the rule of law and dedicated to a multi-party system, parliamentary democracy, and a social market economy. With a population of approximately 10.6 million, nearly 60% of the people lived in four major cities—the primary concentration in Budapest. Yet, as with many European countries, the overall population was declining with the death rate exceeding the birth rate.

Hungary also suffered from fairly low living standards. One of its most acute social problems was a severe housing shortage. Consumer goods were subsidized and automobiles expensive and in short supply. Foreign currency regulations set low limits on private spending abroad; and while the government was looking at privatization of capital and foreign investments to create new job opportunities, overall employment was expected to grow.

Many enterprises were expected to seek external capital (domestic and foreign sources) as well as to divest themselves of assets in the movement towards privatization. As a means of further upgrading the overall business climate, tax relief for the development of high-technology industries were even more generous than those for regional development. The 1988 Foreign Investment Act was passed to further facilitate such investment by eliminating certain impediments and providing a highly favorable legal framework.

No sectors were closed to private investors. While 100% foreign was possible, joint ventures with Hungarian partners had been found to be particularly advantageous. As for potential sources of funds available to foreign investors, high forint, the Hungarian currency, interest rates, and the government's tight credit policy made domestic borrowing by Hungarian companies with foreign participation relatively unattractive. Companies could borrow through domestic foreign banks or through equity stakes financed on international money markets.

The Hungarians were willing and eager to do business with American companies, but after 45 years of communist rule, the business communications and commercial infrastructure taken for granted in the West was virtually nonexistent. A new business had to wait six months to a year to have a phone installed at a cost of about $1,500. The waiting time for a residential phone installation was an even more exasperating ten to twelve years. An apartment with a phone already installed rented for four times the normal rate. The Economic Act of 1988 was one of the most important pieces of legislation governing commercial activities. But much of it remained untested both in practice and in the courts. There was little or no commercial law dealing with East-West transactions. The commercial banking system was only one and a half years old. At the top of this system was the Hungarian National Bank (HNB), which was in the process of transforming itself into a Central Bank modeled after the Federal Reserve System in the United States. Among other things, HNB was trying to encourage commercial banks to take on commercial risk. The payment system was primitive. Most transactions were in forints, and there were no checking accounts. Wages and salaries were paid in currency every week. Large quantities of forints could not legally be converted into a hard currency without the permission and aid of HNB.

However, there were several positive aspects of doing business in Hungary. Like their counterparts in the U.S.S.R., Hungarians had a strong tradition of paying their bills on time. If they said they would pay in 60 days, the bill was paid in 60 days, period. The Hungarians showed themselves able negotiators and picked up on business concepts quickly. For example, the bankers in Budapest, even though they had less than two years of experience as Western-style commercial banks, already sounded very much like their counterparts in London. The large pent up demand for phone service was a very positive aspect for the project and the existing telephone wire network, although decades behind Western systems, was capable of supporting the planned cellular system. In spite of the 45 years of communist effort to thwart development of a quality phone system, Hungarian ingenuity had created a far better telephone system than would be expected.

The Impact Of Cultural Differences

The Hungarian's command of English was limited and the American's command of Hungarian was abysmal. Meetings were conducted in English, often through translators, with 10 or so participants representing the technical, finance, legal, and business development areas. The meetings were often frustrating and unproductive. As John Broach, USWI controller put it, "Reaching consensus on an issue was like trying to shovel steam."

One such meeting focused on identifying the Magyar Posta people who would staff key positions within Westel. Several names surfaced early in the meeting and setting up their transfer should have been a straightforward process. However, the meeting dragged on for the entire day. The USWI participants could not figure out what was holding back progress on what seemed like a simple matter. Finally in the late afternoon, one of the USWI participants figured out that the people to be transferred would be terminated immediately by Magyar Posta and would not be on the Westel payroll for another 4 to 6 weeks. Not being paid for this period was a real problem for these people, however, they were unwilling to reveal this to their USWI counterparts. Once this was apparent, the matter was resolved quickly.

Another series of meetings dealt with the topographical maps that were so important to building a cellular system. Under communist rule, maps were classified as top secret for military reasons and were generally not available. A request for such maps, then, necessitated a major change in thinking by the Hungarians. Should they allow Americans to obtain such sensitive information? Several types of maps were presented by the Hungarians, but rejected by the USWI technical people as not providing enough detail. Finally, after several lengthy meetings, the topographical maps were made available.

Transition from a Centrally Planned Economy

Hungarians, by East European standards, enjoyed a high standard of living. To support this style of living most people worked at least two jobs. Given the lack of incentives in the communist centrally planned system, the result was to do a mediocre job on each. Western companies such as USWI had to deal with this issue to be successful. One accounting firm handled this problem by imposing such long hours that the employees were forced to quit their second jobs. This meant sending people out to talk to the wives and husbands to explain why their spouse was not working a second job.

Transition from a centrally planned economy lead to other major misunderstandings. The concept of a profit was almost impossible to explain, not so much that

Hungarians were against the profit incentive, but they had a hard time believing that an operation could be operated efficiently enough, and the demand could be strong enough to result in a profit. The business cases developed by USWI predicting strong cash flows were often met with disbelief by their Hungarian counterparts.

Marketing was another concept that was foreign to the Hungarians. Trying to convince the Hungarians to spend "real" money on a marketing plan was a daunting task. Their philosophy was, "If you build it, they will come." In fact, for the Westel project the Hungarians were correct. But USWI continually pushed the importance of market analysis and planning. Closely related was the concept of customer service. Again under the centrally planned economy, the concept of customer satisfaction had little meaning.

One area where there were few differences was the technical aspects of designing, building, and operating a cellular system. For decades the Hungarians had labored with an antiquated telecommunications network under a political system that was hostile towards open and free communications. The well-trained Hungarian technicians and engineers worked miracles with the system and took pride in keeping abreast of the most recent Western technologies. So when New Vector, the cellular arm of USW, presented their ideas for the cellular system, there were few differences of opinion between the two sides. In fact, the Hungarians often surprised their New Vector counterparts with some ingenious solutions to some very knotty technical problems.

Legal and Financial Differences

In the contract area, the differences were indeed stark. Under a centrally planned economy there was little need for a commercial code and as a result there was virtually no case law to guide contract negotiations. So when USWI put forward a proposed contract, the Hungarians were not sure how to react. In some sense they felt cornered by the document. It specified such restrictions as Magyar Posta not being allowed to partner with anyone else and loosing control of Westel if capital payments were not made on time. Why, thought the Hungarians, was it necessary to formalize such items when they had no intention of violating their verbal agreements? To some extent they found this American need for specifics offensive. In the end, however, the Hungarians relented and signed the contract reluctantly, trusting that USWI would live up to its word.

The confusion about the government's involvement in the economy was a two-way street. In particular when the USWI people tried to explain the Modified Final Judgment (MFJ for short), the Hungarians could not understand it. The MFJ was the agreement among AT&T, the seven regional bell operating companies (of which US West was one), the U.S. government, and other parties that governed the breakup of AT&T in 1984. Among other things, US West was not allowed to offer long distance and information services nor were they allowed to manufacture telephone equipment. Such restrictions impacted how Westel was structured and managed. The Hungarians simply deferred to USWI on this confusing issue.

Finally, the absence of most of the main features of a modern financial system such as checking accounts, credit cards, a developed banking system, and a stock market made most financial transactions difficult. Hungarians pretty much operated on a "cash and carry" basis. Weekly wages were paid in cash. Phones were purchased with cash. Because of the focus on cash, it was difficult to convince Magyar Posta to borrow money to expand. Their philosophy was that if you didn't have the funds right now, then you should wait to expand. An extreme example of the emphasis on cash showed up in their accounting system. The Hungarians were used to keeping track of all funds to the forint (80 forints to the dollar). At one point, the books were not closed due to a discrepancy of $50. It took considerable effort on USWI's part to convince the Hungarians that such a difference was not material.

The Early Months

It was against this backdrop that in January 1990, the group with the operational responsibility for the project, began assembling the necessary resources. The personnel for the project were mainly Hungarian with the exception of a few Americans in key management positions. Ron Sanders of US West and Joseph Pete of Magyar Posta (MP) were chosen as the co-managers for the project.

As specified in the joint venture (JV) agreement, MP owned 5% of Westel while USWI owned the remaining 49% (Appendix A and B). Hungarian law specified that for infrastructure projects such as this one, a foreign company could not own a majority stake. USWI was expected to provide hard currency for its $5 million share of the initial $10 million funding requirement, while it was expected that MP would provide mostly in-kind contributions such as cellular equipment and land for cell sites. MP cash contributions would be in forints, but it was widely recognized that MP was chronically short of cash. The deal structure also assumed that the Westel venture, once operational, would be funded from its customer base.

Despite the formidable hurdles facing it, Westel met its various deadlines, and in July 1990 began signing up customers. The response was unbelievable. Without any marketing effort whatsoever, people began to line up outside Westel's sales office. They often brought their entire family and waited for up to three hours in line to see a live demonstration of the system and then sign up for the service. Much to the surprise of Westel, most new customers bought two to five phones rather than just one. Initially this was a puzzle, but later it was determined that people were buying phones for relatives and business associates so that they would have someone to talk to. It quickly became apparent that demand was far surpassing the proposed capacity of the system. Sanders was in the unfamiliar situation of having to tell his sales force not to sell. As Sanders said, "This is the only company I've ever been in where you can't collect any cash and you can't sell any product."

In October, the cellular system began operations right on schedule. The "ribbon cutting" ceremony was attended in the U.S. by Vice-President Dan Quayle and in Hungary by the Minister of Finance. With Westel people holding their collective breaths, the Vice-President successfully completed a call to the Finance Minister. The network was off and running.

Strategic Considerations

Reflecting on the developments to date, Mr. Gras took out a pad of paper and outlined what he considered were the key risks and advantages associated with such a project. Despite the potential problems associated with any new venture, things appeared to be going smoothly with the Westel operations. The forint was down 13% by January 1991, representing a concern but not a major problem. Yet, poor performance by Westel during 1991 would significantly hamper ongoing efforts in other Eastern European countries and the U.S.S.R.

Short-term issues that still needed to be addressed included the amount of capital that US West was willing to invest. Mr. Gras felt strongly that investment should be capped at $5 million—given the continued political instability of the region. Hard currency was another concern. Like all Eastern European countries, Hungary was in dire need of currency. It was not unusual for hard currency to "disappear" for two to three weeks in the Hungarian banking system. This was simply a fact of life of doing business in Hungary.

A final short-term issue was the matter of technology transfer. For US West to be a global player, it needed to gain and maintain a sustainable advantage. The key to doing this was to become a value-added player in such ventures. While US West was the first to enter the Hungarian market, others, such as ConTel, a subsidiary of GTE, were preparing to enter the market with a superior product.

As for long-term issues, there were several. While joint ventures such as Westel provided a convenient avenue for US West to transfer its expertise and experience base, it was also important to examine reverse technology transfer. That is, what was learned in this venture could be applied to other areas or units of US West? How does one facilitate this transfer in a rapidly changing environment?

Closely associated with such technology transfer was *reverse business transfer.* There was always the risk of assuming that "our" way was the way others should do business. Perhaps there were particular successful managerial skills and techniques within Westel that could be applied elsewhere.

Beyond the notion of transfer of best practices, US West needed to demonstrate that it could manage and optimize businesses in key areas. This meant that they needed to be sensitive to cultural issues as well as where they could add value. Above all, US West had to view itself in the future as being consultants to international businesses rather than as simply local telephone operators.

Finally, there was the overriding issue of how US West would fit into the so-called "information highway" of the future. The "information highway" was envisioned as a global network capable of delivering telecommunications, entertainment, computer, and information services to a variety of customers via a single line or radio signal. Participating in international ventures allowed US West to engage in activities from which they were barred in the U.S. How, then, did Westel help US West position itself for the coming "information highway?"

As he was finishing his notes, Mr. Gras glanced at his watch and realized that he was late for his next meeting.

Appendix A:

DEAL STRUCTURE

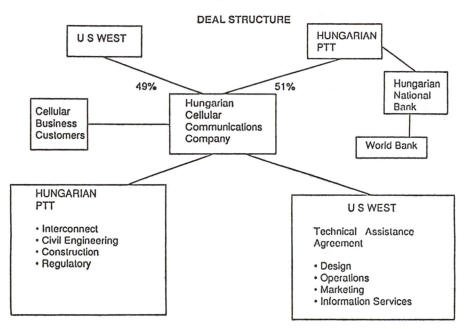

Appendix B: Joint Venture Agreement Highlights

Joint Venture Company (JVC) organized initially as a limited liability company—
  ▶ Initial capital = Ft. 10,000,000
  ▶ Will conduct initial system planning and market studies
  ▶ Will obtain frequency allocation and tariff approvals

Conditions precedent to constructing system—

  ▶ Obtaining all necessary licenses and authorizations
  ▶ Satisfying all conditions of the World Bank credit

Upon satisfaction of conditions, JVC reorganized into company listed by shares—

  ▶ Initial capital equivalent to US $10,363,000
  ▶ Magyar Posta (51%) contributes equipment, other assets, and forints
  ▶ US West (49%) contributes US $

Board of Directors—Magyar Posta 2 and US West

▶ Chairman of board rotates between parties every six months
▶ Chairman has tie-breaking vote

75% Shareholder approval required for:

▶ Change in business objective
▶ Declaration of dividends
▶ Adoption of annual budgets
▶ Entering into contracts exceeding US $100,000
▶ Increase in capital
▶ Admission of new shareholders

Key employees—appointed by unanimous decision of the Board

▶ Managing director—nominated by Magyar Posta
▶ Director of operations, marketing, financial and administration—two nominated by US West; two by Magyar Posta

Each shareholder has first right to purchase shares transferred by the other shareholder.

8
Westel (B): Overcoming Financial Problems

C. Thomas Howard

"Why is this line moving so slowly?" asked John Broach, controller and treasurer for US West International. Mr. Broach was in line for a security check at Heathrow in London. Dave Davis, who was Mr. Broach's traveling companion and vice-president for strategic investments at US West International, began to peer around to determine the cause of the delay; the security guards were body searching everyone and opening every piece of carry-on luggage. In January 1991, this had become business as usual at Heathrow due to the growing tensions surrounding Iraq's invasion of Kuwait.

Broach and Davis were returning to Denver from their most recent trip to Budapest, Hungary, during which they had met with the managers of Westel (see Chapter 7). Westel was a joint venture between US West International and Magyar Posta (MP), the Hungarian PTT (Postal, Telephone, and Telegraph Company). Westel was formed in December 1989 to provide cellular phone service to the Budapest area. What they heard from Westel was encouraging and distressing.

The growth in customers and revenues during the initial months of operation had far exceeded the initial forecasts upon which the project had received its initial approval. In addition, Broach and Davis had the distinct impression during their visit that the organization, composed of Hungarians and a few Americans, had finally begun to gel. But success had created a new set of financial problems for Mr. Davis in particular. To meet projected 1991 cellular demand, additional funding was needed to build the necessary cell sites and to meet working capital needs. For US West, with $26 billion in assets and nearly $10 billion in revenues, this type of request

---

This case is a basis for classroom discussion and not as an example of either effective or ineffective handling of an administrative situation.

would have normally been handled routinely. Broach and Davis had already been told that US West wanted to limit its investment to the $5 million in initial joint venture (JV) funding. Moreover, US West, because of the regulated nature of its core telephone operations, could not provide any loan guarantees. Thus, Davis had to assemble a financing package involving western banks, government agencies from several countries, suppliers from several countries, and Hungarian commercial banks.

Adding to the urgency of the situation was a realization by virtually everyone that Westel was a lynch pin in the company's international strategy, and that 1991 was a particularly critical year for gauging US West's ability to operate successfully outside its main line U.S. telephone business. Without the additional funding, Westel would not be able to achieve its potential as new competitors moved into the now open Hungarian telecommunications market.

As Broach and Davis cleared Heathrow security and headed to their plane, both began thinking about the enormously challenging task that lay ahead of them. It would be a long flight back to Denver, but the exhilaration of tackling such a complex financing problem would keep them awake and talking for most of the trip.

Managing the Capital Account

As specified in the JV agreement, MP owned 51% of Westel, while USWI owned the remaining 49%. Hungarian law specified that for infrastructure projects such as this one, a foreign company could not own a majority stake. USWI was expected to provide hard currency for its $5 million share of the initial $10 million funding requirement, while it was expected that MP would provide primarily in-kind contributions such as cellular equipment and land for cell sites. MP cash contributions would be in forints, but it was widely recognized that MP was chronically short of cash.

One of Broach's responsibilities was to oversee the capital account and to ensure that it remained in 49–51% balance. The initial $75,000 contribution made by USWI to the capital account presented Broach with the first of many problems associated with this account. Broach wired the initial money to Hungarian National Bank (HNB) for deposit in Westel's account. After waiting three days, Broach contacted HNB to verify that the funds had indeed been deposited. Much to his surprise, he was informed that the $75,000 had yet to be credited to the account. Even more shocking was HNB's response to his next request. When he asked that a tracer be put on the funds, he was told that a tracer is not initiated until 70 days after the request. Broach immediately called the chief financial officer at Westel, a Hungarian woman, and asked her to go to HNB, locate the funds, and have them deposited in the correct account. The next day the funds were correctly deposited. What Broach discovered was, like all Eastern European countries, Hungary was in dire need of hard currency. So when the $75,000 showed up at HNB, it was no doubt used to meet other pressing hard currency needs. It was not unusual for hard currency to "disappear" for 2 to 3 weeks in the Hungarian banking system. This was simply a fact of life of doing business in Hungary. Ironically, Broach would later learn that because of the combination of pressing hard currency needs and the tradition of paying bills on time, it was often easier for Westel to get money out of Hungary than it was to get money into Hungary.

Keeping the capital account in balance often interacted in undesirable ways with the vast differences in the American and Hungarian approaches to business. One of the best examples of this was an early request by USWI for Westel to conduct a $200,000 market study in Budapest. Such studies were standard in American markets. But the Hungarians could see no need for it. After all, there was currently a ten-to-twelve-year wait for a phone and the existing phone system was not very reliable. A new system promising immediate connection and reliable service (at least to other cellular customers) would have no trouble attracting an unlimited number of customers. In addition, MP did not have the forints to fund their 51% share of the project from the capital account.

In another similar situation, USWI put forward a proposal for Westel to purchase a $500,000 computer to run the billing system for the cellular network. USWI recognized that such a system was the "nuclear reactor" of any cellular network and thus was an essential component. The people from MP, on the other hand, did not see the need for the computer. They had operated the PTT system without computerized billing for years and so the cellular system should be able to do the same. Besides, the $500,000 was not being used to purchase telephone hardware, the type of assets that would actually produce revenues for the project. Again, MP did not have the forints to fund their share, further complicating the discussions. Broach eventually helped resolve these two issues, but the interaction between balancing the capital account on the one hand, and the often divergent views on business on the other, represented a continuing source of conflict for the partners.

Currency Risk

Another major concern for Broach was currency risk. A company could not convert the forint into a hard currency without first receiving permission from the HNB. The conversion process began by submitting the required documentation to HNB along with the necessary number of forints. After sitting in an account for up to two weeks, the forints were converted to the hard currency and then transferred as requested by the company. Westel had received permission for hard currency conversion from HNB and had tested the system by paying several hard currency bills to European suppliers. Broach was pleasantly surprised to learn that the conversion took place in a matter of hours rather than in a matter of weeks.

Most importantly with respect to currency risk was the possible future devaluation of the forint. Broach quickly learned that reliable information with respect to currency changes was hard to come by. Often, he received conflicting information from officials who were supposedly in the know. At times, the people at HNB would say exactly the opposite of what was being announced by the government. During 1990, it was widely anticipated that the forint would be devalued. On the contrary,

Broach had observed that the forint actually appreciated relative to the dollar during 1990 while falling somewhat against other hard currencies. Given the paucity of currency information, Broach decided to set up his own system for gathering information to make his own judgment about the forint.

Because the JV agreement included a "price to inflation" clause, Broach preferred to see creeping depreciation rather than sudden currency changes followed by price caps. Beyond the "price to inflation" clause, Broach had implemented several other strategies to protect against currency risk. The most important was aggressive current asset management in which cash, accounts receivable, and inventories were kept to an absolute minimum. As Broach described it, "it was the ultimate in commercial hand to mouth."

Another strategy was that once a dividend decision was made, Westel would approach HNB for a currency forward contract. Like forint spot rates, forward rates were not continuously quoted. In addition, the forward rates no doubt reflected the current 35% interest rate charged by HNB for commercial loans. (The current annual Hungarian inflation rate was thought to be in the range of 15 to 20%). For this reason, the use of forint forward contracts would be limited to dividend payments.

Additional Financing Needs

Well before the October 1990 start-up, it had become apparent that Westel would need additional financing beyond the $10 million in initial JV funding. The $10 million basically covered the cost of getting the organization established and building the main switch in Budapest and the first six cell sites. These six sites were completed by December 1990 as demand surged beyond the initial capacity of the system.

Broach knew that Westel could not look to MP for help in arranging new outside funding for several reasons. First, debt was anathema in the Hungarian economy. You only purchased an item if you had the cash to pay for it. This attitude permeated both individuals and businesses alike and created a practical difference in how each partner approached project financing. On the one hand were the USWI operations people from New Vector who, based on their experience in U. S. markets, argued that the only way to succeed was to grow the system as fast as you could pour new financing, including debt, into the system. On the other hand were the MP people who argued just as strongly that the system should be grown only as fast as internal sources would allow. It was a classic clash of two divergent business cultures. It was everything Broach could do to convince the MP side of the urgent need for rapid growth in the system. After many long discussions, MP finally did agree to rapid growth. The second problem with having MP help with external financing was that they had no experience with making financing arrangements other than the standard arrangements made under the previous system.

It was apparent to Broach that the financing package to be negotiated would involve multiple international parties. To help with this task, fellow USWI Vice-President Dave Davis joined the project. Davis had extensive experience in international financial markets, an asset that would prove invaluable in negotiating the complex financial package necessary to fund the continued growth of Westel. After getting up to speed on the project, Davis began to investigate the sources of financing available to Westel.

OPIC Financing

One of the most obvious was the Overseas Private Insurance Corporation or OPIC. OPIC was a U.S. government sponsored organization operated by the Commerce Department to encourage U.S. investment in foreign countries. Before a country could be approved, it had to apply to OPIC to become a "favored nation." OPIC used mostly political considerations in making this determination. For example, companies operating in Hong Kong did not have access to OPIC programs because Hong Kong had allowed North Viet Nam's ships to anchor in its harbor during the Viet Nam War. OPIC offered partial insurance against various political risks such as convertibility of currency and expropriation of fixed assets. Early in the process, Broach had contacted OPIC to reserve insurance for each Eastern European country of interest to USWI. When Hungary finally met OPIC guidelines, USWI was granted OPIC insurance for the Westel project.

In addition, OPIC would provide loan guarantees for up to 50% of the value of a project. That is, OPIC did not actually lend the money, but instead simply provided a guarantee. It was then up to the borrowing company to arrange the actual loan from some other source. OPIC preferred fixed asset projects such as the building of a manufacturing plant. An OPIC guarantee generally meant the company could borrow money at a rate which was 250 to 300 basis points (1/100th of 1%) above the equivalent maturity Treasury Bond rate. Davis felt that Westel would qualify for an OPIC loan guarantee, but that the arrangement might be a bit cumbersome given the ongoing construction and equipment nature of building out a cellular system. Davis was reluctant to go back to OPIC every time Westel added another cell site. Instead, he wanted to arrange for all the financing up front and then have Westel "take down" the funds as needed.

HNB Financing

Another alternative was to borrow money from a Hungarian bank. This would have the advantage of repayment in forints, thus providing Westel a better currency match between revenues and expenses and reducing currency risk. In addition, with MP, one of the largest companies in Hungary, as a partner, Westel could present a very strong case for a loan. Westel would have to approach one of the large commercial banks, such as the Hungarian Foreign Trade Bank or the Hungarian Credit Bank, rather than HNB because HNB was trying to distance itself from commercial activities as it transformed itself into a central bank. However, the going rate for a commercial loan was 35% in a country with an estimated inflation rate of 15%–20%. Furthermore, Davis was not convinced that the Hungarian bankers would actually make a loan to even as low risk a venture as Westel. Old habits die hard.

Whether or not Westel approached a Hungarian bank for a loan, the importance of a strong working relationship with HNB was clear to everyone. From the very beginning, Davis had carefully cultivated his HNB contacts. As a result, HNB had already given Westel permission to borrow in Hungary or elsewhere in hard currencies and had assured Westel currency convertibility. Beyond these two important agreements, Davis was pursuing the possibility that HNB might agree to issue a letter of credit (LC) and/or provide a loan guarantee to Westel. In the case of an LC, HNB would, up to a limit, pay Westel bills submitted to HNB by suppliers and others, and HNB would then in turn ask for payment from Westel for the amount of the bill plus a fee. LCs represented standard practice in international trade in which the credit worthiness of the bank was substituted for the credit worthiness of the importer. In the case of a guarantee, HNB would not be involved in any payments except in the event of a loan default. Davis had already held several meetings with HNB to discuss LC's and loan guarantees. Even though HNB had not agreed to either yet, he felt that if a specific, well-documented need was presented to HNB, they would agree to issue one or both.

During one of his HNB meetings concerning the issuance of an LC, the banker surprised Davis by producing an LC issued by USWI and signed by Broach. In the last months prior to start-up, Broach had found himself in need of additional Westel funding. Because MP could not match new USWI transfers to the JV capital account and because Hungarian law prevented foreign companies from loaning money directly to Hungarian joint ventures, Broach had to come up with some sort of creative financing. He accomplished this by setting up a receivable, in which USWI paid the supplier and in turn billed Westel for the amount of the invoice. To set this up, Broach had a USWI LC issued under his name. As part of the necessary documentation for arranging payment from Westel to USWI through HNB, Broach sent a copy of the LC to HNB. It was this copy that the banker was waving in front of Davis. "Come back in February after this LC expires and then we can talk about HNB issuing a LC for Westel" was the banker's response to Davis. Thus until February 1991, a HNB LC was out of the question.

Supplier Financing

Another potential source of funds was supplier financing. Because all of Westel's suppliers were outside Hungary, such financing would likely involve the Export-Import (EXIM) banks in those countries in which the suppliers were located. The typical EXIM bank was a government sponsored institution that had as its major goal the stimulation and growth of the country's exporting industries. The EXIM bank provided guarantees, not loans and in granting gua. antees was most concerned with the political and economic stability of the importer's country. Generally, the

EXIM bank required a guarantee from the central bank of the importing country or from a substantial firm such as US West before issuing its own guarantee. In setting up the agreement, the EXIM would typically guarantee 80% of the loan value while requiring the supplier to guarantee another 5%. The remaining 15% had to be paid by the importer (Westel in this case) to the supplier in the form of a cash "down-payment" at the time of shipment.

Westel had two main suppliers; Ericsson in Sweden, which provided the equipment for the main switch as well as for the individual cell sites; and Motorola in Germany, which provided the cellular telephones for use by customers. Ericsson was a large, well-run company with many strong customers throughout Europe and the rest of the world. Given this strong position, Davis felt that Ericsson would drive a hard bargain and might very well turn down the request to take on the 5% loan guarantee required by the EXIM bank. Westel was exploring the possibility of using alternative suppliers such as Nokia in Finland. But clearly such a change would significantly slow the loan negotiation process. Motorola seemed much more receptive to the idea of supplier financing through the German EXIM bank.

In any case, the first step in arranging such supplier financing would be to secure a loan guarantee from either U.S. West or HNB. After the resulting EXIM guarantee had been secured, it would then be necessary to form a consortium of Western banks to provide the actual loan. In general, Western banks were reluctant to accept an HNB guarantee but were willing to accept an EXIM bank guarantee. In addition, they were unwilling to loan to Westel without some sort of guarantee. Davis estimated that the interest rate on a guaranteed loan would be 150 to 200 basis points above the equivalent maturity Treasury Bond rate and that up to five-year loans were possible. Davis liked the flexibility that supplier financing offered.

To facilitate the arrangement of the financing package, USWI had retained Bank of America (B of A) to act as their merchant banker. B of A would provide many of the contacts with EXIM banks and commercial banks and would be responsible for assembling the consortium of Western banks that would actually provide the funds. Also, B of A could participate in this consortium and even act as the lead bank. Finally, B of A was one of the few Western banks willing to accept a HNB loan guarantee directly.

The Current Situation

The demand for cellular services continued to grow rapidly. By December, 2,500 customers had signed up compared to an initial plan projection of 1,000. Westel estimated that by the end of 1991, 18,000 customers would be using the system compared to the initial projection of 12,000 customers by the year 2000. To meet this exploding demand in the Budapest area, Westel proposed building, during 1991, an additional 46 cell sites beyond the 6 already in operation. Each site would cost roughly $500,000 to equip. Broach estimated that 600 million forints were needed for 1991 working capital purposes. A portion of this working capital would be telephones held in inventory. The telephones cost about $1,000 each and would be held in inventory for roughly one month before being resold to customers. Westel's December balance sheet was debt free and showed 200 million forints in cash, receivables, and inventory. Operations were expected to generate a net cash flow (not including interest payments) of roughly 50 million forints per month during 1991, while the exchange rate was expected to be 80 forints per dollar.

Even though there were many positive things about the Budapest cellular market, there were also several risks. Competition was coming. ConTel, a subsidiary of GTE, was preparing to enter the market. In October, just when Westel turned on its cellular network, the government released the RFPs for a 900 MHz analog cellular license and a 900 MHz digital license, both representing superior as well as highly complementary technologies to Westel's current 450 MHz analog system. Westel was excluded from bidding on the 900 MHz analog license, thus insuring another competitor. The JV agreement gave Westel the right of first refusal on the 900 MHz digital license, the superior technology. However, formally winning the bid was going to take considerable additional effort on Westel's part. Whatever the outcome, Westel would soon lose its monopoly and would have to be careful not to be out-flanked technologically.

Beyond the risks inherent in the Budapest market, Diversified Group CFO Bob Gras was making his own demands on Westel. First, he made it clear that U.S. West wanted to cap its investment at $5 million. In Mr. Gras' opinion, U.S. West should put as little money as possible at risk in politically unstable regions such as Eastern Europe. In addition, because of the regulated nature of the U. S. telephone business, U.S. West simply could not provide any loan guarantees. The regulators viewed such guarantees for non-regulated subsidiaries as unfairly burdening rate payers. On the other side of the coin, Mr. Gras had made it clear to Broach and Davis that Westel represented a lynch pin in Diversified's international strategy and that 1991 was a critical performance year. Poor performance by Westel during 1991 would significantly hamper ongoing efforts in other Eastern European countries and the CIS. Clearly, Westel was under a magnifying glass.

As Broach and Davis left the plane in Denver after the long flight from London, their bodies were weary, but their minds were alive with the challenge that lay ahead of them.

9
International Gateway Company, Ltd.

C. Thomas Howard
and
Robert P. McGowan

It was a typical gray autumn day in Moscow in 1991. Greg Sadler, the director of international accounting for the US West International and Business Development Group (USWI), was walking through one of the many street bazaars looking for an egg-shaped Gorby doll. Upon finding one, the street vendor asked to be paid in U.S. dollars. The transaction, however, could not occur at his booth because the penalty for receiving hard currency was jail for both the vendor and Sadler. Sadler was instructed to put the currency under his armpit and another gentlemen would take the currency from him as Sadler wandered among the other vendors. The transaction was consummated without an arrest. Pausing to reflect on the incident, Sadler thought, "What a crazy place to do business!"

Of more pressing concern to Sadler was what he would tell John Broach, US West international controller and treasurer, concerning the status of the International Gateway Company Ltd. Clearly the project had been affected by the still fresh August coup. Prior to the coup, USWI had agreed to a deal to install the telephone switching hardware as soon as it arrived in Moscow from Yugoslavia. Now US West would have to reconfirm the deal and, in addition, it was unclear whether the switches would even get to Moscow. Yugoslavia, where the switches were being built, was descending into total anarchy. USWI found itself in the unenviable position of shipping highly sophisticated switching equipment from a country that was self-destruc-

---

This case was written for the purpose of classroom discussion and not as an example of effective or ineffective management. Will Sumners, an MBA student at the University of Denver, helped with the research and initial writing of this case.

ting to another country that had just gone through a coup. As Mr. Broach would later joke, "Other than that, everything was fine!"

In addition, there were several options that needed to be considered. US West could continue insisting that the new Russian ministry honor their agreements, but, unfortunately, this might lead to some bad feelings. On the other hand, US West could convert its investment to a loan that would be repaid over the course of one year, and, as a result, US West would be out of the project. US West could also walk away from the existing agreement and take their chances through the international courts. Finally, US West could renegotiate terms that were satisfactory to both sides; provided they could obtain an acceptable return on investment as well as secure a relationship for ongoing participation in the Russian economy.

The Gateway Switch

The venture was originally conceived in mid-1989 as a way to build a fiber optic system from Moscow to Copenhagen, Rome, and Tokyo known as the Trans Siberian Line or TSL. Participants in the proposed TSL venture were USWI, British Telecom, Danish Telecom, Stet (the Italian telephone company), KDD (the Korean Telephone Company), NTT of Japan, and the Soviet Union Ministry of Posts and Telecommunications (MPT). The MPT was to provide labor and construction of the system, the rights of way, as well as the customers. USWI was to obtain COCOM approval to use the fiber optic technology in the Soviet Union. COCOM, controlled by the U.S. Defense Department, regulated the transfer of technology into communist countries. COCOM approval was not granted and the $750 million TSL project was put on indefinite hold.

While the TSL project was being pursued, the need for long distance gateway switching capacity became apparent. The gateway switch function was to direct incoming and outgoing long distance calls to and from other countries. The call was then passed onto the local Russian telephone network. After approaching the MPT about forming a joint venture to install and operate gateway switches, USWI agreed to form the International Gateway Company Ltd. (IGC) joint venture. The initial goal was to install three switches in two or three cities within the U.S.S.R.

The need for the switches was driven by the fact that Moscow was the only gateway switching point within the U.S.S.R. Additionally, Moscow served as a gateway city for the Baltic states. The existing switching capacity only serviced 1,100 originating international calls from the entire U.S.S.R. with a population of 250 million people, or roughly the same population as in the United States, whose switching capacity was in the millions of calls. Each new switch installed would double the capacity of the existing system.

An alternate way of making a long distance phone call was through the existing satellite system. The system had adequate capacity and was reliable, however, the calling cost was approximately $12 per minute. In fact, USWI's Moscow office of seven people racked up monthly phone bills of $50,000 using the satellite system due to bottlenecks in the land-based phone system. This bill would drop by between 80%–90% if the land-based switching system was used. Thus, there were powerful financial incentives for increasing the existing long distance switching capacity within Russia.

The new switches were to be purchased from Nikola Tesla, a Yugoslavian company operating under a license from Ericcson of Sweden. While these switches were not as efficient as the other switches on the market, they were the only ones compatible with the existing Soviet technology. Nikola Tesla took advantage of this fact by charging a premium price for their product. The switches would cost $12 million apiece. By comparison, a switch with similar capacity being installed in Latvia, only cost $1.5 million and possessed superior technology.

Attracting USWI to this venture was the nature of the switch itself. Once it was up and running, it became a low-maintenance operation, and the overwhelming majority of transactions it generated would be in hard currency. This was because there were more incoming hard currency calls than outgoing ruble calls, at least for the foreseeable future. USWI was not known for its expertise in operating switches, but the company viewed this as an opportunity to establish itself within the U.S.S.R. and gain a foothold for future projects.

One such potential project included a digital overlay network that involved scrapping the existing telephone system and building a new telephone infrastructure over the old one. The size and population of the U.S.S.R. meant that installing a digital overlay would be a once-in-a-century opportunity. It would be like installing a phone system in the U.S. from scratch. Other potential projects were expanding cellular systems beyond St. Petersburg, laying a cable network, directory services, and installing more switches. All of these possibilities led USWI to pursue vigorously the IGC joint venture.

The Joint Venture—Pre Coup

Before the August 1991 coup, USWI was one of the few companies actively seeking joint ventures in the Soviet Union. USWI had developed a relationship with N. G. Trufev, the minister of telecommunications, and his subordinates that had helped in the IGC negotiations. At this time it was clear to USWI who they were dealing with and who could make the decision to put the venture together—Mr. Trufev. USWI and the Soviet MPT were each going to provide $17.5 million in hard currency for the switches. USWI would also supply the technical knowledge, organizational leadership, and export licenses. In addition, they would act as a liaison with the international long distance carriers. MPT would provide customers, labor, construction and rights of way.

Due to favorable tax laws and the reputation as a safe haven for hard currency revenues, the Isle of Man was selected as the legal location for the joint venture company. IGC Ltd. would receive 16% of the net income to distribute equally to the partners in the form of dividends. The partners would receive dividends until the annual internal rate of return (IRR) for USWI reached 18%. After this benchmark was reached, two thirds of IGC's continuing 16% of the net income would be set aside for reinvestment in MPT's international business. The remaining one third would continue to be paid out in dividends to the partners. The business plan that was prepared and agreed to by both parties reflected very attractive returns for both partners.

IGC management would consist of the board of directors, equally represented by MPT and USWI. The managing director, CEO, and CFO would be USWI executives. Work plans, funds flow, and audit plans had to be approved by the IGC board.

By the summer of 1991, both sides had agreed to the joint venture. Each had invested $5 million in hard currency and Nikola Tesla had begun construction of the switches. USWI had also established an irrevocable letter of credit to Nikola Tesla for another $5 million. Broach and Sadler had developed a strong relationship with Mr. Trufev, and they were confident that USWI was heading down the right road. Like nearly everyone else, they were caught flat-footed by the August coup.

The Joint Venture—Post Coup

August 1991—the Soviet Coup—Gorbachev out, Yeltsin in. USWI employees walked around tanks to get to work. All the people and agencies that USWI had dealt with were gone. Mr. Trufev was out and no replacement had been named. Yeltsin declared that all agreements prior to the coup would be honored. Everyone was still showing up for work but nothing was getting done, including in the former agencies. No one knew how the country was running. Appendix A provides a chronology of key events that took place over the next year.

Over the next three to four months, Greg Sadler and Stan Cramton, USWI's project manager in Moscow, spent a great deal of time trying to determine who their partner was, and who was in charge. Speaking to ten different people resulted in eleven different answers. Meanwhile, the switches were still being assembled. The documentary letters of credit, which were previously established to fund the switch purchases, were being drawn against. Broach had made the decision to fund the switches even when the MPT did not fund its portion. The reasons were several, not the least of which was getting the switches out of war-torn Yugoslavia. Moreover, by funding the purchase of the switches, USWI showed a commitment to the venture and to the former Soviet Union. However, such a decision exposed USWI to additional risk. The switches finally arrived and were stored in Moscow and St. Petersburg. One of the switches was scheduled for installation in Kiev, Ukraine but after the coup, Ukraine no longer wanted to deal with the Russian MPT, so USWI found itself with an extra switch.

In November 1991, it was apparent that the original deal was being seriously scrutinized by the new Russian leadership. Complicating this issue was the ever changing role of the MPT. In December, discussions finally began with Minister Rumbak, Mr. Trufev's replacement and the new head of MPT. Much to the chagrin of USWI, Minister Rumbak began to ask why the MPT needed USWI after the switches were up and operating. "The MPT should simply pay off USWI like a lender and be done with them and have the switches and all the associated revenues for themselves," stated Minister Rumbak. The selling point for USWI was its expertise in getting the system installed and in showing Western business people that deals could work successfully in the Soviet Union. Broach felt that while it was true that the MPT didn't necessarily need USWI's help with installing and operating the switches, USWI provided value beyond the hardware. He felt the Russians understood this.

Clouding the issue further was the fact that after the coup several other companies including AT&T, Sprint, and MCI began pursuing ventures with the MPT. They perceived the former Soviet Union as a logical and safer place to do business as a result of the coup. USWI's main disadvantage was that they weren't a long distance carrier as AT&T and Telecon Denmark were, and they could not afford to give away the switches and make their return on the volume of calls. In addition, with the new ministry, everyone had to make new contacts, and it was often difficult to know who truly had power within the ministry to negotiate contracts. This put to the test the relationships Sadler, Broach, and Cramton had built over the previous eighteen months.

Once the discussions moved beyond the issue of needing USWI's involvement, several other deal points became major concerns. First, was the issue of an offshore corporation. This was not acceptable to Minister Rumbak. Instead he wanted a Russian company paying Russian taxes. His logic was that in the old Soviet system corruption was common and officials often funneled illegal profits offshore to protect their wealth. A Russian company was not the preferred corporate form for USWI due to political instability, and would be hard to sell to the USWI Board.

A second disputed point was the internal rate of return that USWI was demanding. The Russians, again perceiving USWI as a lender, felt that 18% was too high, while, on the other hand, USWI felt it was insufficient to compensate for the political risks. This point was bolstered by the fact that the original deal was being reopened by the new MPT people. However, Minister Rumbak clearly did not understand why USWI was demanding such a high IRR on a project that would generate large amounts of cash and could lead to a number of other opportunities within Russia.

Finally, the revenue sharing arrangement was renegotiated from a percentage sharing basis to a per minute basis. IGC would receive $.10 per minute of use after taxes.

The Business Climate After the Coup

Doing business in the new CIS was like sailing in uncharted waters. While USWI had experience in the region through the installation of the cellular phone system in St. Petersburg, that venture had been largely unsuccessful. The same was true for the cellular system in Czechoslovakia. Hungary, however, had been a great success. What made the difference, in Broach's opinion, between St. Petersburg and Hungary was where each region was on the learning curve with respect to capitalism. Hungary was abuzz with people hustling to make money. Hungarians realized the need for communication and were heavily using the system. Business conditions in St. Petersburg reflected the nature of business in all of the Commonwealth of Independent States. The people did not understand the profit motive and lacked comprehension of basic business concepts like IRR and net present value.

Despite the lack of appreciation of profits, Russians displayed a great deal of negotiating skill. As Broach put it, "They didn't necessarily understand how to negotiate the finer points, but they knew where they started and where they wanted to end." In his opinion, the Russians were some of the best "bare knuckle" negotiators in the world.

The Russian people themselves were honest and ethical to a fault. The Soviet government had one of the best records of any nation for paying their bills. But it seemed that the rules of the game changed every week.

The Final Push

By June 1992, the IGC discussions between USWI and Minister Rumbak had reached a critical juncture. Both sides had grown weary of the seemingly endless round of talks. The USWI Board had run out of patience as IGC was beginning to look like a failed international venture. Minister Rumbak was being bombarded by other numerous attractive offers for providing gateway switching capacity. In an ironic twist, USWI's old friend Mr. Trufev reappeared, this time as head of the new Russian telecommunications operating company. Minister Rumbak's MPT was being reconfigured to be like the U.S.'s Federal Communications Commission and would no longer have operational responsibilities. Broach and Sadler viewed this as a positive turn of events as Mr. Trufev would now be the person they would deal with.

USWI also had two other points of leverage. First, they had funded their part to Nikola Tesla. Tesla, in turn, was putting pressure on the Russians to pay their part of the agreement. Second, the ministry was looking for a long-term commitment to Russia and was leery of those who appeared to be "cream-skimming." USWI offered a reinvestment provision as part of a 15-year deal. This latter point took a few meetings with the ministry to explain how it would work and how both sides would profit. Yet such meetings weren't without their problems. "Both sides initially started out wanting the same terms as before," stated Greg Sadler, "but it was obvious we weren't getting anywhere. The Russians came back wanting USWI to fund their position, and they were using other competitors' terms as points of leverage. USWI was finally able to convince them that it was interested in long-term investment and agreed that, on the money side, "USWI could go with a lower rate on a per call basis."

In negotiating with the Russians, Sadler offered the following reflections. "You have to realize that a lot gets lost in translation. It is important to listen to them and go back and work with them. Keep them involved in the decision making process and don't dictate terms to them."

As a result of the frustration on both sides, USWI and the MPT had agreed to a buy-out of USWI's interest by the MPT if a new deal were not agreed to by the end of July 1992. While this buy-out would limit USWI's financial losses, deep in their hearts, Sadler and Broach did not want this to happen. On the other hand, USWI was not willing to pay an extravagant amount to get a foothold in the Russian telecommunications industry. In addition, the current negotiations would set the tone for all future negotiations.

With the July deadline bearing down on him, Sadler boarded the plane for Moscow. As he settled into his seat, he reviewed the issues facing both USWI (See Appendix B) and Mr. Trufev. He knew that substantial progress would have to be made during this trip to salvage the IGC joint venture as the Russian economy grew weaker by the day. "Would this economic weakness lead to another coup?" was one of the questions that constantly darted through Sadler's mind.

Appendix A: Chronology of Major Events Since 1991 Coup

August 19, 1991: End of perestroika

September 5, 1991: Republics declare independence

November 28, 1991: Venesheconom Bank announces bankruptcy

December 1, 1991: Price liberalization (300% food price increases)

December 21, 1991: Leaders of 11 republics form the Commonwealth of Independent States

December 30, 1991: Formation of the Republican Hard Currency Reserve under Russian Law (local businesses must transfer all hard currency into Russian banks and sell 10% of hard currency to the state)

January 8, 1992: Central Bank announces new official market-based U.S. dollar conversion rate at 110 rubles per U.S. $1 (rate in October = 400)

January 21, 1992: Central Bank becomes only authority to grant licenses on hard-currency transactions

February 6, 1992: Package of acts and provisions on privatization of state and municipal entities adopted

March 1992: General price increase for month—38%

April 6, 1992: Selected businesses with foreign ownership released from Republican Currency Reserve

April 30, 1992: CIS accepted IMF

May 1992: General price increases for month—24%

June 1992: Bush and Yeltsin sign new tax treaty. $24 billion aid package announced

July 1992: 60% personal income tax rate established for individuals making more than $4,200.00 per year

Appendix B: US West International Russian Strategy Considerations

The Opportunity	US West's Situation
• 160 M Russian people • Highly educated • Rich scientific and technical base • Great natural resource riches • Huge need for telecom improvement and development • Probably the largest undeveloped market opportunity in a century • Potential to explode and mushroom—if our political relations are solid	• Have established an advantageous position—flowing largely from TSL • Have had a local presence for more than two years • Solid relationships with some key players • Good contacts throughout CIS • No other western company comes close

THE RISKS	"REASSURING" OPINIONS OFFERED	THE "REALITIES"
• Political unsettledness —relationships vulnerable to disruption • Course of the CIS economics highly uncertain • Policies towards foreign investment not yet settled • Ruble not freely convertible • Financial infrastructure not yet established • Cultural dissonance	• "They've just got to make it" • Membership in the IMF eliminates most of the financial uncertainty • The West just won't let them fail • Because of their nuclear capability, the West wouldn't dare let them go down	• No successes yet • Hard currency investment needs are nearly insatiable • Takes a long time to build a relationship of trust • Competent indigenous managers are desperately needed

10
Beijing Jeep Corporation: American Motor's Experience in China

Mary B. Teagarden and Mary Ann Von Glinow

"We believe our Chinese joint venture can change the face of the auto industry in Asia, and give the Japanese the first real competition they have ever had in their own back yards."[18] Tod Clare, vice-president of international operations of American Motors Corporation (AMC), made this bold statement in 1983 after signing an ambitious, twenty-year, renewable agreement with Beijing Auto Works (BAW) formalizing an equity joint venture, called Beijing Jeep Corporation (BJC), to manufacture Jeeps in BAW's Beijing plant. AMC faced strong competition. The Japanese auto manufacturers were eager to build market share in the People's Republic of China (PRC); and the other U.S. and European global competitors were jockeying for market share and scale economies in an industry plagued by overcapacity and inefficiency.

The path that had brought AMC to the signing of this joint venture agreement had been complex and full of twists and turns. AMC was a pioneer in the newly opened PRC market, a new business frontier. From the beginning, AMC wanted to establish a joint venture in which they were deeply involved with their partner. In the following decade, as they initiated, developed and implemented their joint venture, AMC and BAW coped with many setbacks. In the face of these cultural, managerial, technological, and external challenges, AMC, BAW, and BJC had developed innovative responses and solutions.

This case was prepared as a basis for classroom discussion. The case relies on archival research done by Antonis Kounoupis, Lauren Raines, Susan Ellis Richards, and Louise Rohy, as well as interviews at Beijing Jeep Corporation, Beijing, PRC.

At this point, BJC's board of directors was contemplating the direction of their future activities, especially their expansion plans. BJC's work force was committed and the quality of their work was high. Would changes to increase output productivity diminish commitment and quality? Should BJC expand its production of Jeeps? Would expansion into other product lines be appropriate at this time? Should they introduce more sophisticated manufacturing technology? What role should their Chinese engineers play in design modifications, and in management of the technology department? As he prepared his proposal for approval from headquarters, Don St. Pierre, BJC's general manager, contemplated alternative courses of action.

People's Republic of China: A Business Frontier

In 1978, the PRC was a new frontier for U.S. business. Richard Nixon signed the Shanghai Communique in 1972 that reestablished diplomatic relations between the U.S. and the PRC after a twenty-three-year freeze. Commercial relations barely proceeded for the next seven years as Chinese authorities reached consensus on the role of foreign investment in their modernization plans.

The period between 1972 and 1979 could best be characterized as highly uncertain and risky for U.S. business entering the PRC, and most interaction was the exchange of technology or sports delegations. China's authorities concluded that rapid and effective modernization was dependent on expanded foreign interaction. Reforms in foreign economic policy, such as the Open Door Policy and, eventually, the 1979 Joint Venture Law facilitated U.S. business entry under specific circumstances.

The introduction of these reforms resulted in an initial euphoric wave of U.S. investors, but AMC, one of the earliest pioneers, was ahead of this wave by almost a year. BJC, the result of pioneering efforts on both sides, was held out as a model joint venture by the Chinese and received more publicity and notoriety in the Western press than any other Sino-U.S. strategic alliance.

Competition in the Pacific Basin

In the 1980s, the Pacific basin was the most attractive growth region for the auto industry and China was its newest market. As AMC Chairman W. Paul Tippett commented, "The key market will be China. A nation with a billion people, a billion bicycles, but no cars." He continued, "This is a long-term strategic move by AMC . . . It will be a long time before there is much in the way of profit, but the opportunities seem very great to us in the long run."[46]

Japanese Dominance

In 1983, Japanese companies sold 97% of all of the approximately 100,000 four-wheel drive vehicles purchased in the Asia-Pacific basin each year. The Japanese were willing to sell vehicles directly to the PRC, a market they dominated. However, they avoided direct investment in vehicle manufacturing despite offers from Chinese factories to do so. Japanese auto manufacturers used this export market entry pattern throughout the Asia-Pacific basin. Clare, colorfully commented, "The Japanese are beating our brains out there." He continued, "China has the domestic capacity to soak up everything you can build there, but it won't happen quickly."[9, 93] Clare believed that the PRC was an attractive market and that direct investment was key in establishing a strong market position.

The Asia-Pacific Basin Jeep Market

The four-wheel drive market was rapidly expanding in the Asia-Pacific basin and grew at an average yearly rate of 25% between 1980 and 1983. The Jeep, AMC's best known product, enjoyed worldwide recognition as a reliable and durable four-wheel drive utility vehicle. Clare pointed out, "The Chinese believe they've got to get their people on wheels and Jeep is perfect for their needs."[93]

AMC's Rationale for Entering the PRC

AMC produced four-wheel drive trucks in addition to Jeeps. In 1983, AMC sold 2,000 to 3,000 Jeeps in the Pacific Basin and a total of 91,000 jeep-type vehicles were sold domestically and abroad. AMC, the fourth largest U.S. automobile manufacturer, behind General Motors, Ford, and Chrysler, was motivated to enter China by several factors. According to Clare, "The most important strategic advantage of the joint venture lies beyond the borders of China itself . . . Every $1 reduction in cost of a vehicle to be exported built-up to a market like Australia represents a $2.30 reduction at retail price." Additional venture advantages cited by Clare were increased opportunity for AMC exports of vehicles, tooling and equipment; entry and access to the domestic Chinese market of over one billion people; the desire to establish a large, low-cost manufacturing base in the Far East; and the opportunity to build a wedge to compete effectively for more market share in the Far East.[18]

Initial Contacts and Pre-Entry Exploration

The joint venture exploration process began when AMC contacted the PRC government in early 1978 regarding possible business opportunities. They gave their first formal presentation to the PRC government in the fall of that year. Clare, commented, "In those days there was no joint venture law, no Chinese National Automotive Industry Corporation [CNAIC], no hotel rooms, nor any previous examples on how to proceed." A high level of risk and uncertainty surrounded the endeavor.

BAW as a Partner

BAW had been in operation since 1965, and was the only Chinese plant producing light cross-country utility vehicles in 1978, the year AMC began its foray into the PRC. BAW also produced a jeep at that time, the BJ-212 which was a military-type looking vehicle characterized by the Chinese as technically out-of-date, stylistically dull, and not competitive in the international marketplace. That was an understatement at best. In fact, the BJ-212 was a more than 20 year-old Russian design, copied from the military jeep supplied to the Chinese by the Soviet Union during the 1950s. Called a *jipu* in Chinese slang, the Russian original was allegedly copied from Jeep's World War II military vehicle.[22, 23, 96]

BAW's large, sprawling manufacturing complex had slid into obsolescence, and management was eager to secure funds and techniques to update equipment and improve products. Nevertheless, they were cautious about partner selection. After AMC initiated contact with BAW, BAW contacted Japanese, British, French, and other U.S. automobile manufacturers and compared bids from manufacturers from each of these countries before they selected AMC as a partner.[24, 46]

The Entry Mode Decision

Key decision makers on both BAW and AMC's sides were eager to form an alliance. However, there were political and perceptual barriers on both sides that impeded initiation of the agreement and, later, progress of the negotiations. There were a significant number of BAW employees who had serious misgivings about entering into a joint venture with foreigners. "Arguments on the potentially destructive effects of dealing with a capitalist country were debated on all sides before BAW began one discussion with AMC." At the same time there were skeptics among AMC's management who tried to dissuade AMC from cooperating with the PRC because the PRC was seen as unstable and politically risky. Even among those in agreement about pursuing business with the PRC, there was considerable dissention regarding the form that business relationship should take and the terms of the contract that should be negotiated.[24]

AMC concluded that their future partner, "already had the aptitude, the skills, and the facilities to do the job." What was missing was "the proper management of these resources and an injection of technology to come up with a competitive product . . ."[11] Cooperation arrangements, compensation trade, and subcontracting offered neither the security of a long-term commitment nor took full advantage of AMC's strength as a manufacturer."[2] In the fall of 1979, once initial hurdles were surmounted, it only took four days to sign a memorandum of agreement to form an equity joint venture to build Jeeps in China. "We thought the rest would be a breeze," recalled AMC's Ron Gilchrist, general manager of Far East operations.[94]

The Negotiation Process

Negotiations were not a breeze: it was four years and fifteen trips to China before they were complete. The first Sino-foreign automotive joint venture contract was signed by AMC Chairman Paul Tippett and Chinese BAW executive Wu Zhongliang in the PRC's Great Hall of the People. Reflecting upon the signing of the contract, Clare observed that once again, "We deluded ourselves into thinking we were in the home stretch."[25, 94]

The Liability of Newness

The negotiation process was arduous in part because AMC was a pioneer and there simply was not precedent for either partner to follow in hammering out the contract. AMC officials commented that at times "they felt they were negotiating not only their own contract, but China's joint venture law," which was developing while AMC was negotiating the contract.[17]

In fact the joint venture negotiations between the Chinese and AMC are credited with having made significant contributions to the development of the 1979 Joint Venture Law and subsequent modifications. For example, Chinese laws permit joint ventures in China to buy much equipment locally and to pay in Chinese currency (RMB) instead of foreign exchange currency (FEC). AMC officials are certain that their insistence that BJC be allowed to pay for equipment in Chinese currency (RMB) was the basis for this provision in the Joint Venture Law. Tippett commented, "Other companies that follow will have an easier time because of the patterns this joint venture set."[17]

Initial issues that usually present stumbling blocks in joint ventures—equity and profit goals—presented little difficulty to either party. However, the Chinese had different assumptions and expectations about the contract. The Chinese were most concerned with detailing how the joint venture would operate rather than the financial and legal aspects most commonly focused on in American contract negotiations.

Resistance to Boilerplate and Legalese

There was ongoing and constant haggling over standard clauses; standard clauses referring to "Acts of God" met with considerable resistance. The Chinese wanted every act spelled out in detail. Finally a substitute phrase, "conditions beyond reasonable and foreseeable control," was agreed upon.

The standard use of *etcetera* was not considered appropriate by the Chinese and also had to be specifically detailed. "We spent half a day arguing over an *etcetera*," said Richard Swando director of AMC's China project. Gilchrist commented, "American contracts are 35% boilerplate. The Chinese would only settle for zero." He continued, "The 20-year contract is really devoid of any legalese. The Chinese had a real problem with anything that smacked of legal jargon." AMC negotiators were quick to point out that "God" was not the problem. "It was the *etcetera* they objected to."[17, 94]

Differences in Business Practices

In addition, China's long commercial isolation contributed to both sides' lack of understanding and insight into the other's standard business practices. For example, AMC negotiated for quite a while to simply convince the Chinese that incorporating an inflation factor into the contract for the price of parts over time did not constitute "out and out robbery." "We thought they were arguing over the number," said Gilchrist. It turned out, after lengthy discussion, that the Chinese apparently were unfamiliar with the inflation factor concept.[17,94]

Compensation "Equity"

The Chinese insistence that their managers be paid by the joint venture at near the salary of the foreign managers rankled AMC. The Chinese requested a salary of US$ 45,000 a year, about 80% of the salary AMC planned for expatriates. However, the Chinese manager would only receive a tiny fraction of this amount, with the government getting the rest. Finally, AMC agreed upon paying a higher salary to Chinese managers. Because the Joint Venture Law had not yet been published, both parties agreed that the extra salary would be paid into an escrow account until the law was published. In light of the perception that the Chinese managers would not benefit from this higher salary, Gilchrist commented, "It's a tax."[17]

Profit Repatriation

One of the biggest problems encountered in negotiations was the establishment of a mechanism for AMC to repatriate profits. One AMC source commented, "BAW is making money right now. We're buying a percentage of a profitable corporation." AMC officials said they anticipated little difficulty in meeting the export commitments necessary to generate profits.[2, 20] AMC's expectation was that the plant would generate foreign exchange within a relatively short period. Then AMC intended to export some products, such as the four-wheel drive Beijing Tiger utility vehicle, through AMC's sales outlets. Gilchrist commented that the resolution of the profit repatriation dilemma was "the foreign exchange generated by export sales would be placed in a special fund, from which AMC's hard currency profits could be drawn."[2, 96]

Production Goals

The goal of the venture was to produce world-class vehicles for domestic and export markets, and components that could be used in AMC's operations worldwide. The partners agreed to embark on a massive retraining of the work force, to introduce modern management skills, and to retool existing production lines.[2,20,21,46] Although it did not set export percentage requirements, the agreement set out some benchmark foreign exchange targets that the venture was expected to achieve on a "best-efforts" basis, subject to vehicles meeting rigorous quality standards, to changing market conditions, and to other factors.[2, 17, 46]

External Impediments

Negotiation progress was impeded by outside influences as well. Negotiations were stalled for a year while China went through a retrenchment from ambitious expansion plans precipitated by overly enthusiastic local spending that occurred as China decentralized approval to make import purchases within specific limits. This retrenchment and internal reorganization resulted in extensive turnover of Chinese negotiators. When AMC's negotiators returned after the one year delay, they found only one of the original Chinese officials still on the negotiating team. In fact, this was the only Chinese negotiator to remain with the project from beginning to end.[17, 94]

Bureaucratic Impediments

In addition, obstacles came from China's "old economic management system." Feng Xiantang, a BJC vice-president commented that, BAW had more than ten government sections "overseeing its operations and interfering with its work." When it came time to approve a feasibility report, no one in these ten agencies would take the responsibility of approving the plan until more than a year after the report was submitted. An AMC official commented that during the process, "We had four different Chinese delegations come to our country, talk to us, and walk around our plants. They were very cautious."[20]

Between 1979 and 1982, while the contract was being negotiated, factory representatives reported to officials about negotiation progress more than three hundred times, at least once a week, "but heard no response." Finally, in 1982, "the Chinese formed a five-member group of department heads with complete negotiating and decision-making authority in the talks with AMC. The adjustment simplified the procedures and accelerated the pace of the negotiations . . ." AMC sources suggest that the priority designation given transportation by the Chinese government is what enabled the pace of the talks to speed up. On May 5, 1983 the contract was signed.[24]

Contract Details

The contract formalized the creation of Beijing Jeep Corporation Limited. In four years, the negotiators had hammered out many details.

The Board and Executive Management

BJC would have an eleven-member board of directors, including seven members from the PRC and four from AMC.[20] AMC would provide eight to ten employees for three-year on-site stints to fill the roles of president, director of product development, manufacturing engineering, and quality control, finance, sales, and supply managers. Every three years the president and vice-president positions would rotate between AMC and PRC appointees.[3]

Financial Aspects

The contract created a twenty-year renewable equity joint venture. BAW had 68.7% and AMC 31.3% equity stakes in the US$ 51 million investment. AMC negotiated an option to bring its stake up to 49% through the reinvestment of export profits. AMC contributed US$ 8 million in cash and US$ 8 million in technology, which Clare described as a prepaid royalty.[25, 96] The Chinese contribution included land, existing plant and equipment, labor, and local currency, together valued at US$ 35 million.

AMC's approach for valuing each side's contributions was to have an outside auditing firm, Deloitte, Haskins and Sells, evaluate both Chinese assets and AMC technology contributions. "The Chinese accepted the valuation with little fuss." In addition, a formula was agreed upon that would determine what proportion of technology would be "already deemed utilized" should the venture be prematurely dissolved.[2]

The venture would enjoy a tax holiday for two years, followed by a 50% reduction of the joint venture income tax rate for the following three years. In addition, BJC would pay no duty on production-related machinery and equipment, and only 75–80% duty on imported vehicles. AMC's corporate policy was to operate in international ventures as a minority partner, and they developed time tested clauses that they believe protect their interests. BJC's by-laws include a host of these provisions.[2]

Human Resource Management Considerations

Up to one hundred Chinese managers and engineers would receive up to six months training at AMC in the U.S., and additional foreign experts would be brought in as necessary on a temporary basis. BJC would start with a 4,000-employee work force and retrain the workers during the first two years of operations. The venture would have hiring and firing authority and would pay higher wages than other PRC enterprises. An existing bonus and incentive system would be continued with some modifications.[2]

Marketing Responsibility

BJC would sell the vehicles produced to BAW, the Chinese partner, for distribution. The Chinese would handle the distribution and sales within the country and AMC would handle export sales and distribution.

Production Targets

BJC's long-term goal was to eventually produce 24,000 Cherokees a year on a one-shift basis, working the regular Chinese year of 300 days. The total output for 1984 was to be increased 30% over that of 1983. For the first two years, the partners would begin production of "an improved version" of BAW's current four-wheel drive overland vehicle, the BJ-212, and introduce the production of AMC's CJ model assembled from kits. For the first five years BJC would continue to manufacture current products, while both sides would collaborate on the design of a new jeep using only Chinese components. The BJ-212 would eventually be replaced by this jointly designed version of AMC's Jeep CJ.[20, 22–25, 96]

Start-Up Operations

The conclusion of negotiations did not mark the end of difficulty for the partners. Eight months after the contract was signed, on January 15, 1984, BJC went into business, and the early stages of operations were beset with problems. As agreed upon in the contract, BJC's labor force was to be set at 4,000, a 60% reduction in the original 10,000-employee work force.[24, 25] This was accomplished, in part by transferring some employees to other positions within BAW's operations. In addition, the contract required a 30% increase in output value between 1983 and 1984.[24, 74] The Chinese, who had previously followed the "more workers, more production" maxim were confounded by the idea of increasing production 30% while reducing the work force 60%. The Chinese proposed a compromise plan to hire 300 additional workers to see the venture through the start-up period, but the board of directors would not approve the proposal.

Productivity

The BJC work force, three fourths of which worked on a one-shift six-day week, were scheduled to produce 21,000 BJ-212s and 750 Cherokees in 1985. Cherokee production was slated to start at twelve per hour, rising later to eighteen per hour. There was no opportunity to add a midnight shift because buses do not run between 11 p.m. and 5 a.m. in Beijing.[2]

One industry specialist got "a unique perspective of the old Chinese auto-making process." After walking past a table in which several workmen were puttering over some miscellaneous hardware, the industry specialist asked Robert Steinseifer, BJC's director of enterprise management, "Where's the production line?" Steinseifer casually replied, "You just passed it."[27]

St. Pierre, the joint venture manager, commented that productivity in general was poor given the high over-manning and that their strategy was "not to try to shed some of the plant's 4,000 workers but to prevent any increase in the work force as production expands."[12, 25]

Despite these difficulties, BJ-212 production levels increased, quality was improved and productivity increased. Steinseifer observed, "Any assignment I've given them, they've done in just a first-class way. The prime thing for them to do is to improve their productivity. They haven't had to do that before because their prime interest has been to furnish everybody with a job. Now their prime interest is to build a world-class car that can compete with the Japanese in the Japanese backyard and that's really quite a chore."[22]

The New Structure

BJC streamlined its management structure and this restructuring reduced the more than thirty departments into six that would oversee business management, production, finance, marketing, quality and technology, and one office under the general manager. "With only one manager heading each department, the new structure established direct management lines with clear responsibilities for each manager, and eliminated the previously vague management distinctions that occasionally adversely affected production."[24]

Control Processes and Systems

AMC introduced quality control techniques and began monitoring production statistics, finances, and quality measures on a daily basis. Computers were introduced to aid in the management of this information. The introduction of this management information system made "feedback from management and other departments a more integral part of the factory routine and has also improved quality control, while raising the utility rate of each work hour."[24]

Communication Challenges and the War Room

Steinseifer identified an additional challenge. He observed that, ". . . one of the handicaps for Americans is that the Chinese, when making a comment or a criticism, are so polite that the forthright American often doesn't get the point." To get around this obstacle, Steinseifer created a "war room" in which he and his Chinese counterpart or other employees could be completely blunt and even argue if they cared to. The Chinese have laughingly accepted this approach, although they always resume their totally polite "face" once they leave the room.[22]

The Joint Vehicle Design Program

In 1985, the board of directors decided that the new jointly designed vehicle would be based on AMC's YJ type with the Chinese having dominant say over the general body design. However, after several months, the board decided that the vehicle designed "was defective in such areas as its exhaust system, noise, visibility, and speed, none of which could match international standards."[24]

AMC suggested that joint design efforts be postponed until after BJC perfected its production of models from the AMC XJ model series, which included the Cherokee jeep and a four-wheel drive, long axle minitruck, which had been under production in the U.S. since September 1983. The Chinese interpreted AMC's suggestion as "a symbol of the American's unwillingness to cooperate on a jointly designed vehicle, and as evidence of AMC's desire to control China's market." Needless to say, AMC's proposal was "pigeonholed."[24]

The AMC XJ

AMC persuaded the Chinese to reconsider their proposal and eventually, the Chinese surveyed potential clients for a reaction to the AMC XJ series. The response was very positive, and soon orders for AMC XJ models began "pouring in." This very positive response, "along with some needling from the Americans" prompted the board to reconsider. Approval was given for BJC to manufacture the Cherokee, an AMC XJ model, with the intention of replacing American parts with Chinese substitutes as those became available.

Assistant General Manager Zhao Nailin commented, "The readjustment of the product design was a rational move that showed the sincerity of the two sides. The Americans showed their sincerity by letting the Chinese come up with a new design, a move that also demonstrated their faith in China's business management and technical skills."

Both sides benefitted from the decision to manufacture Cherokees. The Chinese could begin production of a new technically advanced vehicle three years ahead of schedule, thus "propelling a portion of China's automobile industry out of the 1950s into the '80s." AMC would realize the beginning of a competitive edge in the Southeast Asian auto market. Clare called it "a triumph of technology and spirit."[17, 24, 25]

Local Content Challenges

BJC has been frustrated in its attempts to introduce local content into the manufacture of their XJ model products. By the end of 1985 only about 12% of the Cherokee was manufactured from local content. AMC official commented that the level of local content must reach 50–60% before the vehicle becomes exportable. BJC timetables called for 80% local content by 1988, and 10,000 exported vehicles by 1990. BJC had problems both finding factories that could make high quality components and in gaining access at reasonable prices to the output of factories that could. The lack of a supplier infrastructure worked to AMC's short-term advantage: within two years of signing the agreement, AMC had recovered all of their initial investment costs through the sale of Cherokee kits to BJC.[24, 74]

The Foreign Exchange Crisis

In 1985, BJC announced that it would begin assembly of the Comanche, another AMC XJ model to be built from imported kits by the fall of 1986. In mid-1985, the Beijing International Trust and Investment Corporation, an arm of the Beijing city government, loaned the venture US$ 8.5 million to buy equipment for a new Cherokee jeep assembly line and to import kits. AMC contributed an additional US$ 6 million for the assembly line. The loan was made under the assumption that the Cherokees would be sold to end-users in China for foreign exchange. Clare commented that at this point, ". . . things were going well."

The business plan to carry BJC into the 1990s was redeveloped, including a localization plan, a capital budget—in excess of US$ 110 million—and an export plan. All these were approved by BJC's board by the end of September 1985. BJC's future looked bright indeed. Within a month, however, that future began to dim, becoming clouded by China's growing foreign exchange problem.[74]

End-users proved unwilling or unable to buy the vehicles for foreign exchange. As one source observed, "chiefly because foreign exchange allocations to enterprises have been slashed across the board, but perhaps also because a 60% duty on imported parts makes the Beijing price considerably higher than the North American price."[11, 74]

During the first part of 1986, local authorities were unwilling to renew foreign exchange allocations or loans to the venture, since the venture's expected foreign exchange earnings were not forthcoming. "BJC's import licenses were not being approved and BJC was forced to default on three purchase contracts with Jeep," said Clare.[21, 25, 74] In April 1985, AMC announced that it had not received letters of credit from the Chinese for additional Cherokee kits. P. Jeffrey Trimmer, general manager of Far East Operations, stated that the existing inventory of Jeep kits would run out in the middle of June. The kits were assembled at an Ontario, Canada AMC facility and shipped to BJC. Trimmer said production of the Cherokee would be suspended for at least two months because of the long lead time needed for kit shipments to reach the plant. In addition, the closure would be extended one day for each day AMC did not receive a new letter of credit. At the point that BJC ceased Cherokee production, Cherokees represented about 10% of BJC's total production.[21, 67]

AMC's Contingency Plan

AMC formulated a contingency plan in November 1985, which Clare described:
First, we would contact Chinese and American authorities at all levels to explain our plight and solicit their help, for unfortunately our partners had proved less than effective in dealing with their own political infrastructure. We felt we had to take matters into our

own hands. Even our traditional contacts with the China National Automotive Industry Corporation (CNAIC) and the Beijing Municipality were initially (read separately) unable to help us. We had to find our own access to those ever present but always elusive "high-level authorities" who could even begin [to] deal with our problem.

Second, to conserve scarce foreign exchange until the crisis was over, we would suspend capital expenditures, which was a devastating blow to our partners, slowing training and the all important technology transfer. We simply started to shut everything down. In addition, we reduced our expatriate staff. People started coming home and we didn't replace them. These actions caused an uproar with our Chinese partners and the government but we were seriously concerned about the very preservation of BJC.

Third, we agreed that we would respond accurately to press inquiries as word got out and world interest grew. The resulting press reports . . . exposed the unadorned problems to the authorities in both countries as well as the global business community. Most people imagined we were distressed about the bad publicity but in fact it was working to our benefit. The world was watching and failures always seem so much more newsworthy than successes.[11, 12, 67, 74]

Resolution of the Showdown

The implementation of this contingency plan "forced a major showdown in which AMC allowed its grievances to leak into American newspapers, and according to a number of reports, threatened to pull out of the venture." The Chinese were eager to keep the shutdown time as short as possible, and they invited AMC officials to Beijing for meetings between May 8 and May 12. "After everyone from Premier Zhao Ziyang to U.S. Treasury Secretary James A. Baker III and David Rockefeller, retired chairman of Chase Manhattan Bank, became involved, AMC negotiated a new agreement under which the foreign exchange has clearly been made available."[11, 12, 67, 74]

According to Chinese press reports, the central government offered US$ 2 million for Jeeps already assembled, in addition to an unspecified amount for further kit imports. Production of Cherokees resumed on August 1, and St. Pierre, president of BJC commented, "There's been a dramatic change in attitudes since May. It's like night and day, there's now a complete spirit of cooperation . . . What took me hours of banging my head against the wall, is now sorted out in half an hour."[11, 12, 74]

As part of the settlement of the foreign exchange dispute, AMC apparently agreed to increase equipment supplies to BJC and to actively work to develop the automotive component infrastructure to speed the localized parts content of BJC vehicles. St. Pierre commented, "We hope to be the first factory producing new car engines and to sell (them) to other joint ventures."[11, 12] A stamping plant was to be set up and the details of the machine tool imports were being worked out.

In addition, an axle-making venture by one of AMC's U.S. suppliers was explored. St. Pierre commented, "Just like Volkswagen, we've brought our U.S. suppliers over to explore cooperation with Chinese partners." AMC expected that about 80% of the 45% AMC Cherokee content would be made in Beijing. The remaining

55% may come from other Chinese suppliers, and St. Pierre said AMC was working hard to assist them.[11, 12]

In June, at the height of the crisis, the Chinese government convened a meeting for managers of joint ventures to discuss their problems and set up a new inter-ministerial office to deal with them. St. Pierre said, "They are now seriously concerned with foreign investment and want to fix the problems." One indication St. Pierre noted was that he was asked to fill out a thirty page questionnaire aimed at improving joint venture relations.[11, 12, 86]

In October of 1986, the State Council, the country's highest government body, issued guidelines that offered qualifying joint ventures lower taxes, reduced labor and land fees, and more managerial authority to combat bureaucratic interference. In addition, the Chinese began promoting an informal practice, foreign exchange swapping, that encouraged joint ventures with excess foreign exchange to trade with ventures that have yuan but little hard currency. ITT's Great Wall Sheraton Hotel in Beijing became a kind of mini-bank. In December, St. Pierre stated that BJC had obtained US$ 2.5 million in hard currency from the hotel in exchange for local currency.[79]

Reflections on the Crisis

St. Pierre was not part of the original negotiating team, however, he commented in retrospect, "Who knew anything about the Chinese auto industry then? Nobody knew how the supply situation would develop or that the foreign exchange crunch would be so severe." He continued that BAW despite making the knockoff Russian BJ-212 for two decades "didn't know how the auto industry worked either . . . We had always thought that foreign exchange would come from the Chinese, as part of their investment. AMC didn't intend to put up any more money." As Joe Cappy, AMC's president observed, "The China venture has been making money from day one . . . China spent all its investment money, panicked, and stopped making payments. But now they're making payments again, and AMC is making Jeeps."[61, 95]

BJC declared and paid dividends to BAW and AMC in 1986 and 1987. In the spring of 1987, the alliance was producing the equivalent of about US$ 120 million in sales revenue annually. BJC had weathered many difficult challenges, and operations were running fairly smoothly. At this point Clare concluded, ". . . it all adds up to a business environment that demands long-term commitment, patience, and flexibility. If your company doesn't have a strategy nor the resources to amply support all three of these attributes . . . then China is surely not the place for you."[26, 36, 49, 72, 95]

The Chrysler-AMC Merger

The unanticipated news arrived at BJC on March 7, 1987: Chrysler, the third largest U.S. automobile manufacturer and Renault, France's largest automobile manufacturer announced that they had agreed in principle to exchange Renault's 46% interest in AMC for US$ 200 million in interest bearing notes and up to US$ 350 million in cash depending on AMC's future performance.[25]

Despite BJC's relative success, AMC had entered a five-year streak of operating losses, and year after year, Renault continued to inject capital to keep AMC afloat. In 1985, because of Renault's poor performance, the French government directed Renault's chairman to return the giant manufacturer to profitability. AMC was one of Renault's largest financial drains. Consequently, Renault began exploration of a way out of the agreement and Chrysler provided the exit.

The Chrysler-AMC merger was touted as a very good fit for Chrysler. Under the merger, AMC was transformed into the Jeep Eagle division of Chrysler and the AMC name passed into oblivion. Chrysler gained control of the Jeep, one of the best known and most profitable brands in the U.S. and a product that would fill a gap in Chrysler's product line; Chrysler also got a network of 1,472 AMC-Jeep-Renault dealers who were to remain independent. Adding AMC's 1% market share to Chrysler's would bring Chrysler's share up to over 14%—not far short of the share Chrysler had in 1979 before it was rescued from bankruptcy from the U.S. government. AMC's engineering and development division would be closed, and Chrysler would add manufacturing capacity at marginal cost by taking over AMC's used assembly lines, including AMC's Bramalea, Ontario plant, which has been characterized as one of the newest and most modern in the world.[30–32, 49, 92, 97]

The Chinese Response to the Merger

The Chinese were unhappy with the Chrysler-AMC merger. They had not been consulted, and they thought they had been "sold out." The ensuing time proved to be difficult as both sides began the adjustment to this change in ownership.

BJC: Post Chrysler-AMC Merger

Behind tall, bleak concrete walls and rusting iron gates, slouching, flea-bitten horses pull creaking wagonloads of high-tech auto parts and, sometimes, automotive engineers. Drab plywood placards along dusty factory roads read: "Time is Money, Efficiency is Life." Managers scold uniformed workers over scratchy outdoor loud-speakers for slow work, messy tool kits and dirty work areas. Perhaps most striking—by American and Chinese standards—are this factory's freshly painted, screaming neon blue walls. "It used to be a pretty deadbeat looking place," Don St. Pierre says of Chrysler's Jeep-making joint venture factory. . .

To St. Pierre the paint job is a trophy, "a symbol of his hard-won fight over day-to-day operations." To the foreign investment community, it is a badge of BJC's survival against extraordinary handicaps. However, St. Pierre and Chrysler Chairman Lee Iacocca are confident about BJC's future.

In May 1988, Chrysler and the Chinese government began talks aimed at expanding the Jeep venture in Beijing, perhaps even doubling it within the next twelve to twenty-four months. The memo of understanding signed by both parties created a joint task force to decide output goals. In the long term, Chrysler wants to take over Chinese production of one-ton pickups and improve their design. Commented St. Pierre, "When I first got here, every day there'd be some guy running in and saying, 'I need 200 people for this job, 400 people for that job, 100 for this.' Then, when I'd tell someone what to do, they'd shake their head, go back to the office and forget about it. It was incredible. Productivity was nil."

However, St. Pierre had no way out. His orders were: Boost productivity or pull out of China. To this end, St. Pierre has introduced wage scales, "a radical new concept." The plan called for paying bosses and key engineers "a fair amount" more than what workers made and "the plan (was) to widen that gap." St. Pierre stated, "Before, 10–20% of salary was based on the type of job someone had, and experience doing it. Now, 68% of salary is based on job classification and seniority."

There has been quite a bit of resistance to this change. BJC's highest ranking Chinese manager declined his raise for fear it would ruin his rapport with subordinates. Yang Fengnian, BJC's director of purchase and supply commented, "Some workers have been afraid Mr. St. Pierre might be wanting to break too many rice bowls." They're right. Cracking his factory's lifetime employment system was St. Pierre's next goal.

Epilogue

In 1992, 5,400 people were working at BJC on two shifts. These salaried workers made dividends if they performed well. In general, the average wage rate was 370 yuan or US$ 67 a month. Workers could achieve an 8% wage increase annually, which was a function of how profitable BJC has been. While profits were still not discussed, "dividends" were. The "dividend" distribution was a complicated equation based on the average base salary amount a worker received, their position, and how well the unit performed.

BJC continued to enjoy some tax reductions, whereas other state-owned enterprises did not. Labor costs continued to be relatively low, and the major costs for BJC were associated with customs duty on imported parts.

The labor quality, according to Yang Gengnian was good, and quality slogans began to appear on the walls of the shop floor. However, BJC still failed to resemble any of the assembly lines at Chrysler or any other U.S. automaker. Young men still stood around, and appeared to have little to do. However, their output was still good, and although the Chinese side was not allowed to make any design modifications, the working relationships continued to smooth over the years. The Chinese wonder, nevertheless, why the manager of the technology department is always from the U.S.

References

1. "AMC Cuts Back Cherokee Output in China Plant," *Automotive News,* February 17, 1986, p. 3.
2. "AMC's Jeep JV in the PRC: Contract Details," *Business China,* June 8, 1983, p. 83–84.
3. "American Motors Corp (U.S.)," *Business International,* p. 2.
4. Apgar, Leonard M., "AMCs Difficulties Are Mounting Again Even as Consumers Prefer Smaller Autos," *The Wall Street Journal,* July 8, 1980, p. 6.
5. "Automobiles: China," *Business China,* July 14, 1982, p. 103.
6. "Automotive Expansion Projects," *The China Business Review,* July/August, 1986, pp. 30–33.
7. "Automotive Joint Venture: China," *Business China,* February 15, 1984, p. 22.
8. Bangsberg, P.T., "Sino-U.S. Auto Venture Gets 2nd Hefty Loan," *Journal of Commerce,* August 24, 1987.
9. Bass, Dale D., "AMC Has Profit Following Losses for 14 Quarters," *The Wall Street Journal,* February 22, 1984, p. 2.
10. Bass, Dale D., "Financing Business: AMC Plans to Issue 24.1 Million Shares to Develop Vehicles," *The Wall Street Journal,* February 27, 1984, p. 36.
11. Becker, Jasper, "Cherokees Off the Warpath, On Production Line," *The Journal of Commerce,* July 7, 1986, p. 1, p. 4A.
12. Becker, Jasper, "AMC Defends China Venture," *The Journal of Commerce,* July 7, 1986, pp. 4A.
13. Bennett, Amanda, "Renault to Get Control of AMC Under Proposal," *The Wall Street Journal,* September 25, 1980, p. 23.
14. Bennett, Amanda, "In the News: Franco-American Motors," *Fortune,* October 20, 1980, p. 23.
15. Bennett, Amanda, "Labor Accepts Ploy to Aid Hard Hit AMC," *Business Week,* October 6, 1980, p. 35.
16. Bennett, Amanda, "France: What Led Renault to Raise Its AMC Stake," *Business Week,* August 31, 1981, p. 34.
17. Bennett, Amanda, "Four Years of Tortuous Negotiations Led to AMC Jeep Venture with China," *The Wall Street Journal,* May 6, 1983, p. 34.
18. Bohn, Joseph, "AMC Launches Attack on Japan from the Rear," *Business Marketing,* September, 1983, p. 24–26.
19. Bronson, Gail, "Ronald J. Gilchrist: Marketer with a China Syndrome," *Sales Management,* January 16, 1984, p. 15.
20. Brown, Warren, "AMC, Chinese to Make Jeep in Peking," *The Washington Post,* May 3, 1983, pp. A1 and A11.
21. Bussey, John, "AMC to Suspend Chinese Venture's Production," *The Wall Street Journal.*
22. Callahan, Joseph M., AMC Faces Challenge in China. *Automotive Industries,* November, 1985, p. 12.
23. Callahan, Joseph M., "China! A Trade Dynasty IS Born," *Automotive Industries,* November, 1985, pp. 58–60.
24. Chuan, Jian, "Joint Venture: Success Speaks for Itself," *Beijing Review,* November 4, 1985, No. 44, pp. 21–25.
25. Clare, Tod O., "Business Challenge in China," *The Corporate Board,* July/August 1987, pp. 16–19.

26. Clark, Laura, "AMC's 33 Years: Good Days, Bad Days; Always a Struggle," *Automotive News,* June 15, 1987, p. 88.
27. Clarry, John W. and Xianfang Liu, "Rough Ride on a New Road: The AMC Joint Venture in China," manuscript presented at the Academy of International Business Annual Meeting, Chicago, Ill., November, 1987.
28. "Chrysler Selling 2.2-liter Tooling to Chinese Maker," *Automotive News,* July 20, 1987, p. 1, p. 53.
29. Cohen, Jerome Alan and Stuart J. Valentine, "Hurdles to Investing in China Are Being Toppled," *The New York Times,* June 25, 1987.
30. Connelly, Mary, "Chrysler Is Planning to Dismantle AMC," *Automotive News,* March 16, 1987, p. 1.
31. Connelly, Mary, "Chrysler's Cost Could Reach $2 Billion, Miller Says," *Automotive News,* March 16, 1987, p. 56.
32. Connelly, Mary, "AMC Offers Chrysler 'Good Fits,'" *Automotive News,* May 4, 1987, p. 1.
33. Connelly, Mary, "Chrysler Comes to Crossroads," *Automotive News,* December 14, 1987, pp. 1 and 49.
34. Connelly, Mary, "News Lines: Chrysler Outlines for Products into 1990s," *Automotive News,* February 1, 1988, pp. 1 and 7.
35. Connelly, Mary, "Chrysler Pushes AMC Sales," *Automotive News,* June 22, 1987, pp. 1 and 61.
36. Ealey, Lance, "Renault Dumps the Comeback Kid," *Automotive Industries,* August, 1987, pp. 39–41.
37. Fannin, Rebecca, "Vroom, Vroom or Sputter, Sputter?" *Marketing and Media Decisions,* July, 1986, pp. 125–130.
38. "Financing Automobile JV: China," *Business China,* September 12, 1985, p. 135.
39. Fleming, Al, "AMC Reorganizes Product Engineering," *Automotive News,* February 27, 1984, pp. D5–D7.
40. "Foreign Investment in China: Blowing Cold," *The Economist,* April 16, 1987, p. 69.
41. Gargan, Edward A., "Investing in China: Still Hard," *The New York Times,* June 26, 1987.
42. Grenier Guiles, Melinda, "AMC to Build Plant in Canada for New Car Line," *The Wall Street Journal,* June 12, 1984, p. 12.
43. Grenier Guiles, Melinda, "Dedeurwarder Succeeds Tippett as AMC CEO," *The Wall Street Journal,* October 1, 1984, p. 28.
44. Grenier Guiles, Melinda, "Renault's $338 MM Loss Doubles 1983 Full Year," *The Wall Street Journal,* October 3, 1984, p. 34.
45. Harding, Henry, "China Trade: Investment Climate," *The Corporate Board,* July/August 1987, p. 19.
46. Holusha, John, "Jeep Maker Plans Factory in Peking: American Motors Expects to Sign Accord on Thursday," *The New York Times,* May 3, 1983, pp. D1 and D19.
47. "How Jeep Hit the Road to China," *Businessweek,* May 16, 1983, p. 26.
48. "How to Win the War," *China Trade Report,* October, 1986, p. 8–9.
49. "Jeep, Jeep," *The Economist,* March 14, 1987, pp. 62–65.
50. Johnson, Richard, "AMC Struggles to Survive," *Automotive News,* April 29, 1985, p. 3.
51. Johnson, Richard, "Dedeurwaerder Maps AMC Survival Plan," *Automotive News,* July 15, 1985, p. 3.
52. Johnson, Richard, "AMC to Build Pickups in China," *Automotive News,* December 2, 1985, p. 16.

53. Johnson, Richard, "Jose Dedeurwaerder: American Motors," *Automotive News,* December 9, 1985, p. E16.
54. Johnson, Richard, "AMC Chief Predicts a Rocky Road Ahead," *Automotive News,* December 23, 1985, p. 28.
55. Johnson, Richard, "One Plant May Replace AMC Toledo, Kenosha," *Automotive News,* February 17, 1986, p. 3.
56. Johnson, Richard, "AMC Talks with China to Revive Jeep Project," *Automotive News,* May 12, 1986, p. 6.
57. Johnson, Richard, "AMC Sale Boosts Renault's Stock," *Automotive News,* March 16, 1987, p. 1.
58. Jones, Bowen, "Peking Slashes Imports," *China Trade Report,* April, 1986, pp. 1–4.
59. Kelly, John, "China Screens Joint Ventures," *The Journal of Commerce,* August 14, 1987.
60. Kraar, Louis, "China After Marx: Open for Business?" *Fortune,* February 18, 1985, pp. 28–33.
61. Kraar, Louis, "The China Bubble Bursts," *Fortune,* July 6, 1987, pp. 86–89.
62. Krebs, Michelle, "AMC Plans New Stock to Raise $187 Million," *Automotive News,* June 15, 1985.
63. Krebs, Michelle and Mary Ann Maskery, "GM Awaits Major Pact with China," *Automotive News,* January 23, 1988, pp. 1 and 48.
64. Lapham, Edward, "Profits Rise for Big 3; '87 2nd Best," *Automotive News,* February 22, 1988, p. 6.
65. Lapham, Edward and Laura Clark, "Chrysler's Profits Decline; Sales Rise," *Automotive News,* January 8, 1988, p. 51.
66. Lee, Mary, "Pekingwatch," *China Trade Report,* January, 1986, p. 2.
67. Levin, D.P., "AMC, China Agree on 2-Month Halt of Jeep Production," *The Wall Street Journal, 1986.*
68. Ling, He, "If Things Go On Like This, There'll Never Be a Chinese Detroit," *The China Business Review,* July/August, 1986, p. 35.
69. Lienert, Paul, "China Upgrades Auto Factories," *Journal of Commerce,* October 1, 1985, p. 1.
70. McGill, Andrew and Richard Johnson, "Renault Chief Vows No More Aid, Will Sell Some Assets," *Automotive News,* June 22, 1987, pp. 1 and 56–60.
71. Meredith, Paul H., "American Motors: Still Seeking a Niche!" in *Cases in Strategic Management for Business,* Hale C. Bartlett (ed.), Chicago: The Dryden Press, pp. 475–496.
72. Moskal, Brian, "AMC Battle to Survive," *Industry Week,* June 23, 1986, pp. 63–64.
73. O'Grady, Thomas, "Automaker Quarterly Report: 1987's Unlikely Winners in Sales and Market Share," *Automotive Industries,* February 1988, pp. 75–76.
74. "Problems at Two Joint Ventures," *The China Business Review,* July/August, 1986, p. 34.
75. Rosario, Louise do and Barnett, Martin, "Still Stuck in First Gear . . . But Foreign Help on the Way," *China Trade Report,* May, 1985, p. 6–7.
76. Rosario, Louise do, "Not Living Up to Promise," *China Trade Report,* January, 1986, pp. 1–2.
77. Rosario, Louise do, "Jolt for Joint-Venturers," *China Trade Report,* March, 1986, pp. 1–3.
78. Rosario, Louise do, "A Myth Is Exploded," *China Trade Report,* December 1986, pp. 4–5.
79. Schiffman, James R., "China Issuing Rules to Mollify Investors," *The Wall Street Journal,* December 24, 1986, p. 12.

80. Simison, Robert L., "AMC Raising $500 Million via Loans, Stock Offer, Planned Sale of AM General," *The Wall Street Journal*, March 24, 1983, p. 2.
81. Simison, Robert L., "Stockholders Briefs: American Motors Corporation," *The Wall Street Journal*, April 28, 1983, p. 42.
82. Sloan, Allen, "Waiting for Renault," *Forbes*, July 21, 1980, p. 31.
83. Sloan, Allen, "Here Come the Franglaismobile," *Forbes*, September 28, 1981, pp. 42–48.
84. Sloan, Allen, "AMC May Drop Its Passenger Cars in Favor of Renault," *The Wall Street Journal*, January 31, 1983, p. 37.
85. Smith, David C., "Chrysler Talks Joint Venture with Chinese," *Ward's Auto World*, May, 1985, p. 14.
86. Sterba, James P., "U.S. Firms Urge China to Make Changes or Risk the Loss of Foreign Investment," *The Wall Street Journal*, June 6, 1986.
87. Stevens, Charles W., "AMC and China Agree to Build Jeeps in Peking," *The Wall Street Journal*, May 3, 1983, p. 37.
88. Stevens, Charles W., "AMC's Loss Widened in Second Quarter; Profitable Unit Sold to LTV Corporation," *The Wall Street Journal*, July 26, 1983, p. 2.
89. Stevens, Charles W., "AMC Sells Well Horse to Group for $8 Million," *The Wall Street Journal*, August 11, 1983, p. 42.
90. Stevens, Charles W., "AMC Says It Is Selling Headquarters Building," *The Wall Street Journal*, August 19, 1983, p. 8.
91. "Still Stuck in First Gear . . . But Foreign Help Is on the Way," *China Trade Report*, May 1985, pp. 6–7.
92. "The Chrysler-AMC Win-Win Deal," *Automotive News*, August 10, 1987, p. 10.
93. "Ward's Wrapup," *Ward's Auto World*, May, 1983, p. 9.
94. "When Capitalists, Chinese Cut a Deal," *U.S. News & World Report*, March 5, 1984, p. 52.
95. Williams, Douglas, "Can AMC Survive?" *Automotive Industry*, January, 1987, pp. 36–39.
96. Wren, Christopher S., "A.M.C. and China Sign Jeep Plant Pact," *The New York Times*, Friday, May 6, 1983, p. D1.
97. Wrigley, Al, "Chrysler Getting Jeep Eagle Division in Gear," *Metalworking News*, August 10, 1987, p. 4, p. 30.
98. Yang, Dori Jones and Robert T. Grieves, "China's Tight Fist May Squeeze Foreign Companies Out," *Business Week*, April 7, 1986, p. 50.
99. Yang, Dori Jones and Maria Shao, "China's Push for Exports is Turning into a Long March," *Business Week*, September 15, 1986, pp. 66–67.

11
Orient—U.S. Leasing Corporation: A Japanese-American Joint Venture in Financial Services

Arvind Bhambri,
John Davis,
and
David O. Braaten

Doug Scudamore, president of Orient-U.S. Leasing Corporation (OUSL), sat at the desk in his office writing notes for an upcoming meeting when Kaz Naganuma, executive vice-president, burst in. Looking visibly upset, Naganuma dispensed with the usual pleasantries and blurted out, "Doug, the credit committee at USLI has done it again. They've rejected the credit application from Noma. Noma is the American operation of one of the Orient Leasing Corporation's (OLC) best customers in Japan. This is a very awkward situation. We cannot build a company this way."

Scudamore stopped writing and looked up at Naganuma. Seeing how upset he was, Scudamore joined Naganuma as he stood by the window. The two of them worked closely together, comprising the office of the president of the Orient-U.S. Leasing Company (OUSL). The issue that Naganuma had just raised on this day in September 1986, was one that had come up periodically throughout OUSL's four-year history, since the Orient Leasing Company Ltd. (OLC) of Tokyo and United States Leasing Company (USLI) of San Francisco had created a joint venture in Los Angeles.

This case has been prepared as a basis for discussion rather than to illustrate either effective or ineffective handling of an administrative situation. Certain names and figures have been disguised to preserve confidentiality.

Concerned, Scudamore responded, "Is the decision final? What reasons did they give?" Naganuma, obviously frustrated, replied, "The usual reasons. Noma is not adequately capitalized. Their balance sheet is not strong enough. They don't meet USLI's credit criteria for a lease of this magnitude in the U.S. But, USLI should realize that Noma's Japanese parent is a blue chip company. The parent is one of OLC's old customers in Tokyo, and they'll stand behind Noma's commitments in the U.S. In fact, I asked OLC in Tokyo to request a letter of guarantee from Noma's parent and, even though it was very awkward for OLC, they got it. But still USLI's credit committee turned us down. This issue gets at the very root of our strategy. Our target market is Japanese owned and managed businesses in the U.S. We cannot approach them like USLI's conventional American businesses."

Scudamore, slowly shook his head, "I'm sorry it's happened again. I'm seeing Gary Stern tomorrow in San Francisco to review our monthly results, and I'll talk to him about the case. But, Noma may only be resolved between Miyauchi (OLC's CEO) and Mundell (USLI's CEO). In any case, we need to work out some policies and norms so we don't keep getting these embarrassing rejections. But, Kaz, you know that the credit committee is only doing its job by applying the guidelines they have on paper."

Naganuma responded, "But that doesn't help me get customers, and it certainly doesn't help us achieve our growth goals. Can't you talk to the people at USLI and get them to change their mind?"

OUSL—Background and History

Established in Los Angeles in October 1982, with a capital base of $1 million, OUSL was a 50/50 joint venture between OLC, the largest leasing company in Japan, and USLI, the largest independent leasing company in the U.S. Set up to specialize in providing leasing services to Japanese owned and managed businesses in the U.S., OUSL was described by one Japanese executive as a "marriage of first cousins," because the history of interaction between OLC and USLI went back over two decades to the founding of OLC.

USLI History and Strategy

USLI was founded as United States Leasing Company in 1952 by Henry Shoenfeld in Oakland, California. The impetus for Shoenfeld's pioneering effort came when a bank, refusing his application for a loan to purchase food processing equipment which, in turn, he offered as collateral, suggested he form a corporation to which they could lend the money. Shoenfeld took the advice, and with $20,000 of his own, and another $10,000 from family and friends, he formed USLI as a way of financing the equipment needs of local business people.

The company's major turning point came a few years later when it established an exclusive vendor relationship with Pitney Bowes. Under this arrangement, USLI provided 100% financing to Pitney Bowes' customers who preferred to lease rather than purchase the equipment. These lessees made regular payments to USLI that covered equipment costs plus USLI's financing and administrative expenses. This type of arrangement had several advantages for manufacturers and sellers who saw the leasing service as an opportunity to attract more customers and expand their market. Termed "sales-aid leasing," this service became USLI's bread and butter and set the company on the path to growth.

By year-end 1985, USLI's revenues exceeded $380 million, and it employed about 1,500 people. It was listed on the New York Stock Exchange and the Pacific Stock Exchange and had sizeable institutional holdings. The company had five principal business segments:

1. *Sales-aid leasing* was USLI's oldest and largest business segment and involved arrangements with manufacturers or equipment sales organizations under which USLI provided lease financing to the vendor's customers such as IBM, DEC, Wang, NCR, Kodak, and Pitney Bowes, among others.
2. *Automotive fleet leasing* involved the leasing and/or operational management of vehicles, mostly automobiles and light trucks. USLI was a principal competitor in the commercial fleet leasing marketplace, and the fleet leasing subsidiary second only to sales-aid leasing.
3. *Operating lease programs* specialized in investment and rental of equipment including data-processing equipment, electronic test instrumentation and railroad stock. These programs required active remarketing efforts, because equipment costs were not typically recovered from initial/or single users.
4. *Lease Financing* represented USLI's participation in the high end of the leasing market where it served as a transaction manager, rather than a direct investor, in multimillion dollar individual leases. This segment was intensely competitive with large industrial-credit companies (GECC, Westinghouse, ITT), investment bankers (Merrill Lynch, E.F.Hutton) and money-center banks (Bank of America, Security Pacific, etc.) who were investors as well as managers.
5. *Associated leasing companies* represented USLI's participation in foreign companies mostly in minority ownership positions. USLI's investment usually dated from the start-up of the foreign company and the training of its senior personnel in the U.S. After the venture was established, USLI continued to provide policy level guidance and to help with middle management training. USLI also had two international subsidiaries, and Los Angeles-based Orient-U.S. Leasing Corporation, which specialized in providing leasing services to Japanese owned and managed businesses in the U.S.

All of USLI's domestic leasing subsidiaries operated nationwide. The sales-aid leasing, fleet leasing, and instrument rental units had national sales organizations and branch-office networks. All were headquartered in or near San Francisco.

Through its three decades of consistent growth, USLI had followed a strategy that was distinguished in its conservatism and focus. It stayed within the leasing industry and selected segments where their marketing or management services could increase the value of the basic financial product. Sales-aid leasing, for example, provided assistance to vendor clients in selling products and to lessees in acquiring equipment by providing intensive field sales and program marketing support. The company also imposed internal guidelines to avoid overdependence on major customers or excessive exposure to single product types. It also minimized the impact of short-term interest rate fluctuations by primarily financing equipment purchases with intermediate-term, fixed-rate borrowings.

Ned Mundell, president & CEO since 1976, and a veteran of USLI for twenty-seven years, described the company's strategy as follows:

> We believe in segmenting and creating niches, being in certain segments in certain markets where we have some value added. We don't believe that we must have a full product line. I also don't believe we must be an international company to grow. We haven't yet reached the limits of our investment objectives in the U.S. In leasing, we don't have a franchise or a patentable product; it's a transactions oriented business, our margins are thin. We must be better at the operating level.
>
> We also don't feel we have to be market share dominant. Most of our competitors have failed because of poor investment judgments over time and too rapid a rate of growth of assets. You can't grow assets in this business in excess of 20% a year for three years in a row and keep it under control, you just cannot acquire the people rapidly enough, or the systems, and still produce a profit doing it. To the extent that we are successful, it has really been based on decisions not to grow too quickly and not to make adventuresome decisions. We have never been driven by size; we've been driven the other way around—Don't get too big!
>
> There is a culture to it, what mistakes not to make.
>
> The question we always ask ourselves is whether the stockholder will be better off. I think there is a certain integrity in having to report to your owners every quarter, to show good earnings quarter after quarter. I've noticed that people who rationalize the short-term focus as being terrible also have long-term poor results. We're happy making money, and we don't see a charter to be multinational.

In keeping with the philosophy espoused by Mundell, USLI had started in recent years to withdraw from some of their foreign minority equity positions and to concentrate instead on majority holdings in a few, selected foreign markets where Anglo-Saxon common law prevailed and English was the native language. Hence, USLI could transfer their leasing expertise and exercise direct control without necessarily tying up with a local partner.

Gary Stern, USLI senior vice-president, commented on the evolution of USLI's strategy:

> When leasing was a very young concept, USLI would leverage its technology. We would trade on our technology and knowledge and find a partner who had the local con-

tacts and financial wherewithal, and that left us with a reasonably good shot at making money on our investment without a lot of involvement.

As the leasing business has matured, however, we don't have as much to sell on a minority basis. We think we still know things that are new and different but our value added is clearer in our minds than it would be in our partner's mind, so we don't get as good a play in a minority position as we got once upon a time. So, if we really think we have something to add to an overseas market, it makes more sense to do it directly.

USLI's conservative culture also extended to its policies for filling senior management positions. In 1986, 14 of the 15 senior managers at USLI had been with the company more than ten years, and nine of them had a tenure exceeding 15 years.

OLC History and Strategy

In 1963, the managing director of the New York branch of the Nichimen Trading Company approached the managing director of the Sanwa Bank to discuss the prospects of a leasing company in Japan. Having observed the rapid growth of the leasing industry in the U.S., he was curious about whether such a concept would work in Japan. As a result, three Japanese trading companies and five Japanese banks decided to form a joint venture that would pioneer leasing in Japan. The new entity, Orient Leasing Co. Ltd. (OLC), was established in Osaka, Japan, in 1964, with initial capitalization of 100 million yen (about U.S.$400,000). USLI, invited as one of the investors, provided OLC the technology of leasing.

Between 1964 and 1985, the Japanese leasing industry grew rapidly. The Japan Leasing Association had three members in 1964, 36 in 1974, and 240 in 1985. The estimated volume in leasing contracts in 1984 was 3,600 billion yen, about seven times the volume in 1974. Even though leasing in Japan was not indirectly subsidized through tax incentives, as in many other countries including the U.S., the ratio of new leasing contracts to private capital investment, though still substantially below the U.S., showed a steadily increasing trend from 3% in 1979 to 6.2% in 1984. (In the U.S., new leasing contracts as a percentage of total private capital Investment was estimated at about 20%).

OLC, as a pioneer in the market, had also grown rapidly. By year end 1985, it was the largest leasing company in Japan with revenues over 166 billion yen and employing almost 2,500 people. Besides a wide range of leasing services, OLC had diversified into consumer finance, housing loans, mortgage securities, and venture capital. OLC had been aggressive in global expansion and, by 1986, had joint ventures or affiliates in 18 countries.

Through a nationwide network of 38 sales branches and sales offices, including two headquarters in Osaka and Tokyo, OLC operated in the following major segments:

1. *Direct financing leasing* was the heart of OLC's operations. OLC focused on office automation and factory automation equipment, industrial machinery, and transportation equipment including ships, aircraft and automobiles, and,

through vendor programs, offered even relatively low-priced items such as push-button telephones, copiers, and personal computers.

2. *Operating leases* like USLI, provided operating leases mainly for certain types of data processing equipment, maritime cargo vessels, and measuring instruments.

3. *Loans and other activities.* Unlike USLI, OLC had become a diversified financial services company. OLC's loan business showed rapid expansion in recent years. It emphasized arranging housing loans through business tie-ups with leading housing developers and brokers. In addition, Family Consumer Credit Co., an OLC subsidiary, engaged in several areas of consumer credit. In 1983, OLC also entered the mortgage securities business, and into the venture capital business aimed principally at start-up, high technology companies.

4. *Subsidiaries and affiliates.* Starting with Orient Leasing (Asia) Ltd. in Hong Kong in 1971, OLC had consistently followed a path of international diversification through joint ventures, wholly owned subsidiaries, and minority investments, leading to participation in the leasing business in 18 countries by 1986. OLC also followed a strategy for expanding its network of affiliates in the domestic market. In 1984 alone, for example, OLC established five joint ventures for leasing in Japan in cooperation with two life insurance companies, two regional banks, and a mutual loan and savings bank. Another company, OSR Co. Ltd., was established to develop software for computer systems because computers were claiming a rising share of OLC's leasing volume. Finally, Family Rental Co. Ltd. was launched with funding from Japan's largest bank-affiliated credit card company, JCB Co. Ltd., to furnish rental services to individuals.

Like USLI, OLC emphasized small-ticket items as a cornerstone of a defensible niche and a stable growth strategy. Unlike USLI, however, OLC had been much more aggressive in diversifying into new services and geographic areas. Miyauchi described his philosophy:

> As a service industry, we have to keep developing new services. We can never relax because the fellow next door can enter the business any time. We have to run fast to succeed.
>
> Competition in leasing is very keen in Japan so, in a sense, we are not a leasing company at all in Japan. Our leasing portfolio only has some 30+% of our total exposure. We diversified into related areas to sustain our growth. These efforts combined with our marketing strength have kept us at the top of the industry.
>
> Like our expansion in Japan, we have built our international network step by step. In 1971, when we'd reached a certain size in Japan, we started a company in Hong Kong because the market there seemed promising. When that venture proved to be profitable, we entered another promising market: Singapore. If a market looks interesting, we move in quickly. If it proves to be profitable, great, and if not, we pull out just as fast. As a rule, we don't begin operations in a new place until the most recently established venture has proved successful. And we will continue our international expansion as long as we think we have opportunities for profit outside our country. At any time, we have a priority list of six or seven countries we are studying and one or two in which we are carrying on negotiations.

Mr. Yasushi Iwai, OLC managing director in charge of international operations and member of OUSL's board, also commented on OLC's international strategy:

> OLC is very aggressive and has two major policies. One, we will go out to any foreign country if we have a business opportunity. Two, when we enter a country that already has an established, advanced way of doing business, and good financial institutions, we do not manage ourselves but link up with established institutions sometimes with minority equity. But in countries with undeveloped leasing industries, such as Asia and Latin America, OLC manages itself and takes as much equity interest as possible.
>
> We have to keep setting up new companies and developing new know how; that way we can maintain our premier status and recruit the best people.

OLC was an unusual "Japanese" company. Because it was a young company, many of its senior managers were also relatively young. For example, Miyauchi was only 45 years old when he became CEO of OLC in 1980. In addition, OLC attempted to blend management systems from the West and the East. To quote Miyauchi:

> OLC does not fit the typical pattern of most Japanese companies. OLC makes greater use of numerical performance measures than most Japanese companies. U.S. companies tend to take this method too far and become short-term oriented and overlook the human element. OLC would like to combine the group-oriented behavior typical of Japanese companies with American-style, profit-oriented management. That is the ultimate ideal, but I don't know if it is possible.

One reason for OLC's American orientation could be traced back to USLI's influence and involvement with OLC since OLC's creation. At OLC's headquarters in Tokyo, a large conference room was dedicated to Henry Shoenfeld, USLI CEO when USLI helped create OLC in 1964. Displayed prominently in the room was one of Shoenfeld's favorite iron golf putters in a glass case alongside his photograph.

USLI was one of the original investors in OLC and had retained their stockholding until 1978, when they sold their equity. As Mundell explained:

> One of the reasons we sold our investment was that in 1977, 23% of our net income and 25% of our net equity was in OLC investment, and we were quickly becoming a passive shareholder in a Japanese company. The dispersion of assets didn't seem right.

OLC, however, immediately bought stock in USLI to continue to maintain its link with the company. In the words of one OLC executive, "the son became the father." In 1986, OLC owned 14% of USLI stock. In addition, Miyauchi, OLC's CEO, was a member of USLI's board of directors and Mundell, USLI's CEO, was an advisor* to

---

* Unlike boards of directors in U.S. corporations, boards in Japan consisted largely of insiders. Ned Mundell was one of two outside advisors to OLC's board.

OLC's Board. Mundell and Miyauchi thus had frequent contact with each other and had developed a relationship that was described as based on "liking and mutual respect."

The Birth of Orient-U.S. Leasing Corporation

In mid-1982, Miyauchi approached Mundell with the idea of setting up a 50/50 joint venture in Los Angeles to provide leasing services to Japanese owned and managed businesses in the U.S. He described the background behind his action:

> We have had equity in USLI for many years and have been very happy with it. However, we saw a new movement emerging with Japanese products being sold in the U.S. in large quantities and we saw immediately that we had to get on the business side of this trend. USLI did not have any particular ideas to handle only Japanese products so we proposed this venture specializing in Japanese products and vendors.
>
> The U.S. leasing market, from a Japanese standpoint, was a highly developed market and it would have been very difficult to enter this market by ourselves. We didn't have any special relationships with any big banks or lending institutions in this country. Also, I personally had very strong doubts about the ability of Japanese business people to manage in this culture. OLC managers are very well trained in managing companies the OLC way, but I want OUSL to follow the U.S. management style because we borrow most of the funds from institutions in the U.S. and also the customers are in this country.
>
> In entering other countries, we have made alliances with banks, but our entry for the U.S. was different. We have known USLI for many years and we have strong confidence in their ability to manage leasing programs, so I brought up this idea with Ned Mundell and we talked about it a few times and decided to go ahead.
>
> We drew up a simple written agreement. I think the important part is that USLI has the right to withdraw after some years, and OLC can increase its equity.

Mundell recalled:

> The idea for the joint venture essentially came from OLC. They had determined they had to diversify out of the Japanese domestic market and they had an investment in USLI for many years, but their investment in USLI probably wasn't large enough if they looked at their asset concentration around the world. So they wanted to increase their U.S. presence, but they also said that to succeed in the U.S. you must have good U.S. management, and you will not keep good U.S. management over the long term if you have 100% Japanese ownership.
>
> When Miyauchi said they wanted to form a joint venture with us to explore the market in the U.S., we said, "Well, why don't you send somebody over here, we'll send a guy, and we'll do a market study." And he said, "No, no. We'll send two people, you send two people, they'll start the company, and after two years they will tell us whether the business is successful or not." That's their idea of a market study; get in the market and see what the guys can do.
>
> We further refined the charter of the company by asking how we would explain to our people at USLI that OLC was setting up a new organization to attack our customer base in the U.S., and they said, "We will define it as Japanese content business." Japanese

content business was described as Japanese companies either having distribution networks here or manufacturing and distribution networks here, so that we would attempt to associate with and set up vendor plans for their products. In addition, it included the direct leasing market where we would call on Japanese customers directly and lease whatever they needed. But both of them had some Japanese content to them.

The agreement that Mundell and Miyauchi reached specified that OUSL's president would be an American, and the executive vice-president would be Japanese. Mundell picked Doug Scudamore as OUSL's first president. Scudamore had been with USLI since 1978. A Harvard MBA, he had joined Deloitte, Haskins & Sells after his MBA in 1967. After working with DH&S for 10 years, Scudamore spotted an advertisement in *The Wall Street Journal* for a job as controller at USLI. He worked as controller in the parent company for 3 years and was working as controller in U.S. Leasing Corporation, USLI's largest operating company, when he was offered the presidency at OUSL in July 1982. He described his initial reaction:

> Ben Maushardt, who at the time was executive vice-president of USLI, called me to his office to discuss the setting up of this joint venture. I assumed he needed to discuss some accounting issues and was asking questions when he said, "Well, we were wondering whether you would go down and be the president." Which was a real surprise to me because 30 minutes earlier I wasn't even aware that a new company was being set up.
>
> That evening Miyauchi was in town and they wanted me to join him for dinner. I already had plans with my wife and some out-of-town friends I hadn't seen since school, but I called my wife and said, "I think I'm going to have to cancel. I may have been given an offer I don't want to turn down." I had decided before I walked out of Maushardt's office that I would accept the offer, even though moving to Los Angeles was not at the top of my list.
>
> The dinner with Miyauchi and Mundell was a very low key affair. Very little business was discussed; I'm sure Miyauchi was basically trusting Mundell and the USLI people to select the right person.

Mundell recalled the dinner:

> When we asked Scudamore to take the job, he was really enthusiastic about it and so the other people involved also became enthusiastic. When Scudamore dumped a whole social evening to have dinner with Miyauchi, Miyauchi knows enough about Americans to know that was unusual, so he immediately got enthusiastic too.

Start-up

Within a week of being offered the job, Scudamore had accepted and begun preparations to move to Los Angeles. The person that OLC chose as the EVP was Kaz Naganuma who worked in OLC's International Department in Tokyo. He had an American aunt, spoke English fluently, and had, at age 23, taken a Greyhound bus trip across the U.S. Naganuma had majored in business administration at Keio

University and had received an offer from one of Japan's most prestigious banks after graduation. He decided instead to join a chemical company which, in turn, he left to join OLC. As he described his choice:

> I did some self-assessment. In my job with the chemical company, I had to market to defense buyers, which I didn't like because they were powerful and expected a lot of flattery. Leasing was a new concept in Japan and OLC seemed like a nontraditional company. If I had joined a traditional Japanese company in a non-entry level position, I would never make it to the top.

In OLC, Naganuma started in sales & marketing, was sent to USLI for training in 1973, and was assigned in 1976 to set up joint ventures in the Philippines and in Australia. From 1977 to 1981, he worked as managing director of OLC's Malaysian joint venture before returning to Tokyo in the international department. In 1982, he was assigned to OUSL.

Scudamore traveled to Japan in September to meet Naganuma. As they worked on the budgeting and planning, they also developed a high degree of mutual liking and respect for each other. Scudamore described Naganuma as "a very unusual person who understood American culture and was very easy to communicate with."

Scudamore recalled his search for office space after his return from Japan:

> Greater Los Angeles has one of the greatest concentrations of Japanese businesses in the country, much more than Northern California. So, we looked up a Japanese directory and found that most Japanese companies were located around the Torrance area close to the Long Beach port. And that's where we initially went to look for an office.

> But when I called Naganuma, he signalled in a very subtle way that he didn't think Torrance was a very good idea. He kept asking me where the Japanese trading companies and banks were, and they were all in the downtown L.A. So I did a 180 degree turn and now I think we are much better being in downtown LA, because image is really very important.

Before Naganuma could come to the U.S., a family emergency caused a change in plans. As a result, he was asked to come to Los Angeles for 2-3 months to assist in the start-up and return to Japan in December 1982. Akira Seko was assigned to OUSL in January 1983. He had worked with OLC for 12 years, first in domestic leasing and then in the international department in Tokyo. His most recent assignment before coming to Los Angeles was managing director of the OLC joint venture in Singapore for four years.

Scudamore and Seko shared overall responsibility OUSL. In practice, however, Seko spent more time calling on potential customers and Scudamore set up the internal systems and policies. On OLC's side, OUSL reported to Yasushi Iwai, managing director of international operations, and on USLI's side, to Gary Stern, senior vice-president of international operations.

Initial Marketing Decisions

At the time the OUSL was set up, it did not have a formal or detailed business plan. The expectations of the two parents were articulated to the extent of "focus on Japanese content." Strategic issues as to whether the company should focus on big ticket or small ticket items, internal growth or growth through acquisition, etc. had not really been addressed. As a result, OUSL's start-up team operated in an opportunistic and entrepreneurial manner. Naganuma had his business cards printed and called on numerous Japanese executives just to let them know OUSL was in business. Naganuma described the start-up months as follows:

> Our strategy in the beginning was to go after the big ticket items, such as computer equipment, machine tools, etc., as the major strategic thrust. However, we also wanted to get visibility for our company name so we also decided to try and write leases for some small items that were widely used, such as Canon Copy machines, Panafax Facsimile machines, Yamaha golf carts, etc., essentially to promote our company name.
>
> We found that the competition in big ticket items was very stiff and the margins were very thin. But, we were having good success with small ticket items so, even though that was not our original strategic intention, we decided to refocus our attention and go after the small ticket segment. And, we tried to identify small ticket items, especially Japanese products in very competitive segments that could benefit from vendor leasing programs, such as copying machines and facsimile machines.

Scudamore concurred with this assessment:

> USLI has found their niche more in the smaller end and I think we are influenced to some extent to be in the same marketplace as far as the size of equipment is concerned, doing forklift trucks and small computers as opposed to big jumbo jets and large computers.

For 1983, OUSL's first full year, the company managed to generate $6 million of leases (equipment cost). Its major turning point came in 1984 when it signed a vendor leasing program with Panafax. For 1984, OUSL's new business shot up to $19 million, of which $11 million came from the new vendor account. The explosive growth in the 1983-84 period resulted in severely straining OUSL's operational systems. Scudamore described the situation:

> We landed our first big fish and had digestion problems. With the vendor program, our dollar volume about tripled and our number of transactions increased sevenfold, and we just didn't have the systems to cope with it. We had a computer service bureau that couldn't handle the growth so I brought in Kent Keigwin (later vp and controller) from DH&S to setup an in-house computer.

By early 1985, an in-house computer system had been set up at OUSL to track lease agreements, billings, and payments. Partly as a result, delinquent receivables had dropped drastically by 1986. In addition, the system had the capacity to support further growth.

During the period 1983-86, OUSL maintained its high rate of growth as shown:

Year-End	Leasing Volume	# of Leases	# of Employees
1983	$6 mill.	400	9
1984	19	3,000	20
1985	22	6,500	36
1986 (est)	29	10,000	43

During this period of rapid growth, Seko and Scudamore had some conflicts and communication difficulties. Personality and cultural differences were exacerbated by the pressures of rapid growth, and communication between them was reduced sharply.

OUSL Culture and Management Structure

Scudamore and Naganuma together made up the office of the president, which had been created after Naganuma's return to facilitate on-going communication and joint decision-making between Scudamore and Naganuma. Though Naganuma had primary responsibilities in marketing and Scudamore in operations, this distinction was artificial as they both influenced the other functions. Frank Anton, in addition to managing credit and administration, was also responsible for business development, which comprised negotiations of big contracts and accounts, such as vendor programs. It had been found that, even with Japanese vendors, American effort was very critical because Japanese companies typically employed Americans as senior marketing executives. Therefore, although Naganuma and his Japanese team were critical in cementing the deal with the Japanese top management, Anton and Scudamore spent a major portion of their time in negotiating and selling the vendor program arrangement. The sales/marketing group focused on getting business from vendor programs after the account was landed, and also in dealing with Japanese users for direct leasing deals. Finally, Kent Keigwin handled the systems for tracking transactions, billings, and payments.

When Naganuma returned to OUSL in January 1985, he found that the company's culture did not encourage free and open communication. Partly because of the differences and conflicts between Seko and Scudamore, a sense of camaraderie had not emerged during its start-up years. In addition, OUSL faced some unique challenges in building a cohesive culture because there were three distinct groups of people in OUSL, namely, the "OLC group," the "USLI group," and the "OUSL group." Scudamore and Anton, for example, received their basic salaries from OUSL, but their bonuses from USLI; similarly, Naganuma and Inabata received their basic salaries from OUSL, but their bonuses from OLC. The rest of the employees received their salaries and bonuses from OUSL. Also, while the Japanese sales &

marketing people were compensated on straight salary, the Americans were on salary and commission.

Naganuma described some of his views on building OUSL's culture:

> A successful joint venture has to be like a marriage. To be successful, there must be a culture of give and take, not take and give. For that to happen, there must first be good communication and mutual respect between top managers and between the two parent companies. That was not always true at OUSL.
>
> Now, Doug and I do not have a clear, formal division of responsibility. In a marriage, how can you have a clear division? We brief each other regularly on what each of us is doing.
>
> To build a better feeling in the company, we have started an inter-department meeting every Thursday. Doug and I attend and raise issues for open discussion. We also have company picnics. But finally, the culture comes from little events that have a big impact. For example, one day I saw a sign on a manager's door saying "Do not disturb"; partly as a joke to tease him and partly to make the office atmosphere more comfortable, I put up a sign on my door, "Please disturb anytime."

Scudamore described his relationship with Naganuma:

> We are operating more like a partnership of two people running the company with the trust that if I am out of town, he is running the show, if he's out of town, I'm running the show, and when we're both in town, we're keeping each other informed of what we are each up to. I don't get surprises of things that are already done or 90% done and this leads to much more consciousness on my part to keep him advised of relatively little decisions. It's just the courtesy and dialogue of keeping the other informed.

In September 1986 there were two Japanese managers at OUSL, in addition to Naganuma; both had responsibilities in marketing, one was based in New York and one in Los Angeles.

Links with Parent Companies

Separate monthly financial reports were sent each month to the two parents. In addition, frequent contacts were maintained between Naganuma and Iwai of OLC, on the one hand, and Scudamore and Stern of USLI, on the other. All four of them comprised OUSL's board that met twice a year.

Due, in part, to USLI's proximity, and, in part to Stern's management style, he played a fairly active role in overseeing OUSL. He visited OUSL about four to five times per year and talked with Scudamore on the phone every couple of weeks. However, as Stern described it, his role was somewhat ambiguous:

> Am I a manager, counsellor, consultant on request, or rubber stamp? How much am I a half owner along with my counterpart from OLC, and how much am I a decision maker in the classical group vp level role where you have a company president report-

ing to you and you're making the call? I'm much closer than OLC so I can make decisions more easily, but when is a decision mine, when should the decision be shared with
my counterparts, and when should it be left down there? I have to think about not only
how Scudamore interprets my involvement but how his counterpart does.

There is a lot of trust in the relationship between the parent companies, but the belief
and comfort in the relationship may actually inhibit issues that would otherwise have
surfaced much earlier. Some of these issues become problems before they come up.

A recurring problem that affected both parent companies, as well as OUSL, had
to do with credit approvals for large lease applications. On paper, credit approvals
for OUSL were structured so that up to $200,000, OUSL could decide locally. For
$200,000-300,000, information was sent to both shareholders, but the final decision
rested with the partner who represented the lessee's nationality, though the other
partner could point out something they felt needed attention. For leases over
$300,000 approval of both partners was needed. It was in this third category that pol-
icy differences often arose.

The application of Noma to lease equipment was a case in point. Noma, in the
U.S., was a highly leveraged Japanese subsidiary that did not pass the usual credit
evaluation criteria imposed by USLI. USLI's credit committee, therefore, requested
that OLC obtain a written guarantee from the Japanese parent of the lessee, a request
that OLC felt was completely contrary to their norms of doing business.

Iwai, USLI's managing director of international operations, remarked:

> USLI sometimes wants a written guarantee from a Japanese parent company, but we
> cannot go to the company and say, "Our partner wants a written statement," there would
> be loss of face.

In Noma's case, however, OLC obtained a written guarantee in Tokyo in support
of the lease application for USLI's consideration. USLI's credit committee decided
that, even with the written guarantee, Noma's application ought not to be approved.
Stern commented:

> For an application of this magnitude, our people do a very careful screening. I under-
> stand the sensitivity of the relationship between OLC and the Japanese parent, but I also
> have people at USLI who say, "If you're going to approve the application anyway, based
> on OLC's support, regardless of the results of our analysis, what's the point in our doing
> a credit analysis?" So we have to tread a very delicate balance.

Scudamore described how these credit policy decisions affected his situation:

> A major portion of our operation is saying yes or no on applications for credit, and
> when OLC and USLI would have a difference of opinion, Naganuma becomes concerned
> about why USLI does not want to do the deal. And, if I cannot convince USLI to approve
> an application, then I'm sure Naganuma wonders whether things would have turned out
> differently if I had tried harder. So, not only do the credit decisions affect OUSL's busi-

ness prospects, they also compromise my standing and position with Naganuma. But, on the other hand, being an accountant, I also understand USLI's position.

Sometimes USLI's policies show immediate results. For example, USLI has always made a lot of money on late charges, whereas OLC seldom imposes late charges. In Japan, most payments are made by automatic bank transfer from lessee to lessor, whereas Americans want to take advantage of float and send in checks. As a society that believes in "saving face," Japanese seldom have payments that come in late. In fact, since our start-up, almost all of our write-offs have been with our American accounts.

OUSL instituted a late charge policy until January 1986. In the first nine months, they collected $65,000 in charges, a fact that Scudamore cited as an illustration of the policy's success.

Concluding Comments

By 1986, OUSL's systems and operations were well established and OUSL had started to become slightly more aggressive in marketing. It had recently signed a letter of intent with a large Japanese consumer products company for its second major vendor program, and new business was expected to show a significant increase. However, competition was also starting to intensify. Many Japanese companies had started to enter the U.S. with 100% owned leasing subsidiaries, for example, Sanwa Bank had bought the leasing arm of Continental Illinois; Fuji Bank had purchased Walter Heller, and independent Japanese leasing companies were also entering the U.S.

Naganuma commented:

Now many Japanese companies are coming to the U.S. It always happens like this. OLC went to China; everybody said OLC was crazy, but now there are ten Japanese companies there. Many Japanese companies are now coming to the U.S. with 100% owned subsidiaries so we need to take defensive steps. We should take advantage of our four-year history and established position in the U.S. and fortify ourselves in the market by increasing our exposure and market share. But our shareholders want to see profits, and chasing volume and profits at the same time is a dilemma.

Scudamore described his concerns:

We are still a very, very young company and reasonably flexible to shift gears and point in a little bit of a different direction, but gradually we are building a structure that commits us to a certain type of business and how we are perceived in the market. Where are the opportunities and what special talents and abilities do we have? How can I stay within some charter that keeps me from really interfering with USLI's market? On the strategy side, where should we go with our traditional products, such as sales-aid leasing? Should we broaden our product/service offerings? Should we offer them *with* USLI? Finally, *how* do we do a better job of landing the fish? We know our market, namely the Japanese segment, but there are still many questions to be addressed.

We have a 3-year plan with a more detailed 1-year budget. My goal is to produce a return-on-equity that is better than USLI's average. We're expecting fairly rapid growth, but should we go after growth per se through acquisitions. There is consolidation going on in the leasing industry and there are many companies for sale. We have two large shareholders behind us and we could finance an acquisition without that much trouble, but what kind of leasing company would fit our charter?

I also worry that the two parent companies are not so close that they view the entire world as partners; how will the dynamics between them unfold and how will they affect OUSL? USLI and OLC have strategic as well as operating differences. The Noma leasing application is just the one example. Strategically, USLI tends to operate companies with a 20% equity component, and a very conservative growth philosophy. OLC maintains a 5% capital ratio and aggressively goes after volume. These differences will become more important once the start-up phase is over. How can I manage the conflicts that are coming up? There seems to be no easy answer.

12
Kuwaiti/Chinese Business Partnership

Youming Ye

It was November 1985 in Beijing. Mr. Simon Sun and Mr. David Wu were sitting in a conference room on the third floor of the China International Trust and Investment Corporation (CITIC) Building, the "Chocolate Building" in downtown Beijing. They were preparing a presentation for CITIC's chairman of the board and the general manager of the business department, Mr. Yiren Rong and Mr. Jun Wang, respectively. For the last three months, Simon Sun and David Wu, had been working on a business proposal made by the Al-Ghurair Group of Kuwait to CITIC. The Al-Ghurair Group wanted CITIC to establish a joint venture trading company in Kuwait. The mood in the room was one of anticipation, excitement, and apprehension.

Three months earlier, Mr. Essa Al-Ghurair, chairman of the Al-Ghurair Group presented the proposal during his visit to CITIC headquarters. The main theme of the proposal was to establish a 50/50 joint venture in Kuwait engaging in general trading operations, to promote Chinese products in Kuwait and its neighboring countries and to attract other wealthy Arab investors to China's new investment climate.

History of CITIC

CITIC has been and continues to be "the best-regarded and most international company in The Peoples's Republic of China." (*Euromoney,* June 1991) CITIC was established in October 1979 to implement China's economic reform and open policy. "It is seen by foreigners as the advance guard for China's Modernization Program."

CITIC is owned by the Chinese government and reports directly to the Chinese Cabinet. The corporation brings in advanced technology and managerial expertise to develop domestic and foreign economic, technological cooperation, and to engage

133

in domestic and international finance, banking, investment, and trade. It has 26,000 employees and total assets of nearly US$ 5 billion abroad.

CITIC acts as a manufacturing enterprise group employing advanced technologies, a financial institution specializing in fund-raising and financing, and a comprehensive trading house for domestic and international transactions. It has, over the first 10 years of its existence, developed into a conglomerate with a diversified interest in production, technology, finance, trade, and services.

CITIC now owns 63 enterprises, and is a partner in 121 joint ventures with foreigners, and 179 joint ventures with other Chinese organizations. It has concentrated on developing natural resources and communications, establishing CITIFOR in Seattle, Washington, to market timber. The corporation now owns large tracts of forest and is one of the major timber suppliers in the northwest United States. It owns 20% of Hong Kong Telecommunications, the local telephone monopoly. It is the second largest shareholder of Cathy Pacific Airline (Hong Kong's major airline company), and owns 45% of Dragon Air, (the second largest airline in Hong Kong). Another possession is the Ka Wah Bank, Ltd. with offices in Hong Kong and the United States. To strengthen its business ties with foreign countries, CITIC has also opened representative offices in Tokyo, New York, Frankfurt, and Paris.

The board of directors is CITIC's organ of power. It consists of 71 members, including senior officials from government ministries and commissions, provinces and municipalities, as well as prominent industrialists and business people, including celebrated entrepreneurs from Hong Kong and Macao. Since 1979, Mr. Yiren Rong has been the chairman of the board.

Mr. Rong is a legendary man. He is widely regarded by foreigners as the "Red capitalist" in China. He was selected by *Fortune* magazine in 1986 as one of the "Top 50 Excellent Businessmen in the World." Mr. Rong's father was a prominent entrepreneur in Shanghai prior to 1949. Their family owned a very reputable business of textile and wheat processing plants in Shanghai. When the communist came to power, most of the family fled to Taiwan, Hong Kong, Europe and United States leaving Mr. Yiren Rong to manage the family business. During the Cultural Revolution, Mr. Rong was jailed by the Red Guard. In 1979, when China was adopting the open door policy, and looking for foreign investment to help its modernization program, Mr. Rong was handpicked by Chinese senior leader, Mr. Deng Xiao-Ping to head the newly established CITIC. In addition to his role in CITIC, Mr. Rong is also a deputy chairman of the People's Congress in China.

As a result of Mr. Rong's extensive experience and expertise in the private sector, CITIC has won international recognition. It was the first corporation in China to issue debentures in overseas financial markets, and the first to provide full-scale consulting services through its wholly-owned subsidiary, China International Economic Consultants, Inc. (the only company in China recognized by the World Bank for its projects in China). It was the first corporation to set up an in-house bank, CITIC Industrial Bank, which broke Bank of China's monopoly on foreign exchange transactions. It initiated and operates its real estate business through its subsidiary, CITIC Real Estate, Inc., which built the first commercial office building in Beijing; CITIC was also the first firm to introduce the leasing business into China, through its subsidiary China Leasing Company Ltd.

History of the Al-Ghurair Group

Mr. Essa Al-Ghurair is the second son of the Al-Ghurair family, a reputable and wealthy Kuwaiti family. He studied at Indiana University in the mid '60s and earned a degree in architecture. After graduation from Indiana, he returned to Kuwait and started his own business, Pan Arab Consulting Enterprises (PACE). He made his fortune in the '70s construction boom in Kuwait. To his credit are some of the major buildings in Kuwait City: Kuwait National Bank Building, Kuwait Hilton Hotel, and Kuwait Department Store Building. To diversify he expanded into general merchandising and currently owns the largest department store in Kuwait City, Kuwait Department Store. He also owns an industrial chemical trading business, and an engineering and contracting firm. Al-Ghurair has companies in Geneva, and owns property in Paris, New York City, London, and Hong Kong. His management team consists primarily of Americans and Europeans, which he describes as "a mini United Nations." In 1984, the Al-Ghurair Group established a representative office in Beijing, China.

In addition to Mr. Essa Al-Ghurair's worldwide business interests, he is involved in a variety of social and government activities in Kuwait. He is the chairman of the Kuwait Safety Society, a government sponsored, non-profit organization supervising and regulating traffic regulations in Kuwait. He serves as a private adviser for the Kuwait royal family, and is a frequently invited guest at parties held by the American, British, and Chinese ambassadors to Kuwait. Over the years, he has established a close friendship with the Chinese ambassador. Mr. Essa Al-Ghurair's elder brother was the Kuwait ambassador to the United Kingdom.

Mr. Essa Al-Ghurair's family is close, although the four brothers all have their own families, they gather at their mother's house for dinner every Wednesday.

The Business Relation Between CITIC and the Al-Ghurair Group

Mr. Essa Al-Ghurair was introduced to CITIC by the Chinese ambassador to Kuwait, Fuchang Yang. In the late '50s, Mr. Essa Al-Ghurair's elder brother and Yang were classmates when both men were studying at Cairo University in Egypt.

In the 1980s, when China was desperately seeking foreign investments in China, the Chinese and Kuwaiti governments reached an agreement that encouraged the Kuwaiti private sector to invest in China. Kuwait Oil Company, a firm owned by the Kuwait government, participated in a multimillion-dollar fertilizer plant in the northern part of China. The Kuwaiti government also held two multimillion-dollar low-interest loans to the Chinese government. To encourage and facilitate the Kuwait private sector to invest in China, the Chinese ambassador worked hard to convince Kuwaiti businessmen to engage in business contacts with Chinese companies. In October 1984, Mr. Essa Al-Ghurair made his first highly publicized visit to China at the invitation of the Chinese Ministry of Foreign Affairs. During his visit, Mr. Essa Al-Ghurair met with the Chinese state counselor, Mr. Zhang Jinfu, the deputy minister of foreign trade and economic development, Mr. Yuming Wei, and other high-ranking Chinese government officials. When Mr. Essa Al-Ghurair was in Beijing, the Kuwait Ambassador to China hosted a banquet to honor him, and repay the Chinese officials for hospitality they extended to him during the visit.

While Mr. Essa Al-Ghurair was in China, he signed an agreement with Poly Technology Inc. a subsidiary of CITIC to develop a villa project located in suburban Beijing. This real estate project, Beijing Garden Villa (BGV), involved more than $70 million. It was one of the largest joint venture real estate projects undertaken in the Beijing area at the time. In anticipation of the growing number of foreigners doing business in China, BGV intended to provide expatriates a more Western-type residence rather than a hotel or apartment.

In collaboration with the representative office of Xinjiang Autonomous region, Mr. Essa Al-Ghurair also expressed strong interest in building an Islamic Center in the northwest part of Beijing City. He was confident that the project could be financed by long-term interest-free loans by the Islamic Bank, of which he was a board member.

CITIC was interested in the Middle East connection because it had been a blind spot on the strategic map of globalizing its operations. Strategically, because of the cease-fire in the Iran and Iraq war, CITIC saw a chance for a foothold in the Middle East. From a marketing viewpoint, CITIC anticipated a huge demand for Chinese goods ranging from construction materials to toilet paper once Iran and Iraq rebuilt after the war.

Also, CITIC felt that wealthy Arab investors would like to diversify their investment portfolio worldwide because there was a growing concern regarding investments in the West for political reasons. The West, especially the United States, was historically a strong supporter of Israel in the Arab-Israeli conflict. For this reason, some Arab countries wanted to shift their investments. Furthermore, the Chinese government had maintained good relations with the Arabs countries, publicly supporting them over the years. The Chinese felt that these reasons produced an advantage in attracting Arab investment.

Because of the newly adopted open door policy, there were some good investment opportunities in China. If CITIC were to set up its operation in the Arabian Gulf, there could be tremendous future payoffs. In the short term, CITIC might acquire and improve its export business, and supply much-needed construction labor for Kuwait and its neighboring countries. In the long term, CITIC might tap into the Iraq market for the reconstruction boom, and be able to attract more Arab investors to China.

With all these strategic intents, CITIC was extremely interested in establishing a joint venture with the Al-Ghurair Group. The top management of CITIC assigned Mr. Sun and Mr. Wu to study the proposal and the feasibility of the joint venture. Mr. Sun, the administrative assistant to the general manager of CITIC's Business Department, and Mr. Wu, with 15 years experience in the export and import business, took the assignment seriously. The two men worked long hours seeking help and insights from many sources.

During a trip to Kuwait, to visit the Al-Ghurair Group, they met with the Chinese ambassador in Kuwait. During this meeting, they were informed that Mr. Essa Al-Ghurair was the first Kuwaiti private investor to commit $50 million as an investment in China. None of the other major players in the Arab world had even bothered to visit China. Therefore, the joint venture between the Al-Ghurair Group and CITIC was more than a pure business deal; it would have political implications. Mr. Sun and Mr. Wu were overwhelmed by the importance of this project and how should they report and recommend the venture to the top management of CITIC.

Decision Dilemma Faced By CITIC

During their stay in Kuwait, Mr. Sun and Mr. Wu learned of a rumor that Mr. Essa Al-Ghurair's younger brother, Mr. Heshan Al-Ghurair, was involved in a Kuwait stock market scandal. According to allegations, Mr. Heshan knowingly misrepresented himself to public investors and he faced criminal charges. Supposedly, the Al-Ghurair Group had to pay a fine of more US$ 100 million. Mr. Heshan himself could not stay in the country, and fled to Iraq to avoid the prosecution.

Shocked by the news, Mr. Sun and Mr. Wu, flew back to Beijing. Before they talked to CITIC management, they met with Mr. Mike Holmes, the general manager of the Al-Ghurair's office in Beijing. They indirectly hinted to Mr. Holmes that if this rumor could not be explained satisfactorily, it could affect the proposed joint venture. Mr. Holmes, a veteran American businessman, empathized his understanding of CITIC's concerns.

In response, a week later Mr. Essa Al-Ghurair sent a letter to CITIC explaining the allegation. According to Mr. Essa Al-Ghurair, his brother was involved in the stock market scandal because of his inexperience in business and was fined US$ 100 million. The Al-Ghurair Group paid the fine to the Kuwait authorities. His brother's behavior was not in any way to reflect the business practices of the Al-Ghurair Group. He assured CITIC that the Al-Ghurair Group would cooperate fully with CITIC and live up to its commitment.

Even with such an assurance from Mr. Essa Al-Ghurair, Mr. Sun and Mr. Wu wondered how to present and recommend the proposal to the top management of CITIC. On the one hand, the joint venture had the full support of the Chinese ambassador to Kuwait, who personally favored full cooperation with the Al-Ghurair Group, and who was concerned about the political implication rather than the financial implication for CITIC. On the other hand, with the knowledge of the stock scandal, would CITIC benefit with such a partner without damaging its own reputation and image? Because there was a very close relationship between Mr. Essa Al-Ghurair and his brothers, did Mr. Essa Al-Ghurair have a part in the stock scandal? Did he know of his brother's activities? Or, as he claimed, did he not have any knowledge of his brother's dealings until it became public? What if Mr. Essa Al-Ghurair was the man behind the scandal? Could CITIC still trust him and go ahead with the joint venture proposal?

If Mr. Sun and Mr. Wu recommended rejection of the proposal, what kind of response could CITIC expect from the Chinese ambassador? What response would it get from the Ministry of Foreign Affairs? What impact would it have on CITIC's strategy in developing the Middle East market? Could Mr. Sun and Mr. Wu personally stand all these political pressures? What impact would it have on their career advancement?

With all these unanswered questions in their mind, Mr. Sun and Mr. Wu walked into the Chairman Rong's office.

Bibliography

Anonymous, "Business Confidence in Hong Kong: Let a Hundred Companies Bloom," *Economist,* Sept. 28, 1991, p. 76.

"Dragon Air to Boost Number of Flights to 3 Chinese Cities," *The Wall Street Journal,* Jan. 17, 1992, sec. A, p. 7B, col. 3.

Baldinger, P., "Helping China Prosper," *China Business Review,* Nov/Dec 1991, pp. 42–43.

Chen, K., "CITIC Pacific Plans to Issue Shares for Acquisitions," *The Wall Street Journal,* Jan. 7, 1993, sec. A, p. 10, col. 4.

Cheng, E., "Under the carpet: Peking's House Cleaning in Hong Kong Leaves Problems Unsolved," *Far Eastern Economic Review,* Nov. 1, 1990, pp. 58–60.

Cheung, T. M., "Crown Jewels Polished: CITIC Flexes Muscle Outside China," *Far Eastern Economic Review,* Jan. 21, 1993, pp. 50–51.

Cheung, T. M., "Companies: Middle of the Kingdom," *Far Eastern Economic Review,* Jan. 21, 1993, pp. 48–50.

Cheung, T. M., "Naval Officer on Deck: CITIC Heir-Apparent Talks of Shake-up," *Far Eastern Economic Review,* Jan. 21, 1993, p. 52.

Cheung, T. M., "State Within a State: CITIC Develops Power to Local Units in China," *Far Eastern Economic Review,* Jan. 21, 1993, pp. 51–52.

Friedland, J. and Westlake, M., "The Cadres' Bargains: CITIC Secures Hong Kong's Commanding Heights at a Discount, with Strings Attached," *Far Eastern Economic Review,* Jan. 11, 1990, pp. 34–35.

Friedland, J., "Prize Fight: CITIC Seeks Hong Kong Trophy but Hits a Barrier," *Far Eastern Economic Review,* Aug. 22, 1991, p. 53.

Glain, S., "Chinese Province Makes Capitalist Moves with Deals Tied to Hong Kong's Future," *The Wall Street Journal,* Jan. 10, 1992, sec. A, p. 5A, col. 2.

Montagu-Polock, M., "Covered Warrants: A New Revolution," *Asian Business,* June 1990, pp. 93–94.

Rafferty, K., "China's Enigmatic Conglomerate," *Euromoney,* June 1991, pp. 24–32.

Tan, L. H., "A Coup for Barclays," *Asian Finance,* Apr. 15, 1990, pp. 14–18.

Taylor, M., "Swooping to Conquer: Hong Kong's Peregrine Spreads Its Wings," *Far Eastern Economic Review,* Oct. 10, 1991, pp. 63–65.

Westlake, M., "Aviation: Pao Bails Out," *Far Eastern Economic Review,* Nov. 16, 1988, p. 82.

Westlake, M., "Out of the Clouds: Cathy Pacific and CITIC Take Control of Dragon Air," *Far Eastern Economic Review,* Jan. 25, 1990, pp. 62–63.

13
International Espionage at IBM Hitachi, Ltd.

John E. Walsh, Jr.

HITACHI LIMITED

In the 1980s Hitachi Limited, Japan's fifth largest industrial enterprise was indicted by a San Jose, California grand jury on a charge of "conspiring to transport property from the United States to Japan." The property was confidential IBM computer information on models 3053, 3081, 3380, and 3880.

Those arrested included: Mr. Kenji Hayashi, senior engineer of Hitachi, Ltd., Japan; Mr. Isao Ohnishi, section manager, Hitachi; Mr. Kunimasa Inoue, programmer, Hitachi America Ltd., San Francisco; Mr. Keizo Shirai, section manager, Nissei Electronics Ltd., Japan; Mr. Takaya Ishida, assistant to the president of Mitsubishi Electronics America, Inc.; and the only American, Mr. Tom Yoshida, president, NCL Data Inc., Santa Clara. The FBI issued warrants for the arrest of nine additional Hitachi and three more Mitsubishi employees in Japan who also allegedly engaged in the conspiracy.

Background

Since 1979, with extensive backing from the Ministry of International Trade and Industry (MITI), Japan's computer firms had been pushing to expand their computer export business to follow the country's export success in other fields. An undersecretary at the U.S. Department of Commerce, Mr. Lionel Olmer complained that the U.S. had a growing deficit with Japan in electronics. "Japanese suppliers had captured, through a variety of direct and indirect government support, 65% of the world market for advanced semiconductor memories, a key element in the fastest growing parts of the computer business," he said. Japan was also working on a so-called fifth-generation computer, that claimed to be closer to human intelligence than present machines.

Analysts felt Japan's development as a major force in the world computer business had been slowed by the language barrier, especially in providing computer software in specialized fields where program costs rapidly escalate into the millions, and where the operating language is English.

Furthermore, "The U.S. computer industry, led by IBM, had been developing software that was not compatible with Japanese computers. The new American system would be a blow to the Japanese companies," a computer company executive said, "because the Japanese had designed and built computers to be compatible with IBM software." While the Japanese had launched a major campaign to capture the American computer market, they had shielded their own market from imports as the local industry became more competitive with American and European manufacturers.

IBM held only a 30% share of the Japanese market, compared to its share of more than 50% in every other major industrial country, except Great Britain. A fact that, according to Mr. Olmer, the United States planned to introduce for discussion at the next meeting of the General Agreement on Tariffs and Trade.

Prior to the indictment, Richard Deacon, a British espionage expert and author of a series of books on secret services around the world, offered these comments to a reporter:

> How many of the world's intelligence services have set out with the prime aim of making their nations more prosperous and improving the standard of living of their peoples? With the sole exception of Japan, none.
>
> More than any other single factor, this total intelligence effort for prosperity has enabled Japan to rise from the ruins of World War II to become one of the world's top industrial powers. Although the Japanese would be loath to use the word "war," they have conquered the world industrially simply by mounting what could be described as a national peace planning effort on a wartime footing.
>
> To do this, the Japanese turned what first seemed a disadvantage into a positive advantage. The Japanese constitution drawn up after World War II restricted both the nation's defense forces and military intelligence gathering operations to a low-profile purely defensive role concerned only with national security. Thus, barred from carrying out cloak-and-dagger type aggressive espionage, the Japanese wisely, sensibly, and without fuss set about organizing a global intelligence-gathering system aimed at making them more prosperous. Eighty-five percent and possibly over 90% of Japan's intelligence gathering is directed towards business, economic, and industrial espionage. The very success of this effort now threatens to erupt into a trade war.

When asked "Don't all nations conduct various degrees of commercial intelligence?" Deacon replied:

> Yes, but none do it as comprehensively and on the scale of a national effort as do the Japanese. One of the reasons for this is that in Japan there is much greater cooperation between private industry and the government. Hence, not only diplomats and members

of trade missions, but executives, students, salesmen, and visitors to the West all provide the country with a steady flow of information on commerce, markets, technological developments, economic research, and almost everything that would produce ideas for improving their living standards.

All of this information is separated, computerized and analyzed, and the results are fed to various "think tanks" which work out future policies. It is believed that there are more than 100 private research organizations or "think tanks" in Japan today.

The Japanese View on Spying

Culturally, Japanese view spying as an occupation requiring courage and daring, much like the qualities of the samurai. In his book, *A History of the Japanese Secret Service,* (1983) Richard Deacon stated:

> Unlike some other nations, the Japanese regard spying as an honorable and patriotic duty, and even in their reference books, do not seek to hide the fact that some of their illustrious citizens have indulged in espionage. In a Japanese edition of *Who Was Who,* for example, there is this remarkable entry:
> "ISHIKAWA, Goichi: Spy. Born 1866, died 1894. Sent to China where he traveled to the Mongolian border. Active in China in Sino-Japanese War, but captured by the Chinese and executed in Tientsin . . ."

Long before Deacon's book was published, the ability of the Japanese to gather information was well-documented. In covering the Sino-Japanese War in his book, *Problems of the Far East,* published in 1896 the Rt. Honorable George Curzon wrote:

> War having once been declared, it was evident that the national spirit was intensely and unanimously enlisted in the enterprise. It was felt that Japan was playing for a high stake, and that there must be no bickering or jealousy at the table. No country, in all probability, ever went to war, sustained by a higher or more unfaltering fervor of patriotism than did Japan. Then, too, it was discovered how ubiquitous and exhaustive, and almost Machiavellian in their patient secrecy, had been her preparations. Skilled topographers in disguise had mapped the high-roads of China, and had plotted their angles over the interior of Korea. Hydrographical surveys, unostentatiously pursued for years, had acquainted the Japanese with every inlet in the Korean coast, and had furnished the chart-room of every vessel in her Navy with hitherto unpublished maps. Her mobilization proceeded with a smoothness and rapidity that excited the admiration of the European military attaches; her organization and equipment were wonderful in their completeness. The Japanese Intelligence Department might have been engaged upon, just as it had certainly been preparing for a campaign for years. Its spies were everywhere, in the offices and arsenals, in the council chambers and amid the ranks of the enemy. The press was manipulated and controlled with a masterly despotism that would have been impossible in Europe.

Mindy L. Kotler, president of the Japan Information Access Project and a member of the Council for International Business Risk Management discussed in the newsletter, *Risk Management Review,* Winter 1990-91, the difference between Japanese and American views of information:

The problem is not that the two sides of the Pacific suffer from any shortage of discrete facts about each other. . . . In the U.S., intelligence is the process of linking information to meaning, whereas in Japan information is synonymous with intelligence. For the Japanese, information connotes purpose; for Americans, it is simply the word for a free good.

In the West, information is defined and thought of as news, facts, or knowledge. Intelligence, on the other hand, is defined as the ability to learn, to cope with a new situation. . . . Whereas for the Japanese, information is not only used to explain, but it is used to reduce uncertainty and to plan strategy.

The Sting Operation

FBI agents were tipped off that Hitachi had obtained confidential IBM computer information. The documents that Hitachi procured were stamped "IBM Confidential" and "Do Not Reproduce." These copies were for IBM's Adirondack Hardware Design Workbook, which contained secret strategy plans for the development of new computers.

Following the tip, FBI agent Alan Garretson, and a confidential source at IBM, began organizing the successful sting operation by posing as businessmen willing to sell stolen IBM materials. FBI agents even set up a phony computer dealership in Silicon Valley called Glenmar from which they operated. The agents then met, telephoned, and corresponded with a number of Japanese businessmen, including top officials at Hitachi and Mitsubishi. The merchandise they offered, and eventually sold, was provided by IBM.

A month later, Kenji Hayashi, a senior engineer for Hitachi, met Alan Garretson in Las Vegas to talk business. Hayashi believed Garretson could provide him with stolen information about computers made by IBM. Hayashi had quite a shopping list. He told Garretson that he would pay $10,000 for various IBM computer manuals, and as much as $100,000 for an IBM source code. Payments would be "discreet," mostly through funnel companies in the U.S.

At one point during the operation another FBI agent, accompanied by a Hitachi top engineer, had sneaked into an American factory complex to secretly photograph the advanced IBM 3380 disc drive and its manuals. The entire episode was a charade, but the Japanese businessmen involved did not know it.

A week later, Garretson met with Jun Naruse, identified as another Hitachi senior engineer, in a Connecticut hotel lobby. From there they visited a company with an IBM 3380, the most advanced disc drive system on the market. Naruse wanted the manuals for the 3380. Garretson pretended to bribe an employee of the firm where the 3380 was installed, so that they could enter the facility and photograph the disk drive system and its manuals. Naruse gave Garretson $3,000 in $100 bills, and promised another $7,000 later if Garretson could also provide the maintenance manuals.

Over the following weeks and months, Garretson supplied the 3380 computer manuals and other IBM documentation in return for thousands of dollars in cash. The series of Hitachi payments culminated in a $525,000 payment to Garretson transferred through Tom Yoshida, president of NCL Data, a subsidiary of Nissei Electronics in Japan. In total, payments for the confidential IBM information by Hitachi amounted to $622,000.

It was not only Hitachi that practiced this type of espionage. Although how Mitsubishi became involved in the operation is not known, they were also clearly interested in obtaining IBM information related to the 3380, for which the company paid some $26,000.

The Japanese Reaction

Japanese Prime Minister Zenko Suzuki expressed shock at the arrest of Japanese executives, and said he hoped the incident would not impair relations with the United States. "It is a very shocking incident. We have to deal with it by thoroughly and prudently investigating and studying what has actually happened," Mr. Suzuki told a parliamentary committee. He added that his government would consider "Japan's national interests" in deciding whether or not to turn over the indicted Japanese executives if the United States requested extradition. The foreign minister, Mr. Yoshio Sakurauchi, observed that the case had come at an inappropriate time during a period in which U.S. and Japan were discussing ways to improve technological cooperation in the future.

Shortly after the arrest, one Hitachi executive said he was "shocked" by the charges against 14 Hitachi employees and he insisted that his company had not engaged in illegal activities. But he said it was "possible" that Hitachi's employees "may have been too eager" in their search for information. Another Hitachi executive, Yasukichi Hatano, chief of Hitachi's computer department, remarked. "If the incident is true, it may be right to suppose that something went wrong in the course of information-gathering activities entrusted to a local consulting company."

Later, Hitachi pleaded innocent on all accounts. Hitachi spokesman Yuzuru Kuramoto said, "Our basic position is unchanged, regardless of the summons." Hitachi claimed it did nothing wrong in paying more than $600,000 for IBM computer technology and said it would not honor any summons issued by the United States.

In addition, one Mitsubishi executive in Japan denied that any of his company's employees had attempted to steal computer secrets from IBM. The Mitsubishi executive director, Hideo Ota protested what he considered entrapment. "We have a strong impression that our employees were cheated by the FBI." In a published statement, Mitsubishi emphatically denied it or its employees had been involved in any illegal conduct.

Speaking at a Boston business luncheon, Akio Morita, chairman of Sony, said that his company had been approached many times by Americans offering to peddle industrial information and that it was normal to buy such information from legitimate sources. However, he added that his company always turned down individuals seeking to peddle information on their own.

The Japanese publication, *Asia Week,* suggested that the charges were motivated to exert pressures on Japan in trade negotiations. In California, the accusation, interpreted as calling one of the pillars of Japanese industry a thief, shocked and hurt millions of Japanese-Americans.

But, in Japan, where a different cultural matrix inextricably binds a man for life to the company for which he works, charges, generally, are viewed as an affront to the collective sense of honor. Mortification ran deep among Hitachi's 150,000 employees. Rage and a feeling of victimization surfaced regarding counter charges that the FBI's action was part of a ploy to discredit the company, and punish it for its success in convincing American consumers that Japanese goods were superior to their U.S. products.

The Japanese found it difficult to accept that the two prominent companies, Hitachi and Mitsubishi Electric, were apprehended by an abhorrently sneaky (to the Japanese perception of propriety) process of deliberate deception on the part of the American FBI. The idea that a governmental agency would go to the extent of establishing a phony company, and engaging the services of undercover agents as "employees" was unthinkable in the Japanese concept of justice. In addition, the Japanese felt that the U.S. federal police were dishonorable to abet Japanese businessmen in doing something wrong for the purpose of arresting them. No Japanese police force would set up such a "sting."

For the Americans, it was all merely part of the process of law enforcement. Defending the operation, U.S. Attorney-General William French Smith declared that "legitimate undercover actions" would continue. If a fine line between legal and illegal procedures in inducing someone to commit a crime existed, the practiced FBI certainly knew best where it should be drawn. Furthermore, the U.S. courts would ensure that this line was not overstepped. Americans liked to believe that no one, neither the chairman of IBM, or even the president was above the law. In Japan, it was consensus, not definitive rulings, that prevail. "Seldom in peacetime had differing cultural value judgments doomed two nations to such inevitable, gigantic misunderstanding," said one academic scholar.

The American Response

According to a computer consulting firm president, Maxwell Paley, the case began with a telegram from Hitachi. Mr. Paley quoted Hitachi as saying that the huge Japanese firm had several volumes of IBM "Adirondack" workbooks, containing the secret keys to the company's future development plans. Hitachi asked if Mr. Paley's company, Palyn Associates, would assist them in acquiring more of the secret volumes.

"'Oh-oh.' that's the jewels," Mr. Paley recalled saying to himself. "I was at IBM long enough to know what that means. They (Hitachi) can't have these. There was a lot of stuff in the gray area, but here's the real thing." Mr. Paley decided, "enough is enough," and he called IBM.

IBM relayed the information to the FBI, and a sting operation was activated. The "firm" then helped Hitachi fill a shopping list of IBM's most secret technology. IBM asked Paley to help and subsequently he flew to Las Vegas for a hotel meeting between Hitachi's Kenji Hayashi and an IBM executive. Paley then bowed out of the case until Hitachi identified him as the person who introduced them to Glenmar during the week of the arrests.

Paley, according to a federal affidavit, called the list of Hitachi's requests "unbelievable," while another consultant, Ken Churilla of Input Inc., estimated that the information was worth US $100 million if Hitachi had succeeded.

The director of the FBI, Mr. William Webster, said, "The investigation was a classic example of the value of an undercover operation designed to ferret out the theft of high technology. I want to commend IBM for the excellent assistance rendered during this investigation."

A spokesman for the Department of Justice reported that both Hitachi and Mitsubishi staff members were involved in separate efforts to obtain confidential information used in the development of computers and related products. Specifically, they were said to have "unwittingly recruited the same undercover FBI agent."

An FBI spokesman, Mr. Bill Barker, who assisted in the investigation said, "The Japanese were trying to thwart the development of new technology going on in this country and greatly increase their own development of computers by quickly obtaining advanced research by IBM." James H. Pooley, a Palo Alto trial lawyer who has represented many U.S. companies in cases of industrial espionage in Silicon Valley, said spies thrive on valuable information because many companies simply do not pay enough attention to discouraging them. The companies often fail to realize that secrets have been lost due to simple carelessness. Sting operations are the only way high-technology crimes of industrial espionage can be detected. It is a perfectly acceptable law enforcement method, and just what we need.

An Objective Response

In an attempt to provide an objective response and identify major areas of misunderstanding, Michael K. Young, associate professor of law and director of Columbia University Law School's Center for Japanese Legal Studies made the following comments in an article entitled, "Japan Stung," that appeared in the *New York Times,* August 17, 1982:

> What is most interesting about the Justice Department's indictments against employees of two major Japanese companies for conspiring to buy stolen IBM computer trade secrets is the light the incident sheds on how little the two countries understand each other.

Americans have treated the 17 indictments, mostly involving employees of Hitachi Ltd. and the Mitsubishi Electric Corporation (and one American) with detachment and faint amusement. In Japan, the news has spawned a national fixation that we would reserve only for a major crisis; it has preoccupied the media, government, and most businessmen.

Why these markedly different reactions? First, the Japanese were astonished that American law-enforcement officers would use a "sting" operation in something other than a drug case. Their astonishment turned to shock when they discovered that the operation was undertaken at the behest of and with the cooperation of International Business Machines, a major competitor of the accused companies.

The Japanese abhorred resorting to formal legal processes to resolve disputes. In Japan, there is about one attorney for every 100,000 people, as compared with one for every 450 in the United States. More lawsuits were filed in California than in all of Japan. This reluctance to resort to formal processes means that such processes, when invoked, are viewed with more seriousness—indeed, alarm in the case of a criminal indictment—than they might be in the United States.

Americans are accustomed to a confrontational, adversarial relationship between the government and business. Japan's regulatory style is based on intense dialogue and extensive interaction that leads to compromise. In Japan, informal and formal warnings precede indictment. As a result the Japanese surprise at the "shoot first, talk later" regulatory attitude was considerable.

Both countries approached conduct differently. Americans emphasized somewhat abstract notions of right and wrong, duty and obligation, asking themselves What is my right? My duty? And yours? The Japanese, on the other hand, emphasize the effect of any act on personal relations, and ask what the act's impact will be on the long-term relationship between the parties involved. Americans stress individual values and attitudes; the Japanese found community values and interests more important. Because they believe that the indictments arose from a deliberate attempt to color long-term relationships, they have taken the Justice Department's action more personally than Americans.

The Japanese identify very strongly with their country as an entity. They attach immense importance to group identity. Ideas of "us versus them" permeate the society. When "we" is one's family or company, "they" becomes all other families and companies. When "them" means foreigners or foreign countries, the "us" is unmistakably, irreducibly the Japanese people and Japan. Thus, the country is debating what "happened to Japan" and is trying to decide how the "country should respond." On the contrary, Americans reactions were quite different when Lockheed was involved in a scandal that compromised the Japanese government. Americans may have been disturbed by Lockheed's conduct, but few had any sense of wounded national pride or much concern over loss of face in the international community.

Japan believes that the U.S. Justice Department's actions against Hitachi were part of a coordinated plan by the entire U.S. government, perhaps to enhance America's position in impending bilateral trade talks. Used to more fragmentation in the government, Americans in general do not believe that the department concocted such a nefarious plot.

Conclusion

The lesson for Japan is essentially what it has been urging upon the United States; when in a foreign country, you must play by all the rules, including legal, political, and social.

For America, the lesson is no less important. Despite supposedly learned commentary to the contrary, Japanese companies, not unlike American companies, are individual units that vary considerably in their ability to compete in the international marketplace. Some are well run, highly efficient and very competitive; many are not. Thus, trade-protection measures directed against the Japanese in general are not only ill-conceived economically, but are almost certainly unnecessary. If this realization of equality of competitive entities is accompanied by vigorous American enforcement of the laws that insure equality of opportunity in the marketplace (such as the antitrust, anti-dumping and unfair trade practices laws), perhaps pressure for specific protective measures would be even further reduced.

If the trade-secrets affair does nothing more than help each society understand the other, mutual relations may be strengthened rather than weakened.

What action should the U.S. government have taken so as not to jeopardize critical trade negotiations with Japan? If the case against Hitachi had dragged on in court and more names had been introduced, what effect would that have had on major technology agreements signed by Hitachi with companies such as Hewlett-Packard and Advanced Systems? What action should Hitachi and Mitsubishi have taken? What action should IBM have taken? What key cultural differences should have been considered in seeking a resolution to the incident? What would be the best way for a global company to protect its trade secrets and classified information from foreign or domestic competitors?

14
Motorola Analog Division: Development of a Shared Global Vision

Ralph Krueger
and
Corinne Pfund

Motorola Analog Division

In the beginning of May 1993 Alison Palmer, consultant for organizational effectiveness in the human resources department of Motorola's semiconductors sector, was looking out of the window of the airplane that just left Phoenix Sky Harbor Airport. She was on her way to Manila, where the fourth phase of the visioning process would occur.

As the plane was penetrating the clouds, Alison reflected on the process the Analog division, part of Motorola's Semiconductor Products Sector, had done to design and create a new global vision for the division. She was partly responsible for initiating this change and she thought of the process as a success. In the third meeting that had occurred in Toulouse, France in October 1992 the shared vision had

This case was written under the supervision of Dr. David O. Braaten, associate professor, and Dr. Robert T. Moran, professor of International Studies at the American Graduate School of International Management. This case has been prepared as a basis for discussion rather than to illustrate either effective or ineffective handling of an administrative situation. Names of the people have been disguised to preserve confidentiality. The authors would like to thank the Motorola Analog division for its cooperation.

been finalized. The development process of this shared vision had been unusual because it had directly or indirectly involved all managers and employees of the Analog division around the world. She was thinking back to how the idea of developing a global vision had begun almost one and a half years earlier.

The History of Motorola

The company was founded by Paul V. Galvin in 1928 as the Galvin Manufacturing Corp. in Chicago. Its first product was a "battery eliminator" that allowed consumers to operate radios directly from household current instead of the batteries supplied with early models. In the 1930s, the company successfully commercialized car radios under the brand name "Motorola." The company developed a broad customer base consisting of consumers and state authorities such as police departments. The name of the company was changed from Galvin Manufacturing Corp. to Motorola, Inc. in 1947. In the 1940s Motorola also entered into contracts with the U.S. government to explore solid-state electronics.

At the time of Paul Galvin's death in 1959, Motorola was a leader in military, space, and commercial communications, it had built its first semiconductor production facility, and was a growing force in consumer electronics. Under the leadership of Robert W. Galvin, the son of Paul Galvin, Motorola expanded into international markets in the 1960s, and began shifting its focus away from consumer electronics. Motorola continued to concentrate its energies on high-technology markets in commercial, industrial and government fields. As a result of the expansion into international markets Motorola's customer base became more and more global. International sales represented 52% of total sales in 1992. Motorola had always placed particular emphasis on product quality, total customer satisfaction, short cycle manufacturing, and training and education of employees at all levels to improve manufacturing, marketing and technical skills.

Motorola in 1993

In 1993, Motorola employed approximately 107,000 people worldwide and was among the United States' forty largest industrial companies ranked by total sales ($13.3 billion in 1992). It was one of the world's leading providers of wireless communications, semiconductor technology and advanced electronics equipment & services for global markets. The company's operations can be described as highly decentralized, with business operations structured into sectors, groups or divisions, depending on size. Motorola's three main activity sectors were: the Semiconductor Products Sector, the Land Mobile Products Sector, and the General Systems Sector.

The Semiconductor Products Sector designed and produced a broad line of discrete semiconductors and integrated circuits (IC), including microprocessors, microcomputers, and memories, to serve the advanced systems needs of the computer, consumer, automotive, industrial, and federal government telecommunications markets. This sector was headquartered in Phoenix, Arizona. The Semiconductor Products Sector accounted for $4,475 million in sales in 1992 equalling 33.64% of Motorola's total sales. The Analog division was part of the Semiconductors Products sector and accounted for 10% of the sector's sales in 1992.

Corporate Culture

Motorola had a strong and homogeneous corporate culture despite the relative independence of the various sectors, groups, and divisions of the organization. All employees act according to certain corporate values best captured in the Motorola global mission statement:

> In each of our chosen arenas of the electronics industry, we will grow rapidly by providing our worldwide customers what they want, when they want it, with Six Sigma quality and best-in-class cycle time, as we strive to achieve our fundamental corporate objective of Total Customer Satisfaction and to achieve our stated goals of best-in-class people, marketing, products, software, hardware and systems, manufacturing and service; increased global market share; and superior financial results.

People at Motorola were empowered as long as they could show adequate performance and aim at total customer satisfaction. Motorola stressed empowered team culture that resulted in complex organizational structures that lead to team decision making. The company recognized the value of its employees. Motorola set priorities in developing the capabilities of its people. For this reason, emphasis was placed on training. Once an employee had worked for ten years in the company, there was an unwritten rule stating that he/she cannot be laid off without the permission of the CEO.

The Analog Division within Motorola

The Motorola Analog division was originally one of several divisions that evolved from the Integrated Circuits division that was formed in 1960 in Phoenix. In 1993, the Analog division was a major manufacturer of analog products in the world, manufacturing linear circuits of all different types and complexities for a broad spectrum of products around the world including AM stereo radio chip, fuel injection in cars, circuits in state-of-the-art cellular phones. The Analog division operated in a $7.5 billion worldwide market and employed more than 2,200 people worldwide. Its sales were expected to reach $500 million in 1993.

In 1993, two thirds of Analog's sales originated from outside the U.S. and consequently, the division had a global presence. It had major business interests in Hong Kong, Tokyo, and Toulouse, France. Design centers were located in these three locations, and in Geneva, Switzerland and Tempe, Arizona, site of the division's worldwide headquarters. Production facilities for silicon wafers were located in France and Japan, while product packaging and final testing was done in Mexico, Malaysia, China, South Korea, Taiwan and Hong Kong.

The worldwide Analog division was organized along the lines of a three-dimensional matrix, in which decision making was shared among product managers, functional managers, and regional managers. The complexity of the Analog matrix organization reflects Motorola's belief in empowerment, shared responsibility, and effective team management.

The Decision to Develop a Shared Vision

Marco Michelotti, vice-president and general manager of Analog, took charge of the division in 1991. He was concerned that the worldwide division lacked cohesiveness. Each of the regions and countries worked almost independently from the others. Marco felt that the idea of a global vision, communicated throughout the whole division, would improve the way Analog was doing business globally.

Keeping in mind Motorola's global mission, he hoped to develop a common goal for the Analog division. When he arrived, the communication among the country managers and the product managers was poor and prevented the division from operating efficiently on a global scale. More specifically, close collaboration between headquarters, the design centers and the manufacturing centers of the division was becoming more and more vital to the division's ability to react to changes in the environment. This created difficulties, because each Analog country manager had different priorities. Marco was looking for a way to bring the worldwide Analog team closer together by giving them a common cause embodied in a vision. An overarching goal would, he hoped, make people communicate and collaborate better.

To achieve his objective Marco asked the corporate effectiveness consultant, Alison Palmer, and the training and human resources manager, John Sherwin, to help him create and communicate a common goal to all the division's employees. For Alison, this was the first time that she would work on an assignment with international scope.

Alison and John discussed the task and identified three ways to convince people to change their behavior and adopt a global vision. The first alternative, which was the traditional way at Motorola, would have been to "train the change." Motorola already had many training programs. Alison knew that the advantage of a training program lay in the fact that it required limited time and effort. But she and John saw a major disadvantage in that the employees would not be involved in the change, rather, the change would be imposed on them. They both knew that change was only truly accepted when it was initiated by the people themselves.

John identified a second alternative; to hire a public relations company to create a convincing advertising campaign around the new global vision and promote it within the worldwide Analog division. Alison agreed that this would be a better way to convince people than the training approach. However, it entailed the hiring of an external organization to facilitate an internal change. This went against Motorola's principles. Moreover, here again, the employees would not be intimately involved.

The third option was to involve all Analog employees around the world in the conception and implementation of a "shared vision." This ambitious alternative was clearly favored by Alison and John. Creating a shared vision was a totally new concept. It did not mean having Marco's ideas communicated to all employees; it meant asking all employees for their vision for Analog and integrating those values into a common statement. The idea was to facilitate a "visioning process," which would require that managers and employees from ten different countries develop a consensus on the future of the division. Alison realized that creating a shared vision would constitute a long process. The potential benefits, however, were tremendous. If the visioning process succeeded, the whole division would be focused toward one commonly created vision. The division would work more efficiently and faster as a global team. Alison and John prepared a proposal on developing a shared common vision. The task was not easy. The problem was to come up with a process that could involve all 2,200 employees.

When they explained their idea to Marco at their next meeting, he was enthusiastic about the idea of a visioning process. He immediately backed the proposal. In several brainstorming sessions after that meeting, Marco, Alison, and John tried to determine how they could get the Analog people excited about the idea and how the process could be designed. It was anticipated that the visioning process would probably have to last between one and two years to involve as many employees as possible. The three had agreed that this process should build on rather than replace the existing mission and objectives that at that point existed within Motorola, i.e., the objective stated by CEO George Fisher that Motorola be the finest company in the world. Marco and his team, though, knew that "finest" might have various interpretations in various cultures. They intended to explore these differences when developing their own Analog vision.

Designing the Visioning Process

Alison and John began to design the initial process for the development of the vision. An external consultant helped on the macro design. At first it was agreed that all employees would be involved either directly and/or indirectly in the visioning process. After reviewing the task it was decided that it was logistically and economically not feasible to bring together 2,200 people. Instead, the Analog country managers (in charge of Analog in each country), along with the Motorola Country general managers (in charge of all the divisions of Motorola in each country) would be directly involved. This was seen as a practical goal, because these managers already had two strategy meetings a year.

Initially, three "visioning phases" were planned. Each phase would last six months and would be started with a special visioning meeting, piggybacking the strategic meeting that involved the worldwide Analog top-management twice a year. The managers would then have the task of communicating the results of the process to their employees at home. The employees were to give their opinions, comments, and suggestions for improvements. Each phase would end when the managers met again six months later and share the insights they had gained from their employees. Alison and John hoped that by the end of the third phase the division would have developed a finalized shared vision statement. This arrangement of piggybacking the strategic meeting was preferred because it allowed the company to limit the costs of the visioning process.

Alison, John, and Marco assumed that, over time, the managers would understand and support this well-designed visioning process. They did not see the ten different cultures represented as an obstacle. Alison hoped that there would be an understanding of the need of leadership and vision. She was, at the time, not overly concerned with the way the managers would communicate the visioning process to their employees in the different countries. The vision idea was, at least in the beginning, a U.S. initiative. She hoped that none of the participants felt this process was imposed on them. For all these reasons it was of utmost importance not to rush the process.

Developing and Implementing the Global Vision

Phase One: Phoenix, October 1991

In late October 1991, thirty-two managers from the ten Analog plants gathered in Phoenix, Arizona for a two-day visioning meeting. Alison and John developed two objectives for that first visioning meeting. First, they wanted to begin to form the various managers into a global team. They knew that it was absolutely necessary to convince the general managers that this process was important to the future of the division. Second, Alison and John wanted them to work on the identification of so-called "essence words" that would be the backbones of the future global vision. Prior to the meeting, the participants were asked to read Kenichi Ohmae's book *The Borderless World*.

To achieve these objectives Alison and John developed a procedure in which participants would work in multicultural teams. These team ventures were reconstituted frequently to encourage a constant exchange of ideas between all managers. This had another advantage in that the managers for the first time really got to know each other. At the end of the first phase the team effort had developed several essence words in English that would be shared by each country manager with his or her local employees. The essence words were:

Global Teamwork	Leadership	Esprit d' Equipe
Unity	Personal Growth	Helping Each Other
Helping Others	Trust	Premier/Finest
Global Family	Respect	
Innovation	Mutual Understanding	

Alison and John knew that the greatest problems during phase one would center around management expectations. All of the thirty-two participants wanted to finish the discussion as quickly as possible. At first, the managers regarded the visioning process as a task to be completed in the same way they completed their daily tasks. Alison remembered one manager saying: "All right, so let's get started. We should be able to come up with a sentence by the end of the day." Also, most of the people believed that a vision was imposed, and, therefore, expected the activities in this first meeting to be "a lot of fluff." The meeting was perceived by most participants as being part of a Motorola training program. One other comment that John heard was: "The company wants top management to get more training." Here again the meeting was seen more as an exercise. Most of it would be soon forgotten. However, once the activities started, the managers discovered they enjoyed the process of talking to and learning about each another. This allowed Alison and John to view this meeting as a success.

Furthermore, Alison and John also had to consider the varying levels of written and spoken English. To accommodate everybody the processes had to be slowed down to avoid losing lose part of the group that typically consisted half of Americans and half of people from other countries. Non-Americans had difficulty with the constant use of English and dialogue was necessary to clarify the meaning of each essence word. For example, the word "family" had very different meanings from culture to culture. For Japanese and Korean managers to be a family meant that each of them would be willing to give up his or her life for the company. On the other hand, for Americans or French it had connotations such as unity, bonds, or nucleus. Asians were more reluctant to use this word. Long discussions were necessary to reach a common understanding of all the essence words' meanings.

Immediately following the phase one meeting, Alison and John discussed the results of the first meeting. John at one point said, "I am convinced that with all these discussions and exchanges, all the managers have a common understanding on what each of the essence words means to the division." In a communique sent to the participants of the phase one meeting, Alison tried to summarize the main findings and to provide guiding questions for the managers to use when sharing the results of this meeting with their respective organizations. Most importantly, Alison stressed that the words selected were less important than the spirit and the shared experiences that generated the words.

Between Phase One and Phase Two

Alison and John knew that the most critical part of the first phase was in the communication of the essence words to all employees in each of the Analog plants. Theoretically, the two effectiveness consultants' role was to ensure that the feedback process was carried out in each country. However, Marco, John, and Alison decided that it should not become a performance issue when a manager failed to involve his or her employees in the process. Marco pointed out: "We will not control our people's actions, we have to build trust and convince them of the necessity of this process." Only a voluntary compliance based on the understanding of the importance of this process would lead to the desired results.

Consequently, the involvement of employees differed from country to country. It was a challenge for most managers to transmit the experience of this first meeting to their people. How could they explain and communicate the discussions shared by managers from ten countries? Whereas the meeting in Phoenix had been planned for them by Alison and John, the country managers were responsible for creating an appropriate feedback process at home. Because Alison and John could not in person facilitate the visioning processes in the different countries, this created a psychological barrier for many managers of non-U.S. operations. Alison and John tried to help the managers as much as possible by putting together an English video and information material including presentation transparencies and a summary of the meeting.

For the U.S. Analog managers who participated in the first meeting, Alison and John were able to take part in the feedback process. Outside the U.S. the various countries took different approaches. The Japanese organization, for example, brought in an external human resources consultant, while the French felt they knew how to handle the task on their own. Neither Alison nor John knew how the essence words were communicated to and evaluated by the employees in the different countries.

Another important issue was the question of continuity. Because Marco had just been promoted to vice-president and general manager of the Analog division, all country managers were eager to attend the first visioning meeting and meet Marco. Therefore, they all participated in the activities. Nevertheless, Alison and John felt that, although most of the participants liked the activities, many of them did not believe that this visioning process represented a significant, long-term change. This attitude also constrained the feedback process. John estimated that only 30% of the participants really did a good job of duplicating the visioning process in their home country following phase one.

Phase Two: Tokyo, March 1992

The managers from the various country facilities met again for two days in Tokyo in March 1992 to bring to the group the feedback from their respective Analog employees. The Japanese Analog division was very honored to host the strategic and visioning meetings because the costs of holding a meeting in Tokyo under normal circumstances would have been prohibitive. The decision to hold the meeting in Tokyo was of symbolic importance and meant to stress the idea of global family.

At this meeting, Alison and John had planned first to develop a rough vision statement using the input from the worldwide Analog organizations, and, second, to start aligning the regional and local mission statements with the vision. To develop a draft of the vision, the participants were divided into six cross-cultural groups. Each of the groups had to review the feedback packages and combine the suggestions into one draft global vision statement. These six vision statements were then shared with the group as a whole. Then, the group discussed how each statement would strengthen the Analog division globally and how far it would build opportunities for the division. In the following session, six new groups were formed. Their task was to integrate these six statements developed by the first teams into one statement. The new set of six statements was then, in a final step, integrated into one rough global vision statement by the group as a whole. The Analog division wanted to be:

> An innovative, responsive and trustworthy global family achieving leadership and mutual prosperity by benefiting our customers, employees and communities.

Based on the shared understanding of the essence concepts, this draft of the vision was developed in five languages including English. Alison and John had told the participants: "We do not want the different countries to have a translated version of the English vision. We want you to develop the Analog vision in your language based on the common understanding of the essence words." Each of the participants was responsible for verifying that the feedback on the essence words received after the first meeting from her/his organization at home was well represented in the statement.

The following day, participants identified how their work and their organizations would have to change to implement the global vision statement. Furthermore, it was their task to review the compatibility between the first vision draft and their regional and functional missions. For this task they used the following set of questions that Alison and John had prepared.

Task One (Friday Evening):
1. Review the Phase One Feedback Packet suggestions from Analog organizations and the ideas from the story board.
2. Are the suggestions clear? Listen for understanding.
3. Based on all suggestions, decide, identify, or recommend what the critical elements of the vision statement should be.
4. Write the suggestions into one global vision statement.

Large Group Process Guide—Review the suggested statements and test against the following questions:
How will this statement strengthen us globally?
How will this statement build opportunities for us all?

Task Two (Friday Evening):
Using the suggested statements and outcomes from the previous discussion, write a recommended global vision statement.

Process guideline—As a large group, integrate final six statements into one statement.

Task Three (Homework—Friday Evening):
1. As a representative of your organization, you are responsible for reviewing the suggested Global Vision Statement from the suggestions your organizations

and the knowledge you have of your organizations ideas about the global vision. Are the ideas and suggestions from your organization well represented?

2. Prepare for tomorrow's discussion by having examples of the following: If this were your global statement . . . If successfully carried out, what might be some results for

- My organization
- My culture
- My country
- My employees
- Motorola
- Myself as a leader

Task Four (Saturday Morning):

Working in a group which represents your function or region, prepare and agree upon a process plan that will ensure that the global vision is shared with your organization in such a way that employees begin to carry out the vision and have the opportunity to react to this recommended statement. Use the following suggested questions:

- How will the global vision help me in my work?
- Will I work differently than I have up until now?
- How will we be diffcrent than we were before within Bipolar Analog?

Identify critical steps and set dates

Task Five (Saturday Afternoon):

1. Discuss your mission with others to ensure clarity
2. Review your regional/functional mission with respect to the global vision. Are there any missing elements with respect to aligning the global vision?
3. Identify and record any adjustments which must be made by you and your organization to ensure alignment.
4. Briefly share your thoughts, ideas or suggestions with the whole group.

Task Six (Saturday Afternoon):
Individual Reflection

Your next task will be to develop a plan for your organization to address alignment of your mission with the global vision. In preparation for that discussion take some time to think about the many discussion points you have shared and heard today.

- What have been the most important or valuable things you have experienced as a participant in a shared visioning process?
- How can you ensure that people in your organization learn the same things?
- What challenges do your organization and Analog face in successfully implementing the global vision?
- How should the mission alignment process be coordinated with the plan you developed to share the global vision?

- What has to be decided upon before you can involve your organization in the alignment process?
- What have you discovered to be familiar or in common across the Analog organization with respect to your mission?

Task Seven (Saturday Afternoon):

1. Working in a group that represents your region or function, using what you have learned from your individual reflection, develop a process plan that will align the various missions of your group with the global vision.
2. Identify critical steps and set dates
3. Be prepared to share your entire plan with the whole group.

(The entire plan includes the work of this morning on the process plan to share the global vision as well as the plan to ensure mission alignment with the vision.)

Whereas almost all of the tasks were tackled in teams, the participants individually had to develop a procedure for their organizations to address the alignment of their local mission with the global vision. In all these activities, which can be considered the first steps of the implementation process, Alison emphasized setting deadlines by which the changes in structure, systems and behaviors within the organizations should be implemented.

Although, in retrospect, she considered this meeting in Tokyo a success, Alison remembered all the problems she and John encountered. First, the decision to let some Japanese Analog employees who had not attended the first meeting in Phoenix participate created some confusion and delay, because the newcomers did not understand why all this was happening. As a result, a few confused participants left the room or did not come back the second day. Alison and John did not consider this to be detrimental to the process.

Furthermore, a polarization in some of the smaller groups was noticed. The groups stuck to their interpretations and ideas and refused to further discuss other groups' statements. Alison was somewhat discouraged when one of the American participants said, "Our statement is the best, why should we discuss it?" In these cases Alison had to lead the participants back to the common ground, namely the essence words, they started from.

These problems made it difficult to keep the groups focused at times. Nevertheless, this meeting must be considered a milestone on the way to a global vision because Marco, Alison, and John recognized that visioning was a process that would not end on a certain date as they had first anticipated. Instead, the phases would continue indefinitely. Marco institutionalized the visioning meetings. They would occur after each strategic meeting, twice a year. Visioning was considered from then on as an ongoing process of positive change. This decision led to a change in the managers' attitude as they realized they were in for the long haul. Their commitment to the process and the implementation of the vision increased noticeably.

Between Phase Two and Phase Three

Having developed the vision statement in five languages, the returning managers did not have to concern themselves with translating the English version of the vision statement. During the second meeting they had individually developed a plan on how to share the experience they had had (see Task Six) and how to involve the employees in the alignment of their local mission statement with the global vision.

In line with these changes, the country managers also had to make sure that their employees started to adapt their systems and structures to the new vision. To facilitate these adjustments as much as possible Alison and John put together a package similar to the one distributed after the first phase. But this time the video was translated into French and Japanese. Furthermore, in preparation for the Phase Three meeting in Toulouse, Alison and John also asked each organization to come up with the symbol that best represents the work done thus far on the visioning process or the vision itself.

Phase Three: Toulouse, October 1992

When the managers met again in Toulouse in October 1992, it became clear that they had been rather successful in creating the vision statement at their last meeting in Tokyo. Almost all organizations in the various countries were satisfied with the rough version that had been developed in Tokyo. Only two minor adjustments were necessary. The finalized English vision statement expresses what the Analog division wants to be:

"A spirited, innovative, responsive and trustworthy global family achieving leadership and mutual prosperity by benefiting our customers, ourselves, and communities."

Looking back at the final wording of the vision, Alison had to smile when she read the words "mutual prosperity." "Prosperity" was a word the Japanese and Korean had fought for. The Americans had preferred the word "success." The Asians disliked the word success because it had a very strong monetary connotation. Prosperity was more long-term oriented and broader in meaning. When she looked at the French draft of the vision, she remembered the comment of the country manager: "In France, we have leaders, but the word leadership does not exist. I have to change the sentence a little so that it fits." She realized once more that the words by themselves were meaningless. The meaning of the vision was the key to the whole process. She was almost sure that by the third meeting everybody understood the vision.

The development of the final statement in all languages was postponed until after the Phase Three meeting. Based on this achievement, Alison and John wanted the group to get a good grasp of what the vision meant in the various cultures. This was particularly aimed at developing the division into a global family that would understand that each culture had unique differences and strengths. For the third meeting, all the managers were asked to bring a symbol that would best represent the shared vision they had developed with their peers. To instill this mutual understanding, Alison once again split up the large group into six smaller groups.

Within these teams, each of the participants had to share what symbol he or she had brought and in what way it represented the vision. For example, one manager from India showed a picture of a salad bowl and explained, "We selected this symbol because we are not a melting pot, but individuals with our own rights. Therefore, this compares well with a good salad that consists of many different ingredients each of them contributing to the whole. So, we are all ingredients of a big salad to which the seasoning is added in form of a global shared vision and a global strategy." A French participant brought a drawing that showed two hands reaching out for each other. He stated, "These two hands reaching out for each other symbolize relationships between two partners like wife and husband or supplier and customer. What we are trying to achieve with our vision is to close this gap between the hands." Expressing the vision in the form of a symbol allowed the participants to get a feel for what the vision really meant to the other culture. This procedure also exposed the participants to the cultural differences and strengths that would have otherwise been difficult to detect.

Having developed a global-shared vision and the necessary mutual understanding, the other main objective that was set for this meeting was to continue the implementation of the vision statement. The global team had already started this process during and after the Tokyo meeting. Local mission statements of each country organization were aligned with the global vision. This process was now pushed further by carrying out a global whole system assessment. This assessment was aimed at designing a strategy meeting that would be more efficient due to the implications and changes occasioned by the global vision. For this reason, this was the first of the semi-annual meetings in which the visioning meeting preceded the strategy meeting. Alison chose a set of questions regarding the task, the culture, and the structure and systems technology, that guided the group to make the strategy meeting more effective.

The same set of questions was used after the strategy meeting to find out how the process and the content of the strategy meeting could be enhanced. This was especially important because it was so easy to fall back into the old way of doing things. Therefore, this whole system assessment was vital in translating the vision into real behavioral changes.

Beyond Phase Three

At the end of December 1992, Marco, Alison, and John followed up Phase Three with an implementation package to facilitate the discussions within the country organizations. In a letter to the global leadership team of the Analog division Marco wrote:

It is critically important, as a leader of this change process, that you consistently present, participate in, and model to your organizations the spirit of the vision we have developed together. This next year will challenge us to be very creative in helping the organization to change the way it works.

Throughout the last year and a half, Alison has spent a lot of time thinking about whether or not the process was perceived to be successful in the various countries. She feared to some extent that the Americans were more positive than the Asians about the whole process. Did all the different countries feel the change in their organization? More importantly, does every Analog employee know and understand the shared vision? Have the managers been able to communicate to their people what was involved?

She now realized that the meeting in Manila would be another challenge. The division was now in the process of implementing the shared vision. Each of the plants had to change its systems and structures to be in line with the shared vision. She knew that the success of the implementation would primarily depend on how well the global vision was accepted and understood by each and every person in the global division.

15
Opening a Closed City: Challenges at the New Frontier

Joseph N. Lombardo

"They can give you all the cultural sensitivity lessons and teach you the basic pleasantries of the language, but nothing could have prepared me for this experience!" These were the thoughts going through Richard Albinson's mind as he took a few moments to reflect on his 5-month stay in Ukraine. Julie Warma, Rich's partner in his rapidly deteriorating consulting business, adjusted his tie while the beads of sweat rolled down the side of his face. The tramway bumped and rocked as it made its way down the ancient tracks into the downtown district of Dniepropetrovsk, Ukraine.

Not twenty minutes ago, Rich's translator, Alexander Ivanovich "Sasha" Savich, had called their employer, Gennady, and informed him that the North Americans were hiring a lawyer to settle the situation that had arisen. For reasons Rich was still having trouble figuring out, the relationship between Gennady and the couple had been in steady decline for the last ten days or so. Now, in a few moments Rich would have to walk into the offices of Trans Atlantic and face what would probably be a very hostile group of managers. He very much wished that the tramway was actually a subway car taking him to his home in suburban Montreal. What would he say? How could he possibly rectify the situation? Did he want to? What were the implications of terminating his "contract" with Trans Atlantic? Rich was too preoccupied to revel in the attention that he and Julie always drew to themselves when they went out in public in their business attire. "Well, no matter what happens," he thought, "it will all be over very shortly."

This case has been prepared as a basis for classroom discussion rather than to illustrate either effective or ineffective handling of an administrative situation. Certain names have been disguised to preserve confidentiality. The author would like to acknowledge Ms. Erin Brennan for invaluable contribution to this case.

History of Ukraine

The origins of Ukraine can be traced to the medieval Kievan Rus' state—the cradle of East Slavic culture that was founded in A.D. 38. When that state collapsed in the 13th century, its territory came under the control first of Lithuania, then of Poland. In the 17th century, Russia began incorporating parts of Ukraine and the tsars undertook intensive Russification campaigns. Subsequently, as these lands became a battleground between Russia and Poland, important religious, cultural, and political differences emerged between the eastern and western parts of Ukrainian territory. The western Ukraine, a largely Catholic area that became part of the USSR only in 1939, acquired a more independent-minded spirit while the largely Orthodox, Russified eastern part of the republic adhered to more conservative values.

After a brief period of independence from Russian rule (1918–1921), most of Ukraine was incorporated into the Soviet Union. More than 6 million Ukrainian peasants died during the collectivization of agriculture under Stalin and a famine brought on by forced grain confiscations. Armed resistance to both Nazi German and Soviet rule broke out during World War II, especially in the nationalistic western Ukraine. As young intellectuals revived the movement for Ukrainian rights in the 1960s and 1970s, the regime reacted with arrests and further oppression.

Second in size to the Russian economy among the former Soviet republics, the Ukrainian economy has substantial agricultural resources and a large and diverse industrial sector. Ukraine is largely self-sufficient in agricultural products and is a net exporter of meat, milk, grain, and vegetables. It is also endowed with a broad natural resource base including iron ore, coal, and manganese. The industrial sector generates about two fifths of the country's GNP, with agriculture contributing approximately one-fourth.

Ukrainian independence was restored on August 24, 1991. In a landslide national referendum on December 1, 1991, over 90% of Ukraine's population supported independence. Ukraine's population totals approximately 51.8 million, which is about 18% of the former Soviet Union. Ukraine is the fifth most populous country in Europe and is about 25% larger in square kilometers than France. Ukraine's ethnic composition is: 73% Ukrainian, 22% Russian, 1% Jewish and 4% other. Most of the Russian population is found in the eastern part of the country.

The New Frontier

Only planning to stay in the former Soviet Union for one month, Rich could not believe that five months had passed since he arrived in Dniepropetrovsk, a Ukrainian provincial capital city of more than 1 million people. Dniepropetrovsk was a closed city for most of the 20th century, for it was home to one of the key intercontinental ballistic missile (ICBM) factories in the former Soviet Union. The ICBM factory now made refrigerators and trolley buses, and the imposing facility, the size of about

7 football fields square, has become a testament to a failed past and a new beginning. Many residents boasted of the fact that not even the CIA knew of the existence of their city until the mid-1970s.

Before *glasnost,* living in a closed city had its definite disadvantages. Travel outside the city was forbidden, with the exception of traveling to a parent's funeral. If a brother or sister passed away in Moscow, for example, travel was denied. Business travel was a three-to-six-week experiment in frustration dealing with the government bureaucracy, and international travel was an even greater nightmare. When questioned about these practices, friends would comment, "that was the way it was." Rich had experienced the legacy of the closed city's bureaucracy while trying to mail packages home or when he tried to renew his visa every six weeks. Rich would later write home, "if there truly exists new and untouched frontiers in this world, this is certainly one of them."

Rich arrived in Dniepropetrovsk after having taught a three-week business fundamentals course in Minsk, Belarus. It was in this city that Rich, along with 12 other graduating students of a well known Canadian business school, taught introductory finance, marketing, and general management to Byelorussian students and executives. His original goal in Dniepropetrovsk was to teach an identical course to a group of senior executives of large state-run enterprises. If his experience in Minsk was to be any indication, Rich had his work cut out for him. Not many of his new students would be able to define profit, marketing strategy, or cost allocation.

Sensing an opportunity to continue the work of educating the Ukrainians on North American business practices, at the end of the three-week course Rich offered his consultancy services to his students. A married couple in the class were co-owners of an engineering firm named Trans Atlantic (TA), and they expressed an interest in having Rich work for them. Rich was shocked when he was informed by Sasha that the couple ran their own business, for they were doing poorly in class and he did not think they were going to earn their certificate of completion.

Rich thought Gennady a bit arrogant upon their first meeting in class. A fervent nationalist who spoke Russian only out of necessity, Gennady, who was in his late thirties, looked to Rich like the typical Ukrainian *mafioso* Sasha had taught him to identify. Gennady wore the same outfit every day, grey slacks, white shirt and a thin black tie. Together, Gennady and his wife Marina were part of Ukraine's growing entrepreneurial class of business people. Since the relaxation of the laws banning private business, workers in state-run companies used key contacts in government ministries and other state run companies to help start and fund new ventures. Before starting up Trans Atlantic, Marina was a housewife and Gennady was an engineer with the Black Sea Shipping Company. Always in a great hurry to get to a next appointment, the couple showed great zeal in their business undertakings.

The following day, the couple presented a list of projects they wanted Rich to undertake. Among the list of tasks to be accomplished were the following:

- Help establish business contacts with Singaporean firms in order to send high-technology hull-cleaning ships from the Black Sea.
- Open a bank.
- Find US $2 billion to fund a super-port project to be built on the Crimean Peninsula.
- Initiate contact with Japanese companies to sell them fish products from the Black Sea.
- Get information and initiate contacts with telecommunications suppliers to upgrade the company's (and province's) telephone system.

Rich thought of himself as a creative, resourceful person who rose to new and exciting challenges, and although he was taken aback by the scope of the projects, he accepted an offer to begin contract negotiations.

Contract Negotiations

Rich relied heavily on his friend and interpreter, Sasha, for his insight and information. He asked Sasha about the salary and benefits that were common for this type of work. "The highest paid executives in Ukraine make 30,000 coupons per month, was Sasha's reply, to which he added, "but I would not ask for this much, for Trans Atlantic does not have such money." As a benchmark, Rich used the compensation he was receiving for teaching; 10,000 coupons and room and board. He felt that if this amount of money and benefits was offered for three weeks for teaching a business course, then this should be the minimum acceptable level of compensation for the projects TA wanted him to complete. Words of support came from Sasha, who, upon viewing the ambitious plans that TA had in store, changed his mind and decided that TA was a very wealthy company. This was the extent of Rich's secondary research on the company. There was really no other source of information available given the inefficient bureaucracy and lack of a Dun and Bradstreet office in the area.

Knowing that the length of the contract would be one year, Rich contacted Julie Warma, who lived in Michigan, and asked her for her thoughts on the matter. Because of Julie's similar desire to gain international business experience, and because she had recently graduated with a degree in international management, it was decided during that phone call that every effort would be made to include Julie in the contract negotiations so that they could work together in Ukraine. After much deliberation and discussion with Sasha and another friend, Rich decided on the following set of conditions:

- 30,000 coupons per month for himself and Julie.
- Full room and board in the current suite.
- Reimbursement for 2 packages per month, either from Ukraine to North America or vice-versa. This was so that the couple's family could send food or other supplies that may be needed.
- Reimbursement for two long-distance calls to North America per month.
- An office for Julie and Rich with fax and computer.

Rich felt that these demands were fair and that they represented conditions that would offset hardships such as not having access to English newspapers, radio stations or newscasts, and the food. Having read somewhere of the Russian's hard line approach to negotiating, Rich viewed these set of demands as "ideal" and was prepared to symbolically "give in" where necessary.

The negotiations were spread out over 4 days and took place in the well-appointed conference room at the exclusive hotel of the former Communist Party's elite, the *Octyaberskaya*. Cognac, vodka, and Pepsi were available throughout the negotiations, as well as three-course meals, every day. All these factors impressed Rich, who began to think that maybe he was asking too little of his potential employers. Sasha received 2,000 coupons for his negotiation translations (Gennady and his wife spoke no English), the equivalent of about three weeks' salary.

The first three days consisted solely of discussions of the various projects that were to be undertaken, and although somewhat frustrated, Rich listened attentively and took many notes. Much time was also spent asking Rich about his goals, ambitions, education, and work experiences. The work to be carried out seemed like an immense amount, but Rich figured that given one year to complete the tasks, there should not be much problem in successfully seeing them through to completion.

Toward the end of the third day, Rich was asked to present his demands. Although initially surprised by the inclusion of Julie into the contract, the Ukrainians were happy to have another Western consultant on their payroll. The ease of negotiations and the amount of money spent on them gave Rich the impression that all his demands would be met. Sure enough, Gennady showed up the next day with contract in hand, which Rich readily signed and told Julie the good news. Unfortunately, neither Rich nor Julie would ever see the signed contract.

Beginning of the End

Things went along without major incident during the two and a half weeks before Julie's arrival. Rich made a relatively successful trip to Moscow with Sasha, where he met with several North American telecommunication companies' executives to gather information and discuss Ukrainian business opportunities, and dined with the Singaporian Commercial attache. Rich had been given train tickets and 5,000 rubles for expenses.

Julie's arrival at the Kiev airport was also handled well by TA. Gennady had a car waiting for Rich at the Kiev train station with two associates who would take him to his various appointments. Rich was only slightly surprised by the fact that the two men spoke absolutely no English. Through sign language and his Russian-English dictionary, Rich told the gentlemen that he had meetings at the American and Canadian embassies. He was to meet the respective commercial attaches to gather information on the financing of Ukrainian projects. After the meetings it was off to the airport to pick up Julie, a lavish dinner at a beautiful restaurant, and then back to the train station for the 10-hour train ride back to Dniepropetrovsk.

The next three weeks went smoothly for Julie and Rich. They had ample opportunity to explore the city and enjoy the cultural attractions together. Without more specific instructions from Gennady, there was not much work that could be done. Rich made the odd phone call to Asia or Moscow to get some information sent, but business did not proceed at an extraordinarily fast pace in a city where it took at least ten hours to place an international call, five for a regional call, and where there was only one fax in a city of over one million inhabitants. The postal system, although relatively efficient, was very slow and the couple had no computer or office space. "Had it not been for the incredible hospitality of the Ukrainians, we never would have achieved what we did," Julie commented. "When we needed to type out a letter to the Singaporean Port Authority, for example, we would have to politely ask the workers at the company that rented a room in the lobby of our hotel if we could use their computer. We spent more time in the company's office than some of the workers!" That was to be the couple's experience throughout, and despite any misgivings they may have developed through their relationship with Gennady and TA, the two would never forget how friendly and generous the Ukrainians were.

The couple had plenty of time on their hands because Gennady did not bother to meet with them for over 20 days. Julie finally met Gennady, more than three weeks after her arrival, when he showed up at the hotel with a beautiful (and expensive) bouquet of flowers for her. The meeting consisted of small talk and, after Julie mentioned to Rich that she wanted to know what her responsibilities were, Rich asked Sasha to forward her remark to Gennady. Gennady's response seemed arbitrary, "she will assist Rich."

Gennady then proceeded to explain that he would be gone for the next week on business. Rich pointed out the pressing need for more details on some of the projects, as well as more direction or focus on others, but the requests fell on deaf ears. Six weeks of teaching through a translator had taught Rich how to carefully explain his thoughts to Sasha to prevent confusion. Assuming their requests were getting properly translated, the couple could not understand Gennady's lack of response.

Hull Cleaning in Singapore, An Exercise in Frustration

Among the various projects to be completed was one that involved starting up a hull cleaning operation in Singapore. Gennady had control over two hull cleaning ships and their crews in the Black Sea, which he said would most certainly be able to clean ships faster and more efficiently than any current method. He wanted the Singaporean market explored because he was aware of the great volume of ships anchored in its ports at any one time. There were no other instructions. The questions Rich and Julie would have to answer would be: How many men on each crew? How much do they get paid? How much food and water is needed on board to get to Singapore? Were these ships ocean-going? What accommodations would these crew members need in Singapore? What licenses were needed? What was the potential market for hull cleaning? All these questions could have been answered in one or two full working days in North America, but with the lack of basic business survival tools, it took months in Ukraine. A call to the Singaporean Port Authority, for example, had to be ordered 10 hours in advance and would generally come in the middle of the night. If the number was busy or wrong, the whole process had to be repeated the next day. It took approximately eight business days and nights to get through to the proper person, who then sent out the information by mail, which took almost a month to arrive.

Disappointments

Two months had gone by and Rich and Julie did not receive their promised office, fax, or computer. They also realized by this time that chances were slim of ever acquiring these items given their relative scarcity anywhere outside of Kiev. The couple kept inquiring as to when they may expect the items, but all they received were assurances that they were "expected shortly." Gennady rarely showed up for scheduled meetings at the hotel, sometimes making Julie and Rich wait in their rooms for days. A further frustration for Julie was Gennady's lack of acknowledgment of her presence at any meeting, which was as equally frustrating as Sasha's habit of only addressing Gennady's remarks to Rich. Many requests put to Sasha did not rectify the situation.

When Gennady appeared for a meeting he would announce the results of his latest deals. One day it would be the acquisition of two cargo trucks that would help haul various products in from other Eastern European countries, another day it would be the installation of a satellite dish at his office. Because of Gennady's unreliability, Rich and Julie would seldom bother to put on their business attire for his arrival. A nice pair of shorts and a polo shirt were the standard fair for the sporadic meetings with Gennady. Rich and Julie would explain to him their accomplishments since the last meeting, and ask for further information. Gennady stiffened and always looked very serious when the couple would recount how difficult it had been working through the Ukrainian phone or postal system. Gennady was becoming frustrated at the slow pace of operations, despite Julie and Rich's constant reminders that "things cannot proceed here as they do in North America."

Among the more humorous and interesting experiences, Rich and Julie had to deal with were the cleaning ladies who liked to sample the various colognes and other toiletries. More often than not, Rich would walk up the stairs to their rooms and smell his cologne or after shave throughout the hallway. Rich also found that if he had any packages of chewing gum lying around, several pieces would invariably go missing while he was out teaching or eating dinner. Sasha explained to him that the cleaning ladies, most of them *Babushkas* (grandmothers), must be taking the pieces as small gifts for their grandchildren, who must have developed a taste for the flavor. Julie noted that cinnamon was most preferred, with peppermint usually having the most chance of not being touched. Although upset at first, Rich accepted these as part of the trials and tribulations of the only resident foreigners.

Vladimir Pakno and the Large Pond

Dniepropetrovsk is a city of over 1.1 million people. However, having been closed for so long, an event such as two North American business people coming to live in the city was common knowledge within days. Vladimir Pakno was an entrepreneur who formed agricultural cooperatives and privatized state farms. He had heard about the couple's presence in the city and sought out a meeting. This was fine with Julie and Rich, for perpetually waiting for Gennady to show up or call back was immensely boring.

Pakno was an amiable person with a great sense of humor. He discussed his operations at length with the couple and then asked for their help in finding contacts who would be willing to sell wheat to Ukraine. "I have never heard of Trans Atlantic," he told the couple, "they are a small fish in a large pond. I am a big fish." With that, Pakno slapped his large belly and laughed. Not only were the tasks interesting to Rich and Julie, but the potential for profit was great. The couple continued to have meetings with Pakno and started to do some preliminary research through the American embassy in Moscow.

Drowning in the Pond

Rich and Julie's hotel bills and phone bills were paid regularly by a transfer of funds from Trans Atlantic's account to the hotel's account. At about the same time that Rich and Julie's second pay was due, eight weeks into the contract, the funds stopped being transferred and the couple's bills began to pile up. Thinking this was a regular occurrence given the incredibly slow bureaucracy, the couple did not worry until the hotel director started to demand the money from them. Gennady, as usual, could not be found, so the couple stalled the director for a week until their boss decided to drop in.

It was during this visit that Gennady informed the couple that he wanted to change the contract. He could no longer afford to pay the couple's room and board and he wanted to renegotiate. Julie and Rich countered that they would be more than willing to negotiate once they received their pay. Gennady left, seemingly in agreement with the pair's demands.

The next day the couple received another visit by an employee of TA. A former student of Rich's, and TA's new accountant, Ludmila (Luda) Chornyk, stopped in at the hotel unannounced. "She was one of my better students," Rich told Julie, "It should be easy working with her." Rich was sadly mistaken. Luda's first words were harsh, "I demand a report on what you have accomplished since you began work for TA." Taken aback, but still firmly in control of his temper, Rich retorted, "When the issue of pay and compensation is dealt with, you will most surely receive whatever you wish, Ms. Chornyk." Things were beginning to get out of control, "You will not receive a cent from this company until I see this report," Luda replied smugly. "I've created a monster," thought Rich as Luda began to criticize the pace of their work and question their ability as consultants for TA. Finally, Rich had had enough. "You are not the person for whom I work, and if Gennady is so displeased with our work, he will tell us himself. Thank you for coming by." Luda left the room and slammed the door. The meeting was quite a shock to Rich and Julie, who were convinced that they were not going to get paid for the work that they had performed, nor receive compensation for the bills they would undoubtedly have to pay if TA decided not to transfer the funds. Although Rich could draw money from his savings in Canada, this would require a 16-hour train trip to Moscow to get to a hotel that advanced cash on his Visa card. The couple was getting short on cash and very nervous.

Valentina the Lawyer

A friend Rich had made while walking through downtown one afternoon paid an unexpected visit shortly after the meeting with Luda. Serghiy was a nice fellow who spoke English fluently. The couple explained their predicament and mentioned that they probably could use a good lawyer. A broad smile crossed Serghiy's face while he explained to his new friends about Dniepropetrovsk's only private lawyer, Valentina Volovik.

It was hard to believe that Julie and Rich were about to begin discussions with a lawyer and potentially start legal proceedings in a foreign country. The couple was convinced that they were not going to be taken advantage of and decided to talk to the lawyer as a precaution. At their meeting, Rich and Julie found Valentina to be warm and friendly with good business sense. Because it was only an introductory meeting, the couple refrained from asking too many questions about their rights and potential courses of action. Instead, they were asked many questions about themselves by Valentina. They were to find out from the lawyer later on that she asked the questions to determine if they were 'good' people or not. Valentina did not work with anyone that did not answer her questions properly.

"Trans Atlantic is an ill company," were Valentina's first words at their following meeting, a day later. "All Ukrainian companies are ill companies," she continued. She was referring to the fact that there were not many business people that understood what it meant to do business in an open market economy. A company like TA was no different, despite Gennady and Marina's propensity to enroll in business courses. The company had no working knowledge of their cash balance or profits for any given period. It was made clear to the consultants that the contract they had signed was only a "gentlemen's agreement" and not a real contract because it failed to include several key clauses as required by Ukrainian law. But, because of the consultant's work it could be argued that they had demonstrated good faith and should be compensated. The meetings, for the moment, were purely informational, Julie and Rich had not hired Valentina, nor did they wish to sue Gennady. They just wanted to explore their options.

The Last Gasp

Gennady showed up one week after Luda's visit to inform the couple that he would not pay the hotel room or the phone bills because they had gone against the spirit of the contract by agreeing to assist another company in Dniepropetrovsk. This confused Rich, because there was no such clause, nor was one discussed. Rich was floored by Gennady's remarks, but told him that if he wanted, the month-end report would be written and all materials would be handed over to TA in good faith. Gennady then proceeded to imply that as a result of their other dealings, the consultants were not accomplishing anything for TA. A cut in pay, a signing of an exclusivity clause, and the omitting of room and board from the contract were essential to continuing relations with TA. The meeting ended rather badly for Gennady did not even bother to shake Rich's hand, as was his custom.

A few hours later, the fateful phone call came. Sasha had misunderstood Rich's instructions and called Gennady and told him of the couple's plans to hire Valentina. Before he hung up, he told the couple that it would be best if they found another translator. Knowing that Sasha would be going to the Trans Atlantic office, Rich and Julie put on their best business attire and ran for the tramway to try to straighten things out.

16
Confrontation or Collaboration: Two Strong Executives

Robert T. Moran

North American Industrial Mining

In his office at North American Industrial Mining (NAIM), Mr. James Richardson, president of the company, reflected upon a troubling situation facing the company. NAIM's relationship with a key German supplier, Wendland, had significantly deteriorated during the past few months and a serious conflict loomed on the horizon. Across the desk, equally pensive, Robert Miller, vice-president of Operations, listened closely.

"Rob," Richardson said, "I'm the person to either patch this thing up or break it up with Herr Wolfgang Wallenburg of Wendland. This situation has dragged on for too long. I need information to deal with this conflict, but I have to go to St. Louis this week. While I'm gone, I want you to listen around, talk to the people who know what's going on, and give me some insight into our options for resolving the problem. And, I need it by Monday."

As he exited the office, Miller considered his next move. "Listening around a little" would require most of his time during the remainder of the week. A good start, he decided, would be to learn more about Germany and German society, because cultural differences seemed to be a significant part of the problem. Next, he intended to interview the employees and associates who were familiar with the conflict with Wendland and its president, Herr Wallenburg. Finally, by Friday, Miller would

---

This case is to be used as a vehicle for discussion rather than to illustrate whether the effective or ineffective handling of business situations. The situation is actual but disguised at the request of the organization.

outline the alternatives available to Richardson and assist in developing a strategy for the upcoming meeting with Wallenberg.

German Culture

Germany, Miller read in a brief country description, is a small country with a population of approximately 79 million. The crowding of many citizens into an area the size of Montana and the exceptionally homogeneous nature of German society result in an environment characterized by strong pressure to conform to societal norms and to adhere to prescribed rules, both formal and informal. Correctness, or the desire to act within the proper bounds of society, however, in no way implies that Germans are anxiously polite. In fact, they do not hesitate to voice a dissenting opinion to other Germans or foreigners when they disagree. However, while German culture deftly shapes the values and behavior of German men and women, much variation in character, temperament, and personality exists.

Germans are described as a serious people, in both private and work settings. This does not mean, however, that they lack humor, only that intense social pressure contributes to a reluctance to appear silly or frivolous. German executives are characterized as highly disciplined, well-educated, neat, and orderly.

Problem-solving in the German culture is conducted according to a precise process, beginning with thorough attempts at acquiring a full understanding of the relevant issues. Conflict and controversy are viewed, not as disagreeable or undesirable, but as necessary to understand a situation clearly. German determination and perseverance result in a tendency to aggressively pursue and adhere to the implementation of an alternative once selected, even if strong evidence exists that the chosen solution may no longer be the most favorable course of action. Germans may continue according to the chosen strategy, unless and until overwhelming evidence proving its undesirability is obtained.

Fair, direct, industrious, and "perfectionists" are other labels assigned to Germans. German directness and frankness are valued by friends and associates, though relations with the Germans are characterized by an absence of social "chit-chat," particularly noticeable in the work environment. German thoroughness in all things great and small is the antithesis of the casual, friendly and unstructured American informality, a difference sometimes responsible for conflict between the two cultures. However, most Americans agree that, while considerable time and effort is required to establish friendships with German counterparts, the endeavor is worthwhile.

Similarly, the German perception of Americans reflects both positive and negative behavioral aspects. Many Germans perceive Americans as overly familiar, historically and politically naive, not particularly well-educated, narrow-minded, and too self-confident. Balancing these negatives, however, is the impression of Americans as friendly, resourceful, energetic, innovative, and successful in business. American society is respected for its resiliency and proven ability to bounce back from difficult times.

Germans are meticulous in keeping appointments and adhering to schedules, an aspect of German culture that contributes to its reputation for efficiency. This tendency to organize the time allotted for activities, in work or relaxation, to optimize efficiency, is accompanied by strict attention to schedules. Thus, a German executive's day is well-structured and productive, although this passion for organization often prevents the typical German from acting spontaneously.

Contributing further to a lack of flexibility within the German corporate environment is the organizational structure of German enterprises. Highly compartmentalized, a facet that contributes to several organizational deficiencies, the German structure inhibits and sometimes constrains information flow. Often, developments of great importance within an organization are known to only a few key individuals. Thus, the ability to quickly and effectively respond to problems within the company and changes in the competitive environment is somewhat impeded.

Privacy and security are important concepts in German culture. Executive offices remain locked at night, with all working papers and reports secured in desks and filing cabinets at the end of each day. Security is rigid and strictly enforced.

In German society, statements, verbal and written, may constitute an unintended commitment. Legally, if an individual can prove that a promise was made or even intimated, though a contract may not have been signed, it is possible to be held liable. This is one explanation for German exactness in business dealings and for the less casual, more distant relationships among associates and partners.

NAIM and Wendland

In 1977, North American Industrial Mining, operated nine mines and employed more than 10,000 persons. NAIM contracts with Wendland, a German supplier, for the provision of PM2's and PM3's, expensive electronic equipment crucial to the mining process. Relations with Wendland are severely strained at present as a result of continual problems with the PM2's and PM3's produced by Wendland's subcontractor, Medici.

After submersing himself in his study of German culture, Miller telephoned John Radislav, a manager with Louisiana Engineering Company and an individual Miller regarded as capable of offering excellent insight into the conflict.

Radislav began with a brief summary of the history of Wendland:

> A number of years ago after Mr. Hahn, the controlling owner of Wendland, died. Mr. Wolfgang Wallenburg took over. At the time, the department heads failed to cooperate and work as a team, sales had declined significantly and product quality and labor problems were rampant. In short, the company was in serious danger of failing, but Mr. Wallenburg turned the situation around.

The Conflict

The problems resulting in the conflict facing NAIM and Wendland can be traced directly to a contractual relationship between Wendland and Medici, a primary Wendland supplier. Medici, the developer of the PM2 electronic systems that NAIM purchases from Wendland, conducts 95% of its business with Wendland. Also, Medici's control over the PM2 market further binds the two companies to one another.

Though the two firms are highly interdependent, Medici's contract to manufacture the PM2's and PM3's for Wendland is now on the line. The production problems causing the controversy center upon the persistent failing of the electronics in the PM2 due to moisture in the system. A new model, the PM3, was developed at additional cost but did not fit the specifications of the previous system.

However, negating the contract with Medici has proven extremely difficult. Essentially, Wendland is caught in a problem-ridden marriage to its supplier. Subcontracting with another company to develop the electronics components would be prohibitively expensive for Wendland's customers and could result in the loss of important clients, including NAIM. Still, the contract between Wendland and Medici is in danger of dissolution.

In the spring of 1990, some time after these problems emerged, Wendland hired Mr. Fritz Kohl to solve the electronics issue, because he had assisted in solving similar problems for NAIM in the past. During the process, Kohl, a technical genius though lacking in interpersonal skills, acted in a highly confrontational manner with Medici, furthering souring relations between Wendland and its supplier. Mr. Kohl, after burning the already fragile straw bridge between Wendland and Medici, was subsequently fired by Mr. Wallenburg.

Recently, confrontations between Wendland and Medici have intensified. Medici has contacted customers directly, completely circumventing Wendland and resulting in threats of lawsuits by the company.

To date, the defective PM2's have been repaired by a Wendland subsidiary, Western Mining Corporation (WMC). Located in West Virginia, WMC is responsible for maintaining and repairing Wendland's products; however, the company lacks the capacity to repair the incoming PM2's quickly enough. During the summer of 1991, WMC informed Wendland that it would be recalling all PM2's and replacing them with a new version of the PM3.

From NAIM's perspective, the situation has become unacceptable and must be resolved during the meetings between Mr. Wallenburg and Mr. Richardson scheduled in the United States on October 23 and 24.

Key Player Profiles

After his discussion with Radislav, Miller contacted Edward Copeland to expand the perspective he had partially developed through his conversations the previous day. Copeland also was well-acquainted with Wallenburg through numerous dealings with him in various circumstances and previous visits to Germany. His description of the situation and the individuals involved complemented that provided by Radislav.

According to both Radislav and Copeland, Wolfgang Wallenburg is a methodical and purposeful individual. Emotionally, he is stable and rarely defensive. Though interested in and open to the opinion of others, Wallenburg is essentially an authoritarian leader with a reputation as a driven taskmaster. Miller noted that this was a characteristic Wallenburg shared with Richardson.

Wallenburg approaches decision-making tasks in a cautious manner, refusing to commit to a course of action without full and complete knowledge of all relevant circumstances and the related financial implications. In particular, he evaluates options on the basis of economics and views cost as an important factor in selecting the best alternative.

As head of Wendland, Wallenburg is credited for turning around a failing company that he at first knew little about and building it into a successful organization. He is committed to manufacturing quality products, but the bureaucracy of NAIM makes this difficult and follow-up is lacking in Wendland at this time.

After speaking with Radislav and Copeland, a profile of Herr Wallenburg as a dedicated and hard-working professional emerged. At the end of his investigation, Miller concluded that Wallenburg had probably attempted to mend Wendland's relationship with Medici, but had simply been unsuccessful thus far.

On the other hand, Miller was less sure about the motives of Medici's president, Karl Strobel. Strobel, though brilliant perhaps to the point of genius, is insecure as a result of his failure to earn a German engineering degree. In the past, Strobel has been caught in lies by NAIM associates and, thus, is less than trustworthy.

James Richardson, like Wallenburg, is professional, dedicated and honest. However, in contrast to his counterpart at Wendland, Richardson is more emotional and prone to bursts of anger. Miller fears that, given Richardsons' intense frustration with the problems caused by the defective PM2s, NAIM's president may further damage the relationship with Wendland, though, in Miller's opinion, it may still be salvageable.

Conclusion

Though Miller felt that his research during the past few days had provided excellent insight into the conflict between NAIM and Wendland and between Wendland and Medici, he knew this was only the initial step in resolving the crisis. Before Monday, he still had a number of issues to address. Could the relationship with Wendland be salvaged? If so, how? What assistance could NAIM offer to help Wendland solve its dilemma with Medici? Miller sighed and said, "There goes my golf game this weekend."

17
AT&T: Technically Brilliant But Interculturally Average

Cheryl Johnson
and
Carolyn S. Younker

AT&T International

With a satisfied look on his face, Henry Kline, vice-president of Ventures and Alliances for AT&T International, hung up the phone. The AT&T Italian office had just informed him that the Italtel bid had finally been approved by the necessary Italian government agencies. AT&T had been selected to enter into a partnership with the state-owned telecommunications equipment manufacturer; gaining the requisite governmental approvals had been the final hurdle in securing the project. After a long and competitive bidding process, Kline was elated to learn that AT&T had finally gained the chance to establish a genuine foothold in the European market.

Henry Kline had been with AT&T for more than 21 years. After obtaining a Ph.D. in engineering, he joined the company which at that time monopolized the telecommunications industry and operated according to a narrow domestic focus. However, increasing opportunities and competition in the global environment necessitated a restructuring of AT&T's international operations. As a result, in 1987, AT&T International was divided into a number of business units, one of which was Ventures and Alliances (V&A). Since accepting his present position as head of V&A, Kline had become increasingly aware of the need to transform AT&T's cor-

---

This case was written as a vehicle for discussion rather than to illustrate either the effective or ineffective handling of business situations. Although this case includes factual information based on actual situations it is presented in this form to facilitate classroom discussion.

179

porate image from that of a U.S. utility to that of a global telecommunications company, a difficult task indeed.

AT&T attempts to establish a strong European presence, which thus far had met with limited success, began in 1984. This year marked the loss of AT&T's monopolistic advantage and the beginning of a series of divestitures as the company struggled against domestic competition for the first time in its history. Progress toward evolving into a truly global corporation had been hindered by a number of high-profile mistakes primarily attributable to inexperience. Expensive lessons, including a hard-fought but failed French bid in 1987, overshadowed several small successes in other countries. At present, the future of a joint project with an Italian company, Olivetti, was in jeopardy and reinforced questions about the success of AT&T International.

Kline picked up the phone and dialed the office of Elizabeth Webber, director of product development and management. As AT&T's chances of securing the Italtel bid appeared increasingly favorable, Kline had been meeting regularly with members of Webber's unit to prepare for the expected alliance that would include joint research and development (R&D) activities.

"Elizabeth? . . . Henry here. Well, we won! I just got off the phone with our Italian office. We need to be in Italy next week to formalize the partnership. If we leave Monday, we can schedule negotiations for Wednesday."

"That's great! Just the news we've been waiting for. And Monday's fine. I'll pull the material together."

Thoughts raced through Webber's head as she finished the conversation. After receiving her degree in engineering from M.I.T. and working for several high-tech firms, she had joined AT&T five years ago at the age of 33. Her life, busy as of late following her promotion to head of her unit four months ago, would now become even more hectic with the upcoming Italtel project.

Webber proceeded to Kline's office, a large portfolio containing the Italtel bid and the department's strategy for joint product development with the Italian company in hand. The partnership's first priority was the upgrading of Italy's outdated telephone network. An investment of $25 to $30 billion had already been allocated toward equipment modernization by the Italian government, but Italtel lacked the necessary technology to complete the project. Realizing this deficiency, the company sought a partner with strong technological skills for the venture. Additionally, the Italian firm hoped to use the project as a foundation that would establish the groundwork for more such partnerships to pursue expansion opportunities throughout Europe.

"Henry, do you have a few minutes?" she queried.

"Come on in," he said. "I was just looking over some of the records from our first venture in Italy. As you know, at present the Olivetti project is no more than an official relationship on paper. We are trying to delicately withdraw from the venture without creating any more animosity, especially from the Italian politicians. If nothing else, we have learned a lesson about the importance of the government in doing business in Italy."

The Olivetti Venture

A few years ago, AT&T entered into an agreement with an Italian company, Olivetti, to produce and market one another's computer products. AT&T purchased 25% of Olivetti's stock, with an option to increase ownership to 40%, received five seats on the board and gave Olivetti's president a seat on AT&T's board. Like AT&T, Olivetti aspired to evolve into a global player and knew that a stronger position in the U.S. was critical to meeting that goal. Access to AT&T's technology was also a key motivation for pursuing the joint venture.

In the beginning stages of the project, the venture proceeded smoothly. Near the end of 1986, Olivetti received full responsibility for the design and production of AT&T's low-end computers. Soon afterward, however, problems began surfacing on both sides. Most importantly, AT&T's Unix operating system failed to meet the shared expectations of both companies that it would successfully compete against IBM's DOS system. A primary reason for the alliance, these unmet expectations seriously threatened the viability of the joint venture.

Most of the computers produced overseas were exported for sale in the U.S.; the remainder were marketed in Italy. Unfortunately, reception by customers was less favorable than predicted, and actual sales were much lower than forecast. While this disappointed both firms, Olivetti was hit especially hard by the declining sales and a subsequent drop in the company's stock price. Last year, Olivetti abandoned the project and introduced its own line of minicomputers using a different operating system. These computers competed directly with AT&T products; thus, the company was forced to discontinue marketing Olivetti's computers in the U.S.

"Looking back," mused Kline, "control was probably a bigger issue than we realized. The way ownership was set up, it was apparent that Olivetti had no real authority over the product. Now, we are discreetly looking for another company to supply our computers. It's obvious that the primary reasons for our alliance no longer exist, and I'm sure Olivetti feels the same way."

"I didn't realize that the situation was that complicated," Webber interjected. "I hope the problems with Olivetti don't affect our meeting next week."

"Yes, me too," Kline concurred, "especially since Olivetti's influential chairman lobbied the Italian government in our favor for the Italtel bid. I'm sure hoping it won't be a problem, since the Olivetti parting seems mutual. We think that they are equally relieved that the alliance is coming to an end . . . So what did you come to see me for?"

Webber started, "I wanted to show you our current product development strategy for Italtel. Joint development is an important part of our work together, but I'm just afraid that if we don't have control of the technical aspects and design, the end product will suffer." Kline nodded and began looking over the plans, but his thoughts had already jumped ahead to the upcoming negotiations.

Negotiations with Italtel

It was a chilly February morning in Italy. Kline and Webber had arrived the evening before and were now on their way to meet with Italtel executives including Richard Costa, director of business development, Elena DeMarchi, product marketing manager, and Antonio Vicari, research & development manager. As the taxi maneuvered through the morning traffic, the two exchanged last minute thoughts.

"Elizabeth," Kline thought out loud, "I'd like to open the meeting with an outline of the points already agreed upon in the bid and then move to a discussion of the partnership. It's important for us to keep our joint goals in mind, but choosing the structure of the alliance is critical. The structure of the project can facilitate or hinder the relationship between the parties involved later as problems crop up or goals change. From the experience with Olivetti, I can see now that, although the structure of an alliance can adapt, an inflexible, short-sighted design significantly weakens an alliance and may lead to its ultimate deterioration."

The taxi slowed and stopped in front of Italtel's headquarters. As Kline and Webber entered the building, they were heartily greeted by Riccardo Costa. "Hello, Mr. Kline," said Costa, shaking Kline's hand firmly. "It's good to see you again," Costa added, patting Kline's shoulder. "And what charming company you have brought."

"Mr. Costa," Kline replied, "I'd like to introduce you to Ms. Elizabeth Webber, our fine new director of product development and management. Elizabeth, this is Mr. Riccardo Costa, director of business development."

Webber extended her hand and said, "It's a great pleasure to meet you Mr. Costa. I'm so happy that we'll have the chance to work together." At the same time, she noted his finely tailored suit and thought again about how important appearance seemed to be in Italy. Kline had once told her that he always took his best suits to Italy; now she understood why.

Costa stepped forward, very close to Webber, and returned her firm, American handshake with a soft, delicate one. "I'm looking forward to our discussions as well, Mrs. Webber. Have you visited our country before?"

The three exchanged pleasantries for a few minutes more before Costa led them into the conference room. Here they waited for more than fifteen minutes, until Elena DeMarchi and Antonio Vicari joined them. After many meetings in Italy, Kline had finally become accustomed to the difference between American and Italian orientations toward time. After introductions and coffee, Costa called the meeting to order.

"First, I would like to thank Mr. Kline and Mrs. Webber for coming on such short notice. As you know, Italtel is pleased to have AT&T as our partner. Since it's been several months since we last met to discuss this venture, I thought we might first review the goals of the alliance as outlined in the bid."

"We will be upgrading and modernizing Italy's telephone network system. As you know, this is a top priority of our government, and the funds have already been allocated for the program. In addition, the venture is designed to jointly develop products and to market them worldwide. This joint development will create mutual economies of scale and eliminate the overlap of our product lines."

"To finalize the venture, we must decide upon the structure of the alliance. One alternative under consideration is for one company to purchase stock in the other, an option we know that AT&T has chosen to use in other international ventures. In our case, however, Italtel prefers mutual ownership, perhaps accomplished through a stock swap. Reciprocal ownership is especially important, since one reason the Italian government approved the bid was to facilitate Italtel's expansion into new markets. What are AT&T's thoughts on such a proposal?"

"We like the idea," Kline replied. "In fact, we've been considering a stock swap ourselves. We prefer mutual ownership as well, since we also view the venture as a partnership, rather than simply an investment. In exchange for a percentage of Italtel stock, AT&T is prepared to offer shares of AT&T Network Systems International stock. As you know, this company is our joint venture with Phillips N.V. of The Netherlands."

Kline proposed this arrangement for several reasons. First, a stock swap with AT&T International would appear inequitable because Italtel would receive only a small percentage ownership in AT&T in exchange for a much larger percentage of Italtel. Because pride and appearance are highly valued by the Italian culture, a large disparity in swap percentages of the highly-publicized venture could reflect poorly upon Italtel and negatively affect relations with AT&T.

Kline continued, "AT&T feels that this stock is an appropriate exchange, since this company specializes in network systems, a key focus of our venture.

After a few seconds, Costa replied with typically Italian hand-waving. "This exchange is something we had not considered. But from what we know and what you have told us, the proposal has merit. If we swap our stock for Network Systems shares, what percentages did you have in mind?"

"Italtel and Network Systems International," Kline answered, "are roughly of the same size and stock value. Therefore, we feel that it would be equitable to swap evenly. We would like to swap an amount that is large enough to show our shared commitment to this venture, perhaps 20 or 25%. These are our thoughts. Your company would, of course, want to investigate the financial aspects further."

"That is an interesting idea. I'll talk to the finance department and have them review the proposal in more detail," Costa replied. "After we analyze the proposition, we can discuss this issue further. In the meantime, why don't we move forward and address the product development aspect of our partnership. Mr. Vicari and Mrs. DeMarchi have some ideas they would like to present."

De Marchi, the product marketing manager said, "One of the points we need to discuss is the location and arrangements for product development and marketing. Ultimately, our goal is to market our products worldwide. However, as we have already agreed upon, it would be best to concentrate our marketing efforts first in Europe before expanding to other countries. Therefore, it makes sense to base our marketing operations here in Italy."

Vicari, R&D manager, continued, "Also, since it would be better to have both the marketing and R&D functions close together, we propose to locate both departments here at Italtel. In fact, we have unused space in our design facility that would be appropriate for research and development operations."

Kline glanced at Webber and immediately sensed her concern. He knew that product development had assumed that all research would be conducted in the U.S. He replied, "I've consulted with our marketing department, and they agree that marketing should be based in Italy. Since your company possesses far more experience here in Europe and is closer to the market, it's natural for marketing to be run from here. However, locating product development here, just to be near marketing, may not be the best alternative. Elizabeth, what is the view of your department?"

"Well, we had planned on the product development activities taking place in the U.S.," she said tentatively. "Technology and innovation are AT&T's hallmark. We have top-rate facilities, and our development labs have worked well with visiting engineers in the past. Our engineers are already looking forward to working with yours."

DeMarchi responded, "Since we are in agreement that marketing should be based here, I think that AT&T should also consider Italy as the preferable development location. Italtel's marketing and development teams have traditionally worked closely together. We have found that this arrangement allows us to create products that closely meet customer demands."

Webber countered, "We believe that the technology should come first. We don't want to stifle innovation by basing research solely on the customer's perceived needs. Our experience has shown that sometimes customers are unaware of the new product developments that are possible until we have already developed the technology. This philosophy toward development has worked well for us thus far."

After more than an hour of discussion concerning the development location, the group adjourned for lunch. Upon arriving at a busy restaurant where there seemed to be no official line for service, Costa quickly caught the maitre d's attention, and they were immediately seated. During the two-hour lunch, Webber attempted to introduce several topics related to the joint venture only to be diverted by one member's remark that lunch was a time to enjoy, not work. When the check arrived, Costa insisted on paying the meal, because the Italians had made the arrangements.

At the end of five days, a final draft of the joint venture agreement was completed, and the negotiations reached conclusion. Kline and Webber returned to the U.S. knowing, however, that it would require several more months, at least, before a final agreement was reached and then reviewed and approved by the myriad Italian government agencies involved.

During the return flight to the United States, Kline and Webber, tired and somewhat reticent, conversed only sporadically. Both were deeply engrossed in thoughts concerning the numerous issues still unresolved. Had they successfully avoided the mistakes AT&T had experienced in its attempts to form other international joint ventures? How should AT&T proceed with its withdrawal from the Olivetti venture? Would the current situation with Olivetti negatively affect the Italian government's final approval of the Italtel alliance? How should the alliance with Italtel be structured to avoid the difficulties encountered with Olivetti? What options existed for resolution of the conflict concerning location of R&D facilities?

Both knew that the path to resolving the numerous issues critical to the success of the AT&T and Italtel joint venture would be difficult and treacherous. Only time would tell if this latest alliance would finally establish AT&T as a global player in the international telecommunications game.

18
Litigation Isn't the Japanese Way: Nippon, Inc. and Raleigh, Ltd.

Alan Goldman

An Intercultural Trainer in Tokyo

Alex Gordon, an intercultural trainer in Tokyo was working his way through the "case study" section of his program with middle managers from Nippon Inc. Part of the pre-departure training required that the Japanese reveal true-to-life conflicts they had personally experienced or witnessed in joint ventures with Western partners. One of the trainees, Roichi Sato, Nippon human resource director, told of his woes with Raleigh, Ltd., a U.S. affiliate. Only several days ago, he had received a letter from the Raleigh attorney, Jules McIver, "threatening litigation" against Nippon, Inc. Baited by the urgency of what appeared to be a managerial crisis, and noticing the smirks on the faces of the other Nippon managers, Gordon gently pumped Sato for more information.

Nippon, Inc. Versus Raleigh, Ltd.

Sato, a forty-six-year-old career man for Nippon, Inc., was noticeably miffed in a restrained, Japanese way. He made it clear to Gordon and the other trainees, that "it is very difficult to be dealing with Americans when they try to resolve conflicts with lawyers and journalists." Upon further questioning, Sato unfolded the letter from the attorney, "putting Nippon on notice . . . that they could be liable for damages . . . unfair labor practices . . . and other work place violations," and further spoke of the prospect for courtroom resolution in a U.S. court. Unfamiliar with the American tort system, Sato asked, "Perhaps you have some opinions, Mr. Gordon? . . . We

Japanese do not see lawyers as the way to make peace in a joint venture . . . at home or abroad."

Sato's troubling remarks were soon abruptly terminated. It was clear that he did not want to reveal anything more within the public forum of the corporate training classroom. While Sato helped set the tone for self- and corporate disclosures by other trainees of Japanese managerial conflicts with U.S., U.K., Canadian, and German companies, there was much left unsaid by Sato.

From "Tatemae" to "Honne:" Moving from the Surface to True Intentions

A few days passed, and Sato invited Gordon to lunch. While they had been to lunch before, it was always with others. In a small back room of a large sushi restaurant at the New Otani Hotel in the Aoyama section of Tokyo, the details of Sato's confrontation started to unfold.

Nippon, Inc. was the majority partner in the three-year-old joint venture, and Raleigh, Ltd. was the U.S.-based final assembly station for Nippon automobiles. Quite a conflict had occurred over what Sato repeatedly referred to as "the group space thing." During the first few months of the venture, there was agreement between the partners that Raleigh, Ltd. needed to tangibly move toward the kind of company-wide team work that the Japanese practice in total quality management (TQM) and just-in-time (JIT) production. A big part of this was what Sato described as "the need to change the physical plant and white collar offices from an individual to a group space format."

Inquiring into the nature of the "group space thing," Gordon offered, "you mean that Nippon, Inc. wanted American management to give up private offices, work in group offices, and rearrange the factory lines and work areas . . . for team work?" Sato nodded his head vigorously. "That is the situation and demands I am talking about . . . you seem to understand me, Mr. Gordon." Trained as a Ph.D. in intercultural and organizational communication, and with additional expertise in international management and law, Gordon quickly recognized the dispute as falling loosely under the category of "proxemics," work space allocations. Lunch took on a more serious and insider tone.

Gordon Is Offered a Consultancy by Nippon, Inc.

Later, Gordon received a phone call from Roichi Sato, asking him to visit with him "in an official capacity" at Nippon's human resource department. A series of talks followed over a three-week period as Sato detailed the events that culminated in the attorney's threat of litigation on behalf of Raleigh, Ltd. Sato wanted Gordon to become a consultant with Nippon and Gordon agreed.

Sato informed Gordon that his official hiring was contingent upon a "few formalities," including a series of *meishi*, or business introductions with key Nippon managers, staff, and personnel. An in-house *nemawashi,* formal and informal discussions, leading up to complete consensus for Gordon's "temporary but strategic role in the future of the Japanese-American joint venture" was necessary. The *nemawashi,* or informal consensus building process, was to be followed by a *ringi,* the formal circulation of a proposal calling for all Nippon members to agree to Gordon's hire and the conditions for his consultancy. Gordon later discovered that there were several middle managers who had serious reservations about a *gaijin,* or foreigner, representing Nippon interests. Only after modifications in the conditions of his consultancy and further talk with Gordon did all managers affix their personal stamps to the printed document (personal stamps are used in Japan in lieu of signatures), resulting in full agreement or *ringisho.*

Also, Sato told Gordon that he wanted to "utilize Gordon's hire as a strategy for showing Raleigh, Ltd. the extent of Japanese good will, and as a vehicle for reopening negotiations between us." In other words, Gordon's hire would also have to be agreed to by Raleigh.

Gordon's frequent talks with Sato soon occupied about 25% of their work days. Gordon learned that after three years into a "five-year plan" the Raleigh human resource director, Mr. Jackson Horvath, told Sato that "we agree wholeheartedly in principle with Nippon's expectation that we get more involved in group work and TQM, but we at Raleigh are committed to preserving privacy, individual offices, and territoriality within our company. We don't feel this is a contradiction." But Sato confidentially showed Gordon statistics indicating that productivity and quality levels were consistently below Japanese standards and expectations, and that it was "due to the excess, waste, unevenness, and the old world mind of American management—a system that puts the individual before the group goals!"

Securing Gordon's Acceptance by the Americans

After securing official approval for Gordon's hire within Nippon, Sato then finessed his acceptance by Raleigh, Ltd., through the good graces of human resource director, Jackson Horvath. Presenting Gordon as an American who had experience with both Japanese and Western corporate worlds, Sato did not call attention to the fact that the consultant had a background with Sato and Nippon, Inc. as a cross-cultural trainer. Diverting attention from the prospect that Gordon might have been hired as a Nippon, Inc. "agent" or "lobbyist," Sato focused on the "objectivity, analysis, and recommendations that Gordon can offer both of our companies."

Gordon remained very quiet during Sato's "pitch" and wondered about his allegiances, biases, and the potential ethical quagmires that might surface during the course of this ensuing consultancy. A detailed, internal, and tedious debate preoccupied Gordon, similar to a cross-cultural ping pong ball bouncing back and forth in his mind. Should he openly reveal his background as a Nippon Inc. trainer to Horvath and Raleigh, or maintain silence? What could the repercussions be? After all, according to Japanese cultural code, the surface communication or *tatemae,* was all in order, while the true intentions or *honne* should not be revealed until firmer relationships were established with the American corporate managers. On the one hand, Gordon considered the moral and ethical implications as he knew them, via his native U.S. national and corporate cultures. But, on the other hand, Gordon was presently living in Japan, greatly influenced by his Japanese experience and client, and felt particularly drawn to the situation-determined ethics of the Nippon, Inc. corporate culture—as revealed through the actions of Sato.

Horvath was genuinely impressed with the good will gushing through Sato's words. There was no question about it, Sato wanted to find an alternative to litigation, and was more than willing to cast most of the blame upon himself for the failure of four previous negotiations aimed at resolving "the group thing."

Gordon was surprised at Sato's ability to switch from "private" to "public" manners of speaking. In private, Sato had relentlessly pursued the "obstinacy of Raleigh and Horvath" for their unyielding positions during the failed negotiations. But in the public venue, Sato seemed to fiddle a different tune. Sato admitted that Nippon, Inc. had been ignorant, insensitive, and ill-prepared for American customs and culture, and the motivations and desires of Raleigh workers and management. Sato wanted to place the brunt of the conflict on the "cultural differences" rather than on the particulars of the dispute. Now Sato and Nippon, Inc. were ready to right all the wrongs of the joint venture through the third party of the consultant.

Won over by Sato's finely-tuned skills at healing a wounded relationship, Horvath even offered to put up Raleigh funding for the consultant. Sato profusely refused, stating that "the fault belongs with me, and it is only fair that my company absorb the expenses of the consultant." At that moment it appeared as if Horvath, on behalf of Raleigh, Ltd., was already willing to go back to the negotiating table and iron out the differences.

Gordon Gains Access to Data for Analyzing the Conflict

Gordon's confirmation was a lengthy procedure with Nippon, Inc. (due to the *nemawashi* and *ringisho*), but was rapidly approved by Raleigh through Horvath and the Raleigh, Ltd. chief executive officer, Mr. Clyde Wyllis. With complete confirmation by both Japanese and U.S. organizations, Gordon requested access to relevant internal documents, memos, correspondence, human resource and personnel files, minutes and notes from joint venture meetings, and interviews with key players.

From the onset, Sato made it abundantly clear to Gordon what his mission entailed; get the lawyers out of the picture—make them obsolete and unnecessary—that is your number one goal. Second, Sato wanted Gordon to find ways that both companies were "guilty" of insensitivities and mistakes in judgment. Third, he hoped that Gordon would be able to discover some "new facts, missing information, or surprises that would cast the conflict in a new light." Horvath had much less to say to Gordon. He simply stated, and frequently paraphrased his objective: "Let's save this joint venture and climb out of the conflict. I'll be real interested to see what you come up with."

The many private talks with Sato made it infinitely clear what Nippon, Inc. was looking for. They in fact wanted Gordon to function as a kind of "mediator" in lieu of an attorney. The success of his consultancy was ultimately contingent upon the diplomatic, above-board removal of attorney McIver. Gordon recognized that McIver was a wedge between the two companies.

In the past, once negotiations had faltered, both companies were ultimately victimized by nasty Western and international press coverage of arguments at the joint venture table (the result of a clandestine admissions to reporters by an unidentified Raleigh, Ltd. negotiator). As a result of subsequent crisis management maneuvers by Raleigh CEO Wyllis, Attorney McIver emerged as the prime player. As the unofficial mediator-consultant, Gordon knew that removal of the attorney from the picture was the key to a renegotiation process.

Although Gordon was well aware of the lack of a Japanese equivalent of Western jurisprudence and litigation, he nevertheless was puzzled by recent Japanese corporate use of lawyers in the U.S. courts. In response to charges of "dumping" and "price fixing," several *keiretsus* populated by Japanese multinationals operating in U.S. markets had recently retained well-respected attorneys. Gordon confronted Sato with these developments, inasmuch as they appeared to contradict Nippon's position in relations to the tort system. Sato responded with an ironic, broad-faced smile, stating that:

> Those are very international Japanese corporations who have much experience in America. They have learned to play your legal game in your U.S. courts. We at Nippon are more typical Japanese. We do not have a lot of knowledge of your legal system, and it is fundamentally against our instincts. Besides, you should realize that the lawyers that those Japanese firms use are American lawyers, not Japanese!

The early weeks of Gordon's consultancy entailed a massive gathering of relevant documents. Surprisingly, he found both sides to blame for the mishaps. Requesting three years of internal memos, letters and faxes, human resource files, minutes from meetings and press releases and coverage, Gordon conducted what he termed a "joint venture, intercultural communication audit." Looking for patterns of behavior, as well as "red flag" situations that led to the conflict, Gordon made some curious discoveries.

First, the most immediate perpetrators of the joint venture dispute were two Nippon, Inc. expatriate managers, Matsuda Fukuzawa and Koichi Miyazawa. In the minds of many of the Raleigh "assembly line guys" they were Japanese "whistle blowers." Out of their element and recent transplants, Fukuzawa and Miyazawa irritated line workers and management alike, as they, in the words of middle manager, Max Justin, "always seemed to be sneaking messages to the Nippon, Inc. headquarters in Tokyo." One of their faxes was "accidently discovered" by Justin, who had it translated by a Japanese friend. The fax letter addressed the "difficulties of individual offices and assembly line worker arrangements . . . the separation of workers is not making group spirit very possible . . ." After the fax message found its way into the Raleigh, Ltd. grapevine, it seriously eroded worker and managerial faith in their Japanese partners. In addition, other faxes from Fukuzawa and Miyazawa resulted in a continual and escalating "gentle pressure" waged by Sato, from the Tokyo corporate headquarters. The conflict was already underway, setting the tone for the disastrous showdown at the table negotiation as well as the final litigation ploy.

Further digging into early memos and minutes of meetings between the two companies uncovered a "red flag." Horvath was a late- comer into the venture. He was preceded by Bill Browning. It was Browning who reached original agreement with Sato and Nippon regarding a five-year campaign to implement a group proxemic format. Browning's firing (one and a half years into the venture) shocked the Japanese partners, and they had difficulty adjusting to the new human resource director, Jackson Horvath. In Gordon's mind, the turnover unintentionally violated Nippon, Inc.'s company and national culture.

When Gordon questioned Horvath about his "inheriting" this agreement, Horvath offered, "Of course I took on a lot of the baggage and some of it couldn't be delivered." Further questioning led to Horvath stating, "You know, I tried to pick up the ball, and circulated a memo about the group space conversion. But all I got was grief . . . formal grievances shot through our system, arguments, threats . . . and we had to table it. Can you blame Ivy League MBAs who don't want to give up their plush offices or blue-collar guys who want a little privacy . . . they don't like these Japanese 'U-shaped lines'. . . they want a little privacy."

On the Nippon side of the fence, Gordon was surprised by Sato's response to Horvath's statements. Sato whispered in confidence, one afternoon at tea at The New Otani Hotel, "It is crazy. The turnover between Browning and Horvath is depressing. U.S. companies and management are so unstable, I think. But I never did hear of Horvath's attempt to convert to group space. It makes me more compassionate. He wanted to comply. He was unable . . ."

Still not satisfied, Gordon pried into Browning's notes and memos and uncovered an oral agreement that had been reached during the fourth month of the joint venture. Three years later, Horvath was stymied by management and workers, and recognized that "there was no written agreement regarding group space, whatsoever."

A Discreet Meeting

After two months of gathering and interpreting data through printed documents and strategic interviews, Gordon recommended a quiet meeting between Gordon, Sato, and Horvath. Clearly, some good feelings had been established during their earlier meetings (over Gordon's hire), and it was time to build upon this.

At this meeting Gordon voiced "there was a lot of Raleigh resentment of Fukuzawa's and Miyazawa's faxed reports—as at least two faxes were discovered in the fax room." When the expatriate Japanese were confronted with their actions they only smiled and said "it is probably a misunderstanding." Horvath said, "The resentment is understandable, don't you think?" While Sato offered, "It was poor judgment for these private issues to have reached public eyes and ears." Both agreed it was "too late" to reverse this source of conflict, but acknowledged the damage done, and wanted to move on.

Also the Browning and Horvath turnover issue was raised. Sato expressed that "agreements made by Mr. Browning must be honored by Mr. Horvath. We Japanese are not familiar with individual personalities in negotiating a joint venture. We feel everything Browning said is the responsibility of Horvath and the entire Raleigh Company." After some mild debate, devoid of harsh language, Horvath recognized that "turnover is deadly with a Japanese partner."

The "oral agreement" problem wound up being the next focal point. Sato and Horvath agreed that "a man's word is very important," but disagreed on the oral versus the written channels. Sato reiterated that he would have showed more patience if he realized "how hard Horvath tried to implement group space." Sato even offered that "perhaps it is very much against the nature of American workers to be in a room together, without their walls, doors and privacy." He nevertheless, still wanted to know from Horvath, "Why did you give up?"

Horvath became irritated. "Do you know the responses I got when I told my managers and workers that their privacy was going to end?" Sato acted concerned and bewildered, all at once. Horvath said, "They used ugly language, cuss words, anonymously threatened my life, and many said they wanted nothing to do with Japanese."

Sato was genuinely moved. Gordon interjected that "both sides have vigorously tried, and have made noble gestures to resolve this problem." Gordon added, "But why, Mr. Horvath, did the negative response put an end to the five-year plan for compliance?"

Horvath was outraged. For the first time it appeared as if Gordon was obviously a Nippon "agent." At least Gordon thought that this must be racing through Horvath's mind. Horvath emotionally stated that "there was no written agreement, period! My own employees threatened me with litigation . . . if it's not in writing . . . bottom line . . . it doesn't hold water . . . !"

Turning to Sato, Gordon asked, "In retrospect, Mr. Sato, do you think that the oral agreement was the best way to reach an agreement? Why didn't a written contract occur to Nippon, Inc., on an issue of such grave importance to you as the spatial arrangements?"

Sato politely offered, "You know the answer, Mr. Gordon. It is not the Japanese way to force things by putting into writing what should be understood among gentlemen and partners. Oral is good enough. Oral agreements are quite good . . . but maybe not in this sad situation . . . maybe something could be in writing."

The Aftermath of the Meeting

Following the meeting, the Raleigh and Nippon human resource departments were in agreement that Gordon would propose a solution that would address the Japanese and U.S. complaints and frustrations. Moreover, it was agreed by both parties that the renegotiation should be a "hybrid solution process," combining aspects of Japanese and U.S. management practices and worker expectations. What was called for was a "new viewpoint" from the "third party" consultant and mediator.

The following solution was proposed by Gordon:

1. A new five-year written agreement should be reached regarding Raleigh Ltd.'s conversion from individual to group space.
2. Proxemic conversions should maintain aspects of both Western and Japanese views of work space.
3. Both sides should become familiar with a German proxemic scheme termed Burolandshaft, as it is an example of a Western country's adaptation to collectivist office and work space.

After inspecting the solutions proposed, Gordon obtained agreement from Horvath and Sato to return to the negotiating table for a renegotiation based on the above. In preparation for the renegotiations, Gordon provided briefings on Burolandshaft, offering both sides hope and a Western prototype for group space.

The Renegotiation

Without any attorneys, both companies resumed negotiations, as advised by Gordon. Several concrete compromises were reached during the second negotiation concerning aspects of Raleigh individualism and Nippon collectivism. The Raleigh team requested that middle and upper management be able to retain their private offices but be gradually expected to spend up to 80% of their time in designated group work areas—away from their offices. This amalgam of Japanese and U.S. views of proxemics emerged as a fairly agreeable prototype to both parties.

Problems began to resurface again, however, when the Raleigh negotiators requested that all agreements be demonstrated in writing, and in precise, exact language, figuring in all possible and probable contingencies. At this point, the Japanese mildly disagreed, in a roundabout, indirect fashion. Sato and the others suddenly lapsed into what Raleigh viewed as a stalling, ambiguous mode of interaction, and Gordon knew what was happening. As soon as Nippon heard that strict written agreements were on the Raleigh agenda, a distance emerged. Nippon wanted the wording to be far more ambiguous "to allow for things that we cannot anticipate, hardships and such."

A Consultant's Nightmare

The nucleus of the conflict resurfaced when the Raleigh CEO, Clyde Wyllis, secretly called in a second attorney, Gaston Curtis, to help draft a new five-year proxemic agreement. Gordon learned about this when he accidently overheard talk between Wyllis and Horvath concerning the contracting with Curtis, a joint venture specialist, during a table negotiation recess.

Gordon was noticeably upset and perplexed. Where did he fail? Why wasn't Wyllis directly included in the interaction from the first day of his consultancy, rather than Raleigh's exclusive use of Horvath as spokesperson? Should he confront Wyllis and Horvath in private? In public? Gordon even considered letting it take its natural course and dealing with the conflict when it hit the negotiating table. Gordon further wondered whether he should raise the issue in private with Sato? He feared most of all that he had let Sato down. Sato's central request clearly rang in his ears, "Get the attorneys out of the picture."

With the joint venture on the line, things were going well until this latest litigator development. Gordon did not want to see the hard-earned renegotiation process flounder. He was convinced that the symbolic reappearance of any attorney would greatly impair all of his damage control to date. Were Wyllis and Horvath playing a win-lose game, figuring that the removal of the first attorney, McIver, now allowed them to bring Curtis to the table? Were they completely ignorant of Japanese distaste for attorneys?

Making His Moves

In about five minutes the third round of table negotiations will resume. Gordon sees Wyllis speaking into his mobile phone. Gordon is sure that Wyllis is inviting Gaston Curtis to appear at the table. Gordon's blood is racing through his body. What should Gordon do to save this joint venture?

19

Testing Solar Stoves in Mexico: Alten Technologies, Inc.

Hendrick Serrie

Solar Energy and the Third World

At Alten Technologies Inc., a small firm specializing in developing and marketing space age products, Dan Farring's engineers created a solar energy cooking stove. Laboratory tests demonstrated that the Alten solar stove produced heat that was equal to the simple cooking fire used in virtually all rural regions of the Third World.

Dan was convinced that this device had enormous market potential. From his worldwide travels, he had seen peasants struggle with the problems of deforestation and diminishing sources of firewood, a main source of energy. Even when rural electrification reached a peasant area, most peasant families could not afford to bring it into their homes. Dan knew that peasants constitute almost 52% of total world population. Surely this was a mammoth market segment!

Of all the developing countries, Dan chose to focus on Mexico as his first target, primarily because he had several powerful friends in the Mexican government who were highly enthusiastic about his new product. In fact, he had already secured a commitment from one of the Mexican ministries to provide most of the start-up costs of setting up a joint venture for mass production of solar stoves, providing that it was established on Mexican soil. Because Dan's firm was small and lacked the resources to manage the venture alone, this seemed like a magnificent opportunity. If everything worked out, Alten Laboratories would experience rapid growth and attract worldwide attention for its contribution to ameliorating one of the most serious ecological problems affecting the planet.

One of the longstanding problems that seriously affects peasants in many parts of the world is deforestation. As the developed nations, and even much of the developing countries rely on petroleum, people in the rural areas of the Third World rely on firewood as a major source of energy, especially for cooking. Excessive population growth in many peasant areas has resulted in the cutting down of trees for firewood at a much faster rate than replacement through deliberate planting of seedlings or natural regeneration. The resulting deforestation results in increasing scarcity of firewood supplies as well as soil erosion, loss of arable land and long-term drying up of the climate and spread of desert areas.

It is clear that peasants have an urgent need for products that will provide them with affordable energy and that will ameliorate the crisis of deforestation.

The Alten solar stove consisted of a four-foot parabolic reflector with a grill crosspiece mounted on a swiveling metal base. During testing in the laboratory, it operated beautifully at more than 50% heat efficiency, producing as much heat as an ordinary cooking fire. Now, Dan wished to test it in a cross-cultural field setting in rural Mexico. So, two of his engineers were flown to Mexico City; but they returned empty handed.

"We drove out to a couple of villages with an interpreter and gave several demonstrations," one engineer reported. "But people just stared and then shrugged their shoulders and walked away. No one even seemed interested."

Anthropology and International Business

Dan then turned to Paul Henser, a young business anthropologist at the university near Alten's research park. Henser agreed to go to Mexico with a dozen solar stoves and carry out a full-fledged anthropological marketing test.

"Look," Dan explained to his staff, "we've got to send someone who understands the culture. We couldn't get to first base trying to fly by the seat of our pants. When you need an expert on culture, you go to an anthropologist."

In a briefing with Dan and his staff, Henser explained that he would take up residence for three-and-a-half months in a typical peasant village. Using the participant observation techniques of cultural anthropology, Henser would study the culture, win the trust of its people, and persuade them to accept the solar stoves on a free trial basis in return for letting him observe their day-to-day usage. In this way, Henser explained to Alten's engineers, he would determine if the technologically proficient solar cookers were in fact culturally appropriate for rural Mexico.

Henser received permission to transport the solar stoves to one of the less developed areas of Mexico, one that he felt would better represent general Third World conditions. He also wanted to conduct the study in an area far removed from the U.S. border, where American culture was a powerful and visible model. Thus, he chose Oaxaca, a relatively isolated state in southern Mexico, and, after arriving in its small capital city and pursuing a number of possibilities, he decided upon Tlacoxochitl, a Zapotec Indian village, one of many without electrification.

Tlacoxochitl, the "Test" Village in Mexico

After several trips to Tlacoxochitl, Henser and his wife Diane had developed a friendly relationship with Raul and Sara Lazo and their family. Raul was an enterprising Zapotec man, among the better-off people in the village, who owned not one but two, one-room, dirt-floor adobe houses. Raul was excited by the novel business idea of renting a house. Moreover, because he earned his living by weaving and selling serapes to tourists in Oaxaca de Juarez, he saw an excellent opportunity to sell his wares to these nice young gringos. Shortly thereafter, Henser and Diane settled in, rapidly became acquainted with numerous people in the village, and commenced work on a general village study.

For several days after Paul and Diane Henser moved into Raul's extra house, the neighborhood children gawked at and whispered about them whenever they went on errands in the village. "Hey, gringo!" the brashest ones would taunt in Zapotec. "Can you see with those blue eyes?" As the shock of seeing white- skinned humans in their village subsided, the blank stares of children and adults alike were transformed by Paul and Diane's friendly greetings into broad smiles, appropriately called *sonrisas*.

The following are excerpts from Paul Henser's field notes from his first week in Tlacoxochitl (Henser is fluent in both Spanish and Zapotec):

Tlacoxochitl is a Zapotec Indian village in the state of Oaxaca. Before the Spanish Conquest in 1521, Zapotecs and Mixtecs, the two competing civilizations in this area, had erected great temple complexes at Monte Alban, Mitla and other sites. Tlacoxochitl itself had been one of the Zapotec administrative centers, and in the center of town stands an imposing church, constructed under the direction of Dominican monks with the rubble of a large pyramid which they had ordered destroyed.

Although Zapotec is the native language of all members of the community and no more than half the population speaks Spanish as a second language, Tlacoxochitl is in most other respects typical of rural villages in the southern Mexican highlands. The mainstay of the economy is agriculture, with corn, sugar cane, and castor beans comprising the dominant crops. Two farmers own a modern tractor with plow and cultivator attachments, but as in all the other villages, the rest rely on teams of oxen, wooden plows shaped like pointed sticks, and the planting of seeds by hand.

Tradition is strong in Tlacoxochitl. A yearly round of festivals, including processions with religious paraphernalia, a small brass band, a pre-Colombian musical group with drum and *chirimia* (a wind instrument), and services in the church, alleviates the boredom of rural life. The biggest events, called *mayordomias,* include feasting, and are paid for by one or several families contributing what may have taken decades to save. This is a traditional leveling mechanism that attempts to keep everyone at a roughly equal subsistence level.

According to several informants, the first crucial confrontation between Tlacoxochitl and the modern world occurred during the 1920s, when a smallpox epidemic ravaged the area. According to Heron Zarate, an elderly man, "People here were dying from the disease in great numbers. The carpenters could not keep up with the work, there were so many orders for coffins." His neighbor, Wenceslao Garcia, also elderly, agrees.

"Especially small coffins for infants and children." Nevertheless, when the Mexican government sent medical teams to the rural villages in Oaxaca, the people of Tlacoxochitl were frightened, having heard stories of the evil sorcery of these teams describing how they punctured people with long needles. Many of them fled into the mountains, and escaped inoculation. But, as the months passed, it was noticed by many villagers that those who had fallen victims to the dreaded needles were not falling ill, and many of those who had run away were now dead. It was concluded from this experience that some of the practices of the outside world might be good.

It is common to see elements of modernization mixed with traditional Zapotec and Hispanic culture. Zapotec women wear factory-made blouses, skirts of wrap-around cloth, and cloth belts woven on small, pre-Colombian looms. They generally braid their long, uncut hair. Zapotec men wear denim jeans, sport shirts, denim jackets and cheap cowboy hats and have the same haircuts as urban Mexican men. Sandals with automobile tire soles are common, and children and many women often go barefoot.

Villagers have been buying industrial products for many years. The preferred laundry detergent is Fab, Coca-Cola is everywhere, and one of the available cigarette brands is Marlboro. Coin by coin, many families have managed to save enough money to buy a special item. There is no electricity in the village, but transistor radios have become popular, and there is great interest in the Mexican soap operas and popular songs called *rancheros*.

A faded, dented, and dusty bus provides service several times a day to the capital city of Oaxaca, twenty-six miles away. A few men have managed to purchase bicycles, those liberating machines that allow one to travel to the market in Tlacolula, six miles away or to visit friends and associates in any of the villages in the area in a fraction of the time required to walk.

Introducing Solar Stoves in Tlacoxochitl

At the end of the third week when the shipment of twelve solar stoves arrived, Raul gave Henser permission to set up a solar cooking demonstration in a vacant lot next to the Lazo houses. It was no accident that Henser chose a house and lot on the only road into Tlacoxochitl. Everyone entering the village, whether walking or riding the second class busses, would notice the solar stoves.

Zapotecs in Tlacoxochitl proved to be very responsive to Paul and Diane Henser's friendly natures and to their genuine interest in acquiring knowledge and understanding of Zapotec culture. They were curious about the outlandish contraptions that Henser and several of their neighbors tinkered with every day in Raul's lot. On the first day, they allowed their children to run to the Lazo home and stare at the wide, curved reflectors. "Don Pablo," they asked Henser. "What are those big round mirrors for?" The children duly reported back to their families, and this somehow made it safer for the adults to visit Henser's demonstration site.

Henser was only too happy to show off his solar stoves. Focusing the reflector, he would take a sheet of newspaper and hold it on the grill, which was suspended a foot-and-a-half over the reflector. Immediately, an intensely bright disk of light, two inches wide, glowed through the newspaper from underneath. Within a few seconds, the bright spot would begin smoking and the newspaper would burst into flame.

"Ahhhh," said the watching Zapotec men, women, and children, nodding their heads. Henser would then take one of the standard *ollas* or pottery jars used for cooking beans, place it on the grill, and add some water. In eight or ten minutes the water would be boiling, and he would invite the villagers to look into the pot and see for themselves. "You can use this machine for cooking," Henser would explain. "It uses the sun, instead of fire on the ground. You don't need to burn firewood."

A strange-looking man, very frail and wrinkled, said in an irritated voice, "It is not good. There is a wise admonition, never leave a mirror face up on the ground. For it will burn the sun, and the sun in revenge will bring destruction upon you."

"How much are they?" various people started asking. Henser had arbitrarily set a price, in pesos, that was equal to the retail price of one of the serapes woven in the village. A serape took at least one week to weave, and more than half of the selling price went to purchase the raw wool. At this point Henser was not trying to sell his solar stoves, but rather he was screening for individuals that were seriously interested in acquiring one.

"I want to buy one," a man named Pedro Martinez said. "I'm sick and tired of wasting all that time up in the mountains hunting for firewood."

"I tell you what," Henser responded. "Don't give me any money at this time. You take this one to your home on loan, and use it as much as you can. I'll visit you every day and see how things are working out. After one month, if this solar cooker serves you as well as we think it will, you can buy it from me at that time for half price."

Word spread rapidly that Pedro Martinez was now the proud possessor of a solar energy cooking stove, and immediately everyone in the neighborhood was clamoring to have one. Because Henser had only twelve solar stoves for his market test, he judiciously placed the cookers among families with higher and lower social status and within various kinship and social subdivisions. Henser then settled into a daily routine of visiting each home and recording the patterns of usage.

His preliminary observations and conclusions were as follows:

All heat analyses conducted around the noon hour, when sun is highest in the sky and solar radiation is at a maximum. Heat efficiency drops drastically with significant clouds and/or wind. The months of April, May, and June are the rainy season; the rest of the year is dry with not much cloud cover.

Heat efficiency of the 12 solar cookers tested in Tlacoxochitl range from 45–62%. Anything above 50% is considered satisfactory, and above 55% is excellent.

It was estimated that over the course of the entire year, there was sufficient solar radiation to power solar energy cooking stoves for continuous cooking use on eight out of ten days during the mid-day hours.

A Big Leap for Alten Technologies, Inc.

At the end of their fourth week in Tlacoxochitl, Paul and Diane Henser drove twenty-six miles to the city of Oaxaca. From there, Paul was able to telephone Alten

Laboratories. Minnie, the receptionist, said that Dan Farring was out but would be back at 1:45 p.m. "Okay, tell him I'll call back at 2:00." After Henser hung up, he turned to Diane and said, "Great! We can do our errands and still have time for a cold Dos Equis and fried grasshoppers in the *portales* of the Marques del Valle!"

Of all the beers in the world, Dos Equis was Paul's favorite, and of all the pleasant places to drink one, he thought the outdoor cafes on the main plaza of Oaxaca city were among the best. Paul and Diane watched the world go by, and at 2:00 o'clock Paul went inside the lobby of the Hotel Marques del Valle to use their telephone. This time Minnie was able to summon Dan Farring immediately.

"Hey, Paul, how's it going?" Dan asked.

"Great, Dan. So far the response of the people in Tlacoxochitl has been terrific. We had to repair a few of the cookers, but they're all working fine. One's down to 45% efficiency, but it still works. Just a bit slower."

"Something happened with the crate?" Dan asked.

"Yeah, I don't know," Paul answered. "It looked like maybe a truck had accidentally backed against it. Don't worry, we got 'em fixed. Listen, I have more people wanting cookers than I know what to do with. All twelve are with Zapotec families, and I've just started collecting data on daily usage."

Dan Farring was tremendously excited. This was what he had been waiting to hear. "That's wonderful, Paul. I'm going to move ahead now with my friends in the ministry."

"Dan, as I said, things are going great. But, I would still recommend that you wait just a little longer. Everyone's so excited out here, they think hunting firewood is a drag, but I still need to observe daily usage just to be sure these cookers are going to work out. We know they are a damned nifty little technological device, but we don't know for sure yet if they are appropriate for rural Mexican culture."

Dan felt in his bones that the solar energy cooking stove was going to be a tremendous success, but he had traveled around the world and learned enough about cultural differences to know that Paul was right about this. Mass production of solar stoves would involve the expenditure of millions of dollars, and Alten's reputation was on the line. He wanted to be very sure before making this big leap forward. Hiring a business anthropologist was his idea in the first place, so Dan decided to let the guy do what he's supposed to do. "I can wait another month or two," Dan thought to himself. "If there are unforeseen cultural problems, this guy will have saved our necks. Alten Labs is up and coming with a great reputation, and several innovative products. I'm ready to bet the company on solar cookers, but I want to hear everything Paul Henser has to say before I take the plunge."

Testing Solar Stoves in Tlacoxochitl

The following are excerpts from Paul Henser's field notes for the fifth week in Tlacoxochitl:

I accompanied Pedro Martinez to his home near the stream that runs through town. When we arrived, he introduced me to his wife, Maria, and we explained what the devil this strange thing was we were carrying.

It was around ten-thirty in the morning, with a strong sun blazing down, and I suggested to them both that we try out the cooker. Maria had already made her tortillas for the day, but proposed to make a pot of beans. She went inside her bamboo kitchen and emerged with a medium-sized olla. We decided what spot in the yard would be a good location for the cooker, then moved it there. I helped Maria place the olla on the grill that is suspended on a crosspiece over the parabolic reflector.

Then I explained to them both how to focus the cooker, first orienting it so that it faced the sun, then adjusting the reflector that swings underneath the crosspiece so that the sun's rays are concentrated in a small disk of light that strikes the bottom of the olla.

After Maria filled the olla with water, she put in the dried beans she wished to cook. Already the blazing focal point was burning away a bit of grease on the bottom of the olla, and giving off a little smoke. Maria and Pedro were immensely impressed. So were a small group of six or eight neighbors, who had found reasons to pay a neighborly visit to the Martinez yard at this very moment.

I explained to everyone that we could leave the cooker to do its work, and I was invited inside the Martinez' house. After chatting a while, Maria remembered her beans, so we all went out into the yard to inspect them. The water in the olla was just coming to a boil. Maria had a wooden spoon and, with this, she stirred the beans.

I pointed out to Maria and Pedro that the solar cooker had to be refocused every fifteen or twenty minutes, in order to track the sun as it moved across the sky. I also showed them both how to make these adjustments, which take less than a minute.

I stayed with Pedro and Maria until quarter after eleven, to watch them check and refocus the solar cooker. There were a few clouds in the sky, but they blew by in a minute or two and did not impede the progress of the beans.

At 3:30 in the afternoon I returned to the Martinez home to see how things had worked out with the beans. Maria and Pedro were both pleased. "Perfecto," they beamed. It had taken about three hours—the same amount of time needed on a standard cooking fire. Maria offered me some in a bowl and they were delicious.

The following are excerpts from Paul Henser's field notes for his sixth week in Tlacoxochitl:

Sara Lazo usually pan bakes her tortillas in the early morning, but yesterday I asked her if she would as a special favor, use the solar cooker that I placed with her and Raul to make tortillas. "All I need is just two or three," I added. "Como no," she replied. Why not. "However," she added, "I have no corn dough left for today. I get it fresh at the molino, the corn mill, early every morning, and then I come back and use it to make tortillas for my family for the whole day."

"Well," I said, "How about tomorrow? Could you save some dough for later on in the morning when the sun is up in the sky a ways?" "Como no," she replied.

So, today at ten thirty, when the sun was strong enough, we went out to the solar cooker in the yard, with Sara carrying her comal, a curved pottery pan, and corn dough already prepared for baking. We put the comal on the solar cooker. It is quite wide—almost 45 inches across—and I was concerned about how much solar radiation would be lost from its shadow. Nevertheless, the sun was strong, and we proceeded. Sara patted out the corn dough into a pancake shape and placed it on the comal.

As we watched, the part of the tortilla dough at the bottom of the comal began cooking, but the rest remained uncooked. Tlacoxochitl tortillas are not small in size—they are over 12 inches in diameter. What was happening was that the solar cooker created a hot spot at the bottom of the comal, and was not able to distribute the heat evenly over the entire pan.

When the hot spot had fully cooked the center of the tortilla, the wide part still remained uncooked. We left it on longer until the center part started to blacken. The outer part remained uncooked.

We repeated this once again with new dough. Same results. It is clear: Solar cookers are technically unable to pan bake the large Tlacoxochitl tortillas on the traditional comal.

Alten Technologies' Decision

Back at Alten, Dan Farring was pondering the implications of Paul Henser's weekly reports and field data from Tlacoxochitl. Dan had just finished speaking long distance with his friend Jose Mendoza in Mexico City. Jose was with the ministry in charge of rural development, and it was through his leadership that the ministry had decided to provide funding for a joint venture with Alten Technologies, Inc. for the mass production of solar energy cooking stoves in Mexico.

"Amigo," Jose had said over the phone, "There are some political changes going on here that I will tell you about another time. But the bottom line is that we need to make a decision very soon about manufacturing the solar stoves, or else we will lose the opportunity. So what is it going to be?"

"Jose," Dan replied. "I think I understand what you are saying. How soon is very soon?"

"Can you call me back tonight at my home?"

Six weeks had passed, and a clear picture of how culturally appropriate the Alten solar energy stove was for villages in Oaxaca and probably for many other rural parts of Mexico had emerged. Clear, but complex.

Dan Farring knew he had very little time to make the right decision about the mass production and distribution of solar energy stoves for the rural Mexican market.

20
The Alpaca Industry of Peru

John E. Walsh, Jr.

Introduction

Robert Morris, an entrepreneur from the United States, had observed that the finest and most expensive alpaca sweaters were knitted in Austria. Yet more than 90% of the world's alpaca fiber came from Peru and Bolivia.

For alpaca sweaters to be knitted in Austria alpaca fiber had to be shipped to Liverpool, England, the major seaport for alpaca imports. At the Liverpool auctions alpaca fiber was directly sold to spinning companies in England or companies in Europe. Wherever the yarn was produced, it would be sent by rail to Austria for knitting. The sweaters would then be sent by rail to a European port, probably Bremen or Genoa, and shipped to New York or Boston. From there they would be sent by rail or truck to eastern, southern, and midwestern cities.

After Robert Morris calculated the shipping and handling costs, duties, and middleman profits, he concluded that a profitable business could be developed if high-quality alpaca sweaters could be knitted in Peru.

A Visit to Peru

Robert Morris wasted no time in following up on his idea. He flew to Lima and through the efforts of the commercial attaché of the U.S. Embassy in Lima, he hired Jose Bermudez, a Peruvian, who had many years' experience in buying alpaca products for sale primarily to tourists. Jose Bermudez pointed out that alpaca sweaters were knitted in Peru in large numbers in several cities of the south as well as in Lima. These sweaters were the weight of light ski sweaters but were more coarse. Sometimes they would shed, especially over a white shirt. More attractive, lighter, softer, multi-colored baby alpaca sweaters were also sold in Lima. They were sold in the better tourist shops and some were exported to specialty shops in the United States. The fine solid colored alpaca sweaters promoted in the United States by golfer Arnold Palmer, however, were knitted in Austria.

In a conversation with Robert Morris, Jose Bermudez detailed some background about the alpaca sweater business:

> I think that tariff escalation keeps Peruvian alpaca sweaters from being exported to the United States for the mass market. The escalation of tariffs in developed countries is often a substantial barrier to the development of industries elsewhere based on local raw materials. By escalation I mean the existence of one tariff for raw materials, a higher tariff for semi-processed goods, and an even higher tariff for fully processed goods.
>
> It is also possible that, in the special case of Peruvian-made alpaca sweaters, limited overall production is not sufficient to justify advertising. And don't forget, alpaca is a difficult fiber to handle. I understand that it is more like hair than wool and builds up tremendous amounts of static when being spun.
>
> Within a few minutes, they were on their way to Morris' first appointment. For the rest of that day and all of the next, they visited business offices and organizations listed on his schedule.

Robert Morris recorded in a notebook the most important and representative information gained from his visits in Lima:

1. Alpaca fiber is like human hair but not as wiry.
2. Currently, the most common end use of the fiber is in coatings and pile fabrics. Synthetic fibers have been tried as substitutes for alpaca, but they lack the quality requirements demanded by the public. Alpaca is a live fiber; it will bounce back if wetted and will not mat down as many other lining fabrics do. In the U.S., alpaca is used for pile fabrics in low-priced coats. In England, many yards of fleece coatings are made for women's wear. These markets differ widely. In the U.S. 95% of alpaca imports are of fleece and 5% are of inferior grade; in England the market will use 50% fleece and 50% inferior.
3. Fads using quality fibers—such as alpaca, camel hair, cashmere, and many others—have normally lasted a few seasons at best. There is no vital need for them anywhere, despite their inherent advantages. It is not unusual for these fibers to not return to the market in worthwhile quantities. The market for alpaca for high-styled sweaters and coatings has had its good and bad years. The current fad for alpaca sweaters, beautiful as they are, may be starting to decline. High-priced, 100% alpaca is being adulterated with other fibers; the results are price reductions, inferior quality, and decreases in demand.
4. The only people presently promoting alpaca are the dealers, who go to the mills and try to interest the manager, stylist, superintendent, or designer in using the fiber in a salable article either in the knit or woven line. The efforts of the dealers to get alpaca into the mainstream of fabrics lack organized support in the form of promotion or advertising campaigns.

5. Some efforts have been made in Lima to develop handicraft programs. I expect to see similar programs in other cities.

The next day, Robert Morris and Jose Bermudez flew to Arequipa, an ancient Inca city and the major industrial and trading center of southern Peru. On the plane, Bermudez explained to Morris the distribution and processing of alpaca fleece and the importance of Arequipa as a processing center. Bermudez said:

> Alpacas are sheared during the warmest months of the year, November and December. The fleece is then gathered at important collection points, such as the cities of Cusco, Puno, and Juliaca, where they are wound into small bundles for ease of handling and transportation and shipped to Arequipa. There, examiners empty the sacks and check carefully to see that the contents have been properly represented and that sand has not been added to increase the weight, since the Indians frequently add sand. The fleece is then weighed and sorted into seven basic colors—piebald, black, dark brown, light brown, fawn, gray, and white—and graded for quality by skilled women. The two basic grades of quality, fleece and inferior, are sent to presses for baling, each bale weighing 220 pounds or 100 kilograms. About 80% of the total yearly yield of alpaca comes to Arequipa and then goes by rail or truck to the port of Mollendo, 100 miles away, for export to world markets. The remaining 20%, primarily inferiors, is shipped from Callao (the seaport of Lima) or Tacna.

For the next two days, they visited business offices and alpaca scouring and sorting plants. Many of the discussions were in English, but Jose Bermudez served as an interpreter when the persons interviewed spoke only Spanish.

The discussion with Mr. George Bentley, general manager of the Harrison Company, a manufacturer of alpaca combed yarns, tops (semi-processed wool), and waste, is recorded for the light it throws on Morris' investigation:

Robert Morris: "Mr. Bentley, why are the highest-quality alpaca sweaters knitted in Austria?"

George Bentley: "Simply because the most efficient knitters, like Lemmermeyer, are in Austria. The most experienced topmakers and spinners are in Bradford, England, the traditional market for alpaca. In order to produce a high-quality sweater of luxury style, the knitters require a highly elaborate yarn, and spinners in England specialize in the production of these yarns."

Robert Morris: "What are you doing to improve Peruvian yarn and knitting techniques?"

George Bentley: "Two combing and spinning plants are already operating, and others are planned. There are also several smaller and medium-sized knitting factories in Arequipa, but they do not produce articles of high quality for export. Several projects are under study to improve the production of sweaters in Peru."

Robert Morris: "I have been told that prices for alpaca fluctuate widely. Can you tell me why?"

George Bentley: "While we have no exact statistics about price fluctuations during the last two years, white fleece has been sold at less than $1.00 per pound and up to $4.00 F.O.B. Other colors have different prices, which also fluctuate according to supply and demand, depending on the fashion trend."

Morris and Bermudez flew to Tacna to visit the Harrison mill on Saturday afternoon. Later they caught the Southern Railway's overnight train to Puno. When the train reached Puno, 12,506 feet above sea level, the air was chilly and thin causing the men to feel somewhat lightheaded.

Gathering Information on the Alpaca Industry

On Monday and Tuesday Morris and Bermudez visited organizations, banks, and a technical university in Puno and hired a car to visit two organizations and a handicraft cooperative in nearby Juliaca.

Morris made notes on the most important and representative information gathered in Arequipa, Tacna, Puno, and Juliaca:

1. An issue that must be confronted is the change in manufacturing that has occurred in the past two decades. Mills of modern vintage, which have only high-speed, high-productivity, fully automated machinery are not appropriate for a fiber like alpaca. The breakdown of the entire alpaca clip into grades and colors results in "small-lot" production units. Large production plants refuse to process fabrics of small quantities.

2. Many people in southern Peru are of the impression that Peru should get into the manufacture of top (semi-processed wool). The bulk of production is shipped in the raw state.

3. The present system of grading and sorting alpaca fiber is based on the use of hands and eyes.

4. Workers in the higher altitudes have difficulty adjusting to indoor machine work.

5. A plentiful supply of good water is necessary. Filtration and softening are too costly.

6. Adequate and reliable power sources are basic, because in any of the processing stages of alpaca, a power failure can cause an operational breakdown, which is expensive.

7. Proper climatic conditions, whether natural or built-in, are necessary. Temperature and humidity should be kept constant.

8. Alpaca fiber in its natural color will not fade. The largest end use is in pile fabrics for low-priced coatings and inner linings in inexpensive raincoats.

9. The present Peruvian export tax on alpaca is almost equal to the producer's price.

10. Efforts have been made in the cities outside Lima to develop handicraft programs.
11. Approximately one million people in Peru depend on the alpaca crop in one way or another.
12. There has been extensive criticism of the exporting of alpaca fiber by Bolivia in small amounts at a distressed price to the Liverpool auction, which established a new world price affecting the alpaca industry of Peru.

The next morning, Morris and Bermudez departed for Lima. Robert Morris continued on a flight that represented the first leg of his return trip to the United States. He would have considerable time to reflect on his experiences in Peru.

The emphasis many Peruvians placed on alpaca top (semi-processed wool) bothered him. He believed there was no shortage of top combing machinery in the world and with the duty differential between raw fiber and top, which is considered a manufactured product, as well as the quality problem which would take years to overcome, it did not seem practical to put up plants in Peru to produce as an end product alpaca top. It would only be a "white elephant." The machinery cost would be high, and the training of workers would be costly. Considerable time and money would have to be expended to produce a quality product good enough to export. For top to bring an adequate return, it would require advantages that he did not see in Peru at present. Quality and price would have to be advantageous to a buyer in the world market.

On the other hand, if yarn could be produced, a ready market in mills lacking machinery could be expected.

He arrived in the United States shortly after midnight. On Monday morning, he called Mr. Harold Norden of the Durant Corporation, a friend of George Bentley's. Harold Norden introduced him over the telephone to Dr. Ricardo Lopez, who ran a wool fiber testing laboratory.

Realities of the Alpaca Industry

Comments of Harold Norden

The Durant Corporation is a major American producer of alpaca top from Peru and Bolivia. The alpaca fleece is shipped from Peru to New York City, where it passes customs and is then sent to scouring mills for scouring and combing. Two years ago alpaca top sold for $5.60 per pound. Today, it is selling for about $2.90 per pound. The alpaca combing mills are located in Rhode Island and New York. Importers like myself pay these mills a combing charge. Alpaca before it is scoured is called greasy alpaca. Scouring takes out the dust, dirt, and vegetable matter in the fiber. As a rule of thumb, there is a 12% loss in fiber weight after scouring. At one time, there was a 9¢ import duty charge per pound for clean alpaca. The rate was reduced to 6¢ per pound clean and 5½¢ per pound greasy. As of November of last year, it was further reduced to 4¢ per pound clean and 3½¢ per pound greasy. I suspect in five years there will be no duty on alpaca fiber.

Alpaca fiber is the strongest natural fiber in the world. It can replace wool or be combined with wool. Further, it has a lustrous sheen.

Alpaca fiber is used today primarily in the manufacture of sweaters and alpaca pile. No woolen mills in the United States today will use it. The darker shades of alpaca are usually used in coats, the lighter shades for sweaters.

Comments of Dr. Ricardo Lopez

Complete vertical integration is needed in the alpaca industry. In concrete terms, this means myriad support industries. For example, the following are needed for a vertically integrated knitting operation: a scouring mill, a top-making mill, a spinning mill, a dyeing mill, and a finishing mill. The scouring mill and the other support mills require extensive capital investment, but they do not provide a large enough price advantage. Unfortunately, there is only peripheral support for investment in Peru. Moreover, mere possession of the plant and equipment is not enough. Scouring, combing, spinning, and dyeing are about half science and technology and half art. Alpaca fibers differ in color, texture, and chemical properties. When finished products seem uniform in color, it is because they were dyed by highly talented and skilled persons who were able to blend various lots of alpaca with different dyes to make a uniformly colored product. This skill and art cannot be learned quickly, and those who know it do not give it away freely.

In addition to the costs involved for supporting facilities and the skill and techniques required, there is still another problem. Colors and styles for alpaca products are affected by the vagaries of fashion. The alpaca business is evanescent. Several years ago black, charcoal gray, and dark brown were the desired colors in alpaca sweaters. The cheaper colors, such as piebald and light brown, could be used. Today the emphasis is on lighter and brighter colors for which the white alpaca fleece must be used. If the manufacturer is too far away from the market, which is primarily the United States, he may be too slow to react to changes in fashion. The result, of course, will be unsold finished goods inventories.

The situation in Peru is analogous to that in Turkey. Most of the world's mohair, and the highest quality mohair, comes from Turkey, but the yarn is not woven there because the country has no scouring, sizing, dyeing, and finishing plants. There is no capital for investment, and Turkey is too far removed from the European and American markets.

Don't forget, the alpaca trade is self-defeating. It is a greedy trade. There is no reason in the world why an alpaca sweater should sell for $100 or more, but it is considered a luxury item. As the demand for the item goes up, the price of the fiber escalates rapidly. With the increase in price you would expect the Indians to produce more fiber. Quite the opposite, they produce less or stop completely. They are not concerned with enlarging their incomes beyond their customary level. I wish there would be some way we could increase their desire to want more things, because their attitude causes alpaca fiber prices to fluctuate wildly. The price for alpaca top now is about $3 per pound, but several years ago it rose to as high as $7 per pound. It takes about one pound to make a man's cardigan sweater.

Wool is a more stable product. Unlike alpaca, it is produced in several areas of the world. There is much greater competition and hence more price stability.

I suspect that Peru and Bolivia could produce 30 million pounds of alpaca a year, but there is no market for it. Consequently, the Indians do not collect all that is grown. Further, the government places a high export tax on the product. The government and the growers appear to cut off their nose to spite their face, because each wants a high percentage of tax and a high percentage of profit. The difference between alpaca and the better grades of wool is not very great, although alpaca is superior to wool and alpaca and wool blends are superior to wool itself. The large American companies, like Burlington Mills, are afraid to handle alpaca because of its price variations. In fact, in addition to the Durant Corporation, there are only three or four companies in the United States that import alpaca fiber.

Time for Decisions

Now, Robert Morris was ready to decide whether he should invest in some segment of the alpaca industry in Peru. He knew that 96% of the total alpaca fiber exported to the U.S. was fleece as opposed to 4% of inferior fiber. On the other hand, the United Kingdom imported 56% of inferior fiber and 44% of fleece. His interpretation of these percentages was that the present use for alpaca fiber in the United States was for sweaters. In the United Kingdom the inferior fibers were used for lining in coats. He would still have to explore other profitable uses of the fiber.

Morris would have to investigate the best way to evaluate marketing and promoting alpaca products in the United States and possibly Europe. He would also have to motivate Peruvian manufacturers to keep up with the latest fashion trends in the United States and Europe. He recalled that when looking for an alpaca tie in a department store in Lima, the width was not in keeping with lapel sizes of suits and sportcoats sold in fashionable American and European stores.

He planned to contact U.S. government officials in the Agency for International Development (AID) to seek industrial incentives. Companies processing alpaca might provide him information on processing, training, and licensing costs or even a joint venture partner. They might even recommend specific production stages suited to the Peruvian alpaca industry. Regardless, he would soon have to make a decision on what investments, if any, he should make in the Peruvian alpaca industry.

21
Motorola's Attempts to Increase Market Share and Profits in Japan

John E. Walsh, Jr. and William P. Coon

Motorola Corporation

In the early 1990s, Motorola's top management had to make a decision on a new strategy for increasing market share in the Japanese consumer and industrial markets. Between 1982 and 1990, Motorola had vigorously pursued sales of semiconductors and telecommunications equipment in the Japanese markets, while aggressively defending its U.S. market against Japanese dumping and predatory pricing. Motorola's successful dumping suits in the United States had brought them additional business with certain companies in Japan. Their Japan strategy had been to take a leadership product position with superior technology and quality, but they found out that these required great patience and very large up-front investments. As the executives considered all of the time and money that they had invested in selling to Japan, they concluded that they were less than satisfied with their previous return on their investment.

Product Lines

Motorola's business consisted of an integrated technology triad of semiconductors, communications, and computers. Their products included two-way radios, pagers, cellular telephones, and other electronic communications systems, semiconductors, defense and aerospace electronics, automotive and industrial electronic equipment, and data communications and information processing hardware and software. In 1987, the company registered worldwide sales of $7 billion.

The company had long been considered a powerhouse in land-mobile communications. In the early 1990s, it was one of the largest suppliers of two-way radios and assorted mobile electronic communications equipment in the world, with market share estimates of 65–75%. Motorola, General Electric (GE), and E.F. Johnson controlling about 85% of the U.S. two-way radio market, with the remainder going to very large, diversified Japanese firms such as NEC, Matsushita, and Fujitsu. In some categories, such as communications gear for police departments, Motorola accounted for approximately 90% of the total U.S. market. The company expected major growth to come from cellular radios. About half of the expected $2 billion revenues forecasted for the next five years would come from equipment for major stations that would transmit the radio signals, and half from the smaller terminals that individuals would use to communicate with one another.

The primary customers for Motorola's communications products included public safety agencies, utilities, transportation companies such as taxicab operators, and institutions such as schools and hospitals. Product development pressures in communications were high, and increasingly stressed the use of advanced electronic components. Competitive factors facing communications firms included price, product performance and quality, and availability of service and systems engineering. Because the equipment configurations demanded by its customers were diverse, Motorola found that none of these factors was dominant overall.

Motorola's product sales and leasing took a number of forms: primarily through a company distribution force, but also through independent distributors and commission agents, and through licensing of independent companies. One important variable affecting the firm's telecommunications operation was government regulation. In the United States and Japan, the government's allocation of frequencies could significantly affect the two-way radio business, particularly in congested urban areas.

The semiconductor industry was a rapidly growing, highly fragmented industry. Motorola faced intense competition from larger, vertically integrated Japanese firms. Motorola's semiconductors were used in a variety of products, including mass-market video and audio receivers, computers, automotive controls, industrial automation systems, and defense equipment. Like most companies in the industry, Motorola's sales were heavily oriented toward original equipment manufacturers and were typically channeled through both in-house distribution forces and independent distributors. Chips were supplied to other operating units within the company, a common practice at other diversified companies. Although its semiconductor sales tended to be sharply cyclical, Motorola had one of the most diversified semiconductor product lines in the industry.

Company Organization and Markets

Motorola's early history strongly emphasized consumer products. Founded as the Galvin Manufacturing Corporation in 1928 by Paul V. Galvin, two years later the firm introduced the first commercially manufactured car radio under the brand name

Motorola (Motor + Victrola = Motorola), and subsequently in 1947 adopted that name for the corporation. Over the next 40 years the company was involved in several consumer lines (as well as its communications and semiconductor businesses), including car and home radios and televisions. But in the early 1970s the company's focus shifted to high-technology industrial electronics, including advanced mobile telecommunications (e.g., cellular phones) and advanced semiconductors (e.g., microprocessors).

Motorola's leap from the consumer electronics field was unusual. As one business analyst noted, "What must be appreciated is that Galvin did this proactively. There was no crisis at Motorola; the company and the industry appeared to be in good shape. Galvin did something highly unusual for an American executive—he anticipated the need for future change even though the company was not in imminent trouble."[1] Galvin decided, in effect, to "bet the company" and make Motorola number one in semiconductors and retain the top spot in two-way communications over the next ten years. The overhaul at Motorola involved putting in place a mix of high-growth businesses, decentralizing the company allowing each division substantial autonomy while building up internal controls, establishing a long-term New Enterprises operation, introducing new personnel programs, and committing employees to very high quality—the formal goal was zero defects.

The company was run by the triumvirate of Bob Galvin (the founder's son), Bill Weisz, the vice-chairman and chief operating officer, and John Mitchell, the president and chief financial officer. The three men retained independent spheres of authority with responsibility to make any decision that had to be made in the corporation. If conflicts reached a stalemate, Galvin tipped the scales one way or the other. But the company had a democratic flair and had traditionally been a first-name organization. New employees were told to call the CEO "Bob." Galvin's managing style is a participative one. He relegated a good deal of the operation to others who were clearly more expert in certain details of operation than he was; he put his emphasis into leading the institution.

Evolution of Motorola in Japan

In the 1950s, President Eisenhower advised American business to increase its commercial dealing with Japan. Galvin took Eisenhower's suggestions seriously and encouraged Motorola to purchase electronic components from Japan and help Japanese companies set standards and improve quality in consumer electronic businesses such as car radios, home radios, and televisions. But things had changed drastically by the late 1970s. Motorola officials had witnessed strong Japanese inroads in the electronic components, portable radio, stereo system, car radio, brand name television, and citizen's band radio industries. "We can see the writing on the wall,"

[1]James O'Toole *Vanguard Management: Redesigning the Corporate Future* (Garden City, N.Y.: Doubleday & Co., 1985), p. 91.

one said, and "we know that the firm's survival will depend on how we confront the Japanese challenge. Japan has the second largest market in the world for our products (semiconductors and telecommunications) and some of the biggest and best competitors." Yet Motorola had run into one road block after another in Japan in the 1970s. Each division had attempted for years to sell into the Japanese market, but thus far they had little success.

Telecommunications

By the end of the 1970s, changes in U.S. regulatory policies ended the prohibition against plugging non-AT&T equipment into the U.S. telecommunications system. This shift in policy led to increasing inroads by foreign firms into the U.S. telecommunications market at a time when foreign countries retained strict clamps on their telecommunications sectors. To redress the growing trade imbalance in telecommunications equipment, the U.S. government negotiated a bilateral agreement with Japan in December 1980. The basic point of the agreement was that Nippon Telephone and Telegraph (NTT), Japan's state-owned telecommunications monopoly, would "for each proposed procurement, invite applications from the maximum number of domestic and foreign suppliers consistent with the efficient operation of the procurement system." The agreement stated that foreign firms responding to the requests for proposals (RFPs) would "be treated in a manner no less favorable than those domestic [firms] responding to the NTT-issued RFPs."[2] NTT was also obligated to supply complete information on both the product and the procurement process in the RFP and in supplemental documentation. A bilateral dispute settlement mechanism was set up to enforce the agreement, and the United States agreed not to bring any disputes to an international forum.

Galvin decided in 1979 that Motorola had to do all it could to enter the Japanese pager market—a market thought to be growing by as much as 10% per year. Before the bilateral agreement was penned, Motorola had made inquiries to NTT. Motorola was the worldwide market share leader in pagers, so company officials were certain they had the highest volume and probably the lowest cost in the world. Galvin also recognized that telecommunications systems were part of the lifeblood of advanced industrial countries, but pagers were a modest technology that NTT could not object to on grounds of national security.

Initially, Motorola's telecom group was unable to schedule an appointment to see the people at NTT and had to ask the United States Trade Representative to send cables just to get the appointment. The first meeting was not fruitful and convinced people at Motorola that they were going to need additional assistance from the American government. The Motorola officials had no idea what the specifications

---

[2]Cited in Stefanie Ann Lenway, *The Politics of U.S. International Trade: Protection, Expansion, and Escape* (Boston: Pitman Publishing, 1985), p. 188.

were, how to make a proposal, or how to sell a product to NTT, and NTT wouldn't tell them.

The communications division ultimately received a contract for $9 million worth of pagers in late 1981, 18 months after the first contact. The initial NTT contract was for 50-60,000 units. After providing NTT with an acceptable product, Motorola still had to undergo long negotiations on price and share. Historically, NTT reserved 60% of the market for NEC and Matsushita, the prime suppliers. Four other firms were to divide up the remaining 40%.

Motorola had experienced other problems in entering the telecommunications market. Japanese middle managers didn't want to "buy American" because they looked to retire to the big "family firms" like NEC, Fujitsu, Oki, and Hitachi. Moreover, NTT made no multi-year purchases. This was important because Japanese companies would enter a nominal bid to design a particular product, being reasonably sure that if they got that one contract from NTT they would get subsequent business. But a U.S. firm had neither an assurance that there would be follow-up work nor a commitment on future prices if they got a design contract. Companies had to take NTT on faith. Motorola was willing to take the risk because of its commitment to selling to NTT. For example, Motorola set up a separate pager production line for selling to NTT at a significant cost (Japanese specifications for telecommunications products frequently differed from worldwide standards). Indeed, Motorola expected it would take several years to show a profit with the pagers.

The company also had a long history of difficulties with the Ministry of Post and Telecommunications (MPT), which disallowed some of the services offered in other countries around the world. Japanese companies on MPT committees were not interested in rocking the boat by pushing for changes in the frequency allocation. Another problem was that standards tended to be set by MPT and a committee of Motorola's competitors, and MPT wouldn't allow competition on standards. This process gave Motorola's competitors a year's edge in getting from design to manufacturing.

Motorola had found it extremely difficult to crack other markets. While there were few discriminatory barriers, a major problem was that advanced products were regulated out of the market. This included products such as alphanumeric display pagers, digital voice privacy radios, "intrinsically safe" portable radios, and portable computer terminals with built-in modems. Several of these products had higher frequencies than the frequencies allowed in Japan. In product areas that were permitted, Motorola salespeople also found that strong social pressure from Japanese companies was placed on organizations considering foreign goods.[3] Motorola had achieved a very substantial share of the U.S. market in police two-way radios, but its police radios were invisible in Japan, despite extensive sales efforts.

---

[3]The owner of a trucking company told Motorola salespeople that "we would not buy a pager unless [Prime Minister] Nakasone himself called me and said it was worthwhile."

Semiconductors

Disputes in semiconductors dated back to the mid-1970s, starting with the founding in the United States of the Semiconductor Industry Association (SIA) in 1977. Articles such as "The Japanese Spies in Silicone Valley" charged the Japanese with using unethical means to gather intelligence on U.S. production methods and set a bitter tone early on.[4] Later, American producers complained that while the U.S. share of the Japanese market had remained mired at about 10% for over a decade, the Japanese had managed to increase their share of the American market steadily in a few years, rising to over 12% of the non-captive U.S. market in 1981 (44% in 1985).

One major difference between Japanese and U.S. firms was that Japanese semiconductor manufacturers tended to be very large and diversified while their U.S. counterparts were more likely to be specialized semiconductor companies. In fact, the Japanese firms challenging Motorola in semiconductors were for the most part the same firms challenging it in telecommunications. In semiconductors, however, firms such as NEC, Matsushita, Fujitsu, and Hitachi were major customers of Motorola as well as major competitors.

Semiconductor Manufacturing

Motorola decided in 1979 to buy a Japanese company as a way to advance its position in the Japanese semiconductor market. Local manufacturing in semiconductors would serve two purposes; provide local support for local problems, and help promote an image that Motorola's products were Japanese products. According to one official, the further down the technology curve in the semiconductor industry the more important it was that manufacturing be done in a local market. Customers were increasingly demanding that there be local manufacturing to support their local production operations. Texas Instruments (TI), the foreign market-share leader in Japan and Motorola's major U.S. challenger in semiconductor components other than microprocessors, had four Japanese factories and publicly expressed satisfaction with its access to Japanese customers.[5]

Galvin, Weisz, and Mitchell shared a general preference for a wholly-owned strategy because the company had bad experiences with joint ventures in earlier years in a number of countries. In 1980, Motorola's head of strategic planning identified Toko as a potential company in which Motorola might get involved in MOS wafer processing but didn't have the financial resources to fund these operations. A joint venture agreement was reached in November 1980 that included buyout options for both partners. Motorola was responsible for design and manufacturing, the Japanese were responsible for people matters, and both firms were to share sales and finance

---

[4]*Fortune,* February 27, 1978.
[5]TI invested in Japan before all other American manufacturers (1968). However, TI paid a high price for its rights to produce locally. The Japanese government demanded, and TI agreed to provide, licenses to all Japanese companies for some of its leading edge technology.

responsibility. However, by the end of 1981, it was already becoming clear that Toko was not going to be able to contribute their 50% of the capital spending.

Cultural Problems Encountered by Motorola

To provide a background on Japanese business culture, a consultant was hired to lecture to Motorola executives. The consultant pointed out that Japanese culture was quite different from America's. Often an American business person had difficulty comprehending the responses of a Japanese client or corporate audience. He then provided an example indicating typical American thinking in the midst of typical Japanese behavior.

> Alan, an American employee of a Japanese company, was looking forward to attending his first staff meeting. Because the agenda included an issue that would be controversial in an American office, Alan expected to encounter an interesting discussion.
>
> The meeting, however, ended up being pretty dull: there were no pro and con arguments. Instead, people asked a few questions about the issue, and some made brief comments in favor of one proposed solution. Alan had heard that some of the staff disagreed with this proposed solution, but they merely raised a few minor questions. One committee member did state his objection; there was a moment of silence, and no one responded. Then the chairperson asked if there were any other questions or comments and brought the issue to a close. He didn't even call for a vote! In the end, Alan thought, they hadn't discussed anything substantial at all.

The consultant continued:

> What Alan didn't realize was that, although company staff meetings in Japan can include lively discussion, group involvement in projects typically required much consensus-building before formal decisions are made. One was expected to figure out that a "pointless question" or silence meant reservations or disagreement. Sometimes a lone dissenter was ignored because he or she had not made the effort to get constructive criticism along horizontal lines (among peers) before formal statements were made. Due to a strong Japanese group identity, group approval was often secured by more informal maneuvering prior to the meeting. This process was called *nemawashi,*[6] an important skill in Japanese society. The process involved in settling the means by which a problem is solved informally between different sections and departments is call *uchi-awase.* During *nemawashi* and *uchi-awase,* Japanese consciously try to get a feel for the other person and his or her character by a non-verbal communication termed *hara gei,* or "belly art."

---

[6]A gardening term used to describe the process of digging out the roots of a tree to prepare for a successful transfer to another location.

The Motorola executives were certain that Japan engaged in protectionist tactics designed to protect its domestic markets. What caused this "keep out the foreigner" attitude? The consultant attributed it to the fact that Japan was an island nation.

A Sketch of Japanese History

Through much of its history, Japan had been isolated from the rest of the world, both because of geographical position and historical circumstances. Japan had sometimes been compared to England, another island nation, but the distance separating Japan and the Asiatic mainland was about six times as great as the Straits of Dover, and the journey from Japan to Korea was never lightly undertaken. Moreover, for very long periods Japan was closed to virtually all outsiders by deliberate policy of the government. During the two centuries before Perry's visit in 1853,[7] the Tokugawa Shogunate, a military government that ruled Japan from 1603 to 1868, kept the country closed. Unlike England, Japan was never conquered by a foreign power and the only foreign influences on language, customs, and institutions were those that the Japanese themselves chose.

Remoteness from the rest of the world, and the infrequency, over the centuries, of contacts with foreigners had made many Japanese timid and awkward in their personal dealings with foreigners who came from countries more highly advanced in technology and industry. These feelings were reinforced by the organization of Japanese society as a family system.

The family system was extremely deep-rooted in Japan. During the period of seclusion (1630 to 1853), the Tokugawa *shoguns*[8] deliberately fostered the teachings of Confucius, a Chinese sage who taught that filial piety (*kô*), duty (*giri*), and obligation (*on*) were sacrosanct. These teachings were believed to promote stability through the creation of four classes—*samurai*,[9] farmers, artisans, and merchants— who knew and accepted their societal rights and obligations. Even after Japan adopted many Western ideas in the late 1800s, filial piety was proclaimed to be the source of all virtue. The state was often discussed as if it were a huge family headed by the emperor, and the identity of the loyalty due him and the filial piety due a father was frequently stressed.[10] These feelings existed in the modern Japanese corporate world. A Japanese firm did well if it was successful in obtaining technology or market share in foreign markets while, at the same time, fiercely protecting Japan's home markets from any "foreign invasion."

The consultant commented that during the previous forty years, Japan had given the West many excuses for maintaining its trade barriers: in the 1950s Japan claimed

---

[7]U.S. Navy Commodore Matthew C. Perry sailed to Japan with three gunboats under orders to force the Shogunate to engage in international trade.

[8]Military leaders who actually ruled Japan during this period.

[9]The warriors or soldiers.

[10]Dr. Donald Keene, *Living Japan,* 1979.

to be a poor country that couldn't effectively compete with the Western business powers; later, Japan claimed that Western products would not satisfy the different tastes of the Japanese (Western cherries were too sweet, the oranges were too orange, or foreign beef was harmful to Japanese stomachs); recently, the claim has been that Western products don't meet the stringent Japanese standards of quality. Whatever the reason, the results were the same: the Japanese domestic markets were protected by various means against foreign products reaching the Japanese consumers.

For Motorola's managers to intelligently design and implement their long-term strategy for Japan, it was imperative to understand the nuances of the Japanese style of doing business. Could Motorola succeed where other American firms had failed? Its executives quickly found out that there were many barriers, formal and informal, to doing business in Japan; among these obstacles were:

• Japan was the most expensive country in the world for foreign companies.
• There were many difficulties in locating and hiring qualified personnel; should those personnel be Japanese or American?
• Japan presented Motorola with a system of business based on intricate relationships that drive business and government-making processes.
• Selling in Japan meant entering the multi-tiered distribution systems characterized by exclusive trading arrangements, cross-ownerships with manufacturers, and high-cost physical distribution.
• Government-sanctioned cartels marked by close interdependence within a vertically-integrated cartel group.
• Purchasing discrimination against foreign companies by Japanese managers and government officials.
• The Japanese excluded many American products on issues of quality.
• Motorola found that they needed pressure from the U.S. government to pressure the Japanese to open certain markets.

To deeply understand the cultural differences that were critical to success between the U.S. and Japan was not easy. One common mistake made by Motorola executives was believing that if they understood the cultural differences, then they would be able to use the same sales techniques that proved successful in the United States. Even when you spoke the Japanese language and knew their customs well, you might still fail.

The consultant mentioned the problems of Ryusuke Hasegawa, an American who attempted to help his company enter the Japanese market with a product that was both superior and less expensive to its Japanese competitors. Mr. Hasegawa, a naturalized American, had been born in Japan 49 years earlier. He attended college there and didn't leave until he had earned a Master's degree. No one could complain that he didn't know the language or customs.

He returned to Japan with a high-tech product to sell, a $12 billion corporation, Allied Signal, to back him up, and a partnership with some blue-chip Japanese companies. Yet, Mr. Hasegawa returned to the United States after four years of frustration. He thought:

> This is ridiculous. I speak the language, I understand the customs, this can't happen to me. And then things didn't go as I expected. The Japanese like harmony. You say, "Buy ours, it's cheaper," and they won't. And you say, "Why not?" And they say, "Because we're happy. You're destroying our harmony. Everything was harmonious until you came along."
>
> I spent much of my time defending Allied's invention against patent challenges by Japanese competitors and meeting and drinking with potential customers who never seemed quite ready to buy. I later found out that the Japanese government had been funding research to catch and surpass us. I feel bad for American companies. We do a lot of basic research, and when we're about to be successful, a Japanese company comes in and gets the business.

Like many foreigners before him, Mr. Hasegawa ran into invisible cultural trade barriers, a Japanese instinct, official and unofficial, to protect its industry from foreign competition, and the willingness of Japanese firms to invest huge sums in research rather than cede any ground to competitors.

Mr. Hasegawa came to feel that Japanese companies regarded his venture with suspicion because it was foreign, despite his Japanese partners and his own Japanese heritage.

> The Japanese have this strange custom. They have to do everything themselves. Why do they have to make scotch whiskey? Why do they have to make wine? They don't even have a grape suited to wine. I was born in Japan. I was brought up in Japan, but I still don't understand it.

Mr. Hasegawa's story was given further credibility by another American businessman, Ivan P. Hall, quoted in the *Asian Wall Street Journal,* July 6, 1987:

> The truth is that the Japanese view the participation of foreigners in the working institutions of their society as a threat to their value system, social relationships, and way of life. Without steady outside pressure, they are not about to give foreigners the same access to their market and society as Japanese businessmen, bankers, lawyers, journalists and scholars now enjoy in most Western countries.

Business historians believed that the prevalent Japanese attitude towards protecting its markets against foreigners had been part of the Japanese culture for many years. "No foreigner can compete against the pampered Japanese manufacturer in his own land, except under peculiar circumstances," wrote F. Coleman in his book *Far East Unveiled,* published in 1918. Twenty-six years earlier the British philosopher Herbert Spence advised Count Ito, the prime minister, through a letter to Baron Kentaro, to keep Americans and Europeans at arms' length as much as possible.

The *Keiretsu* as an Impediment to Foreign Exporters

Japanese society was organized by the grouping of familial structures of common interest—in businesses, government bureaucracies, political parties, and even universities. The nation was largely tied together by a web of informal interrelationships (the cartels), as well as their formal derivatives, the *keiretsu*. Politics, society, and business were ensnared because the Japanese believed that these insular arrangements maintained the society of the nation, provided full employment, and distributed the burden of financial and R&D risks.

Despite the often touted Japanese desire for *wa,* or harmony, there was nothing sentimental about these business groups; they could be ruthless. Each *keiretsu* resembled a fighting clan in which business families, typically consisting of a bank (which provided capital at minimal expense), a large trading company (that facilitated export trade), and a large manufacturing company, joined together to help the members acquire and maintain market share. *Keiretsu* and cartels recognized one another as competitors. Virtually all business activity was part of one or another *keiretsu* or cartel. Some cartel-like activity, like price-fixing within an industry, could be blatantly illegal. Yet most cartel practices were legally tolerated by the Japanese system. Hundreds of cartels had been established to set prices, rationalize industries, and respond to depressed markets or threats from foreign competition.

Japan's *keiretsu* ranged from very small affiliations to enormous, well-known, horizontally and vertically-organized corporate networks that included close to 200 of the nation's biggest and best-known companies (Mitsui, Sumitomo, Toshiba, Mitsubishi). Among the tactics used to prevent market share penetration by foreigners were:

■ Control of the flow of products, accessories, services, and prices from factory to the consumer. Shops agree to sell no other brands; dealers agree to sell at manufacturer's recommended prices; rebates to retailers are based on the degree of brand loyalty.

■ Related companies receive loans, investment capital, technology, and long-term supply agreement from customers within the *keiretsu*. In exchange, they integrate their operations and those of their suppliers directly with the final assembler. They agree to make their plants and inventory systems conform to schedules passed down from above. They absorb losses and layoffs when business conditions tighten higher up in the pyramid and find positions for executives seeking second careers.

Motorola correctly identified *keiretsu* trade practices as structural barriers to free trade. It also recognized that Japan would not change its deep-rooted, multifaceted cartel system. Motorola decided in the mid-1980s to exploit the Japanese cartel strategy by forming an alliance with a major Japanese company. It anticipated triple benefits: the capture of new sales in the Japanese market, increased knowledge of the demands of the Japanese marketplace, and the gaining of a position in the cartels that serve that marketplace.

In 1986, Motorola entered into a partnership with Toshiba. After forming a manufacturing joint venture in Japan, Motorola traded medium-level microprocessor capability for Toshiba's one-megabyte DRAM[11] process. Toshiba even provided the employee who became president of Motorola Japan. As one Motorola official stated: "We needed this partnership to gain access to Japanese R&D, stay close to Japanese chip buyers, who consume over 40% of the world's semiconductors, and teach them how to relate to a major Japanese corporation." There was one other reason for Motorola to form the alliance; there were virtually no other alternatives.

Motorola's Alliance with the U.S. Government

The Japanese were acquiring market share in the United States at the expense of companies like Motorola while maintaining its phalanx of trade barriers in Japan against foreign market penetration. Motorola decided to attack on both fronts. It could not afford to trade 50% of its U.S. market share for an additional 5% of the Japanese market.

Motorola was concerned about the effects of Japanese industry-promotion policies on competition in the U.S. The Japanese policies that most concerned Motorola were identified by Weisz as a "set of differences," the sum of which gives them a major competitive advantage that can't be matched by U.S. companies. The differences in the government-supported activities included the "targeting" of specific industries by Public Laws 17 and 84 (see Appendix A), promoting and occasionally requiring cartelization of Japanese companies to meet national goals, and the financing of many activities whose aim was successful commercial results, such as joint research by Japanese competitors.

The financial system, in Weisz's view, through bank and government support, provided essentially a guaranteed flow of relatively cheap capital to big companies, thus minimizing their risk of failure. Unlike American firms, Japanese firms did not have to fund their growth through their internal cash flow.

Motorola employed an aggressive defensive strategy to ensure fair competition in the U.S. telecommunications market. They filed three successful suits: copyright and patent infringements on pagers, pricing below cost on Japanese export of pagers, and dumping of cellular mobile phones. In the pager case Motorola knew the prices charged by its Japanese competitors for NTT business because NTT required each firm to submit a bid and match the lowest price. Thus, Motorola knew what the Japanese firms were selling the pagers for in Japan, and after a detailed cost analysis study, knew what price they could charge and still make a profit. The duties imposed by the U.S. government were very high in the pagers case.

---

[11]DRAMs were dynamic random access memory chips, the world's best selling computer chips.

Motorola devoted considerable energy to a highly visible and aggressive campaign of persuading government officials and business executives in articles, speeches, and testimony that the Japanese challenge to American industry was of dire importance. They believed that U.S. industry was just as capable as the Japanese and produced products of equal or better quality. Motorola was instrumental in forming the Coalition for International Trade Equity, a multifirm group seeking wide-ranging trade reform to counteract foreign industrial "targeting."

Japan's legendary attunement to *gaiatsu,* or pressure from foreigners, suggested that it did heed and even responded to criticism. Motorola had found that, by allying itself with the U.S. government, its market share in Japan had increased. Motorola was instrumental in convincing the United States Trade Representatives from 1985 until the present to threaten the use of, or actually use on three occasions, trade sanctions against Japan authorized under Section 301 of the Trade Act of 1974. Motorola's semiconductor share of the Japanese domestic market had increased from less than 1% in 1985 to over 9% in 1992. Its third-party radios, used by taxis and security firms, now held 23% of the Japanese market share. Company officials freely admitted that these results would not have been possible without the pressure from the U.S. government.

Charles Cook, an MEMC[12] executive, talks about his company's efforts to increase their Japanese market share:

> We were extremely frustrated that Japanese customers would not want our products. After all, we had world leadership in several key developments, but found that our Japanese market share for those items was less than one percent! Even after we hired local distributors, set up local warehouses and technical support, there were still no signs that Japanese buyers would accept our products. We knew our products were good enough—our specs were superior to anything the Japanese were buying.
>
> During this period, we contacted Senator John Danforth (Missouri), who was chairman of an important subcommittee on international trade. MEMC prepared several brochures to document its concerns, and distributed copies to the staff of the U.S. Trade Representative (USTR) and the Department of Commerce (DOC) who needed to be made aware of these activities.
>
> In Japan, we met with Ambassador Mansfield. Detailed background information was provided to him and his staff. Contact was also made with MITI officials to document our concerns and to advise them of the general approach being taken. This latter point is essential to sustaining a working relationship with those who must become your allies if you are to be successful in Japan. The first benefits of our political actions appeared when Japan reduced a discriminatory duty on one of our semiconductors. Our additional profits were several hundred thousand dollars per year—they were welcome, but were still small potatoes compared to the benefits of an open market.

---

[12]MEMC is a global producer of silicon wafers, the material on which almost all semiconductors are made. It was an operating unit of Monsanto Company until April 1989, when it was acquired by Hüls AG, a large German chemical company. The period covered by these comments is 1984–1992.

The effort to involve multiple sources of help required much more time coordinating and communicating than was originally anticipated, but the benefits soon became evident. Several senators, during committee meetings and interviews, used MEMC as an example of a U.S. firm being excluded from the Japanese markets. Ambassador Mansfield made several comments to senior Japanese government officials, one of which resulted in the visit of a high-ranking MITI official to MEMC's new plant in Japan. Regular comments by USTR and DOC staff to their Japanese counterparts were extremely helpful in keeping the issue active. The press began soliciting MEMC's Japanese staff's opinions in interviews, and even Japanese and American TV stations occasionally included our circumstances in their broadcasts.

While these results sound inviting, it is important to remember that they resulted from a sustained five-year effort, and were always supported by unflagging commitment to satisfying customers' demand (whether reasonable or not). While this level of commitment is, of course, critical to cracking any new customer or market, it is particularly sensitive when political activity is involved.

Today our continuing battle for market access uses political activity primarily to sustain the support of key staff within MITI. These bureaucrats are very sensitive to the ever-growing American public's concern over Japan's trading practices. Focus has shifted from absolute barriers to the extremely slow—and therefore, costly—rate of progress.

Was it worth it? Yes, it was. There is still a long way to go, but we have had progress in critical areas. Whatever damage might have been done initially to relationships with Japanese customers and government officials seems to have given way to grudging respect in the realization that our company is a tough, determined, and increasingly effective competitor. And, in the long run, this is all that counts.

Motorola's detractors thought that a highly publicized trade offensive with the Japanese would backfire. However, Motorola's overall aggressiveness on the trade issue earned it a reputation in Japan as one of the most politically connected and powerful companies in the United States. A Japanese semiconductor trade magazine in 1990 cited Motorola as "the vanguard" of those companies that were pressuring Japan and the "key company" on trade issues. The article also reported that "executives of a few Japanese semiconductor makers were alarmed by Motorola's intense campaign . . .," and advised its readers to "keep track of Motorola."

The Issue of Quality

One of Motorola's first shipments of semiconductors to a Japanese customer was rejected due to the poorly-applied Motorola logo on the top of the chips—the paint was faint and difficult to read. Motorola protested that the logo had nothing to do with the chip's performance; the Japanese considered it a reflection of the poor quality of most American products. Eventually, Motorola replaced the shipment with new chips with freshly-applied logos.

This Japanese predilection with quality was a hurdle many American firms failed to clear when attempting to enter the Japanese market. Motorola decided at the outset that they would do whatever was necessary to gain access to the world's second largest consumer and industrial market. They even dedicated, at great initial capital outlay, a separate manufacturing line at their microprocessor plant to the making of high-quality chips for the Japanese.

The Japanese showed American companies how to use quality as a marketing tool. In 1989, Hewlett Packard, a major scientific instrument and computer manufacturer, announced that the failure rate of Japanese chips was one-fifth that of U.S.-made chips. It was not that U.S. quality was poor—it met the specifications of the buyers; but the Japanese *had surpassed* the specs. In the 1970s, the Japanese focus switched from price to quality. They had poured effort into education to raise the skill level of their workforce. Now they were able to move the basis of competition from the cost of labor to the skill of labor. Their emphasis on quality had become legendary, and its results became evident between 1980 and 1986 when Americans gladly paid premiums for Japanese cars in preference to the products of Detroit.

Motorola initially had a difficult time in securing the specifications for pagers being purchased by NTT, the giant Japanese telephone company; Motorola at the time was the unquestioned world leader in quantity and quality of pager manufacturing. When the specifications were eventually released, company officials soon discovered that NTT emphasized product design as well as product performance and expected designs to be followed explicitly, regardless of whether there were alternative ways to do the same thing. When Motorola originally proposed to change the electric current used from the battery in pagers, NTT refused. After prolonged negotiation, this change was eventually allowed. Motorola ran into another problem because it used a microprocessor that recirculated a timing mechanism every 11 times the pagers performed a certain task rather than every 10 as listed in the specifications. NTT considered the request to allow such an exemption a very poor reflection on Motorola and was firm in its opposition, despite the negligible influence the change would have on the pager's performance. Again, Motorola adapted to the demands of this particular market and became the dominant foreign supplier of pagers.

Interview with Bob Galvin

The Motorola chairman spoke about why some American companies were destined to fail in Japan:

> Why did most U.S. companies fail to penetrate Japan? A lot of companies didn't have a good entry strategy. They selected a Japanese trading company to distribute their products over there, but the company they chose may not have had a wide-enough network. If you didn't form a joint venture with a giant company like Toshiba, then it was better to use several trading companies. Also, too many American firms just went over to Japan to work out a deal. Then they forgot about what was happening there. Most semiconductor companies had 15-25% of their business in Japan, but they usually only based 1-2% of their people there.

How did you establish a real presence in Japan? The biggest challenge was attracting Japanese intermediate managers. People in Japan didn't change companies very often. Experienced managers, those in their late 30s to mid-40s, were already established in the big Japanese companies.

The Japanese market opens only when pressure is applied. It only responds to influence, pressure, and prying things open. I suggest the application of pressure to open markets isn't Japan-bashing or protectionism.

If we are going to have more balanced trade with Japan, the professional buyers in Japan must act more like some of the role-model companies in Japan, like NEC, that do in fact seek more balanced trade with the U.S.

People always asked me whether Japan played "fair" or not. It was not an issue of fairness. Japan had a game plan. It intended to be the leading manufacturing and trading nation, and all of its decisions were based on that. Its objective was to have the best products, the best global market, the best-educated populace and a growing economy. It didn't make a secret about that. The question wasn't whether Japan was playing fair. The question was whether we wanted to compete or not.

I always thought that our success in Japan helped us in other global markets. It didn't matter if it was high tech, low tech, or no tech. You had to compete with the Japanese around the corner or in global markets. After having competed in Japan, we improved our worldwide sensitivity to customer service, raised our quality standards and reduced our inventories to just-in-time. Most U.S. firms had a tough time in global markets because they didn't have the standards that they would have developed by competing in Japan.

With hundreds of millions of dollars in additional investment being considered for the Japanese market by Motorola's semiconductor and telecommunications divisions, Motorola management faced some tough strategic choices. Motorola had been one of the world's most successful firms in mobile telecommunications and semiconductors over the previous two decades. They had devised a strategy for every previous problem that allowed them to remain independent and profitable. But Galvin sensed that Japan was a different challenge. So he called together his entire top management team, asking "what are the range of strategic options, and how should Motorola respond?"

Appendix A
Excerpts from Japan's Public Law No. 84, July 1978

Article 1: Purposes. The purposes of this law are to develop specific machinery and information industries by promoting, among other things, improvement of manufacturing technology and rationalization of production thereof, and thus to contribute to the sound development of the national economy and improvement of national standards.

Article 3: Advancement Plan. The Competent Minister must set up a plan concerning advancement . . . with respect to the following industries . . .: (a) those industries manufacturing such electronic machines and tools specified by government order, the manufacturing technology of which has not yet been established in Japan and which especially require the promotion of experiment and research . . .; (b) those industries manufacturing such equipment and tools specified by government order, the industrial production of which is not conducted in Japan or the production quantity of which is extremely small, and which especially require the promotion of the commencement of industrial production or increase of production quantity; (c) those industries manufacturing such electronic machines and tools specified by government order, which especially require the promotion of rationalization of production, such as improvement of performance or quality or reduction of production costs, etc. . . .

Matters to be set forth in the Advancement Plan for those industries described in (a) include content of the experimentation and research and the target year of its completion; matters concerning funds necessary for the experimentation and research . . .; With respect to the industries in (b), such matters which are fundamental for the promotion of the commencement of industrial production or increase of production quantity, including . . . the production quantity for the final target year; the kind and numbers of facilities to be newly established . . .; With respect to industries in (c), such matters which are fundamental for the promotion of rationalization of production, including target of rationalization, such as target of performance or quality, production costs, etc. for the final target year; kind and number of facilities to be newly established; matters including proper scale of production, introduction of cooperation of the business or specialization of the kinds to be produced; matters concerning funds necessary for rationalization; and other important matters concerning promotion of rationalization.

Article 5: Procurement of Funds. The government shall make efforts to procure the necessary funds set forth in the Advancement Plan.

Article 6: Direction Concerning Practice of Concerted Acts. The Competent Minister may direct that persons engaged in the business of the industries described (above) . . . should practice concerted acts with respect to the restriction of standards or the restriction of technology, in case he deems it especially necessary in order to accomplish the target of rationalization set forth in the Advancement Plan concerning such industries.

22
Client Development in Japan: Elcolab, Inc.

John Zerio
and
Bert K. Tsutakawa

Dan Jensen sat back in his chair to contemplate the past six and a half months and the progress he had made. Dan had been given the opportunity to market medical equipment to Japan and wanted to review his efforts. After finishing final negotiations with a Japanese distributor and arriving by plane from Tokyo, his boss, Mr. Hong, had asked Dan to prepare a summary of activities and results, and asked Dan directly whether or not Dan thought the distributor would actually purchase the product. Because the negotiation was agreed upon by handshake and not by contract, Dan strongly believed that the distributor would follow through on his promise. However, Dan knew he had to carefully retrace his steps to understand why his marketing plan had been successful in some areas and unsuccessful in others.

Dan's Background

Over a year and a half ago, Dan had met Mr. Hong, the president of Elcolab, Inc., in Los Angeles at a friend's dinner party. In subsequent meetings, Mr. Hong explained that he needed an operations manager to assist Elcolab's Tokyo sales office in the introduction of a new medical device in Japan. Mr. Hong also had mentioned that he had hired a young Japanese man one year before to assist him in product licensing, market research, technical support, and sales. However, the man recently had written a letter saying that because he couldn't seem to sell the product

This case was prepared as the basis for class discussion rather than to illustrate effective or ineffective handling of an administrative situation.

at all or find any data on the existing market, he had given up. Furthermore, when Mr. Hong attempted to fax messages to the man, there was no reply.

During one of their meetings, Dan was shown the latest product, the Elco-1, product literature, and an elaborate marketing plan. Dan was a natural problem solver, so he was very interested in Mr. Hong's new venture; however, he had just started an engineering job with a major aerospace firm. Mr. Hong was persistent, and after a year he directly offered Dan the position of operations manager. Dan accepted after several days of contemplation.

Although Dan had no international business or cross-cultural experience, he had taken several import/export classes and introductory Japanese language courses. However, Dan felt he did not know the language well enough, and planned to have a young Japanese man act as an interpreter during his stay in Japan. Dan, who was 27, felt that his most important attributes were his B.S. in electrical engineering, his organizational, project planning, and problem solving skills, and his five years of technical experience in the United States. Mr. Hong arranged a six-month visa for Dan to work in Japan.

Just before Dan was about to leave, Mr. Hong took Dan aside and explained that due to contract agreements with his manufacturer, he now wanted products sold within two months. He also explained that there were two scenarios for success. The first scenario was for Dan to succeed in selling products, and for Dan to eventually take over operations in Japan. The second scenario meant that Dan was to quickly close the operation, and rapidly salvage the situation by selling products, licenses, and the corporation to the highest bidder, while recycling the money to a new project. Dan indicated that he preferred the first scenario, and to Dan's surprise, Mr. Hong offered him a 25% stock share in his Japanese operations as an incentive.

In early January, Dan arrived in Japan and was picked up at the airport by a young Japanese man, Mr. Iwase. Mr. Iwase was polite, however, Dan could tell that the man felt threatened by his sudden arrival in Tokyo, but Dan gave him the benefit of the doubt because his mission was to revitalize operations.

As promised, Dan provided Mr. Hong with a financial status report, budgeting projections, equipment and product inventory, and a PERT chart indicating what steps he would take to improve operations at the site. He spent the first week and a half listening to Mr. Iwase's problems with selling the Elco-1. During their conversations, Mr. Iwase told Dan that he had experienced a lot of frustration with Mr. Hong's conflicting directives toward price setting and commitment to on-going projects, which always seemed to end with Mr. Iwase loosing face to friends, business associates, and potential end-users. Dan also had extensive and lengthy conversations about the Japanese market and sales with Mr. Sato (Mr. Hong's father-in-law) who lived in Nagoya and headed Elcolab Japan. His sales office was in central Tokyo.

Mr. Hong provided Dan with a preliminary market plan, however, Dan felt it was inadequate and made efforts to update. Dan started by reviewing the firm and its product.

The Product

The product to be marketed to Japan was the Elco-1, a Microcurrent Electro-Neuro Stimulatory unit (MENS), which uses micro-amperage current to stimulate pain relief. The product sends an electrical current through muscle tissue to temporarily reduce pain and swelling and creates a healing environment within the area to promote permanent pain relief. At fourteen pounds, the unit is light and portable. The Elco-1 has three outputs that allow up to three patients to use the machine at the same time. Applications and uses for the Elco-1 (by priority) were as follows:

1. Accidents treated by rehabilitation and medical hospitals
2. Geriatric related aches and pains
3. Olympic and professional sports related aches and pains
4. Stress and relaxation treatment
5. Health and fitness

Dan compared the Elco-1 to other competitors to determine its advantages.

Advantages

The most important advantage of Elco-1 was that it was the only micro-amperage device in Japan with both Japanese Kouseishou and United States FDA approval. Obtaining approval through the Kouseishou is difficult, usually taking several years and mountains of paperwork, but through Mr. Sato's connections, the Elco-1 had been approved in less than a year. Dan believed that Kouseishou medical approval constituted a substantial barrier for other competitors, and gave Elcolab a major time advantage. There were other companies that had machines with similar technology as the Elco-1, but they were still awaiting Kouseishou approval. Additionally, the U.S. manufacturer of the Elco-1 had awarded exclusive distribution rights for the Japanese market to Elcolab.

Other important advantages of Elco-1 included a one-year product and service warranty from Elcolab Japan and the U.S. manufacturer. Elcolab provided a bilingual instruction manual and four notebooks with U.S. technical and medical recommendations and authorizations. The company also offered an airfare-paid, one-week, training trip to Elcolab's headquarters in San Diego. The Japanese would be trained to operate the Elco-1 efficiently and would have the opportunity to meet with Elcolab executives and researchers. Furthermore, the unit was attractively packaged and endorsed by a major U.S. track and field multi-gold medalist.

Competition

In the Japanese market, there were ten companies promoting large TENS (transcutaneous electro-neuro stimulatory) units that dominated the market and were considered to be serious competitors to the Elco-1. The difference between MENS and

TENS units is the amount of current that the devices use. TENS products use milli-amperage, which has a thousand times stronger current than the micro-amperage of the MENS units. Patients using milli-amperage actually feel the muscle twitch as the current enters their body. However, Elcolab researchers, after doing extensive investigation, concluded that that much current was actually too strong for the body and could possibly retard healing. They believed that a more subtle current, produced in the micro-amperage product, would create a healing environment in the painful area. The only other MENS competitor in Japan was the U.S. manufactured Electro-Acuscope, priced at 5 million yen, which was five times higher than the Elco-1. Dan believed that there was a niche in the market for a good machine like the Elco-1.

Client Profiles

As a first step, Dan developed profiles of the two types of customers who would actually be purchasing and using the Elco-1. Dan's first group included acupuncturists and machine-using chiropractors who were usually men in their 30s or older, characterized by their experimental, modern, creative, and innovative attitudes toward new medical developments. The acupuncturists and chiropractors were located in central Tokyo. Most had a moderate operating budget, but Dan felt that they would be able to afford the Elco-1 and receive a tax write-off for the training on the product.

The acupuncturists/chiropractors were entrepreneurial and usually had tight appointment schedules. Minimal certification was required and therefore, the educational and technical level varied within the group. Furthermore, some practitioners were able to speak English. The acupuncturists/chiropractors typically used TENS technology, which meant Dan would face the challenge of promoting MENS technology as well as the Elco-1 itself. In addition, because stimulation from the Elco-1 one was non-invasive, and some customers were afraid of the AIDS virus through acupuncture needles, an additional selling point could be raised.

The second main customer group that Dan profiled were medical professionals, including doctors and hospital administrators. Like the acupuncturists and chiropractors, they were usually males in their 30s or older, located in central Tokyo. In contrast, however, their attitudes toward new medical devices were extremely conservative and traditional. Medical professionals typically were associated with large organizations that had central administrators, high operating budgets, and were not taxed. Therefore, Dan believed that this group could afford many units. Like the acupuncturists and chiropractors, the medical professionals had very tight appointment schedules and used TENS technology. However, the medical professionals all had medical degrees, extremely high education levels (most spoke English), and were very technically literate.

Direct Mail Campaign

To initiate contact with these two groups, Mr. Hong recommended that Dan implement a direct mail campaign to sell the Elco-1s. Mr. Hong was unsure of how to price the Elco-1, because the Electro-Acuscope was selling for many times more than retail in the United States. He was also unsure about how end-users would perceive the product due to the newness of the technology. Mr. Hong's plan was to find a buyer and slip into the market without being detected by Japanese medical equipment manufacturers. Mr. Hong felt that by slipping in, he would avoid a major confrontation with larger and more established operations.

When Dan mentioned Mr. Hong's idea about direct selling to Mr. Iwase, Mr. Iwase reacted negatively, but Dan decided to proceed because he knew that similar direct mail campaigns in the U.S. had been very successful. Dan saw merits to a direct mail strategy as a good way to gather information about how the market perceived the Elco-1. He felt that although this strategy would require a greater initial effort and possible a longer start-up time, the profit margin would be much better because there would be no middlemen. Dan realized that the direct mail approach would not be a good idea if he needed to sell a large number of units in a short time.

However, Dan wanted to concentrate his marketing efforts on client development, not on achieving a rapid sales volume, and, therefore, decided to go ahead with the direct mail campaign. Most of the Elco-1 unit data was written in English, so Dan first planned to send information to rehabilitation hospital general managers and doctors because most could read English. Also, medical professionals did not have to pay the heavy Japanese tax, which might make a purchase decision easier.

Dan's plan was to first secure a mailing list and to send the prospective end-user a package, including a business card, introductory letter, color English brochures, medical and technological recommendations, and a mail-back card that the client could use to request additional information. After the direct mail package had been sent, Dan would follow up with a phone call to make an appointment to conduct a demonstration. Dan then planned to work closely with the client to close the sale.

To begin, Dan selected the names of twenty acupuncturists and chiropractors from the Japan Yellow Pages, an English telephone directory of businesses in Japan. The next set of eighty names comprised medical professionals, acupuncturists, and chiropractors that were sourced from addresses left by Japanese doctors attending microcurrent seminars in the United States, contacts provided by JETRO, the California State Trade Office in Tokyo, the U.S. Embassy Commercial Attache, and referrals from previous sales efforts.

Dan was surprised that only one individual sent back the self-addressed stamped envelope to the office expressing interest in the product. However, all of the mailings were followed up with a call from one of Elcolab's Japanese sales representatives, who provided further information and offered a free demonstration. Although all of the businesses contacted said they were interested in the new technology and requested additional data, they declined any sort of demonstration or person-to-person contact. Typical answers were that "they were very busy" or "that they wanted to see Japanese data" or "they needed to study the information further."

Dan was disappointed that the direct mail campaign had not produced any sales leads. Furthermore, he felt that the end-users contacted were simply bringing the information packets that he sent to the competition. Because each package was very expensive to mail (approximately $4.20), Dan reluctantly decided to reduce the size of the direct mail campaign. Furthermore, for efficiency's sake, clients were now to be called first before sending any information.

After two months, Mr. Hong and Mr. Sato were beginning to feel that it was probably time to close operations. Dan wanted to continue exploring the market and Mr. Hong agreed to fund one more month's effort and raise Dan's share in the company to 35% if Dan would agree to continue. Dan's next step was to attend trade shows with the hope of directly contacting possible purchasers for the Elco-1.

Trade Shows

Dan Jensen attended four trade shows to build contacts because he found out that trade shows in Japan attract businessmen interested in seeing the latest products. The largest trade shows in Japan, with participants from around the world, are held at the giant Makuhari Messe Center in Makuhari, Chiba. With a Japanese friend, Ms. Tanaka, to translate (Dan preferred not to attempt speaking Japanese), Dan met numerous medical electronics salesmen from various Japanese companies, some were even interested in representing Elcolab in Japan. From the four trade shows, he collected over 35 business cards. Additionally, Dan was able to see the plethora of other innovative health products offered in Japan.

Follow-up on these business leads led to meetings with the salesmen, letters from manufacturers, and telephone conversations. However, Dan was still unable to arrange any direct meetings with company management. Most manufacturers wanted Dan to loan them the equipment for a trial period. Although this seemed to be a common practice in Japan, Dan declined these requests because his predecessors in Japan had found their loaned equipment disassembled and overhauled by seemingly friendly manufacturers.

Dan was frustrated after the trade shows because none of his well-planned efforts seemed to be going as he had hoped. Mr. Hong was pressuring Dan for results since three of the six months had already passed. Luckily, at this point, Dan's friend, Ms. Tanaka, suggested an old contact of her's who might be able to assist in arranging a meeting. Through this contact, Dan was invited to give a demonstration to several managers at the Iken Institute, Japan's leading institute for machine-using acupuncturists (supposedly 15,000 members). Dan finally had the opportunity he had been seeking to personally promote the Elco-1. Dan was told that the Iken Institute had a milli-amperage device on the market, and that they were interested in seeing new technology.

Iken Institute

Upon arrival at the site, Dan was surprised to see twenty members of the institute as well as ten representatives from DBC Trading Company. Dan expected to be shown to a large modern conference room and was startled when he was led to an old disheveled laboratory with a tiny table for the demonstration. Dan felt a belligerent attitude from the audience, although he could not quite surmise why. He accepted tea from a female member of the audience, however he put it aside. He proceeded as scheduled and asked his friend to pass out his business cards, which he had prepared in Japanese and English with no business title. The onlookers seemed concerned.

Dan had a well-practiced presentation and video ready, however, members of the audience continually undermined his efforts to present data by devaluing the quality of American data, and by demanding that they receive an immediate product demonstration. They indicated that they did not have a VCR on hand, and as Dan tried to continue, the audience seemed to completely disregard some of the equipment features, which Dan thought were major selling points. Other features, however, increased their desire for an immediate demonstration. Dan had spent a lot of time practicing with his interpreter, however he felt that she was not repeating what he was saying, and finally they asked her if she was the one selling the equipment.

Unfortunately, a few of the gentlemen had experimented with the equipment during setup, and the Elco-1's audio kept malfunctioning. Stunned, Dan spent a very long 60 seconds recovering his thoughts and resetting the machine, which had been moved to a 5-second single pulse setting. The Japanese were eager to feel the microcurrent stimulation from the equipment and were excited to hear the audible feedback of the Elco-1. The members roughly handled the brochures with American data and endorsements until they found the Kouseishou documents, which they studied meticulously. The Japanese indicated that all American data was invalid mainly because Japanese physical body structure was different than American body structure. Moreover, they insisted there was also a chemical problem due to the diet differences between the two countries, which they said affected capillary and even physical dimensions. The audience claimed that the institute actually started the electrostimulatory sciences and showed Dan a book written in English by the Iken Institute in the 1950s. They felt that the equipment was priced many times more than their own device, and Dan was told there would have to be another meeting with "more doctors."

Mr. Ohara, the vice-president, directly requested that Dan send him data on the exact wave characteristics of the Elco-1 and how they affect the body. Dan was shocked at this question because the very marketability of the equipment was based on this feature. Dan's friend's contact, Dr. Saki, gave Mr. Ohara a look and several nods, and Mr. Ohara seemed satisfied. The Japanese suddenly went quiet, which Dan interpreted as a need for additional information, and he rapidly pointed out several more points about his brochure. As a new group entered the room and started negotiations at another table, Dr. Saki warmly said that Dan would have to improve his demonstration technique, and said he was "just a good boy." As Dan left, Mr. Ohara bowed to Dan's friend, but refused to exchange bows with Dan. Later Dan's friend said she had introduced him as a technical support representative, because he didn't have a title on his business card.

Dan Jensen discovered that indeed a Dr. Tani from the Iken Institute had brought electrostimulatory acupuncture to the U.S. in the 1950s, and a Dr. Wu had improved the technology in the 1970s and 1980s much beyond Japanese advances. Dan also discovered that the institute had their own microcurrent device on the market waiting for medical approval. Thus, Dan realized that there would be little chance of developing a client relationship with the Iken Institute.

Hakutsuryu Company

Luckily in May, Dan was given a second opportunity to promote the Elco-1 after his friend made a successful direct call to Hakutsuryu Company, an acupuncture equipment supplier in Shinjuku, near Dan's office. Dan was invited to come over the next day. He and his friend arrived at the location, a small store with rows of shelves containing very Chinese-looking acupuncture items. He was asked to come into the office where he met three Japanese gentlemen: Mr. Hoshi, Mr. Mori, and a man (hereafter to be called Mr. Otsuka), who never indicated who he was. Dan exchanged his newly purchased business cards prepared by his bilingual telemessaging center. These new cards were white, purposefully thicker and higher quality than the average, and identified him as the "Executive Managing Director," as prescribed by one of the "Doing Business in Japan" books. Dan handed each gentleman his business card with his right hand and carefully repeated each of their names, as they said it. However, when he reached Mr. Otsuka, he refused to give his card to Dan. Dan immediately sensed something was wrong, although he did not know the reason.

The Japanese started by asking Dan several unusual questions about Elcolab. They wanted to know about the company's capitalization, the number of members working for the company, and the numbers of employees working for Dan. Mr. Hoshi, who was in his late thirties, was very direct and gave immediate eye contact. His business card indicated that he was working for or with a German company in Coln, Germany. He appeared to advise the youngest man, Mr. Mori, who was the manager of the store. Mr. Mori appeared to be under stress or pressure even though Mr. Hoshi conducted most of the discussions. Mr. Otsuka was an older, grey-haired gentlemen who spoke very little. He seemed knowledgeable, yet appeared to also advise Mr. Mori. Dan was very confused by the relationship among the men. Worst of all, Dan was unsure which one was actually in charge and who had the decision-making authority to purchase the Elco-1.

In the middle of the meeting, all three suddenly went silent. Mr. Otsuka and Mr. Hoshi then abruptly left the meeting without a word and returned later in a state of slight exhaustion. The gentlemen sat down and then continued with the meeting as if nothing had happened. Luckily, Dan was well-prepared for this through his experiences with the Iken Institute. He simply told his Japanese friend, who was startled, not to worry. Dan performed a quick demonstration of the equipment, and in response, the Japanese men indicated that Dan's U.S. data was unacceptable. They gave Dan's friend their lab equipment catalog, and they suggested that Dan send his equipment to a research institute they knew in Kyoto to provide Japanese data.

The meeting ended abruptly and as the Japanese left, Mr. Hoshi mentioned that he would contact Dan's friend, Ms. Tanaka, regarding a future meeting. Later, Dan wondered if Mr. Hoshi and Mr. Otsuka had suddenly departed from the meeting to personally verify that Elcolab really existed. To help reassure them, Dan had Mr. Hong send a personal letter to the Hakutsuryu Company to further legitimize Dan's cause. In addition, Dan wrote a letter in English to each individual thanking them for their hospitality and stressing the features of the Elco-1.

Shinjuku Acupuncture Clinic

Meanwhile, Dan also followed-up with the only client who had returned the direct mail information card, Dr. Tsuji of the Shinjuku Acupuncture Clinic, who requested that Dan make a presentation the very next day. After Dan's previous experiences with unfriendly Japanese clients, he was somewhat surprised that Dr. Tsuji and his assistant were extremely friendly and hospitable. Furthermore, Dan was pleased to note, from Dr. Tsuji's business card, that he was the president of the Shinjuku Acupuncture Clinic. Unlike Dan's other Japanese contacts, Dr. Tsuji did not seem puzzled when Dan presented his new business card.

Dan was determined to get off to a good start with Dr. Tsuji. He knew he must be able to competently, knowledgeably, and spontaneously answer the questions from his host, and he also knew that he must be able to strongly communicate the perceived advantages of his product. To accomplish this, Dan's friend, Ms. Tanaka interpreted, while Dr. Tsuji used the equipment on a chronically ill patient. Dr. Tsuji and his assistant were extremely excited when they saw that the patient received immediate pain relief and promptly wanted to negotiate for distribution of the Elco-1.

Dr. Tsuji conducted business in a very friendly fashion and explained that he had lived in Florida for several years. He shared his extensive knowledge of the industry and of specific medical equipment with Dan. In fact, he gave Dan brochures of all the new entrants to the market in exchange for Dan's Elco-1 information. Dr. Tsuji even admitted that earlier in the day he had investigated Dan Jensen's office to verify its existence. Moreover, Dr. Tsuji frankly explained that the Japanese product literature format of the Elco-1 was not done in the most appropriate Japanese way and suggested that Dan have the documents done again. He implied that to be more successful, Dan should try to find more Japanese data instead of mainly using U.S. articles and recommendations to promote the Elco-1.

In the following weeks, Dr. Tsuji decided to simply become a mentor for Dan instead of distributing the Elco-1 himself. The doctor seemed suspicious of the product's pricing, and he did not want to become a distributor because of Elcolab's requirement that distributors contract for a set volume. Dr. Tsuji was willing to introduce Dan to some of his friends at another company, which turned out to be the Hakutsuryu Company. Tsuji told Dan that he didn't know that Dan had talked to them before, and that his friends said that Dan wanted a demanding contract arrangement with a small working margin for distributors.

Dan decided to take Dr. Tsuji's advice about the Japanese data problem by doing additional research. Dan knew that in the 1950s a Japanese medical doctor, Dr. Yasuda, was the first person to ever discover that microcurrent was generated through pressures from a healing bone.

Dan went to the famous Diet Library with his interpreter, and after three long days he found twenty-four articles on microcurrent stimulation by Japanese medical doctors and acupuncturists. The Japanese themselves did not even know they were the experts on microcurrent stimulation on bones. In fact, Dan considered that he now had the greatest concentrated package of data on microcurrent stimulation assembled in Japan. As a follow-up measure, Dan sent these articles to his current client list. Dan was convinced that this information would help advance his client development efforts.

Dan sent eight packages of the aforementioned articles to his company contacts. Six of the eight companies did not respond at all. One company asked Dan to search for an obscure article by the equipment's inventor from the 1970s. Dan had the equipment's inventor, manufacturer, and sponsors all search for the article in the U.S., yet no one was able to locate it because the article had long ago gone out of print. He made profuse apologies by fax to the company, yet they refused to respond.

In contrast, Dr. Tsuji of the Shinjuku Acupuncture Clinic was ecstatic and offered to do his own personal study of the equipment. Dr. Tsuji no longer complained about not having data on microcurrent studies, yet he still expressed concerns about the equipment's features, the equipment's unfounded effectiveness, and the brochure format. Dan was extremely disappointed that the Japanese scientific articles did not elicit a better response. Because each package cost approximately $17 per mailing, he decided not to send any more.

Dan recalled how at this point everything seemed to go downhill. Dan's friend needed more time on her own business and was only available for translations of mail and business cards. Dan did not feel comfortable speaking Japanese and was not sure how much he could accomplish alone. To make matters worse, Elcolab's exclusive distribution rights for the Elco-1 were expiring, and Mr. Hong was frantically trying to negotiate to keep the Japanese distribution rights. Dan's six months were nearly over, and he knew he had to succeed at all costs.

Dan, therefore, decided to approach the kindly Dr. Tsuji for advice. Dr. Tsuji gave Dan brochures, which the doctor had received from competitor mailings. This gave Dan an idea of the current status of the Elco-1's competitors. The Iken Institute was marketing several microcurrent devices that were still waiting for medical approval, and the Electro-Acuscope, Elco-1's American competitor, was no longer available. There was a copy-of-a-copy of the electro-acuscope on the market still awaiting medical approval, and there were approximately 15 more instruments waiting for approval. This understanding of the competition provided Dan with some hope that an opportunity still existed to promote the Elco-1 in Japan.

Kin International

Just before the end of six months, everyone, except Dan, had totally given up on the Elco-1. As a final incentive, Mr. Hong offered Dan a 49% share of Elcolab Japan. Dan was tired and dispirited, however he kept reminding himself to look out for opportunities. Dan returned to his office and as he was cleaning up to move operations to Nagoya, he came upon an old fax message from the year before. A certain Mr. Fututake of Kin International, a facial stimulation machine distributor, had expressed interest in marketing the Elco-1 to break into the medical market. After debating all night about how to proceed, Dan decided to fax a message the next day. Ten minutes after sending the fax, Mr. Fututake faxed Dan back and set a meeting for the next day.

At this point Dan was very realistic, and collected all his paraphernalia, an Elco-1, and selling material for a lone journey across Tokyo. He knew time was against him, but he had arranged to extend his visa by two weeks.

The Kin International office was located in Nibancho in Chiyoda-ku, a very wealthy district. Dan found Mr. Fututake to be very congenial and friendly, and a graduate of the University of Michigan. Mr. Fututake immediately asked Dan about the terms of sale. Dan let Mr. Fututake ask for a unit price first, because he knew that this was Japanese strategy and that Mr. Fututake had previously been in direct contact with the manufacturer of the Elco-1. By fax, Mr. Hong and Dan had strategically planned valuation strategies, drop back, and hold fast prices. From Mr. Hong's description, Mr. Fututake's present facial equipment design was a copy of the facial unit Elcolab had designed years before. Mr. Fututake was a bit surprised with Dan's price and counter-offered. Dan then said he would have to speak with Mr. Hong to get confirmation. Mr. Fututake asked that Dan leave an Elco-1 unit for demonstration purposes the next day. Not only did Dan entrust a unit to Mr. Fututake, he left a complete set of manuals and brochures for his staff with the exception of the official company Kouseishou documents, which Mr. Fututake very much wanted to see.

The next day, Dan returned to Kin International to train Mr. Fututake's staff on the Elco-1. He was surprised that Mr. Fututake had separate suites for office space, lab equipment, repair, training, and beauty treatment. Because Dan had only seen a single secretary at the first meeting, he was stunned at the size of the facilities and Mr. Fututake's staff. Over the next several days, Dan spent hours demonstrating the many healing techniques to each member of the staff. During that period of time, he met six different people including the sales manager, Mr. Fututake's wife, three very attractive models, and an in-house clinician. He was extensively questioned by the clinician and Mr. Fututake's wife. Conversation with the sales manager was polite during which Dan noticed the manager's extensive business card collection.

Although there were some English to Japanese translation problems, Dan was generally able to communicate. The in-house clinician asked Dan if he was ready to give a demonstration to a group of 50–60 people. Dan gladly said he was ready, but because there was a shortage of brochures, the meeting size was reduced to twenty.

Both Mr. Fututake and the clinician extended lunch invitations, which Dan happily accepted. During lunch with the clinician, Dan was asked various questions about the equipment, how many brochures he had, and his background. When he had lunch with Mr. Fututake alone, Mr. Fututake made direct eye contact and conducted a serious business discussion on pricing, distribution, shipping, warranties, and the basic terms of sale. Mr. Fututake wanted to buy all Elco-1 assets in Japan including all units, Kouseishou approval, and Dan's stock shares in Elcolab Japan. He eventually wanted the entire title of incorporation. He told Dan that Mr. Sato was an old man, and that he needed a younger man, Dan, to stay in the country to ensure reliable distribution and technical support. Dan was not expecting to discuss business during what he assumed was a social engagement, yet he assertively made compromises and agreements. Mr. Fututake wanted a written contract from Dan, which Dan agreed to. Because Mr. Hong happened to be in Hong Kong, Dan arranged for a meeting during the week so that Dan and Mr. Hong and Mr. Fututake could meet and discuss the details.

During the subsequent meeting, although Mr. Fututake liked the contract, he refused to sign it. He mentioned to Mr. Hong that the Chinese are nice to deal with, but they often hold back their true intentions. He then told Dan and Mr. Hong that the Japanese go beyond the call of duty for their customers by immense sacrifices through customer service, quality, and thus "win the heart of their customers." He also explained why his own facial model had to be produced by a local manufacturer. An American, Mr. Suzuki of Seattle, five years before had given many Japanese dealers exclusive contracts on the same facial equipment. When the Japanese found out what was going on, Mr. Suzuki provided little product support, thus Mr. Fututake currently felt very cautious about the Elco-1 and Mr. Hong. Once the meeting concluded, Dan and Mr. Hong were still unsure whether Mr. Fututake would agree to sign the contract. Mr. Hong left the country disappointed; however, Dan had come very far and refused to let this become an obstacle.

Meanwhile, Dan was still scheduled to present the Elco-1 to the medical manufacturer, Chiba Medical Company. Before the actual presentation, there was a lot of checking and rechecking to make sure that each staff member of Kin International was well informed on the Elco-1. It was as if one were preparing to perform in a play or a show. Dan and the clinician exchanged techniques on microcurrent therapy, and Dan was asked if he was prepared, and when he replied positively, this seemed to please the clinician who was apparently "responsible" for the performance. Instead of taking the train, Kin International traveled by company car across Tokyo. The sales manager drove, while the clinician sat in the front passenger seat. Dan sat in the left rear passenger seat, while Mr. Fututake sat in the right rear seat. No business was discussed during the trip, only small talk. Mr. Fututake spoke of his family background, and Dan described his own personal work experiences and future plans.

Upon arrival, Dan was warmly greeted by a Chiba Medical vice-president and various staff members. The vice-president spoke perfect English, while the others greeted Dan in Japanese. The meeting was held on old cafeteria tables and metal chairs, and there was a cart for the equipment. Various engineers and staff entered the room, and Dan individually traded business cards with each member using both hands, while repeating their names and bowing. They were genuinely congenial and offered tea. For most of the meeting, Dan listened to Japanese conversation. The Kin International staff and the Chiba Medical staff conducted a very friendly and relaxed meeting regarding the equipment that Chiba Medical Company produced for Kin International. There was an intense session comparing their equipment with the Elco-1, which started with the clinician going point by point down a chart. This was followed by discussion of their current products. A defective plate cover was passed to an engineer, and this concluded with a presentation of the actual device. Dan was then asked to demonstrate the Elco-1 because it seemed the clinician was not quite confident with it. Dan then gave the best demonstration he had ever given in Japan and answered spontaneous questions about the equipment's wave forms and basic statistics. He made extensive use of the room's chalkboard, knowing that all members of the room most likely were able to understand written English. When the subject of interferential therapy came up, a Chiba Medical Company engineer became so excited that he stood up and actually explained and drew the wave form phenomena for the rest of the audience. Mr. Fututake, the clinician, and the sales manager were extremely pleased and impressed by Dan's performance and signaled their approval over the table, because Dan had contributed along with the rest of the team.

The rest of the meeting was about various random topics, which Dan did not understand. During the middle of the meeting, a Chiba Medical staff member, who Dan had not previously met, arrived. Dan made direct eye contact, which seemed to annoy the man. The members of the meeting started to pass various types of equipment around the table. They let Dan participate in the ritual of looking at competitor's equipment. At the end of the meeting, Chiba Medical members came up to congratulate Dan on his performance. He was invited to meet the president of Chiba Medical Company. Unfortunately, Dan explained he had to leave Japan in several days because he couldn't arrange another flight for another month, and thus he was not able to arrange a meeting. The presentation was considered a success, and after arriving back at Kin International he was bid goodbye with the promise of future communications later.

Winning the Heart of the Customer

After Dan arrived home at his apartment in Chiba, he received a call from the Chiba Medical Company vice-president, who subsequently offered to deal directly with Elcolab and Dan, while cutting out his good friend Mr. Fututake. Dan was surprised, yet politely promised to extend the message to Mr. Hong and to think it over. Mr. Hong was currently in flight to the United States, and Dan was in an ethical dilemma, but he remembered that his international business advisor had told him that "international business was based on trust." Thus, Dan immediately called Mr. Fututake and informed him that his "communication chain" needed to be straightened out. An emergency meeting was then arranged.

Dan explained that he had worked hard with Kin International's staff and that he had spent considerable time training his people, and that he didn't know the vice-president very well. Mr. Fututake truly appreciated Dan's loyalty and would immediately call his friend, the vice-president of Chiba Medical to solve the matter. He explained that these things were fairly common in Tokyo and it was better if these things were stopped quickly. He wished Dan had not seen or experienced it. Mr. Fututake personally escorted Dan out, and he told Dan he had done an incredible job selling the product. He asked Dan to call him from the airport when he left.

Dan thanked all his business contacts by fax. He also sent packets of the famous Toraya Yokan to all his close business friends including Mr. Fututake. When he called Kin International, Mr. Fututake was very touched and pleased and he warmly thanked Dan for the gift and wished him well on his trip.

Conclusion

Mr. Sato's accountant was now ready to make arrangements for sale of product with Kin International. Now that Dan had a chance to review the events of the past six and a half months, he had a clearer idea of his progress. His experience enabled him to analyze his successful efforts as well as his mistakes. Dan's objective was to include this invaluable information in his summary report for Mr. Hong before leaving to attend Thunderbird, the American Graduate School of International Management.

23
Anheuser-Busch (A): Developing a Global Brand in Germany

John E. Walsh, Jr. and William P. Coon

Jack Purnell, chief executive for Anheuser-Busch International (A-B), had a goal to globalize A-B's best-selling brand, Budweiser, and to make it as popular worldwide as Coca-Cola, Marlboro, and Levi's. He told a reporter from *USA Today:*[1]

We're not sure, but we're going to give it a shot. Lately we've been hurt by overall U.S. revenue, which has been flatter than day-old draft since the late '80s, so we've decided to tap into the fast-growing foreign markets. We'd like to build a global brand, but I'm not sure if it'll happen. But right now, we don't know how high we can go—we want to take it as far as we can.

Unlike distinctly American products such as soft drinks, cigarettes, and blue jeans, our beers hold little cachet in many traditional beer strongholds like Germany, Australia, and Brazil. That's because our beers tend to be lighter, sweeter, and less robust than foreign brews. You know, we've been spoiled by the availability of fickle Americans who favor faddish brews like light and dry beers. So far, at least, drinkers in countries such as Germany are loyal to brands that are centuries old.

Right now, we're doing our best to globalize our beer business. We're almost forced to by the fact that the U.S. beer market is projected to grow at only 1% annually for the next ten years, while the international market will increase anywhere from six times to ten times faster. We also have to keep ahead of our two main rivals, Miller and Coors—they've both expanded to Mexico, Canada, East Asia, and Europe.

A-B is looking at a half-dozen development deals in Latin America, the Pacific Rim, and Western Europe in addition to the agreements we just signed in Japan, Mexico, and Italy. The big problem with expanding to Europe, the most stable and second-largest world beer market after the United States, is that we can't seem to negotiate a deal with the Czech brewer Budvar, which holds the rights to distribute Budweiser (theirs, not ours) in most European countries.

---

[1]March 24, 1993.

Our domestic business generates about $400-million in excess cash each year, so developing the international beer business is a good use of funds. Clearly, that's where our focus is going to be. But then I have my market research people tell me that, while we have an 8% worldwide market share now, we may be able to capture only 5% more. They tell me that we'll be limited by the local loyalty people have to their home brewers. People in the Netherlands will drink Heineken, in France, Kronenbourg, and in Germany, they'll drink thousands of local brands from little fiefdoms.

But the way I see it, A-B's beers, especially Budweiser, could ultimately become bigger abroad than at home. We've been right for 120 years—Bud has taken over North America. It may as well take over the world! We know how to market our products—I don't see any reason why we won't be just as successful in other countries.

Background

Anheuser-Busch (A-B), headquartered in St. Louis, Missouri, was the world's largest brewer, having sold an all-time industry record 86.8-million barrels of beer in 1992 for a 44.3% share of the United States beer market, including imports (see Figure 23-1). A-B had led the world brewing industry in sales volume and market share every year since 1957. In 1992 A-B marked the fourteenth consecutive year the company had increased its market share lead over its nearest competitor.

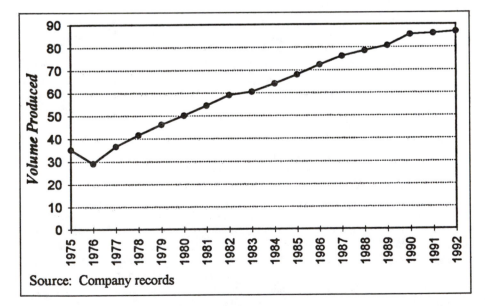

Source: Company records

Figure 23-1. Anheuser-Busch beer production, millions of barrels. (Source: Company records)

Anheuser-Busch produced 13 naturally-brewed beers, as well as a non-alcoholic brew, and imported three Carlsberg brands from Denmark. The company operated 13 breweries throughout the United States and licensed the brewing of Budweiser in 6 foreign countries. The company exported beer to 65 countries worldwide through its Anheuser-Busch International Division.

During the 1860s, Eberhard Anheuser and his son-in-law Adolphus Busch, partners in a small St. Louis brewery, were having trouble persuading consumers to buy their beer. They tried a new approach. They began paying taverns to promote their brew. They even bought some taverns, which began to serve their beer exclusively.

In the years ahead, such tactics served the partners well. A-B made good beer, but the knowledgeable people in the industry believed that the main reason for its success was that the beer giant was tougher, rougher, and shrewder than its competition. Its marketing tactics sometimes resembled military assaults. When Miller Brewing Company, its main rival, threatened its lead in the 1970s, for instance, A-B launched a campaign consisting of 10,000 separate sales-promotion programs that divided the country into not only cities and neighborhoods, but also individual streets and bars. A-B had been accused of such hardball tactics as illegally monopolizing beer sales at ball parks, racetracks, and arenas. Retailers would agree to sell A-B beers exclusively, and, in return, the company allegedly would give them fixtures, advertising services, and other inducements. While the company had denied some allegations, in other cases it admitted such tactics, claiming they were used "for competitive reasons."[2]

Adolphus Busch immigrated to the United States from Germany in 1857 with an allowance provided by his father's estate. He was a born huckster and a canny businessman who married Anheuser's daughter, and then turned this connection into gold. Under his management, the brewery that soon became Anheuser-Busch rose to national and, in his descendants' time, international prominence. He and Anheuser produced beer under the company name, The Bavarian Brewery. Adolphus always strove to improve his product. He read every technical journal he could get his hands on about advances in Europe. In 1868, he traveled to Europe to study the brewing industry. He focused his attention on the Pilsener beer brewed in Bohemia, then part of Austria and now part of the Czech Republic, where beer had been skillfully brewed in the southern region for more than 600 years. The brewery in Pilsen was the largest, with cellars carved out of solid rock stretching for more than five miles.

Adolphus meticulously noted the Pilsener process, right down to the name of a brand of beer that was being produced by a brewery in Ceské-Budêjoviçe, 65 miles south of Pilsen. During the reign of the Hapsburgs, the town was known by its German name, Budweis. Its famous beer was sold in Vienna, Yugoslavia, and Bavaria; some even reached New York in kegs and bottles bearing the name Budweiser.

The brand name was first registered in the United States by Conrad, an importer of wines, champagnes, and liquors. The Anheuser brewery produced the brand for him under contract. In 1882, Conrad went bankrupt. An arrangement was worked

---

[2]Chris Welles, "The Kings of Beer, Froth and All," *Business Week,* July 8, 1991.

out in which Anheuser-Busch assumed control of Conrad's company—and the brand name Budweiser.

A-B's tenuous claim to the name Budweiser was kept under wraps for many years after that. But when it filed documents in 1907 to register the name as a U.S. trademark, a German brewery stepped forward to file a complaint, arguing that the St. Louis company could not use Budweiser, because it was a geographical name, and because the German brewery had used it first

In 1911, Adolphus settled the matter by paying the German brewery 82,500 kronen. That same year a similar settlement that included a large payment was reached with the Czech brewery in Ceské-Budêjoviçe. Under the terms of the arrangement, A-B could use the name Budweiser on beer sold in the United States. The European breweries could use it on beer sold in Europe and they could sell "Imported Budweiser" in the United States. But A-B was not allowed to sell its Budweiser in Europe. In 1939, A-B obtained from the Czechs the right to use the name exclusively in North America, the United States, and all of its possessions.

Diversification

During the late 1980s, when U.S. beer sales for A-B flattened, they attempted to diversify into the theme park business. The company, in late 1989, paid $1.1-billion for four Sea World complexes and two other amusement parks. The deal made A-B, which already owned the Sesame Place and Adventure Island theme parks and Busch Gardens in Tampa and Williamsburg, Virginia, the second-largest operator of such parks in the country, trailing only Disney. The Sea World purchase was expected to increase the number of people the company entertained from 5-million to 21-million a year. "We get a feel for what the consumer thinks," Chairman August Busch III said. "We get a pulse on that. So we like the entertainment business."

Unfortunately, it could be a notoriously fickle business—especially if public attitudes change regarding keeping dolphins in captivity at places like Sea World. Loud protests had been raised by conservationists and animal rights activists, one of whom referred to Sea World and other marine parks as "dolphin amusement parks." Although many experts praised Sea World for its breeding programs, it was roundly criticized for keeping killer whales in captivity.

Such criticism notwithstanding, A-B professed to be pleased with Sea World and similar ventures. In fact, it was building a $300-million theme park and resort near Barcelona on Spain's Mediterranean Coast. Five years in the making, it had been one of A-B's boldest ventures. With American beer consumption down 4% since 1981, the idea was to give A-B a toehold in the tough European beer market. August Busch III liked to call the Spanish park A-B's "footprint in Europe."

The company spent heavily on its marketing—not only in total but also on most of its brands—and the average Anheuser-Busch distributor handled more than twice the volume of other wholesalers in the industry. The company lavished a lot of attention on its wholesalers and did not, for example, short circuit them by dealing direct with national retailing chains. It was very selective about its wholesalers, many of whom could thank the company for making them millionaires. A-B liked small family businesses rather than big corporations and loyalty to its products was amply rewarded.

Competition from Other Brewers for European Market Share

Adolph Coors Co., America's No. 3 brewer at home and No. 10 in the world, was acutely aware of the need to acquire market share in Europe. Mark Stankovic, Coors' director for international marketing said, "As the number of players got smaller, we could have been locked out of some distribution channels that were better than others."[3] With this in mind, Coors began selling its Coors Extra Gold in Greece and was looking into other European deals.

Meanwhile, Miller Brewing Co., the No. 2 U.S. brand, owned by giant Philip Morris Companies, purchased a small Belgian brewery in the hopes of gaining a toehold on the continent. They entered into a distribution agreement with Bass Brewery in England to counter A-B's moves there.

American brewers couldn't afford to be fainthearted. Europe represented a growing beer market, whereas North American sales had plateaued. In 1990, Western Europeans downed 241 million barrels of beer, while Americans drank only 206 million. U.S. brewers made plans to boost overseas sales, which remained small when compared to their European counterparts (see Table 23-1).

At least one U.S. brewer tasted success in Europe. C. James Koch, founder of tiny Boston Brewing Co., tried to export his company's Samuel Adams beer to Germany in the early 1990s. German beer officials wouldn't let it in, claiming his beer contained a meat tenderizer sometimes used as an additive and thus violated the coun-

Table 23-1. The Global Scope of Selected Brewers

Brewer	1990 Volume*	Foreign Sales as Percent of Total
Anheuser-Busch (USA)	85.5	3%
Miller (USA)	43.5	1% or less
Coors (USA)	19.0	1% or less
Stroh (USA)	16.4	1% or less
G. Heileman (USA)	12.0	1% or less
Heineken (Netherlands)	43.4	85%
BSN (France)	21.3	57%
Carlsberg (Denmark)	17.0	75%
Guinness (Britain)	17.0	65%
Interbrew (Belgium)	11.0	55%

*Millions of barrels of beer
Source: *Business Week,* February 4, 1991

---

[3] *Denver Post,* March 29, 1993.

try's stringent beer purity law. Koch hired a consultant who found that the enzyme occurs naturally in both Samuel Adams and German brews. Three thousand barrels of Samuel Adams beer were shipped to Germany the first year.

The Netherlands' Heineken began buying interests in European breweries in the late 1970s, betting on the eventuality of a single European market. The world's No. 3 brewer made its well-known product in breweries in France, Greece, Ireland, Italy, and Spain. Equally important, Heineken dominated other premium beers on Europe's supermarket shelves.

Trademark Problems with Budweiser

The cloudy origins of the Budweiser name continued to haunt A-B into the 1990s. As it set its sight on world markets, the brewery found itself legally prohibited from selling Budweiser in most of Europe. A-B had grown into a colossus, producing 250 times the amount of beer brewed by the little brewery of Ceské-Budêjoviçe. But the Czechs still had exclusive marketing rights to sell Budweiser in Western Europe; they resisted A-B's offers of cash, joint-venture production and new territorial division.

In 1990, as communism gave way to a free-market economy, workers at the Czech brewery went on strike trying to force management to merge with A-B. But the suggestion of a merger created protests around Ceské-Budêjoviçe. The local paper reported that beer drinkers would rather die than see an agreement with a company whose beer is "a weak imitation of the original product." An irritated young businessman said, "You'll never see our beer in cans—we use cans for sauerkraut only."

A-B continued to expand overseas. The company was licensed to brew in six countries and exported to sixty-five others. But the big beer-consuming countries of Europe, particularly Germany and Great Britain, had proved tough nuts to crack. England was especially inhospitable. Despite heavy marketing since 1984, Budweiser claimed less than 1% of the world's fourth largest beer market.

Meanwhile, A-B's latest offer of $2-million to the Czech brewery for the use of the Budweiser label was rejected. A-B sold Budweiser in Finland, the Netherlands, and Great Britain. It was also sold in France, Italy, Russia and Spain, but only as Bud.

International Operations

American brewers share was less than 1% of the market outside the United States. For the first ten months of 1992, Germans drank only 64,000 cases of American beer. That included everybody—Budweiser, Miller, Coors—combined. During the same period, Americans drank an estimated 9.8 *million* cases of Beck's beer alone.[4] Anheuser-Busch had already launched its international division in 1981 to develop new markets. Initial export numbers were impressive, but they were misleading. Of the 5 million barrels of beer U.S. brewers exported in 1992, only 2.5 million were

---

[4]Lawrence Delaney, Jr., "Beer Brawl," *World Trade,* March 1993.

actually drunk by foreign customers (the remainder were sold in Puerto Rico—considered a foreign market for the industry—and to US military bases abroad). A-B had licensing agreements in several countries (see Table 23-2).

Figure 23-2 shows the major export markets for American beers in 1992, excluding sales to Puerto Rico and U.S. military bases abroad.

Recently, Paine-Webber's beer-industry analyst Manny Goldman said, "Unless Anheuser-Busch acquires operations overseas, (exporting beer) doesn't mean too much. The payoff is not in what they license or export. For overseas to matter, they have to acquire some good-size operation. If A-B is to make a major international move, it will have to do it soon."[5] Stephen Burrows, A-B vice-president for interna-

Table 23-2. Budweiser Beer Brewed Abroad*

Country	Volume (barrels)	Licensee
Canada	1,400,000	Labatt
Japan	400,000	Kirin
UK	400,000	Watney Mann & Truman Brewers

*Note: About 200,000 barrels were brewed by licensees in Ireland, Korea, and Denmark
Source: M. Shanken Associates and Anheuser-Busch

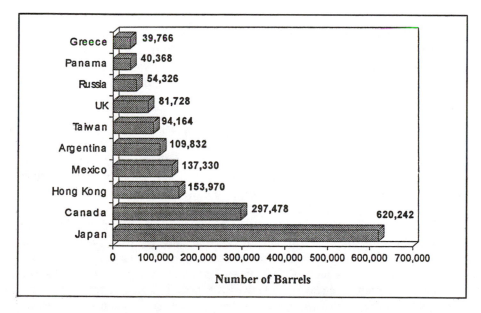

Figure 23-2. Top ten export markets for U.S. beer. (Source: U.S. Dept. of Commerce, Beer Institute)

---

[5]Ibid.

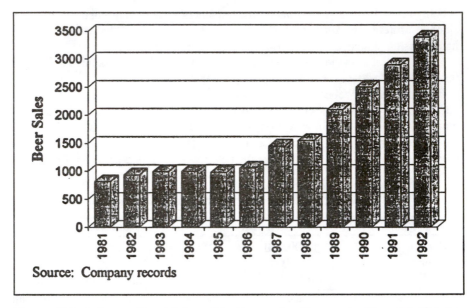

Figure 23-3. Anheuser-Busch International beer sales (thousands of barrels). (Source: Company records)

tional marketing, affirmed that A-B was always looking for "opportunities for partnerships or acquisitions . . . building partnerships on foreign soil was a key part of our strategic plan."[6] But even if A-B did make a play for a foreign brewer, Burrows noted that the beermaker's overriding goal was to make Budweiser the first truly universal beer.

A-B's principal reason for overseas expansion was that, contrary to the flat growth projections for the domestic American market, international markets enjoyed (and according to projections will enjoy for many years) rapid growth in the number of beer drinkers. A-B exported to over 65 countries. Anheuser-Busch's overseas expansion included not only the European market, but the whole world as well. The volume of beer sold outside the United States was more than 3.5 times the volume sold in the U.S. market. A-B International's sales volume had been rising at an annual rate of 20% for the past five years (Figure 23-3). In addition, two A-B brewmasters resided permanently in Europe to ensure that all licensed products brewed there met A-B's exacting quality standards. Sales increases were led by Japan and Korea, with both markets up more than 50%, while two other large volume markets, Canada and the United Kingdom, also recorded increases despite overall industry softness in those countries. A-B placed three brands among the top ten best-selling beers in the world (see Table 23-3).

Table 23-3. World's Most Popular Beers (1992)

Brand	Country	Barrels (millions)
Budweiser	USA	48
Miller Light	USA	19
Kirin Lager	Japan	18
Brahma Chopp	Brazil	18
Antarctica	Brazil	16
Coors	USA	16
Heineken	Netherlands	13
Bud Light	USA	13
Polar	Venezuela	10
Corona Extra	Mexico	10
Busch	USA	10

Selling to the German Beer Market

Before any company attempts to sell any foreign products, and especially beer, in Germany, the cultural differences must be understood. Children were taught to drink beer lemonade (a drink that was three fourths beer and one fourth lemonade) and dinner was often followed by a trip to a local gasthaus. In a way beer was consumed in Germany like soft drinks were in the United States. A professor at the University of Heidelberg commented on the problems an American company might incur:

> Every aspect of German life is steeped in tradition and conservatism. A company from the United States hoping to conquer the German markets overnight will be disappointed. Look at some of the differences:
>
> Our educational system is a traditional European one. The professors lecture—the students listen. There is very little discussion, if any. Most courses are very segmented and demanding. The number of students committing suicides has been increasing for some time. Entrance to the universities is so competitive that only one person in ten will be admitted.
>
> Politics has strong influence from labor unions. Our democracy consists of more socialistic concepts than the American version. Nationalism is very strong in places like Bavaria and northern Germany. The government plays a significant role in business—they and the central bank help certain industries that are deemed important. In Germany, the same government usually stays in power for at least 12 years—sometimes longer. You don't see many political outsiders attain power here. In the U.S., the system is designed to protect the rights of the minority from the majority, while in Germany, the rights of the majority are protected from the minority.
>
> We Germans consider our technology to be very advanced. Improvements in efficiency are very important to us. We take pride in our modern possessions.

Socially, our family ties remain strong throughout one's lifetime. Children should be seen, but not heard. There is a wide distinction between friends and acquaintances. Our professional titles are more important to use than our social rank. You don't see many Germans laughing in public or dancing on tables, except at the proper time, like *Octoberfest.* There is a popular saying: "Work is work and schnapps is schnapps," business and pleasure never mix. A Sunday afternoon might be spent dissecting the day's weighty issues. We, of course, gave the world the word *angst,* or a feeling of dread or anxiety.

Even our language is formal, ordered, and polite. We use the formal past tense in written documents. The vocabulary is usually technical, but always precise. Take *technik,* for instance. Germans use the term to refer to engineering knowledge and craft skills. It should be noted that more Germans are qualified in engineering than in anything else; engineers enjoy higher standing in Germany than in Britain. This one word, *technik,* dignifies and even glamorizes engineering under its distinctive rubric.

The German worker is diligent and disciplined. Loyalties to the company are strong. The typical worker is fiercely conservative and politically moderate. Once you are a German's friend, you will remain his friend for life.

We expect everyone to obey the law. Take bicycles, for example. You must stop at all stoplights and signal if you intend to turn. If you don't, you'll probably get a five-minute lecture from the *polizei* (police).

Formality played an important role in the German personality. Virtually every social situation has been formalized, and individual reaction to it was typically judged against an established code of behavior. This characteristic led to a social system in which political, economic, and social institutions were highly organized and of decisive influence. Political parties, government bureaucracy, labor movements, employers' associations, religious societies, social groups, clubs, and fraternities were numerous and strong. Germans tended to be comfortable only in situations in which an institutional framework was explicitly formalized and within which they could carry on social relationships with a minimum of dependence on personal initiative.

The social structure in Germany was based on traditional foundations. The division into upper class, upper middle, lower middle, urban working, and peasant classes was generally applicable. Each individual was constantly preoccupied with the evaluation of his or her status in terms of that of neighbors, fellow workers, and others he met in daily life. Titles, dress, accent, manners, and interests served as guides. The complexity of the criteria brought forth the comment from some Germans that no one is the equal of anyone else.

The Germans were a family-oriented people. The tradition of the home as an important center of the activities of all family members remained strongly instilled. The family spent much of its leisure time in shared activities. Important events such as birthdays, name days, marriages, anniversaries, and holidays were family affairs. Sentimental attachments between grown children and their parents were strong and lasting. It was common for several generations and laterally-related families— cousins and so forth—to gather for important family celebrations.

Germans also valued friendship highly. The bonds of friendship are extremely strong and sometimes make demands on the individual's loyalty equal to those of family ties. For this reason, such friendships are not undertaken lightly, but once formed are warm and usually lifelong. They are not so likely to be based primarily on mutual interests as are friendships among Americans, but more on strong emotional ties that lead to close identity.

Anheuser-Busch executives were confident that they could successfully sell their beer in Germany, even though they knew the social and emotional makeup of the Germans was different from Americans. They decided to test market a light, American-style beer in West Berlin. A-B wanted to exploit the trend of the Europeans away from the heavier, darker beers to the lighter, lager beers. The fact that Germans drink three times more beer per capita than Americans was not lost on the St. Louis-based giant brewer (see Figure 23-4). The beer, marketed using the "Anheuser Beer" label, used a recipe developed by A-B brewers in conformity with Germany's stringent "purity" law. The purity decree, or *reinheitsgebot,* has been on the German legal books since 1516, making it the oldest health law in the world. Briefly, it states that beer sold in Germany must contain only malted barley, hops, water, and yeast. Almost all other beers in the world use adjuncts such as sugar, wheat rice, or unmalted barley—such ingredients were banned under the purity law, but were necessary to ensure even quality and to prevent beers from going flat. German beers last less than 3 weeks after being bottled. The law was overturned by the EC High Court in 1992 as an obvious barrier to free trade (it was likened to the Japanese import barriers).

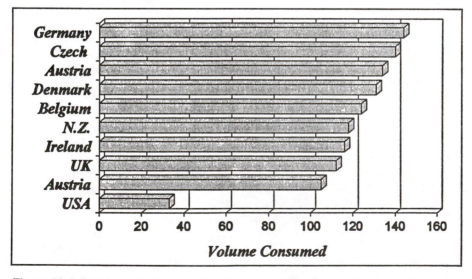

Figure 23-4. Top beer-drinking countries, liters per capita. (Source: Business Week, Oct. 17, 1992)

The "purity" law had effectively excluded most foreign beers, which usually contain a variety of additives and might be brewed from other cereals such as rice or corn. Germany until recently had allowed in the relatively few foreign beers brewed to German standards. Danish brewers in particular have been successful in selling beer in the German market. But the law has ensured that, overall, the balance of beer trade had been tipped heavily in Germany's favor. Even though the EC High Court had relaxed the standards a bit, foreign inroads into the German market were likely to be slow due to the heavy domestic competition and because most German beer drinkers were intensely loyal to local brands. Foreign beers had the strongest impact in supermarkets, where the lower price of foreign beer was likely to be more of a factor in buyers' decisions.

Beer drinking Germans typically drank the lighter lager-type beers called *pilseners*. Pilsener beers, which take their name from the Czech city where they were first made, were the most popular beers in Germany. They formed a creamy head and had an alcoholic content of about 4%.

Kolsch, another type of light beer, was also popular. And there was *export,* a full-bodied beer; *bock,* a strong, dark beer; *alt,* or old, beer, which was heavy on hops; *weizenbier,* which was made from wheat rather than barley malt; and *Berliner weisse,* which contained only 2.5% alcohol.

Germans like to see their beer drawn very carefully, with three to four "layerings." A stein of beer might take as long as 10 minutes to prepare before it was considered ready to serve. Americans, on the other hand, were accustomed to ordering a cold beer and having it served up in a jiffy. They downed it almost as quickly, and they could get impatient waiting. A typical American response would be, "Germany produces a great beer, but you could die of thirst waiting for it."

Peter von Eckardt, Anheuser-Busch's manager of the West Berlin test, explained the rationale behind the decision to attempt to penetrate the German market:

> It was decided in St. Louis to package and promote the beer as "American." We wanted to take advantage of the then-current craze for products with an American flavor: Levi Strauss blue jeans, American college sweat shirts, and McDonald's hamburgers. The American cowboy image in the Marlboro ads helped make that brand the most popular cigarette in the world. We wanted Budweiser to become part of the alluring American mystique.
>
> True to the German markets' tastes, we sold the beer in bottles. It was priced at a premium level. Well, to tell you the truth, the test failed miserably—we pulled out of the market after five months. We didn't anticipate the formidable obstacles coupled with the fact that Germans are notoriously conservative.
>
> One principle reason for the failure was the German distribution system: restaurants and bars are often bound to a local brewery by long-term contracts that makes it nearly impossible to switch or carry a second brand. For German beer drinkers, switching brands often means switching bars.
>
> Another reason came to me from my friends at the Association of German Brewers—they thought A-B underestimated the vagaries of the fragmented German

market. Did you know that there are over 1,200 breweries here? Every little town has one or is close to one. We were a little brash thinking we could overcome that in a five-month test. The attitude was almost like: "We need American beer in Germany about as much as we need a Pilsener from Afghanistan!" Germans perceived all American beers as weak, gassy, and tasteless.

A-B was effectively kept out of the world's largest market by the trademark fight over the use of "Budweiser." Foreign beer brands occupied only 0.8% of the German market and the potential for increasing sales was enormous. It was estimated that the average German derives up to one-third of their daily nutrition from beer. However, Germans were extremely loyal to their own local drinks—beer drinking was almost a religion there. Over 4,000 local brands awaited any foreign beer producer. Germany's two largest supermarket chains, COOP and Tenglemann, had gone on record as saying that they would boycott foreign brews that did not conform to the purity laws. Additionally, German government officials stated that they would stringently test imported beers for impermissible chemicals and would insist that additives be clearly stated on labels. The German legislature passed a resolution urging the German electorate to "stand firm and not yield to the temptation of chemical beer just because of the price."[7]

A-B's Purnell understood the nature of the challenge:

> Even Heineken, the world's largest brewer after us, was practically next door to Germany and they hadn't made a move into the market. It would take us a long time to build up sales. It would be impossible to enter the German market until we had established a good distribution network there. We hadn't done that and we wouldn't get it that quickly. Germans still wanted to drink traditionally-brewed beer and that would take some time to change. But we were not too far away from trying to get back into the market there. We hoped not to repeat the mistakes we made before. We still felt that it made little sense to try to sell a beer in Germany, or anywhere else, that was not the same as the beer produced for consumption at home in the United States. We had found that we needed to sell an authentic American product to be successful. In England, we sold Budweiser as "The Authentic Beer." We could never do that in Germany.[8]

It was possible that A-B could capitalize on the changing attitudes of German beer drinkers towards lighter beers, especially the younger generation. Richard Burt, the ex-American Ambassador to Germany, talked about German attitudes:[9]

> The attitude of the German beer drinker is that his or her local beer is the best in the world, and other beers are inferior to German beer. Generally, Germans prefer heavy alcoholic content beers. Although the United States produces more beer than any other

---

[7]*Business Week,* February 4, 1991.
[8]*Modern Brewery Age,* February 8, 1993.
[9]*TWA Ambassador,* October 1987.

country in the world, Germans do not think of Americans as beer brewers. To get an American taste, American-grown barley would have to be exported to Germany.

While many Germans look at Americans as pushy, rude, overbearing and impatient, most of the younger people are fascinated with the American. Psychologists say that Germans identify the American with freedom and opportunity and a less structured life, which is lacking in their lives. In Germany, children's lives are planned in large measure by their parents at age eleven when the decision to go to a *gymnasium* for a professional career is made.

Young people now coming out of the universities are very open minded about the U.S. They have an image of a dynamic and energetic America that is very attractive, a country that emphasizes economic growth and entrepreneurial activity, which is very exciting to young Germans who want to be innovative and want their society to be more competitive.

Acquiring, Building or Licensing a German Brewery

Buying a German brewery would be costly because of the low dollar. Still, by buying a brewery, A-B would have a distribution network and consumer acceptance. Already big competitors like Heineken and Guinness were acquiring small breweries throughout Europe. Further, McKinney & Company had recommended that Anheuser-Busch buy or build its own breweries. A onetime Anheuser-Busch executive said the company had ignored the recommendation.[10] Anheuser-Busch had been successfully licensing the right to brew Budweiser in other countries and its management could consider this option if no acquisitions were made or no breweries were built. If sales were slow in Germany, Budweiser might do well in countries with weaker beer tradition like Italy or Spain.[11]

From his office in St. Louis, Purnell looked out the window at the Mississippi River and contemplated possible answers to some of the questions likely to be posed by August Busch III, the company's chief executive, regarding the nature of A-B's European expansion:

• How should we increase our sales in Germany? What lessons were learned from the test in Berlin? Should we buy a brewery or should we license one of the German breweries to produce Budweiser? What would be the best way to penetrate the intricate distribution system there? Can we overcome the historical tie of the German citizens to their local brands? How? Would American-style advertising work? After all, American "lifestyle" advertising was popular for consumer products because many Europeans assumed that Americans knew how to relax and have fun. Would a cowboy theme work? What should be done about the German Purity Law? Should the beer be heavier or a normal light beer as sold in America? Would Budweiser sell at a premium price? Were there other groups to target besides the young generation?

---

[10]*Business Week,* February 4, 1991.
[11]Ibid, p. 93.

- How should we resolve the trademark problem with the Czech brewery? The use of "Budweiser" would certainly enhance sales, because the name was so well-known. Was a merger the answer? What other alternatives were available?
- The amusement park idea seems to be working in Spain and the United States. Should we duplicate that strategy in Germany? Or should we put that money into a sales campaign?
- If we buy a brewery, will we have labor problems? How can we guarantee a consistent product? Should we import American hops and barley?

24
Anheuser-Busch (B): Developing a Global Brand in Great Britain

John E. Walsh, Jr. and William P. Coon

Anheuser-Busch (A-B) market research showed that the British beer drinkers were changing their tastes from the traditional ales and bitters to the kinds of lagers that A-B made. The company was confident that Great Britain was a logical choice for international expansion primarily due to the large volumes of beer drunk by British consumers and because English was the national language. However, there was the potential for misjudgments, for as George Bernard Shaw once said: "Britain and America are two nations separated by a common language." Great philosophical and cultural differences existed that were obscured by the conception that a shared linguistic heritage would substantially reduce problems. Jane Walmsley, a television broadcaster in England talked about the British mentality and how it differed from its American counterpart:[1]

> Our "first floor" is your "ground floor"; your "french fries" are our "chips"; what you call a "pickup," we call a "van." But the vocabulary notwithstanding, there are other differences between the American mind and the British mind.
>
> In Britain, one rolls with the punches. It's fruitless to try to take control; bad form to get too involved; arrogant and self-important to attempt to outwit destiny. Lives are to be lived with a certain detachment and a sense of distance preserved.
>
> Events must be allowed to run their natural course. Stay cool, and *never* be seen to try too hard, since anyone with half a brain should recognize the central absurdity of existence and accept the inevitable. Success—if it's to count—must appear effortless. Since nothing matters very much anyway, think twice before making important sacrifices. Never run for a bus. Never skip tea.
>
> The British are more at ease when the range of personal choice is strictly limited. This is reflected in the retail industry, where dresses come in four sizes, shoes in one width,

---

[1]Jane Walmsley, "Oceans Apart," *TWA Ambassador,* July 1992.

and ice cream in three flavors. Too many options only confuse people and encourage them to behave in a greedy and selfish way. It's part of human nature to be happier when our horizons are limited, someone else is in charge, and we know what's expected of us. That's why monarchs are so useful, and the class system survives.

The theory is that money can't buy taste, or style, or a sense of priorities—which are things you're born with. Your spending habits are seen as a reflection of breeding and the quality of your mind, and allow others to make judgments about your background and personal style. People should concern themselves with loyalty to employers, or duty to the wider community. It is the custom of the wealthier Brits to periodically remind the masses of the virtues of self-denial and restraint. This is called *noblesse oblige*. Brits of most persuasions are happiest talking about "self-reliance" and the "common good," which reminds them of the War, the Crown, and the BBC, in no particular order.

Culturally, socially, psychologically, and *literally*—Brits form orderly queues. They like to keep things nice and cozy. Unpredictability carries with it the risk of change and general social turbulence ("No shakeups, please—we're British").

In addition to any cultural differences, A-B had to negotiate around the complex distribution system in Great Britain. Most of the nation's beer was sold through 70,000 pubs, which were traditionally connected to breweries through the historic British beer tie. Tenanted or leased pubs were obligated to stock their owners' brands of beer to the exclusion of other beermakers' brands. The tied system was covered by a European Community (EC) block exemption rule, but this block might come up for review in the future when the EC would have to decide whether to limit the ability of brewers to sell their own products through their own outlets.

The UK Beer Market

Figure 24-1 shows the major breweries in Britain and their relative market shares. The 37.2-million barrels produced in 1992 was the lowest total in 20 years and represented a decline of 3% from the previous year. Reasons cited for the drop were an increased awareness of stiff drunk-driving laws in Britain and a trend towards healthier eating and drinking habits. However, the "Take Home" segment of the beer consumers was in the midst of a dramatic increase in market share (from 12% to 25% in 5 years). The "Drink in Pub" segment was declining due to the increase in the cost of beer sold in pubs compared with purchases in supermarkets. Traditionally, costs were 1 to 1—now they were 2 to 1, with the supermarkets selling beer at lower prices. However, beer consumption "on-premises"[2] still accounted for 75% of all beer consumed in the UK. Other factors that contributed to the decline in beer consumption were general recessionary conditions (exacerbated by higher government taxes on alcohol), a price war begun by the five largest brewers in an effort to force many smaller breweries out of the market, and the effect of a women's movement began in

---

[2]"On-premises" refers to pubs, wine bars, restaurants, and clubs. "Off-premises" refers to all other locations, but principally at home.

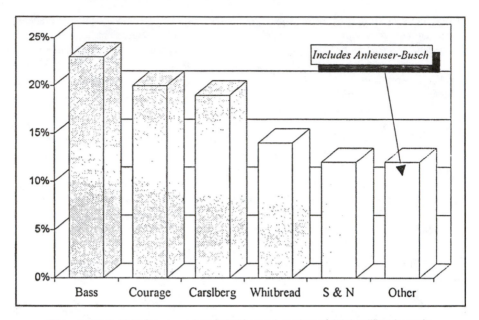

Figure 24-1. U.K. beer market (1992); market size of 37.2 million barrels.

the late 1960s and early 1970s, denting a pastime that often excluded and offended women. Jonathan Murdoch, a researcher at the Centre for Rural Economy in Newcastle commented on the role of women in the level of beer consumption: "If their husband was a beer-swilling oaf who came home drunk every night, most women won't stand for it now."[3]

The women's movement resulted in an increase in numbers visiting the pub, not less, as they joined their male counterparts on an equal basis to drink. While this may have resulted in some curbing on male consumption, it is far more likely that it sent overall volumes up, when one added the additional spirits and beers that women were now drinking.

This official also stated that when no-alcohol (N/A) and low-alcohol (L/A) lagers were first introduced in the 1970s, brands were supported with heavyweight advertising. In the mid- to late 1980s the initial interest in this sector faded because of three reasons:

1. The process for reducing the alcohol for these beers resulted in a poor taste profile.
2. Drinking N/A and L/A beers became associated with the idea of "not having fun."
3. The rise in the popularity of mineral water as an alternative to N/A and L/A beers further damaged that sector.

---

[3]Chuck Freadhoff, "Public Houses Adapt to Changes in Lifestyles," *BNA Electronic News,* April 16, 1992.

Many of the smaller breweries attempted to combine forces to combat the larger breweries. Greenalls, owner of a brewery in the Manchester area and owner of about 1,500 pubs tied to exclusive distribution agreements, purchased all 550 pubs from the Devenish chain to create a U.K. chain of more than 2,000 pubs. The Greenalls chairman, Andrew Thomas, said that "It is our strategic aim to become a national pub retailer, improve our margins by gaining from cross-fertilization of retailing concepts (with Devenish), create more economies of scale, and reduce overhead."[4] The larger breweries all had at least 10,000 pubs in each distribution network.

Competition in the U.K. beer market was fierce (see Figure 24-1). Budweiser faced stiff competition from large domestic breweries that had loyal pub distribution systems. Among these were Bass, Watney's Carlsberg, Courage, Harp, and Guinness. Several beers were brewed under license in the UK—among them were: Carlsberg (Denmark), Fosters (Australia), Heineken (Netherlands), Kronenbourg (France), Lowenbrau (Germany), and Stella Artois (Belgium). Holsten Pils was brewed in Germany and packaged in Britain. Dortmunder (Germany) and Pilsner Urquell (Czech Republic) were imported, but were basically insignificant factors in the UK beer market.

The History of Pubs

The British public house, or pub, was an establishment of social and economic importance providing alcoholic beverages to be consumed on the premises. English common law imposed social responsibilities for the well-being of travelers upon the inns and taverns, declaring them to be public houses, which must receive all travelers in reasonable condition who were willing to pay the price for food, drink, and lodging.

In Tudor England (1485–1603), selected innkeepers were required by a royal act to maintain stables; in addition, some innkeepers acted as unofficial postmasters and kept stables for the royal post (the country's mail system). In the mid-1660s, some public houses even issued unofficial coins, which the innkeepers guaranteed to redeem in the realm's currency.

By the 1800s, many of these establishments were divided internally to segregate the various classes of customers. Public houses—inns or taverns—were considered socially superior to alehouses, beerhouses, and ginshops.

The early inns or taverns were identified by simple signs, such as lions, dolphins, or black swans. Many colorful pub names (e.g., Bag o' Nails, Ghost and Compass, and Elephant and Castle) were actually corrupted forms of historical, ecclesiastical, or other proper phrases and titles (e.g., Bacchanals, Great God Encompassing, Infanta de Castile, respectively). In the 18th century, the word "Arms" was append-ed to many pub names, indicating that the establishment was under the protection of a particular noble family, although some heraldic signs were references to the orig-

---

[4]*International Herald Tribune,* May 28, 1993.

inal ownership of the land on which the inn or tavern stood. Some 200 of the old coaching and posting inns, including a few which date back more than 400 years, are still operating in England and Wales under the management of trust companies, groups begun in the early 20th century to prevent the old inns from becoming merely local taverns.

Beer-Drinking Habits in Great Britain

A former English pub barmaid and several punters (customers) were interviewed about the pub culture and British drinking habits. All but one of the interviewees had been away from England for several years. The barmaid had worked in a pub north of London. Their comments are summarized:

> There are three main types of beer in Britain—beer, lager and real ale. Beer is a flat, brown drink which is served at room temperature and sometimes called bitter (there is a variation called mild bitter). Lager is much lighter and fizzy (carbonated). Ale is a variant of beer and comes in several guises like mild or stout; many of the new "designer" beers are called real ales.
>
> Drinking habits were dictated by the social class, sex, and age of the drinker. In America the legal drinking age was 21—here in Britain it was 18. There were no rules which hold fast for the whole country, and there were also some strong regional preferences.
>
> Being in a pub was as important as the drink itself—passing time in this manner was a major social activity. A pub was selected for its social ambiance and its type of clientele. The British were extremely traditional about their drinking patterns and were loathe to change the habits of a lifetime. They would remain loyal to the same beer and the same drinking establishment, if at all possible, for their whole life.
>
> Lager (the lighter beers) tended to be drunk by younger men of lesser social status. They were nicknamed "Lager Louts," as they were infamous for their rowdy behavior. I would say also that it tended to be drunk more in the south, but it was consumed in vast quantities by the student population of the north and northeast. The older generation would generally not drink lager, as they perceived it as a modern drink. Younger men consumed it as generally it was cheaper than the old-fashioned pint of (dark) beer—it was also less alcoholic so it was possible to consume in larger quantities. Part of the male macho thing was to shout about how many pints one was able to drink in one evening—anything over ten was considered quite impressive.
>
> The new half liter measure, as opposed to the good old-fashioned British pint glass, caused some consternation when it was first introduced. It is now part of the European Community (EC) regulations that there has to be a gap at the top of the glass and a certain amount of froth on the top of the beer. However, the British have been resistant to the ultimate change of buying their beer in liters rather than pints.
>
> Ale was a drink for older people and was definitely becoming old-fashioned. It was similar to stout, the most famous being Guinness, which was the mainstay of Eire [Ireland]. Among the younger generation, Guinness had become rather fashionable and had been successfully marketed as the "thinking man's" beer.

The barmaid is a stalwart of the British pub. It is an ideal job for women, as the hours are flexible and the pay is low—this low pay does not attract men, although you will find male students behind the bar, and most of the proprietors were men.

The barmaid would make the punters (customers) feel welcome, chat with them if they are unaccompanied, and know the favorite tipple (drink) of regulars to the pub—she was like the hostess. This is not a job for the fainthearted or the shy and retiring types. If there was a problem or an argument, which can often happen with the heightened emotions of those who have over-imbibed, then she would have to smooth the ruffled feathers. She was also expected to know all of the different drinks and to be able to pull a proper pint (obtain a draft beer from the barrel or keg), which was a skill in itself. She would have to know how to pour the bottled beers, know how much residue to leave in the bottom of a bottle of White Label, ensure that the bottled lagers do not have too much froth (head) on the top of the glass, and know the difference between a "black and tan" (half Guiness stout ale and half bitter), a "black velvet" (half Guinness stout ale and half champagne), and a "half and half" (half bitter and half mild bitter).

There were seven or eight national breweries (the two largest are Watney's and Bass) which all offered a variety of beers, but there was an increasing demand for premium beers, once called "boutique" beers. The large breweries had traditionally sold their beers through their own chains of pubs or public houses, which served only their particular brands. It was becoming more common to see "Free Houses," which could offer whatever beers they liked, but tended to serve the regional specialities.

Regional tastes varied enormously. Kentish beers would be "hoppy" as the hops were grown locally. Yorkshire beers tended to be stronger and heavier. The beer sold in the highlands and Scotland was darker and less fizzy.

Beer drinking had usually been perceived as a male preoccupation, but this was changing with female emancipation. Younger women often drank lager and many would be offended if they were only offered half-pint glasses (the smallest size available). It was now totally acceptable for women to enter pubs on their own or with a couple of female friends. Pubs used to be almost exclusively male—it was an opportunity for them to escape the drudgery of the home. There always had been a strong association between working men's groups and the local drinking establishment.

Because of this predominance of the working class in the public houses, the pricing of beer was particularly sensitive. An increase in price would reduce consumption temporarily—the breweries would never consider a price increase of more than a few pence (about 3–5¢) at a time. Beer tended to be cheaper than many other drinks available in pubs—this was one of the reasons why beer-drinking has developed into such a strong British institution.

A popular way to drink beer is to drink several pints and follow these with a 'chaser" of a shot of whiskey. The alcoholic content of beer is relatively low for most of the big name brands, so a whiskey will give the beer a "kick."

The premium and "designer" beers are much more expensive, since they are brewed in far smaller quantities and with higher alcoholic content than the standard beers. This market segment used to be the domain of small and very localized breweries, but in the last several years the large national breweries have spotted the growing popularity of these beers, especially in the more monied and middle class areas—they have now started to produce their own types of "boutique" beers to be sold solely through their own public house chains.

The growing popularity of the "designer" beers has been followed by the development of new chains of pubs with their own identity—these new chains are far fewer in number than the large chains like Whitbread or Bass. The most famous of these are based in and around London, and have names like The Slug and Lettuce or The Fox and Firkin. They cater to the "yuppie" market which developed in the last decade.

The busy times in a public house are Friday and Saturday evenings and Sunday lunchtimes. Some people will stop to have a drink on the way home from work—others will come out for a pint after they have finished their evening meal. Weekday lunchtimes are also relatively busy for pubs that serve food and also are within walking distances of factories and other workplaces. Now that the drunk-driving laws in Britain are so strict, people are very wary about losing their driver's license. Another popular time is on pay day, when many of the punters tend to have one (beer) too many.

Pubs can also be very lonely and, yet, very friendly places at the same time. Often people will come in on their own and then start talking to someone else at the bar. The barmaid will always act as everyone's friend. When someone is buying another beer, it is rare not to include the others standing in the immediate vicinity—of course, the barmaid would always be counted in. Buying a round of drinks is the norm for friends. Having bought your round, it is normal for everyone who has benefited to return your compliment—not to do so is considered bad form. Persons visiting pubs or infrequent patrons are not expected to buy rounds of drinks.

Drinking habits in Britain are changing, and pubs are having to adapt to cater to the new market demands. In more affluent areas pubs are being replaced by wine bars. Drinking is becoming more associated with the consumption of food. Some newer pubs or wine gardens offer play areas or facilities for children in order to attract a new family clientele. With beer becoming more widely available in the supermarkets and with more people keeping beer at home, the purpose of pubs purely as a place to purchase alcohol will change. They will become more social places for the gathering and the meeting of people. The local pubs will always be in Britain, as they are part of the very fabric of British tradition.

An industry source interpreted the U.K. market in a different light. He stated that the barmaid's comments appeared to be extremely dated and, in some cases, inaccurate. He said that beer was divided into stouts, ales, and lagers. Stout was a black beer, the color coming from roast barley being introduced in the brewing process. The market for stout was dominated by Guinness. While it was a very traditional drink, it had regained popularity among younger consumers. Ales were lighter in color. While some were served at room temperature, the majority of ales were chilled. There were varieties of ales in the market such as bitter, real ale, and mild. Lager was lighter in color and tended to be served at a low temperature (5–9° Centigrade). Like some ales, it was carbonated, but not "fizzy."

The source also commented that while lager had appeal among younger men, and had, in the past, been associated with rowdy behavior, it had, in reality, a much broader franchise both in terms of age profile and social status. He said that drinking could have a macho aspect, but no more in the U.K. than any other country. He added that men do not tend to "shout" about how many pints they have had in one evening. Moreover, he added that the half-liter measure is not the standard in the U.K. Consumers still order and receive their beer in pint and half-pint glasses.

The official concluded by commenting that, while many women work as barmaids, it was not a female-dominated role; many men carried out the same function as their full time occupation. In city pubs, the turnover rate of bar staff, coupled with the volume of customers, resulted in service without the personal touch. Buying rounds of drinks was a U.K. and Irish feature among friends and colleagues. It was not rude to buy a single drink when alone at a bar. Buying drinks for barmaids was becoming rare.

Different Types of Pubs

There is no description of a "typical" British public house. Any such description by a British beer drinker would bear a strong resemblance to the individual's favorite drinking establishment. Drinking in Great Britain is a very personal preoccupation and everyone has their own ideas of what makes a good pub. However, pubs can generally be categorized as being one of five major types:

- **The Country Pub:** Tucked away on the back street of a small village or down an obscure country lane was a country pub. They tended to be very old, small, and served a loyal and local following. Some had been upgraded to small country restaurants serving old-fashioned English cooking. The newest of these pubs would probably offer a selection of "designer" beers. The country pub was a preferred destination of city dwellers on the weekends.

- **The Local Village/Small Town Pub:** Any town of more than a few thousand inhabitants would offer a selection of pubs vying for different market segments. The "personality" of each pub was dictated by the landlord and the type of customer he wanted to attract. Video machines were placed in pubs catering to the younger crowds. Family-oriented pubs offered good selections of food. A pub for the working class usually had sawdust on the floor. Trendier pubs played loud music. Regular customers were on good terms with the proprietor, and often their drinks would be served before they reached the bar.

- **Inner City Pubs:** These establishments varied enormously in their decor and clientele. Although some had regular customers, most of London's pubs had primarily a transient crowd with no special relationship between the pub and the customers. There was no unique identity similar to that of the country pubs.

- **Roadside Pubs:** This type of pub catered to travelers and businessmen making sales calls away from their home offices. Often they offered "bed and breakfast" accommodations—the food was not always first-rate. The Railway Inns fit into this category.

- **Red Brick Pubs:** This type of pub was built in heavily populated housing estates and tended to reflect the neighborhood where it was situated.

The Introduction of Budweiser to Great Britain

Budweiser entered the British market in the early 1980s. Basically, A-B wanted more "hands-on" control of their marketing destiny. They would import Michelob and let Courage, a large English brewer, brew Budweiser under contract; in addition, Courage would be appointed distributor of Budweiser to its network of more than 5,000 pubs. A-B intended to unleash a media blitz as they attempted to convince beer consumers in the British Isles to switch brands.

They increased their advertising spending budget 100% to $20 million—all U.K. brewers spent about $180-million in 1992. They were getting ready to launch their first national TV campaign for Budweiser: two 30-second spots would feature blues music and continue the successful "Budweiser, the genuine article" theme.

A-B was marketing Budweiser and Michelob in the U.K. at what would be super-premium pricing in the U.S. The products were priced higher than most local brands. We hoped to link Budweiser to American cultural icons, while tailoring the choice of icons to local tastes. Consistent with their advertising compaigns in all European countries, they were trying to say what was good about America. Budweiser, with the premier position in the U.S. and the red, white and blue label, was as wrapped up with America as Levi Strauss. But what appealed about America differed from country to country.

However, the British market, while not nearly as difficult to penetrate as Germany, represented beer drinkers with different habits and idiosyncrasies than the typical American consumer. The English drank most of their beer in the thousands of neighborhood pubs. Their most popular drink was the lager, or lighter beer, which was served on draught.

In the late 1950s and early 1960s a marketing pitch to have a "cool, frosty Budweiser" probably would not have worked in the U.K. Most pubs of that era were not centrally heated. The average afternoon temperatures in northern England and Scotland were quite cool. For most of the year the temperatures in London, which is in southern England, were 5°–15°C (41°–59°F) lower than in St. Louis, Missouri. This cooler climate had contributed to the predilection to consume most beers at room temperature. The American custom of drinking beers at 40°–45°F in a chilled glass was not generally preferred in the UK.

In recent times, however, most pubs maintained their inside air at a comfortable temperature comparable to bars in the United States. In the mid-1970s the British drinkers began to demand that their beers be cooled. This trend occurred because most Englishmen vacationed in Spain or southern France during the months of July and August, when local beers were drunk cooled. They began to appreciate a chilled drink. Now in Britain, many bitters are served at 46°–52°F. Most lagers were now consumed at 44°–48°F (although Budweiser was still served at even cooler temperatures: 40°–45°F).

In the past, Englishmen would eat their dinners at home and then retire to their favorite pub for several hours. However, this changed once women started to work in greater numbers. Many English couples would now go to the pub before going to a wine bar or an establishment that served food. Wine bars were normally found in large cities. They were upscale, often having a theme. They catered primarily to singles and young couples. Scotsmen followed the basic pattern with the exception that the drink of choice was a stout ale, a dark brew that contains more alcohol than the English lagers.

The U.K. Marketing Philosophy of Budweiser

When Budweiser originally debuted in Great Britain, it was positioned as a premium lager, i.e., a brand with a high-quality image and an alcohol level of between 4.5% and 6%. During the late 1980s, A-B's constantly-changing ads led to consumer confusion and left Budweiser with a superficial "fad" image and a reputation of poor quality. As a result, the U.K. strategy changed from portraying Budweiser as a "glitzy" American brand to a commercial message that focused on the authentic American heritage of the brand coupled with higher quality values.

An A-B executive stated that, in terms of the differences between the marketing of Budweiser in the U.K. versus the marketing of the brand in the United States, there are really two points that were important. First, in the U.K. the brand's personality was based on the fact that its roots were American. The success of the brand was a result of fine-tuning those images of America, which were particularly appealing to the U.K. consumer. Second, Budweiser had a very defined target audience, unlike the American situation where the brand had a far broader appeal in terms of social class and age profile. The U.K. marketing plan could focus on this target audience in a very cohesive manner.

The following illustrates the Anheuser-Busch strategy for positioning Budweiser in the British market:

- Lager Segment: Premium Lager
- Strength: 5% Alcohol by volume; draught and packaged
- Pricing: Top of premium lager range
- Source of volume: Recruitment of new drinkers; premium segment growth; brand switching; new distribution
- Target audience: Primary—Men, 18-34; secondary: all men; B, C, D social class (A is highest; E is lowest)
- Packaging: 330 ml non-return bottle; 330 ml can (4, 8, 12 multipack); 11-gallon kegs

The Use of TV Advertising in Selling Beer

When Budweiser was first introduced into the English market, the typical TV ad about beers was focused on humor. These ads were produced with large budgets and the viewing audience found them to be very entertaining. Consumer awareness was also quite high. One brewery, Carling Black Label, attempted to capitalize on the extreme popularity of Levi jeans. A Levi ad showed a young man in a laundromat removing his clothes piece-by-piece and putting them into a washing machine. At the end of the ad, all he had on were his undershorts—the ad gave Levi one of the highest awareness ratings on any TV ad that year. Similarly, the beer ad showed a young man removing his clothes in a laundromat. However, this time, he removed *all* of his clothes and had a beer. This ad became very popular and helped the brewery sell its beers.

Anheuser-Busch also used humorous ads, but wanted to change its image to that of a company with a quality product. Therefore, their advertising began to communicate two key messages:

• The authentic American heritage of the brand.
• The quality of ingredients and the consistently high-quality brewing that goes into the beer.

* * * * * * * * *

If you were the Budweiser brand marketing manager in the UK, what marketing strategy would you choose? Why? How would this strategy differ from a marketing strategy in the United States? What kind of information would you consider critical to your marketing effort?

25
Cross-Cultural Collaboration at EUROSYS

**Robert T. Moran,
John Kerschen,
Geke Rosier,
and
Jacqueline Wagner**

EUROSYS

In March of 1987, the chairmen of the member companies of EUROSYS, Association of European Office Systems Wholesalers, met for the bi-monthly management committee meeting at EUROSYS headquarters in Frankfurt, Germany. The management committee planned to discuss how to improve the deteriorating cooperation within the coalition. During the meeting, the presidents of two new member companies, Denmark and The Netherlands, dominated the discussions severely criticizing EUROSYS policies. Meanwhile, the other six CEO participants and Patrick Durand, the secretary general of EUROSYS, remained silent. Finally, the CEO of the EUROSYS Spanish member company interrupted the two newcomers and accused them of acting presumptuously. A heated argument ensued, the Spaniard stormed out declaring that EUROSYS was no longer a team. Another management committee meeting ended in a total fiasco.

This case has been prepared for educational purposes. The characters and situations are based upon real people and events; the names and details of the events, however, have been changed and altered at the request of the companies. Assistance in critiquing and modifying this case was provided by Pamela Unternaehrer.

Patrick Durand (Appendix A) was once again forced to mediate a dispute. Highly respected by the EUROSYS members, Durand was once again called to preserve the increasingly fragile unity of EUROSYS. Durand saw clearly the necessity of developing a collaborative spirit among members to facilitate the achievement of the group's goals.

Increasingly acute divisions between the members were apparent, especially between the older and younger representatives, owners and the managers, and, not surprisingly, between individuals from different cultures. Resolving these disagreements, in Durand's view, was critical so that EUROSYS could meet the challenge of increased competition, both within the industry and throughout Europe, as a result of the establishment of the European Community (EC). The success of each company in its domestic market contributed to an overly confident attitude about the threat of competition.

Coalition Background

EUROSYS, a coalition of European office systems wholesalers, comprises eight member companies from Switzerland, United Kingdom, Denmark, Germany, Greece, Turkey, Spain, and The Netherlands (Appendix A). All members are involved in the distribution of modular office systems including office partitions, desks, filing cabinets, safes, and lighting systems. Some members also operate furniture manufacturing facilities, household furniture distributorships, and retail furniture outlets.

In 1982, the six founding members wrote and signed the EUROSYS Agreement. Its major objective is to enhance the profitability and competitiveness of member companies through the sharing of information and management expertise and volume purchasing to facilitate members' operations, sourcing, and marketing activities. Also, the association was established, in part, to address the opportunities that the EC posed.

Most of the member companies are national market leaders and all have been profitable since 1978. The coalition offers unique opportunities not attainable by non-coalition competitors. One such advantage is access to economies of scale in purchasing, marketing, and research and development. For example, to reduce purchasing costs from office furniture manufacturers, EUROSYS maintains a frequently-updated database containing price, quality, and descriptive information for office furniture available from European manufacturers. Each member has access to the database and is assigned responsibility for ensuring that the system is updated as new information is received. However, some members have complained that not all members are complying with this responsibility, thus, the veracity of the database information is questionable.

In return for a nominal annual fee and a share of central coordination costs, EUROSYS' members also gain access to centralized staff development and training programs. However, given member companies' individual successes and management styles, some owners do not perceive the need for management training.

Until 1989, no major competitors operated in the EUROSYS marketplace, a non-incentive for members to work toward a common strategy and team unity. Another coalition of office furniture wholesalers, however, was founded in Europe in mid-1989, and Durand believes this new competitor might eventually threaten the growth of EUROSYS.

EUROSYS Leadership

The EUROSYS management committee, comprising the presidents of the member companies and Durand, advises the general assembly (GA) on operations management issues. The GA membership consists of 26 company representatives; each company appoints three or four key personnel to attend the semi-annual meetings. During these conferences, led by Durand who serves as chairman of the management committee and GA, participants discuss and decide major issues concerning EUROSYS' operations. Committee decisions are made on a non-voting, consensual basis, except in the case of urgent decisions. Responsibility for hosting GA gatherings rotates among members, and recently, an element of competition has entered both the settings for the meetings and the social activities.

The heads of the EUROSYS member companies range in age from 40 to 55 years. Most inherited their leadership role and are the dominant or sole owners of their enterprises. A few possess solid academic backgrounds; most have acquired managerial expertise through numerous years of hands-on experience in their firms (Appendix A). In general, the group members are not academically inclined; they do not regularly attend seminars and conferences, nor do they read current management literature. Most openly resist changes in organizational structure, particularly those involving the hiring of outside management potential. Contributing to this resistance is the past unquestionable success of the individual member companies.

Several additional factors have prevented the EUROSYS leaders from achieving a more cohesive working group. Although the need for and benefits of greater cooperation is recognized by most members, the varied, and often conflicting, management styles, cultures, and individual company priorities have proven difficult obstacles to overcome.

In 1989, in an effort to improve deteriorating group cohesiveness, Durand contacted a consultant with expertise in international management and team building and arranged for a seminar designed to enhance the collaborative spirit of EUROSYS members. Reaction to this proposal was mixed, but the group decided to attend a workshop given by an international management consultant.

The Collaboration Seminar

The seminar consisted of several parts, including short written exercises and role-playing activities. During one session, Orhan Akbil, the Turkish member, expressed his discomfort with these methods. To this remark, the consultant replied, "I was not paid to make you feel comfortable."

The workshop helped many members recognize that cultural differences when collaborating must be respected. Moreover, most members began to realize that changing one another was an impossible task and that learning to work together within individual cultural parameters was a more effective alternative.

Cross-Cultural Issues

Until 1985, members relied on simultaneous translators to communicate, which resulted in a cumbersome discussion process and numerous miscommunication problems. After much deliberation, English was adopted as the group's official business language, a move resisted by many members for several reasons, including pride in their native tongues. Ultimately, this solution failed to achieve its goal because members' varied levels of English fluency continued to be a barrier to cross-cultural understanding.

In addition to cross-cultural barriers to group effectiveness, EUROSYS members' attitudes about the group contributed to the lack of cohesiveness and effectiveness of the organization. Most leaders viewed membership in EUROSYS as having certain privileges but lacking clear obligations. Each was motivated to join for two primary reasons; the prestige of affiliation with an international organization, and the desire to protect domestic markets from other members' growth across borders. A major non-incentive for membership stemmed from members' resistance to sacrifice their independence to achieve closer cooperation within EUROSYS.

Social Activities

Each year EUROSYS organizes several social activities for the group, including sailing, skiing, and hunting trips. These are designed to provide the opportunity for members to become better acquainted in relaxed, non-business settings. It is hoped that these purely social outings will improve communication and build trust between the members, thereby facilitating collaboration.

A typical EUROSYS social excursion occurred during the Easter vacation of 1990. Participants signed up for a ski trip to Austria, an outing most were eager to attend. All member companies were represented, except Enrique Gonzalez, president of the Spanish member company, who chose to remain in Spain with his family during Easter.

The ski group met in St. Anton, Austria. Everyone but Markos Stavrapoulos, the Greek member, arrived at the St. Anton airport on Saturday morning. Stavrapoulos flew in late Saturday afternoon. A bus transported the group from the airport to the four-star hotel in St. Anton.

At the lodge, dinner was served between 5:00 and 7:00 p.m. However, unaccustomed to dining at this time, Stavrapoulos and Orhan Akbil, separately, went out late in the evening for a snack. Akbil also had to follow a special diet, in accordance with the traditions of his Islamic religion.

After dinner, several of the members usually played a game of bridge, and one evening a small tournament was organized. The German, Andreas Schuette, and the Brit, Jonathan Williams, played in the finals against Lars Christensen from Denmark, and Werner Buenzli from Switzerland. All four approached the game seriously. After approximately an hour, it became clear that Schuette and Williams were in the lead. Suddenly, Buenzli stood up and slammed his cards on the playing table. Complaining that the rules differed from those in his country, he stated that he had therefore played at a disadvantage from the outset. Dismissing his charges, the others simply laughed at his outburst, gathered the cards, and went to bed.

Most of the EUROSYS leaders were good skiers, especially those from The Netherlands, Germany, Denmark, and Switzerland. The latter four were always the first ones at breakfast and on the ski slopes. After a tiring day of skiing, the skiers met for an "après-ski" drink. While at the bar, Akbil drank tea instead of Gluehwein, a famous Austrian beverage. Christensen and Marc Bartels, a Dutchman, often missed dinner, preferring instead to talk and swap jokes with other skiers they met in the bar.

After nearly a week in St. Anton, it was time to fly home. Akbil and Stavrapoulos took an early flight home Friday morning, and Durand, Buenzli, and Williams left Friday afternoon. Bartels, Christensen, and Schuette opted to extend their vacation another day.

Database Conflict

In late 1990, a dispute concerning the EUROSYS database arose between the presidents of four member companies, including Stavrapoulos, Williams, Akbil, and Schuette. Schuette and Akbil wrote a letter to Patrick Durand voicing mutual suspicion about Stavrapoulos' misuse of the EUROSYS database (See Appendix B). Other members had previously leveled similar accusations, but this was the most serious to date.

Durand quickly responded to the complaint of Schuette and Akbil with a memorandum calling for a discussion of the matter at the next EUROSYS meeting (see Appendix C). All members of the management committee attended this meeting, held at the illustrious Hotel Waldhaus Dolder in the hills surrounding Zurich. Acutely aware of the tense atmosphere, Durand opened the meeting with the following words:

Dear colleagues, I welcome you to this special meeting today and thank you for attending. The circumstances under which we meet today are unfortunate, and I would like to ask each one of you to reflect carefully on the information we learn here. Mr. Markos Stavrapoulos, president of Delphi, Inc. in Athens, Greece, stands accused of falsifying and withholding information from the EUROSYS database. We are here to discover the facts and to make a decision, but we also are here to act in fairness. Please think carefully before making any decisions. I now give the floor to Mr. Williams who will present his information regarding this incident. Thank you.

Williams relayed the story of the Greek customer who was more informed than he. As he finished, the room erupted in heated conversation. Enrique Gonzalez, the Spaniard, became angry and began shouting at Stavrapoulos. Others gathered in groups of two or three and began talking to one another in hushed tones. Everyone agreed that they had long suspected Delphi of withholding information from the EUROSYS database and that Delphi should be expelled from EUROSYS.

Stavrapoulos finally was given an opportunity to present his case. He was obviously uncomfortable but spoke clearly and calmly. He did not deny that the information to which Williams referred was missing from the database, but stated that the information was not purposefully withheld. He explained that the discrepancy was simply an oversight on the part of a clerk and assured the group that a similar situation would not recur. He strongly refuted the group's allegations that Delphi had been withholding information for a considerable time. He continued by accusing the group of discrimination and claiming that the charge was really a trumped-up means to eject Delphi from EUROSYS because it was a Greek company.

Stavrapoulos expressed his anger and disbelief that the group was prepared to ask him to resign on the basis of one mistake. He spoke eloquently about his past contributions to EUROSYS, reminding them of a recent occasion when he negotiated a substantially lower price for office partitions from a Greek manufacturer for the group. By the time he finished, most members felt slightly ashamed for having judged him without first hearing his explanation.

Durand then called for a decision by management committee ballot: Should Delphi be punished? The conference room was filled with tension as Durand silently read the ballots; the majority voted against punishing Stavrapoulos or Delphi.

A month later, however, the management committee obtained new evidence from reliable sources indicating that Delphi was again entering misleading price quotes into the EUROSYS database. Durand's frustration grew. He was worried that these repeated incidents would further erode the unity of EUROSYS if not dealt with swiftly and equitably.

The Expansion of Wuerth KG

Before joining EUROSYS, the German member company, Wuerth KG, operated furniture distributorships in Germany, Austria, The Netherlands, and Switzerland.

The Wuerth distributorships in The Netherlands, and Switzerland primarily handled household furniture; and, thus, did not compete directly with the EUROSYS Dutch and Swiss member companies.

In 1983, the Munich-based Wuerth was presented with the opportunity to acquire a small German manufacturer of file cabinets, desks and other items for office and household use. During the previous nine years, Wuerth had purchased 30 to 45% of this manufacturer's annual production and was consistently pleased with the product quality, competitive prices, and punctual delivery. In late 1982, however, this supplier experienced a severe financial crisis, and Wuerth tendered and won a bid to rescue the company.

Only after Wuerth began pursuing an aggressive acquisition strategy, including the purchase of a medium-sized wholesaler in Vienna, a small furniture manufacturer in Milan and finally a major EUROSYS supplier in 1987, did the group express any reservations. Upon hearing of the purchase of an important Italian EUROSYS supplier, however, some EUROSYS presidents began to question Wuerth's growing international presence. Schuette, however, reassured them that they would continue to receive the same service, and even offered a 1% discount on future orders, from the Italian suppliers. This calmed the Spanish and Greek presidents and seemed to settle the issue. Schuette's company, however, soon became entangled in another EUROSYS disagreement.

The EUROSYS Dutch member company, Meubels B.V., headquartered in Amsterdam, began diversifying into general household furniture in 1988. This activity sparked a direct conflict between Meubels' and Wuerth's subsidiaries in The Netherlands. Meubels' president, Marc Bartels, complained to Durand that Wuerth was encroaching on the Dutch market and stealing his customers. Schuette defended his company's actions, justifying them on the basis of Wuerth's presence in that sector of the furniture market for some time before Meubels' entrance.

Durand attempted to mediate the dispute with three weeks of "shuttle diplomacy" between Munich and Amsterdam. His efforts, however, went unrewarded as both Wuerth and Meubels refused to modify their actions or arguments. The conflict culminated at a GA meeting in June of 1990 during which Bartels called for the immediate expulsion of Wuerth from EUROSYS. Durand exercised his power as the group's secretary general and countered Bartel's proposal by persuading the assembly to postpone a vote on the matter until the GA meeting scheduled for February of 1991. A committee to help investigate solutions to the controversy was appointed by Durand, who privately wondered which, if any, of the member companies really belonged in the coalition, which he believed may be approaching its final days.

European Community 1992

The economic integration of the European market in 1992 served as a major stimulus in the development of EUROSYS. With the removal of trade barriers between European Community (EC) countries in 1993, common pricing strategies become imperative. With lower transportation costs and less paperwork at the borders, cross-border shipping increases. EC financial markets will converge, providing European companies with new financing alternatives. Furthermore, in the long term, the European marketplace is expected to experience converging customer preferences and demands that will necessitate greater cooperation between the member companies. Though not all EUROSYS member companies are located in an EC country, the economic integration will affect each and result in greater competition for all.

Proposals for the Future

On numerous occasions, Durand submitted proposals to the EUROSYS Management Committee outlining alternatives to strengthen the coalition's competitive position in Europe through greater collaboration. In late 1990, he sent the following letter to management committee members.

> December 15, 1990
> For the Management Committee:
> As you all know, since I became the Secretary General in 1985, I have been concerned about the future of EUROSYS, especially with respect to the changes that will take place in Europe. Until now, EUROSYS has faced little competition, but this is changing as potential competitors are preparing to enter our marketplace.
> During the last few years, you and I have discussed many scenarios for achieving greater mutual cooperation between our member companies and increasing profitability. 1993 is fast approaching, and, as important players in the market for office furniture distribution, we must begin to implement some reform measures as soon as possible.
> I would appreciate your comments on the following proposals. Please give your views on the future of EUROSYS and suggest any other measures that you think might help EUROSYS prosper.
>
> * Development of managerial training programs for all EUROSYS managers.
> * Establishment of a EUROSYS franchise system.
> * Use of the EUROSYS name more frequently or requiring use of an EUROSYS trademark.
> * Offering of a more uniform line of products at member company distributorships.
> * Establishment of a system for fair evaluation of member contribution to the coalition.
> * Increased financial integration by using common financial sources and establishment of a commission system for EUROSYS.
> * Implementation of a voting system for Management Committee and General Assembly meetings.
> * Initiation of EUROSYS buy-outs of member companies.
>
> I would appreciate hearing your comments and ideas before February 5, 1991.

With conflicts on the rise at EUROSYS in late 1990, Durand was beginning to lose patience with the coalition. Through his experience as a business consultant and as a director on the boards of several European and American companies, he accurately foresaw the threat to EUROSYS members as a result of the EC. His professional and personal goal was to facilitate and guide the group to successfully meet the challenges of the new competitive environment. However, he was plagued with doubts about the fragile cohesion of the group, the continued conflict between members, and his own ability to continue to successfully promote the benefits of EUROSYS within the group.

Appendix A—Profiles of Characters and Countries

Patrick Durand

Forty-five years old and from Dusseldorf, Germany, Patrick Durand holds both an undergraduate degree from the University of Cologne in economics and a master's degree in business administration from Stanford. He has worked as a business consultant throughout Europe and the United States for more than 15 years and has a strong interest in the European Community.

Durand is single, thus somewhat more flexible in his ability to be available at a moment's notice. He has an open, friendly personality that accounts for the excellent relationship he enjoys, not only with past employers and clients, but with each of the EUROSYS members. He believes in frequent and honest communication, visits each member-company at least twice a year and stays in close contact by phone, letters, fax, and E-mail. He also attends all management committee and general assembly meetings, as well as most social outings planned for EUROSYS leaders.

Durand believes that keeping up-to-date on business trends and practices is important and frequently attends seminars and classes on European integration and new management techniques. In particular, the teachings of Michael Porter particularly impress Durand.

Denmark

Lars Christensen, president of the EUROSYS Danish member company, Jensen Kontormobler A/S, is 52 years old and a lifetime employee of the company. Without a college degree and just a few evening courses at a business school in Copenhagen, he has worked his way up through the hierarchy. This may explain his tendency to hire outside managers only rarely and his belief that experience is far more important than education. He has a keen sense of humor and a relaxed personality but does not hesitate to voice his opinions. Christensen, in accord with Durand, perceives the need for closer cooperation between the EUROSYS members and openly implores them to this end.

The Netherlands

Marc Bartels, age 40, has served as president of Meubels B.V. for more than ten years. Since joining the company upon completion of high school, he has not pursued further academic training. His father, a former president of the company, Hans Bartels, retains ownership of the company, although he was forced to relinquish the presidency as a result of a heart attack in 1986.

Bartels places great emphasis on punctuality and is hard-working, honest, and loyal to his company and employees. As a manager, he prefers quick decisions and action. To him, "business is business," and he refuses to allow his personal life to become intertwined with business.

Bartels supports and encourages cooperation between the members of EUROSYS, although he sometimes causes conflicts as a result of a stubborn streak. On the other hand, he is approachable and possesses a good sense of humor.

Spain

Enrique Gonzalez joined the Spanish company Mobiliario de Oficina, S.A. at the age of 20, after completing high school. At that time his father, Sergio Gonzalez, was president of the company. During the next 20 years, Enrique worked his way to the top of the company to attain his present position as president and major stockholder of Mobiliario.

Gonzalez acquired his managerial expertise through years of hands-on experience. Described as an intensely hard-working man, he is known to put in numerous hours of overtime. As president and majority owner of the company, he feels great responsibility to all areas of the business and experiences difficulty in delegating authority.

Under Gonzalez's leadership, the company has flourished. Seemingly content with the status quo, Gonzalez appears almost indifferent to the urgency of cooperating with the other EUROSYS members expressed by Durand. However, his nationalistic tendencies and his company's position as a market leader in Spain contribute to his concern regarding other members' growth across national borders.

Gonzalez considers personal relationships to be important. He takes pride in his sense of humor, although his rather casual attitude sometimes annoys the more serious EUROSYS leaders.

Switzerland

Werner Buenzli is the CEO of Schmutzli Enterprises AG, headquartered in Bern, Switzerland. He has worked his way through the ranks of the company, which he joined at age 16. After a three-year apprenticeship, he received a business diploma and was promoted to assistant manager of the purchasing department. The consistent quality of his work led to several other promotions and eventually, to the position of CEO. Under his seven-year tenure, the business has maintained profitability, but growth has been somewhat stagnant.

Buenzli's management style is efficient, and he uses a top-down approach to decision-making. He expects his employees to be punctual, disciplined, and willing to extend themselves for the good of the company, even at their own expense. Buenzli has carefully selected his management team: each is experienced, middle-aged, male, conservative, and resistant to change. Though all have traveled extensively, they continue to prefer life in Switzerland and believe that their way of conducting business is best.

United Kingdom

Jonathan Williams, CEO and owner of the British member company Williams, Ltd., inherited the company from his father after completing an undergraduate degree in business. The second largest of the EUROSYS member companies, the company has remained in the Williams family for three generations.

Reserved and polite, Williams occasionally employs a condescending manner of speech that annoys the bosses of the smaller member companies. Although Williams regularly assures EUROSYS of his loyalty, he often irritates other bosses by paying more attention to the needs of his American customers than to his EUROSYS commitments.

Turkey

Orhan Akbil, age 48, is the CEO of Safurni, A.S. in Turkey. He married the daughter of the company's owner and has been with the company since he was 22 years old. An engineering degree from a French university and a solid family reputation characterize Akbil as a member of Turkey's upper class. Akbil, while he considers himself a westernized Turk, continues to maintain excellent relations with Turks who possess more traditional values.

He has four children and regards family matters and personal relationships as more important than his work. For Mr. Akbil, relationships are a critical factor to success. He likes to know people intimately before conducting business dealings with them and, even then, avoids entering into quick decisions. In general, he likes foreigners, with the exception of Greeks, and is easy-going and friendly.

Greece

Markos Stavrapoulos is in his mid-fifties and has been president and owner of Delphi, Inc. for 21 years. Like his father, Stavrapoulos joined the company, founded by his grandfather in 1915, immediately after finishing high school. Starting as a warehouse manager, Stavrapoulos assumed the presidency twelve years later upon his father's retirement. An authoritarian manager, Stavrapoulos delegates little power and responsibility to others, a management style in line with the company's bureaucratic, rigid organizational structure. Modern management, marketing, and finance theories find little or no application at Delphi.

Stavrapoulos is shrewd and street-smart, but lacks openness to new ideas, unless they can be proven to increase profitability. Risk averse, like many of his countrymen, Stavrapoulos' primary business objective is the maximization of short-term profits, a goal he strives toward to the exclusion of all else. He does not perceive contracts as binding and will break them if doing so is in his best interest.

Mr. Stavrapoulos realizes that, with European market integration in 1992, cooperation with other EUROSYS members will provide numerous competitive benefits, but he feels uncomfortable relinquishing control to the group. At management committee meetings, he rarely participates, instead he prefers observing and listening to others.

Germany

Andreas Schuette is a successful businessman and owner of Wuerth KG. In 1981, after completing two years of college, Schuette inherited the position of CEO from his father in 1981 and now directs the more than 320 employees. Like his father, Mr. Schuette plans to retire at age 70. Thus, he will preside over Wuerth for more than 21 additional years before turning the presidency over to his son.

Schuette enjoys a positive relationship with most of his employees and associates. In keeping with company tradition, employees are free to openly express any concerns about the company and its future to top management. Schuette also has an excellent network of professional associates including many top managers in Germany and throughout the world.

Appendix B

October 27, 1990
Dear Patrick:
We are writing this letter to inform you of a disturbing development. We have reason to believe that Markos Stavrapoulos has been withholding pertinent information from the EUROSYS database. We had previously suspected that some of the database information on Greek furniture manufacturers was false, but we lacked proof.

Two weeks ago, Jonathan Williams made a social call on a Greek customer of Stavrapoulos, who also happens to be a friend of the Williams family. This customer asked Williams what he thought of the new, significantly lower prices of the Bereta Office Systems. To his chagrin, Mr. Williams had to admit that he was unaware of this change.

While this was embarrassing for Mr. Williams, the president of the second largest EUROSYS company, it provided the necessary proof to file a complaint against Delphi, Inc. Please let us know how you wish to resolve this problem.

Sincerely,
Andreas L. Schuette   Orhan Akbil

Appendix C

To: The Management Committee
From: Patrick Durand
Subject: Meeting on November 20, 1990
Date: November 3, 1990

Members of the management committee have notified me that they believe that open and honest communication regarding pricing among EUROSYS members is not occurring.

Mr. Markos Stavrapoulos has been accused of falsifying or withholding information from the EUROSYS database. I am therefore calling an extraordinary meeting on November 20, 1990, to give Mr. Stavrapoulos an opportunity to explain his position regarding the complaints before the management committee.

The meeting will take place during the weekend of November 20, 1990 at the Hotel Waldhaus Dolder in Zurich. In addition to the members of the management committee, Hans Waldmann, our corporate lawyer, will also be present to clear any legal questions that might arise during the meeting.

I urge everyone to attend this special meeting.

26
Between a Rock and a Hard Place: A Question of Ethics

Julian H. Allen
and
Gerald Parkhouse

Hathaway Electronics

Charlie Dixon eased the small Peugeot 304 around the closely parked cars in the sub-basement garage of his Neuilly apartment house and headed carefully for the up-ramp. He rolled down the window, stopped at the foot of the long ramp, reached out, and pushed the button that opened the overhead door at the top of the ramp. As he accelerated, the engine stalled. After three tries on the ignition switch, it finally coughed to life with a more promising sound, but by this time the automatic door at the top had run its automatic cycle and closed, so he had to back down and press the button on the wall again.

Charlie reflected that this was not a very auspicious start to what he had hoped would be an important day. He and his family had been in France two months. Most of their time had been consumed in getting settled into the apartment in an attractive suburb just west of Paris, getting the kids established in the American School of Paris, and establishing his work routine at the Hathaway plant near Orly. Getting acquainted with the people at the plant, the layout of the city, and where to buy what, had taken much longer than he had anticipated. He had a nagging feeling that not much had been achieved thus far.

This case is adapted from the book, *Hathaway Electronics* by Julian Allen and Gerald Parkhouse. For further information contact Gerald Parkhouse at Elmira College, Elmira, New York.

Today was to have been different. The company was well into its annual trauma of setting next year's budget, and Charlie had a proposal for reconciling the French and the American budgeting techniques that he thought would help toward resolving one of the problems he had been transferred here to fix. Today he was scheduled to make his presentation to Frank Miller, the American general manager of the subsidiary, and to the French managers who reported to Miller.

Because of the importance of the meeting, Charlie wanted to get to his office earlier than normal, so the car stalling irritated him. He decided to forego his usual route to Orly that took him through the heart of Paris—up the Avenue Charles de Gaulle, around the madcap racetrack circling the Arc de Triomphe, down the Champs-Elysées, through the Place de la Corcorde, past the Tuileries and the Louvre, crossing the Seine by Notre Dame Cathedral, on to the Boulevard Saint Michel, and then southward out of the city. He thought he would never tire of the beauty of Paris. Today he decided to take the slightly longer but faster route via the Périphérique, the high-speed multi-lane beltway that circled Paris. By now Charlie had driven in France just long enough to know that all French drivers were not as crazy as they seemed at first, it was just that they all followed a set of driving rules that seemed incomprehensible to Americans.

Once ensconced in his office, Charlie's plan to review his notes and charts for the meeting was not working out well. His secretary insisted that a rather large stack of papers and reports required his immediate attention, some to be signed, and some to be answered with short dictation. When finished with this chore, she announced that Mr. Patterson was pacing in the other office, insisting that he must see Charlie on a matter of great urgency that could not wait until the afternoon. Dick Patterson was an American working in Paris for the branch office of one of the Big 8 U.S. auditing firms that did Hathaway's auditing on a worldwide basis. Charlie saw that he still had twenty minutes until the meeting, so he reluctantly consented.

Patterson came in, frowned, plopped in the chair opposite Charlie's, and abruptly announced, "Charlie, you've got a problem."

"I know. I've got an important meeting in a few minutes and you're interrupting my preparation."

"No, I mean a real problem. Our crew has turned up something hot, and I felt you should be notified immediately even though our investigation is not complete."

"You make it sound pretty serious."

"In spot-checking your invoices to customers, one of our auditors noticed what seemed to be errors on pricing to a certain customer, so he began to cross-check the prices for the same items billed to other customers."

"Maybe there's a contract with that customer with a lower price based on a larger annual volume in total," said Charlie.

"No, we checked that. Not only is there no contract, but other customers, both last year and this year, bought larger quantities than this one. In checking this we made another interesting discovery. The production scheduler in the factory had told us that there had been a sudden upsurge in total orders for one of your items and the factory was running behind in its ability to handle this load. Customers were being given shipping promises of ten weeks, but this customer was getting his orders filled in one to two weeks. Over the last three months, this customer had taken 60% of your total output, even though in total they represent slightly less than 10% of your sales."

"What's the name of this customer?"

"It's a relatively small distributor in Lyon named Le Clerc Frères."

"Never heard of them. Well there's probably some logical explanation for all this. Have you asked Jean Duval about it?" Duval was the company's sales and marketing vice-president and a director of the company. Charlie didn't know him too well yet, but he seemed to be competent, diligent, and hardworking, and one of the most fluent in English of all the French managers. Charlie had been told that Duval had spent several years in the U.S. acquiring an MBA degree from Stanford, and had several years of marketing experience with one of the Silicon Valley firms in the semi-conductor business.

Patterson replied slowed, "No, we haven't asked Duval about this."

"Why not?"

"When one of the production schedulers was questioned about the apparent high priority awarded to Le Clerc Frères' orders, our auditor couldn't get a straight answer. All he got was a wink and a wave of the hand toward Duval's office. So on no more evidence than just that, our man made a quiet investigation of the public records on Le Clerc."

"Did he find anything?"

"He found that Duval personally owns 33% of Le Clerc, and that Duval's wife, whose maiden name was Le Clerc, owns another 33%. It seems Duval bought out one of the brothers a few years back."

Charlie's secretary opened the door and poked her head in. "Your meeting is in three minutes, Mr. Dixon."

"Yeah, I'm going. Look, Dick, I've got to go, but let's get together this afternoon. How about 2:30?"

"OK."

"In the meantime I'd like to have your gumshoes take a look . . ."

"Charlie, our employees are not gumshoes. They are professionally trained and accredited auditors who . . ."

"Whatever. I'd like them to take a quick look at Duval's expense accounts over the last year to see if there has been a disproportionate amount of travel to Lyon and/or entertainment expense connected with this Le Clerc firm. Next, I want your people to see if there's any evidence of an undue amount of time being spent by our customer engineering assistance people in Lyon. See you at 2:30."

"I'm not sure we'll have all that by 2:30, but we'll give it a whirl."

After his budget meeting, Charlie hurried back to his office, closed the door, and immediately dialed John Lancaster, a junior partner at the Paris branch office of the New York law firm that Hathaway retained. Lancaster had been very helpful to

Charlie, and others before him, in guiding him through the whole legal and bureaucratic jungle for obtaining official government permission to live and work in
France. He had also been helpful in the exhausting process of finding an apartment
and the associated negotiating involved in that step. John was about the same age as
Charlie and they seemed to be able to work well with each other.

"John? Charlie Dixon here. Say, by any chance, are you free for lunch today?"

"Sure, if you're buying."

"I'll flip you for it, but look—I have a real problem I need to discuss with you
right away."

"Personal or business?"

"Hathaway business. How about that place we went to a couple of weeks ago? It's
about halfway between our two offices."

"Great. See you in ten minutes."

The restaurant wasn't very fancy or busy, both conditions suited Charlie fine.
After ordering, he proceeded to recount what he knew to date about the Duval matter and Le Clerc Frères. He concluded by asking John what legal aspects he should
consider in presenting all this to Frank Miller.

"Before I answer, Charlie, right now what do you think you want to do?"

"Fire him! Or rather recommend to Frank that he fire him."

"That's what I thought. And I'm sure that's what would happen in the States. But
let me throw a couple of things at you that make it a little different here."

"Isn't preferential pricing a clear violation of the law?"

"Maybe. But if you were to charge him with it, either in or out of court, it would
not be too difficult for him to come up with several different defenses. He could
argue that the special pricing and favored delivery schedules were part of an overall
marketing plan whereby Le Clerc Frères would help to develop the market for this
line or new product. Perhaps he could argue that this was a special deal based on
annual total volume percentage increase over last year, and that the same offer had
been made to others but not accepted. Or if he's inclined to be nasty, he could blame
the whole thing on a subordinate and claim he didn't know about it."

"But his actions are a clear violation of the company's written policies on conflict
of interest."

"Again, he might be able to claim ignorance of those policies. And a case of helping one's family through slight deviations from written policies would not be regarded as any big deal here. Furthermore, I'm sure you're aware that nepotism is alive
and well in the United States."

"What if the auditors find solid evidence of expense account abuses?"

Lancaster shrugged. "I'm afraid the courts would see that as your problem and
possibly the tax man's but not theirs. There's no French law that makes a company's
extravagant expenditure illegal. However, there is an illegal act on Duval's part. At
least I think so from what you've told me. Under French law all members of a board
of directors are required to disclose to that board any and all other business ownership they possess, and that disclosure must be a part of the official minutes of the

board. That may take some checking because I suspect that Duval's membership on the board precedes not only yours but also Frank Miller's. But if he has never formally disclosed that ownership you have the basis for a legal action.

"But there's another angle about legal action you should be aware of. In France the legal liability of directors of a company is greater than in the United States. If you get into any kind of court battle you're not always sure what the other side might bring up. If Duval could show that the company, not himself, had perpetuated the illegal pricing actions, the directors could be held liable—even if they were not aware of this action. The odds are low that all this might happen, but you may want to evaluate very carefully before you run the risk of dragging your French outside directors into court."

"Boy, you're just full of happy tidings today."

"There's more. If Frank decides to fire him, he is still entitled to what we would call severance pay, and historically this is much greater than you might imagine. What usually happens is a negotiation. The amount of severance, of course, varies with the length of service of the employee. If the negotiations are stalemated, he can take you to court."

"You've got to be joking. This guy cheats the company and can wind up taking us to court!"

"If you go through it step by step it's all very logical. There's still more. You could go through all this and find that the people who worked for him relate more favorably to his position than to yours, and you'll have a morale problem on your hands."

"On top of all this good news I suppose you expect me to pay the check."

"The client always pays in the end. Look on the bright side, the food was great and the waitress didn't say 'there you go' when she brought it."

Back in his office Charlie found Dick Patterson waiting for him.

"Did your team turn up anything?" asked Charlie.

"Nothing very incriminating or conclusive. Duval's own expense accounts don't show anything unusual in either amounts spent or frequency of his calls to Le Clerc Frères. There did seem to us to be an increase in the number of days Duval's customer service engineers spent there in the last three months compared to the same period last year."

"How much of an increase?"

"About 20%. It could be a coincidence, or there could be a half a dozen logical explanations."

"Or," said Charlie, "he could be using Hathaway engineers to help Le Clerc more than they help other customers."

"Maybe, but at this point we can't prove that. So what's next?"

"I have an appointment with Frank Miller at 3 p.m. I'd like you to come with me to spell out for him what you've found and answer any questions he may have."

"Let's go then; it's almost three."

No sooner did they get into Frank's office than there was an overseas call for Frank from someone in Hathaway's research lab. When Frank finally hung up he looked at Charlie, then at Dick and said, "Well you two look as though you have just discovered a multimillion dollar accounting error that wipes out any potential profit for the next ten years. What's the bad news?"

Charlie told him. Dick filled in the details of the audit and Charlie covered his luncheon meeting with John Lancaster. Frank listened attentively throughout but asked no questions. When they finished, he growled. "Duval's a helluva good marketing man. He doesn't need to do this kind of stuff to make a lot of money. Let me sleep on it. I'll tell you what I want to do tomorrow morning."

27
SSA Mexicana: A Korean Prescription for Success in Mexico

David O. Braaten

Introduction

Mr. Park, president of SSA Mexicana (SSAMex), a Korean-owned maquila assembly plant, stole a precious few moments of quiet reflection before he made his second daily walk along the assembly lines. He stood, hands tightly clasped behind his back, gazing out his office window over Otay Mesa, a site for industrial development outside of Tijuana, Mexico. He could see the dust cloud blowing toward his office from the construction site of one of the area's newest maquila plants several hundred yards away. He braced himself, unconsciously, against the unfelt wind, for his thoughts were about the presentation laying on his desk that he was to give next month at SSA Group's international annual meeting of all overseas operations.

It was a great honor to be one of three overseas plant presidents chosen to report, in person, about the success of his operation. Out of the ten SSA Electronics International operations, this plant had been ninth in productivity and last in sales three years ago. Since assuming his position two and a half years ago, the plant was first in both. Yes, he did deserve this honor. He had worked hard to overcome the disadvantages of working in Mexico.

This case has been prepared as a basis for discussion rather than to illustrate either effective or ineffective handling of an administrative situation. Names of the company and people have been disguised to preserve confidentiality. The author would like to acknowledge the assistance of Maria De Lourdes Ballina, Joseph Lombardo, and Oscar Mundia in the preparation of this case.

A seedling of doubt had been planted in recent days that could not be uprooted. Were his efforts really a success? He needed to assure himself that he could accept that award with integrity. His philosophy of consistency and his expectation that his employees always gave their best effort demanded that he find the answer to that question.

Looking out over the grassy plateau, Park thought back to the first few days after his arrival, walking the plant and reading the reports on personnel and production. The picture he had seen in those documents was that of a sick patient, and he found that image insightful. With this image in mind, he had consciously undertaken steps to acquaint himself with the patient—the facility and its personnel, identify the symptoms of the illness, and then diagnose the problems. He had felt that only then could he effectively treat the patient and bring it to health. The honor being bestowed upon him by the parent company was testament to his effective management of the Mexican maquila industry. Or so it seemed.

The Maquila Program in Tijuana

Maquilas, meaning "twin plants" or "in-bond companies," refers to Mexican assembly and manufacturing plants producing primarily for export. Maquilas resulted from a dedicated effort by the Mexican government to encourage foreign capital investment in the country. Under the program, the Mexican border was declared a processing zone in which maquilas could manufacture, process, and/or assemble an array of products. In fact, to encourage foreign investment, significant financial incentives were provided.

Most maquilas are located along the U.S./Mexico border to take advantage of special Mexican and U.S. tariff provisions. Tijuana has two thousand maquilas, comprising 65% of the total number of maquilas operating in Mexico. Plants are located in Tijuana for several reasons. The metropolitan city of San Diego, California, is across the border, giving access to major U.S markets such as Los Angeles and San Francisco. The proximity to U.S. markets facilitates lower distribution costs and transport is easy because of the extensive U.S. infrastructure. Situated on the western coast of Mexico, Tijuana's port facilities at Ensenada permit shipping of goods from port to port, across the Pacific. In addition, a large population and low wage levels make labor relatively inexpensive. The intent of the maquila program was also to encourage investment in Mexico by giving access to this labor pool. One of many expected positive effects for Mexico was that the jobs created would allow the economically disadvantaged northern Mexican states to join the economic mainstream.

Maquilas employ over 65,250 people in Tijuana, where the labor force is not unionized. With no unions, most labor complaints are handled between each company's human resource manager and the appropriate governmental authorities. Workers have little recourse outside of this process.

Each maquila in Tijuana is a member of the Association of Maquilas. This body handles labor dispute negotiations between employers. The personnel departments of association members also compile and share among themselves lists of employees who quit or are dismissed. In this way, they are able to discourage and limit the "wage shopping" of workers between maquilas.

SSA Mexicana

A part of the SSA Group, SSA Mexicana is a television assembly plant for SSA Electronics North America, whose parent company is SSA Electronics Company, which is one of the 32 SSA Group affiliates. The SSA Group, one of the world's twenty largest companies, is a Korean *chaebol,* family-owned conglomerate, with annual sales worldwide of US$ 50 billion from electronics, chemical, textile, food-processing, information services, and international trading activities with 200,000 employees.

Table 27-1
SSA Mexicana Profile

Company Name	SSA Mexicana, S.A.
Established	Spring, 1988
Capital	US$ 4,000,000
Investment	US$ 11,500,000
Land Building	310,000 sq.ft./8,700 pyong 116,000 sq.ft./3,260 pyong
Production Start	#1 Line: Fall 1988 #2 Line: Spring, 1989 #3 Line: Early Winter, 1992
Product	CTV: 13" 19" 20" 25" 27" 31" MVCR: 13" 19" 20"
Annual CAPA	800,000 Sets/1993 (1 Shift) 1,000,000 Sets/1994 (1 Shift)
Market	USA, Canada, Mexico, Panama, Colombia, Chile
Employees	398

SSA Mexicana was established in the spring of 1988. By fall, the first assembly line was producing six hundred 13-inch color televisions per day. Second and third lines were started in spring 1989, and early winter, 1992. By 1993, these lines were producing 3,200 TV sets of various sizes per day. Projections for 1994 are for the production of over one million sets per year (Table 27-1).

The televisions are made in the SSAMex facility, an L-shaped building of 116,000 square feet, constructed in six months in 1988. The length of the building holds the product assembly lines, inventory, and shipping docks, with production lines almost running the length of the plant. Along one wall are charts and data on current levels and proposed management-by-objective (MBO) targets. Their purpose is to constantly remind workers of current production levels.

The plant produces 13-in., non-labeled, television sets for retailers. Larger sets are also produced for the SSA label. A new product is a 13-inch television with built-in VCR. Because production is for retailers and distributors, slight adjustments to cabinet, logo, and boxes are necessary. The PC boards, a major input in the television sets, also are marketed in Korea and Latin America. The plant operates one shift.

Because Mexican labor laws limit the work week to 48 hours, SSAMex operates five days a week, 9½ hours per day. Work periods are 140 minutes, with ten-minute breaks between periods. Lunch is one half hour. All time periods are strictly monitored for tardiness.

SSA Mexicana has a reputation among workers for better wages and benefits, as well as motivational programs, than other Asian-owned maquilas. This should make hiring an easier task than at other maquilas. Korean companies have a reputation for demanding more work from employees than other employers.

Management and Personnel

Overall management of the plant personnel and operations is handled on site by the president, Mr. Park. However, management, marketing, and strategic planning decisions come directly from SSA Electronics North America, Inc., headquartered on the East Coast of the USA.

SSA Mexicana employs approximately 398 people, including line workers, management, and support staff. Of the twelve managerial positions, eight are held by Koreans and four by Mexicans. Two hundred eighty-five people are employed on the assembly lines, with the remainder employed in supervisory roles, engineering, maintenance, training, cafeteria, etc. The three men with the most interaction with workers are Mr. Park, Mr. Gonzalez, the personnel manager, and Mr. Suarez, the Production Manager (see Appendix A).

The company has a horizontal hierarchical structure, which is characteristic of SSA Group in general. Under the president are two general managers. The controller oversees personnel, marketing (production planning), data processing, accounting, and materials. The plant manager oversees engineering, maintenance, quality control, and both production lines (see Figure 27-1). In each area of the production floor are supervisors, one to every 15 to 30 line workers, who report to line production managers. Each line section has a line leader who is subordinate to the supervisor. Wages of line leaders are 150-300% higher than employee base wages and supervisor wages are 250-400% higher. Managers' contracts are valued on U.S. dollars.

Ninety-five percent of SSAMex employees are Mexicans who come from several states of Mexico to work in the maquila industry. Women are preferred for employment (80-85% are female) because they are believed to have greater manual dexterity for the intricate work that is done assembling the electronic

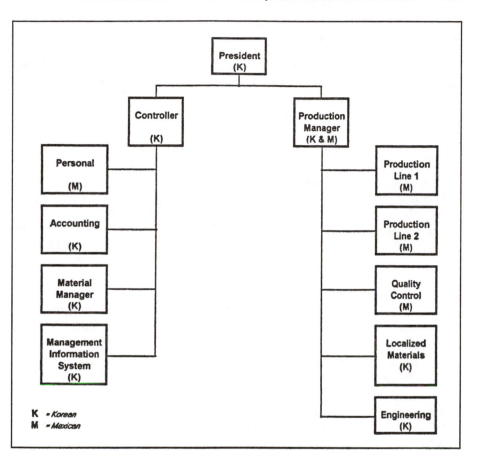

Figure 27-1. Management structure of SSA Mexicana.

components. Most of the workers are relatively young, 65% are females between 15–20. Young women are hired for line work because it is felt that they give more attention to detail and are better disciplined, which promotes high quality levels. Also, women are preferred who are "thin because they have thin fingers and get tired less quickly." This is important as they work long hours doing detailed soldering and positioning work in the delicate TV/video assembly.

The workforce is educated, though not to the degree desired by the management. (Ninety-nine percent of Koreans have a high school education). Forty percent of the workers have an elementary level education. These workers are viewed as more emotional and volatile. Forty percent have a junior high level education. The remaining 20% have been in, if not completed, high school, or have college degrees (managers and engineers). Feelings are mixed about working for SSAMex. Workers with higher education levels are most likely to be promoted.

Seoul Searching

As the cloud of dust blew over the SSAMex building, Park relaxed, letting his gaze rise over the horizon of Otay Mesa and carry his thoughts West, over the Pacific, to home in Korea. Occasionally, he thinks about working at home, where managing a production work force is much easier. He smiled as he pictures the Korean worker, disciplined, loyal, hardworking, and dedicated to his company.

Park reflected that the Korean worker approaches work this way because it is his nature to do so. Ingrained in him is the Confucian ethical code establishing the priority of relationships and responsibilities between superiors and subordinates. His dedication to the fulfilling of commitments is due to a concern for maintaining his "face," or other's perception of him as a moral person.

A particular environment has created this mentality among Koreans. It is born out of the harsh economic and political realities that followed the years of Japanese occupation and the devastation of the civil war with the North. Overcoming the depressed economic conditions of the 1950s, as well as a constant war economy due to the permanent state of civil war with North Korea, formed an intense drive to increase the economic position of the country. This harsh environment is intolerant of error and mistakes, for these threaten security and "face." Workers labor long hours to assure that company goals are met, thus helping each other and the nation.

Korea is a small, tightly organized country. Interdependence and protection within family relationships is generalized to the company and nation. One is part of both "families."

As he finished his musing about Korea, Park recalled that the founder of the SSA Group *chaebol* had passed on his own personal philosophy to his company—he did not pursue money, but strove to do his best. Park had tried to manage this way and pass it on to his employees.

The Symptoms

Mr. Park did not notice the changes in light moving across his face as the sun was covered by the passing of the afternoon clouds. He slowly shook his head as he remembered what this plant was like when he arrived in Tijuana in January 1990. He had anticipated some problems with production, but was surprised at the extent of the mess. But, he never criticized, then or now, the former management. When asked about it, he would only say that the management in 1988–1989 was focused on the start-up and had done a good job at that. He knew, coming to the plant, that problems with quality and control existed. After some investigation, he soon categorized the reasons into four areas: logistical communications with Korea, personnel, training, and operations.

Logistics. Almost from the start-up, the Mexican managers complained about poor communication with the central plant in Korea. Parts with the wrong specifications were sent, wrong materials were supplied, etc. In turn, the Korean office complained about technical and quality problems with the finished product, lack of discipline in the Mexican employee, and poor language translations by the Mexicans that caused misunderstanding. It seemed to Park that everyone was pointing fingers of blame, but no one took responsibility to deal with the problems.

Personnel. In many ways, the personnel problems at the SSAMex plant were similar to those at most maquilas in Tijuana, but worse. The monthly turnover of 13–15% was higher than the city average of 9.8%. The daily rates of both absenteeism and tardiness averaged 4–5%. Park was aghast because this irresponsibility and lack of company loyalty was unheard of in Korea.

Training. The training program was too short, a half day, and did not sufficiently train anyone. No employee screening existed and almost all applicants were hired. With minimum training, new hires were put on the line anywhere vacancies existed. There was no selection and matching of people's skills and abilities to job needs.

Production and Control. The plant was running at only 40% capacity and had the highest defect rate of all SSA overseas operations. No management accountability program existed, but a lot of blame giving did. There were no job descriptions. In addition, Park thought he saw a surplus of manpower on the lines.

The Diagnosis

As Park analyzed the operations of the plant, he had determined that two overlapping problems seemed to be the sources of all the difficulties he had identified, (1) the attitudes of the Mexican workers, and (2) the poor management of production. Park knew that if he could correctly deal with these two concerns, he could turn this operation around within three years.

To better understand the workers of the company, Park, shortly after his arrival, undertook a two-month analysis of the Mexican culture. He concluded that the "Mexican people" had the merits of closely following instructions and being very sincere. They were simple and childlike in this way. He observed negatives as well. Park thought that the problems with the local labor force resulted from the "nature of the Mexican people." This nature included laziness, little sense of responsibility, lack of concentration, little creativity, and no sense of company loyalty. Mexicans were unwilling to work long hours for the good of the company, like a good Korean worker would do. He felt that part of the reason for this overall lack of discipline was that "Mexico is an agricultural society." Therefore, SSAMex seemed too strict to the Mexican laborer and they resented it.

Because Mexican workers did not identify with this company, it was difficult to motivate them to put in the hard work needed to make a quality product. He decided they needed incentives to encourage a sense of "SSAMex family" and help create a sense of discipline. He also needed to teach the SSAMex vision and philosophy so the workers would feel that they belonged to SSAMex.

A lack of creativity was also an issue with which he struggled. Park was frustrated that Mexicans did not think creatively about how to improve their jobs. They did not submit group ideas on how to increase quality or productivity. They just followed what they were told to do. In addition, he couldn't believe that they also insisted that they worked hard just because they showed up for work. Even with the condition of the plant, they actually resented what they considered small raises, complaining to one another bitterly. He could often feel the discontent. Park felt he needed to institute a program of employee accountability that would demonstrate, in a measurable way, the amount and quality of work being done. This needed to be in place from top management down to the line worker.

Park concluded that the high defect rate was the result of several weaknesses. A lack of training and the high attrition rate combined to place many workers on the line who made too many mistakes. Also, line workers had a lack of concern for quality because there were few repercussions for mistakes. He would have to use both a carrot and a stick to get these people to work at the level of quality that was necessary.

The surplus manpower on lines left idle hands, reduced efficiency, and increased costs. If the workers were challenged by having to do more, they would work better. Of course, this would lead to a greater sense of self-satisfaction for a job well done. Finally, Park told his training team that he would need some sort of slogan, phrase, or set of words that the workers could understand and that would motivate them to improve their efforts.

Treatment and Prognosis

(See Appendix B for policy changes.)

Unclasping his hands, Park placed them on the window sill, relaxing his posture as he leaned forward toward the window. He thought back with pride about how quickly and carefully he had implemented several personnel, policy, and production changes. He knew that some resistance would exist because he was challenging the Mexican nature. But, he was confident that, over time, people would come to own the sense of SSAMex family he was trying to build. They would come to see it was good for them and good for the company.

1. A new three-day training program was initiated. Candidates for hire were put through a series of steps to provide them the information they needed to be a good employee. They were interviewed, indoctrinated, and skills tested. A 30-day probation period was instituted to assure that the candidates were able to apply skills and had the appropriate attitude before permanent hiring. This also created a sense of exclusivity about SSAMex's hiring practices.

2. Several personnel policies were changed or new policies instituted. The purpose of the changes was to develop company identity and to create a sense of loyalty. To accomplish this, Park felt that employees must be encouraged to understand the importance of discipline and conformity by learning to create good work habits. Also, for Park it was important that the workers come to own the company vision and philosophy. Many of the changes, such as incentives and recognitions, regular employee meetings, and required wearing of uniforms, were put into place to facilitate these goals.

3. Park was surprised at the management system, or lack of, present upon his arrival. To get control over the production process, develop a sense of responsibility and accountability in employees, and encourage company loyalty, he started several new programs for managers and workers. The purpose of these programs was to provide measurement tools to evaluate activity and performance.

4. Analysis of the production lines revealed several areas that could be changed or eliminated. These actions increasing capacity, shortened assembly time, decreased motion activity, and began to eliminate what Park called the "surplus manpower." As Park finished running through the list in his mind, he felt proud that his changes and incentives had paid off for the company. Employee attitude looked to be less aggressive toward the company. People were assuming more responsibility for quality and showing more discipline. Monthly turnover rate was down to 4.2%, compared to the industry rate of 9.8%. Absenteeism and tardiness were significantly reduced as well. Workers were making suggestions for improving the product and the process. With quality now the responsibility of all workers, productivity had increased dramatically. Defects were down to 2% and still improving, due to the training program and selection process. The many changes in the production process had a great deal to do with this success as well.

The Patient's View of the Prescription

Mr. Park abruptly turned from the window and walked out the door of his office. He had indulged in his reverie for too long. It was time to check on the floor and encourage, by his presence, hard work. As he walked down the hall to begin the afternoon rounds of the plant, his doubts about the authenticity of his success came back to him. Several days ago, he had slipped into one of the men's bathrooms off the assembly line floor to wash his hands after helping a slow part of the line. He had seen some graffiti on the wall. He scowled as he recalled the word he had seen scrawled there, "*Negreros.*" He thought he knew its meaning, but had called to one of the line managers to come and translate it. With obvious discomfort, the fellow had told him it meant "slave driver." Park had let it go at the time, but the word, and the manager's reaction, had come to his mind on occasion, and more so lately. He wondered about the morale of a person who would write something like that, and he wondered if others felt that way. If so, then these Mexicans were more difficult than he had thought.

To a certain extent the word that Mr. Park saw that day in the bathroom was but a small indication of a much more serious reaction to the SSAMex philosophy.

The resilient Mexican spirit knew how to handle oppressive foreigners; by adapting. But, you kept your soul Mexican. During the work day, the workers would mouth the company line and do the amount of work for the job appropriate to demonstrate an understanding of the company line, but, the Mexican workers at SSAMex did not accept the perspectives of the Korean management.

Working for SSAMex was considered a very hard job, compared to many other maquilas. People came to SSAMex because of the training, wages and, for some, the type of work. The training program offered information that made getting hired at other plants easier. Many came just for that. The attrition during the demanding probation period was moderate to heavy, and was not counted against the turnover rate, because trainees were not employees.

Seniority kept people at SSAMex. It was well known that "the longer you worked at the same company, the better the salary you earned." Once a comfortable level of wage was reached, it was difficult to start at a different maquila at the base wage. Those employees who had been at SSAMex before Park arrived shrugged off the talk about family, accountability, and loyalty. To them, the managing of the plant had not changed in the past three years, so why should they. Indeed, the workload had increased substantially due to the closing of several line positions over the years.

Most of the workers listened politely and accepted the talk of loyalty, dedication, and hard work preached at them during employee meetings. But, they did not necessarily believe it. In fact, those that seemed to buy into it all were distrusted for their ambition.

The Mexican production managers were not popular, nor thought of as true Mexican managers, but were considered to be almost Korean. It was not uncommon to hear the managers referred to, disparagingly, as "*negreros*," when workers complained about the arduous tasks and relatively inflexible management system. Management enforced the harsh rules of the plant. For example, people were not enthusiastic about wearing uniforms and tried to make it tolerable by personalizing them. Constant reminders, even reprimands, were given to discourage these displays of uniform individuality. It was not uncommon for the production managers to point out or call aside people for uniform infractions. Another example was the strict enforcement of the 140-minute work periods and the brief, ten-minute breaks. Within the break's ten minutes, one had to take care of any personal or physical needs and then try to relax strained muscles and minds. People were chided or written up if a minute late in getting back to the line. Also, leaving the line during the work period was forbidden, even to get a drink or go to the bathroom. Permission had to be asked, and then granted, first.

Though some workers did make an effort to receive the bonus incentives offered by the plant, most thought it was pointless. They felt that the incentives were impossible to get because the goals were made impossible. Even if you were a minute late to work only once, you lost your previous count toward the goal. Also, even excused absences or emergencies caused you to start the count back to day one.

Birthday parties initially generated some excitement, but after word got out how stiff and formal they were, it became a chore to go, especially because they were given after work at the expense of the employee's time. It was embarrassing to sit at a table with your managers and the president. You couldn't relax, be yourself, like you would at a real party. The company present, given formally and solemnly by the president, was a nice idea, but awkward, as was the picture of the party group taken with the president. Also, sitting in front of your managers and being asked by the president of the company to give suggestions, ideas, or complaints was uncomfortable. If you wanted to say something, you couldn't because your manager was there. In fact, the president really didn't want to hear problems because he would tell you to take care of it yourself. He must know that a worker can't change anything.

Workers felt that one of the most unfair policies was determining raises based on the score on the individual defect, quality, "Five As" daily check-off sheet (see Appendix B). Many of the problems for which you were marked-off were beyond your control, caused by someone else or by the parts you used. If you took the extra time to correct a problem, you were penalized for holding the line, and if you didn't take the time to fix it, you were still penalized for defects. This system was resented by many of the workers.

Some of the employees worked hard to get ahead within the SSAMex system, and a few were successful, usually those with a high school education, but, most of the line workers just put in their time. Though they "worked to live," they quickly learned how to play the Korean work game and do what was expected. For them, the *jefe* was in charge and you took his orders if you ate his bread.

Conclusion

The buzzer echoed throughout the plant, sounding the end of the work day. Walking past the stream of workers flowing down the hall, Park headed back toward his office. As he looked at his people, he wondered if his observations about them and their change of heart were accurate. The morale at the plant looked good to him. But, when it came to determining the success of his efforts, his standards were high. He expected much. He saw that people acted in appropriate ways, they did their jobs, and were involved in the process. They laughed and joked.

But, that recent doubt crept into his mind again. Something he saw that swiftly crossed the faces of the workers just before they smiled and said a respectful *"Buenos dias, señor,"* in response to his friendly *"Buenos dias."* What if his reading of worker morale was inaccurate, or his efforts to instill loyalty and dedication in the Mexican workers was not having the effect he had thought? Would he deserve the honor being given him by the parent company next month? Would he consider himself a success?

He wondered how he could determine if the workers had a problem, and, if they did, how to respond to their needs. If attitude problems were still rampant, what else could he do? His answer to these questions was important, because Park knew, from the experiences of others that if the workers were still undisciplined, he was sitting on a time bomb that would blow up if this little doubt of his was true.

Appendix A
Primary Management Personnel

Mr. Park, President

Mr. Park joined SSA Electronics as a foreign purchasing agent in 1972, after completing his compulsory military service and graduating from Korea University. He moved into export administration in 1978, and by 1986 had become a general manager in Singapore, where he oversaw 36 countries in the Middle East, Asia, and Africa. In 1988, he was promoted to plant and division vice-president, when he was assigned to the East Coast USA electronics facility. His climb up the management ladder was steady. Regarding this latest assignment, he had been advised that heading the Tijuana plant might be a career risk. But, with his years of international managerial experience, Park was confident that his hands-on policy and personal philosophy were well-suited to successfully managing Mexican workers.

His management style resulted from his personal philosophy. He believed a manager should "Treat every employee evenly and consistently, with sincerity and soul. I can melt iron with sincerity." He also realized that, because Korean regulations for the plant reflected the Korean's high degree of discipline, he needed what he called a "soft touch" with the less disciplined Mexican employees. He would personally be involved in the operations. He would walk the floor twice daily to show his concern for quality and for the workers. He would encourage an "open door" policy to all employees. And, he would create an atmosphere of problem solving, not blaming.

He felt that if his own efforts were consistent, then the various policy changes he made would have a good chance for success in improving production, quality, and in changing the nature of the Mexican people working for him.

Sergio Suarez, Production Manager

Sergio came north from his home in southern Mexico to work in the maquila industries. He was employed in both Japanese and Mexican maquilas, learning English while working at a Japanese company, before coming to SSA. Sergio came to SSA, from a Mexican maquila, because of its reputation for discipline and opportunity.

In some ways, Sergio feels more at home in the Korean culture of SSAMex, than in Mexican culture. He will often say that, "Mexican culture lacks a sense of discipline at home, as well as at school. Therefore, their work habits hinder Mexican development in business." He feels that because Koreans respect discipline, have a strong loyalty to their company, and a high sense of responsibility, they have much to teach Mexicans. Also, he believes that, "unlike the U.S. maquilas, Asians work very hard. They don't care about lunch time, break time, and stay to work. When they set a target, they do what it takes to make the target." He feels he can learn much about successful management from this Korean company, and he hopes to work in Korea.

These attitudes have led to problems with the Mexican employees. He takes a strong company position on expectations for worker discipline, loyalty, effort, and responsibility. In his relationship with employees he is considered condescending and unMexican-like. He knows many employees do not like him, but they have performed under his management.

At the direction of Park, Sergio will often check on worker relations with their families in an effort to show that there is a big family at SSA. He feels that this must work because it is the only company where 80% of people who leave in good standing come back.

Jesus Gonzalez, Personnel Manager

A Tijuana native, Jesus went to college in Tijuana and graduated as an Industrial Relations Specialist. In 1989, he came to SSA from a Canadian maquila.

When he first arrived, he was going to quit after two weeks, but stayed. He had initial problems with the differences in the Korean's perceptions of discipline and status. Also, the lack of private office and special allowances contributed to initial feeling of having lower status than in other companies. But now he feels that, "This democratic style breaks the ice among employees and transforms them into a cooperative group."

His first impression of the Korean managers was that they were aggressive by nature. One of the Korean managers, Mr. Kim, the controller, seemed to be angry and yell most of the time. But, eventually he saw different Korean personalities and came to understand that "you can't generalize."

He often notes that the perception in Tijuana is that people are afraid to work for a Korean company because of the strict discipline, the expectation for hard work, and total lack of company product perks. But Jesus, from his past experience, feels this company is a good one to work for because "Koreans are more humane than the Japanese."

Appendix B
Personnel and Production Policy Changes for SSAMex

Training Policy Changes

The events during the three days of training are extensive. They are developed to ascertain how best to use the abilities of the candidate, as well as to check whether the person understands and can be a part of the SSA way. Physicals are given and candidates are interviewed by the production manager, personnel manager, and line manager. A video on the philosophy and spirit of SSA is shown, detailing what is expected of a SSA employee. A training manual was created and all prospective hires have to learn it. Manual skills and mental ability are tested. Temporary hands-on training on the assembly line provide a trial period to determine where one's skills can best be used. Also, a 30-day probation period is instituted to assure that the candidate has the appropriate skills and attitude before permanent placement. During the period, one is a trainee and wears a badge signifying that status. This extensive process also creates a sense of exclusivity to the hiring at SSA.

After testing, all employees are put on the line where their skills are best suited. Park believes that this improves production and the satisfaction levels of the workers. Also, those older employees with good attitudes are placed in less arduous line positions to help in their retention.

Personnel Policy Changes

Several changes are made to help create a good work habit, ingrain conformity, and provide recognition:

- A bonus system is instituted to "create the habit of" attendance and timeliness. Perfect attendance, which also meant being punctual, is rewarded. For three months' perfect attendance, one receives a $60 gift, such as a CD player; for six months' a $100 gift is given, along with a certificate; for one year's, the reward is a 13-inch color television set and $200 cash. Awards are announced at bimonthly meetings of employees.
- Uniforms are required by all employees, even Mr. Park. All uniforms must look the same; the modification of the uniforms, i.e., wearing of pins, badges, rolled-up sleeves, etc., is forbidden and reprimanded.
- Physical appearance is noted and hygiene is important. For example, though long hair is not forbidden (because of local laws), it is expected that the men follow the Korean plant rules and keep hair off the collar. Those who have long hair are taken aside by Park who explains that, although long hair is not forbidden, it is important for all employees to follow the rules posted at all Korean plants. Attitude is considered in raise considerations.
- Birthday parties are given after work for employees on a biweekly basis. At the party, people are individually called up, by name, and given a gift by the president. The company supplies the drinks and cake. A picture is also taken of the group with the president and each person is given a copy. The managers of the "birthday people" are also in attendance. A highly structured affair, the party goers sit in a "U" shaped table arrangement across from their managers, with the president at the head of the tables. During the "party," workers are asked to share with the president, and their managers, any problems, suggestions, ideas, and other input from employees.
- Employees participate in monthly meetings at which the president announces the company's visions and plans and asks for suggestions from employees. A goal in this meeting is to teach the SSA philosophy and spirit. Park explains to the employees why they must work hard, "So we can produce more. When the company makes a profit we will be willing to share it with you." Park feels proud that "I kept my promise." The company supplies gifts to all employees. Also, a special December bonus is given to group leaders and supervisors.
- A bounty policy is started to reward people who recruit good workers to apply at SSAMex. If a new hire remains after the probation period a cash bounty is paid to the recruiter.

Control Policy Changes

To promote accountability and responsibility among all employees, several management programs are instituted.

- Management-by-objective (MBO) is instituted for all employees, including Mr. Park. All employees are evaluated by MBO objectives. Standard job descriptions are written for all positions, top to bottom, and targets are set based on these descriptions. Each manager sets his own target levels, which are evaluated by Park and usually increased. Promotion and raises are based on the targets, not on actual numbers. Each line worker is judged each day of the week on quality, defects, inspecting sequence, punctuality, and the "Five As": Arreglo (Order), Acomodamiento (Organization), Aseo (Cleanliness), Acostumbrase (Follow the Routine), Ambiente Limpio (Clean Work Place), as well as Attendance and Uniform. Sheets are collected each day and tabulated.

Park believes in MBO, because the SSA Group as a whole uses it. He believes that the process demonstrates in a measurable way that hard work is rewarded; the compensation system is fair; that all employees have control of their own fate in the company; and people can feel secure in their jobs because they know what is expected of them.

To assure the effectiveness of the compensation system, Park meets with each manager to go over their goals and measure how hard they have worked to meet them. He gives a grade based on the accomplishment of meeting targets for various sets of items, i.e. one set is an "A" and gets 95%, another set might have rated a "B" and receives 75%, so the final grade is 85%, which gives the percent of salary increase. Park decides salary for managers and supervisors based on the grade given.

- Quality circles were started to get the line workers involved in increasing productivity. But this quickly failed. Park attributes the failure to the low education levels of most employees. It seems that they cannot handle their responsibility in the quality circle system. In addition, the lack of loyalty and concern for the company leads to an inability of the workers to contribute to the groups.

- Park initiates what he calls "management through committee." Weekly manager meetings are held, including both Korean and Mexican managers. English is used as the medium of communication, which makes these meetings tedious at times because much time is taken for translating among the Mexicans and the Koreans. Targets are checked against actual records, discussed and evaluated. Facility and production problems are discussed. After establishing symptoms and finding causes for the problems, managers agreed on counter measures and actions for every member of management. Follow-up is then set for a specified period of time.

- From the top of the organization to the bottom, Park institutes a policy of "don't find blame, find a solution." He insists that people take responsibility to solve problems by saying "don't pass on responsibility. If a faulty part causes delay, you used it and shouldn't have because you should have inspected it. Don't blame the vendor, solve the problem." He won't listen to blame. If anyone needs help solving a problem he has an open door policy and expects people to come and see him. It is his belief that as people are involved in problem solving, management becomes more mature and develops management skills. Park sees this as a long-term goal. For some reason, "Mexican people pass on problems to others, then they don't have to solve problems. They feel they don't have the influence to make them responsible."

Production Changes

Production activity is analyzed resulting in a revision of the production lines by simplifying of some processes and combining others, including manual motion and machine activity. The revised process layout creates a 30% shortening of the length of both lines 1 and 2. The result is a reduction, through attrition, of workforce and process time. During the past year, some robotics has been added to the lines. These have the advantage of being operated 24 hours a day with little down time.

28
Motorola, Inc., CPSTG: Performance Management as Process for Change

David O. Braaten
and
John P. Millikin

Introduction

"How can I breath life into a billion-dollar global group that, while still growing in sales, is simply too big and too fat to move effectively in this rapidly changing world of ours?" Jacque de Savoie, the tall, spare general manager of Motorola's Communication, Power & Signal Technologies Group (CPSTG), was voicing his thoughts to Pete Johnson, his vice-president of human resources, and to Cathy Dayton, their training and organizational development director. He was describing the major challenge of his career, the task of revitalizing this group that he had been in charge of for almost two years now. Jacque made this comment in frustration as he was looking over monthly reports, preparing for the monthly operations review that was to begin the next day. Johnson and Dayton had been working with de Savoie in addressing this question and understood his comment, but today they had a proposal for him that would make his day.

This case has been prepared as a basis for classroom discussion rather than to illustrate either effective or ineffective handling of an administrative situation. Certain names and figures have been disguised to preserve confidentiality.

Setting Group Focus

At the monthly operations review meetings, Jacque and his staff would match current CPSTG accomplishments against the short- and long-term goals and strategic plans set at the annual world-wide CPSTG staff meeting in December. The annual meeting in Phoenix, Arizona (CPSTG headquarters) included the business managers from France, Japan, and Hong Kong, as well as the manufacturing facilities in Korea, Malaysia, and Mexico, who were brought to CPSTG headquarters in Phoenix, Arizona. The strategic meetings provided managerial agreement on the focus and strategic thrusts for the group and then build a vision, mission, and plan to get there. Recently, the global staff had established new initiatives on scrap reduction, quality improvement, capacity expansion, new product development, and employee empowerment (which came to be known as the "Vital Few"), but still something was missing. It was one thing to set goals for a global business, it was another to ensure that the goals were accomplished throughout the organization.

Previously, Johnson had asked Cathy and a group of HR professionals to form a task team and examine the whole issue of integrating individual performance planning and management into the overall business strategy and goals process. CPSTG's parent corporation had developed a series of performance appraisal processes and tools with a clear-cut corporate-wide philosophy of "paying for performance." Today, Cathy was about to explain HR's new recommendation for institutionalizing performance management as an enabling initiative that would accelerate change throughout the global business group.

Motorola, Incorporated

One of the 40 largest industrial companies in the U.S., Motorola, Inc. was a leader in electronic equipment, systems, components and services for markets worldwide. Its 107,000 employees worldwide, produced $13.3 billion in sales in 1992. Research and fixed cost expenditures were $2.26 billion. Motorola's non-U.S. revenues were about 50% of its total in 1992, demonstrating its global customer base.

During the 1960s, Motorola changed its focus from consumer electronics to high technology markets. Interest in Europe and Asia was demonstrated by investments in facilities, distribution, and sales efforts. In recent years, the company had shown major growth in component and equipment electronics technologies and the business truly had become global.

Product quality and total customer satisfaction were emphasized at Motorola. These had been institutionalized through the Six Sigma Quality Initiative in which a maximum 3.4 defects per million (or statistically zero defects) was implemented as the minimum acceptable result expected throughout the company. A concept of Total Customer Satisfaction also was institutionalized and constantly emphasized in company in-house literature, training, and performance appraisals.

The Motorola, Inc. corporate culture had always emphasized innovation, quality, and service and had been innovative from the beginning. Paul V. Galvin set a goal of "direct dealing," dealing directly with employees, and had then set out to eliminate the reasons for potential employee unionization by developing employee satisfaction and loyalty. A "Service Club" was created whereby employees of ten years or more service were assured employment continuity, as long as they continued to perform. Wages were kept at or above market, and working environments were built and maintained as healthy and worker friendly. Downsizing was accomplished through attrition when possible. A sense of Motorola family was engendered. This had recently been enhanced by the corporate-wide adoption of an empowerment philosophy. As the Motorola president had written in his 1991 letter in the 1991 Annual Report, "The Team Culture at Motorola was founded on basic beliefs in uncompromising integrity and respect for the individual. These traditional values create an environment that nourishes a creative, cooperative culture focused on quality and customer service."

Believing in the importance of an educated workforce to remain economically competitive, Motorola required 40 hours of continuing education or training for all employees, from top to bottom. The company maintains a "Motorola University," with branches worldwide, for employee education and training. Employees are considered a valuable asset of the company and treated as such.

Issues in Overseas Operations

The facility in Korea, the first of CPSTG's offshore facilities, had been in operation for twenty-five years. Over this period of time, the Korean management had adapted its management style. They had incorporated CPSTG's direct dealing approach and strong people values, based on a core belief in individual dignity and the value of each employee, with the traditional Korean management style based on a strong hierarchical framework for decision making. While the direct labor population within this plant had turned over frequently, the indirect population regarded their affiliation with CPSTG as a lifetime investment; more than half had been with the facility for more than ten years. Recent years, however, had brought a series of double digit wage increases putting heavy pressure on the manufacturing margins available to CPSTG in Korea. As the oldest manufacturing location, the Korea facility contained some of the most mature product lines. Jacque and Harley Sanders, his manufacturing chief, were developing plans to put new products into the facility that had higher manufacturing margins to maintain the economic viability of the venture.

The Malaysia plant was among the newest of the semiconductor manufacturing operations and had been in operation for approximately fifteen years. The plant population here mirrored the local complexity of the three cultures of Malaysia: Malays (Bumiputras), Chinese, and Indians. In this complex and exciting new nation, the corporate culture at the Motorola plant represented a common focus for these employees. Over the years they have developed into a vibrant and successful, award-winning work team. In terms of recruiting and training, some issues had needed to be addressed because working at the plant was the first job outside of their villages for many of the line operators.

The Guadalajara facility had been in operation for twenty years. This particular plant had struggled under a succession of leaders. Its yield rates were among the lowest in the manufacturing group and its scrap and quality incident rates were far behind the others. Two years ago, with support from the human resources department, the plant's general manager had undertaken a transformation initiative to bring the plant, within a short time, to world-class standards in productivity and yield. The principal vehicle for this transformation effort had been a focus on empowered work teams and developing a higher sense of team work among the employees across the factory, and with employees in Phoenix.

At the Toulouse factory (which Jacque had led prior to coming to the United States) the HR director had just returned from a two-year assignment on Pete Johnson's staff in Phoenix. He had been a key player in the task team to develop the Performance Management concepts.

Problems with Appraisal: Why Performance Management?

Current Personnel Practices

As with any large multi-national, CPSTG's HR processes had evolved over the years. The performance appraisal process used throughout the group, was, at least in theory, drawn from MBO (management by objective) concepts. The supervisor and employee met at least once a year to review the accomplishment of basic job expectations for that period as well as any disappointments, and then jointly to establish short- and long-term goals oriented toward both the job and the individual employee's career development. In the course of the discussion they would agree upon a numerical performance rating, based on a zero to four scale. (At least in writing, a rating of 2.0 represented a solid and consistent performer who was meeting job expectations). Both the manager and individual employee wrote up their versions of the review, then would meet to discuss and agree upon the appraisal outcome. Managers were offered training on the performance appraisal process.

In recent years, Jacque and his management team had felt a growing frustration with the group's performance. A system was developed, therefore, for rating and ranking subordinates by staff levels to get relative comparisons of performance and potential for growth. These ratings were fed back to the employee. This rating and ranking process was used to offset the growing tendency for reviews to became relatively useless discussions in which deficiencies or real constructive feedback were seldom documented. As a result, the CPSTG's average rating was a "gentleman's B" of 2.7. Jacque and Pete both agreed that a 2.7 average did not represent their assessment of the overall performance of the group against its business objectives. By insisting that the rating and ranking process be fed back to the ratees, the individual managers and supervisors were forced to discuss with their poorly rated employees why they were so rated and how to improve performance to meet or exceed expectations.

Additionally, during each year an individual development plan was written as part of a corporate-wide imperative to ensure at least forty hours of training for each employee during the course of the year. As part of the training planning process, the manager and the employee reviewed skill levels against the skill requirements of the job and used the discussion as the basis for planning individual training objectives that were then rolled up into an organizational-wide training/planning process.

Compensation planning was only indirectly tied to the performance appraisal process. The salary planning was done for everyone in the fourth quarter. Exempt salary increases were then established for the coming year by the managers who had flexibility within their budget range to award different levels of increases, or no increase at all, depending upon their perceptions of performance and position in salary grades of each of their employees. While the salary planning sheets generated by the human resources department contained the most recent performance appraisal score, the only control on reviews and their correlation to pay was the requirement that two levels of management co-sign the increase plan. The HR department would audit these plans and discuss discrepancies in philosophy and approach with the manager in question, and, if necessary, gain concurrence from the senior management on Jacque's staff.

Problems with Goal Linkage and Focus

However, Pete had determined that there was a central problem with these reasonably well developed and sound HR practices. A lack of linkage existed between goals of individuals and the strategic objectives established by the group's management. The performance appraisal process was done on an annual basis that varied in timing by employee, often driven by the timing of the preceding year's review, which often was related in some way back to the original date of hire. While these reviews were often helpful discussions providing sound career counseling and feedback on improvements, the goal setting was solely related to the individual employees and their manager's own perceptions of job and departmental goals. Essentially people would say, "This is what you said you'd do; you did it. Good!" Individual goals were not tied on any systematic basis to the strategic objectives of CPSTG. Additionally, the linkage between the performance appraisal process and the merit increase process was informal and unstructured, as was the linkage with the individual development plan and with the strategic planning process.

During previous discussions, Cathy and Pete had identified several personnel issues, also connected to the appraisal process, which could negatively affect the productivity of the group, some of them related to globalization. Redundancies and job overlap may have existed between home and offshore support personnel and operations, increasing costs. Distance and the resulting reduced interaction could foster a loss of focus on the group's strategic goals and priorities, thus enhancing a loss of organizational focus that could affect the whole group. In addition, it was common for people to react to and focus energies on whatever were the immediate personal and/or departmental goals, initiatives, or needs of the moment, which led to loss of focus on longer term corporate goals. As part of a mature product group, with well over 50% of the population being Service Club members, some of these employees may have felt they had entitlements regarding job assignment, raises, and promotions. Questions arose whether the current appraisal process could address these issues.

Recognizing these problems, Cathy had asked her task team of HR professionals to come back with recommendations to tie the programs together and link them with the business objectives in a comprehensive performance management system that would help focus the attention of each employee within CPSTG. She reminded them what Jacque had said about the group's history, "Things that get measured get done. We need to get and keep our people focused on the Vital Few." (The Vital Few were the critical success factors established by Jacque and his staff). Pete had made it clear that he wanted a means to "cascade" group goals and culture down through the organization so the whole group was heading in the same direction toward the same initiatives, with the ability to have each employee accountable for the management of actions toward those goals.

Change at CPSTG: Performance Management Process

Cathy and the others on the task team discussed various means to change the performance culture of the CPSTG. Their conclusion was to create and implement a new systems approach, involving a process of continuous planning, coaching, and reviewing by management, referred to as performance management. Of course, several considerations needed to be addressed. How to get the support of several managers of the different divisions and facilities to make the process work; where to begin the process; and how to treat offshore facilities?

The first concern would be handled if Jacque would buy into the plan. When that happened they would first implement the process in the Phoenix facilities. In addition, they would work from the assumption that the performance requirements at the offshore facilities were no different than those in the U.S., not unlike the fact that production requirements are the same in any location.

The Performance Management Process

"Jacque, we have a proposal I think you're going to want to hear," Pete said with a smile. "Cathy's going to show you a way to make CPSTG respond more quickly and effectively to 'this rapidly changing world of ours.'" Pete looked over to Cathy who excitedly began to describe the performance management process to Jacque.

Cathy emphasized that she and her team were recommending more than a change in the current performance appraisal process. She made it clear that the concept of performance management was a radical departure from existing programs involving changes in thinking, behavior, and planning.

To begin the process, she proposed that after each year's fourth quarter planning cycle, Jacque meet individually with each member of his staff to develop specific individual goals for the next year and how to measure their accomplishment. An 80/20 rule would be established whereby 80% of each manager's activities must be focused on the strategic thrusts set for CPSTG as a whole. Thus, 80% of each person's job related activity would directly apply to meeting the "Vital Few" concerns set by the group. The managers would repeat this process with their staffs, who in turn would repeat it with their personnel, cascading the group's goal setting process throughout the population in a relatively rapid order, completing the process in the first quarter of the year.

During this goal setting session, each employee would set objectives, behavioral expectations, and agreed upon measures for accomplishing the goals set with the manager, whose own goals were tied to those above. One result would be that each individual's behavioral expectations would drive the development of the empowered team concept that Motorola had adopted. In addition, this would foster a participative style of management, the development of leadership, and reinforcing of the corporation's commitment to individual growth and development. At the same time, as part of the planning and review process for each employee, an individual development plan would be established. This would be based on a gap analysis of one's current skill levels and those skills needed to meet the objectives agreed to in the planning process.

It was Cathy's recommendation that quarterly discussions be held with each employee to review progress towards these goals. As changes in the business climate warranted, these goals would be living documents that could be adjusted as long as they met the focused targets of the group as a whole. After the reviews were all finalized, the individual salary planning for the coming year would be completed in the first quarter. By moving the salary planning process from the fourth quarter to the first quarter, after the performance appraisal and goal setting sessions, there would be a much higher correlation between merit increases and the actual performance of the individual employee.

Cathy also asserted that there was an additional benefit of tying the systems together so that employee goals, objectives, and appraisals were bound in a systematic, focused way to the group's business objectives. The management team would better be able to identify redundant staffing and non-value added work. People would analyze their job descriptions with the group goals in mind, thus redirecting their energies to the "Vital Few." Also, individual employees would get a much clearer focus for their own objectives and what the group's expectations were for them.

She insisted, however, that for this particular plan to work, each manager and supervisor must be totally trained in the process. They must understand the approach, embrace it, and be able to set comprehensive and meaningful goals that could be measured with and by each employee. An added benefit would be that the proposed training would strengthen the individual manager's ability to provide fair, honest, and objective feedback to employees that encouraged their job commitment and growth.

A key factor in this recommendation was the focus on establishing specific goals for behavioral expectations as well as concrete measurable business objectives. How an employee performed his or her job providing leadership to subordinates and working as a team in the performance management process, thus enabling everyone to succeed, was at least as important as the traditional business indices for long-term sustained success.

Implementing Performance Management

As Cathy described her recommendations to Jacque, he became excited. After hearing the potential of the process, he readily agreed that performance management would be the enabling initiative that would provide the focus for each employee within CPSTG to accomplish the strategic initiatives set out by the worldwide staff. In the past, these initiatives had been treated as goals and good ideas. They lacked the driving force of measurable actions within each organization to which mangers were held strictly accountable. Performance management would change that. In fact, Jacque was so enthusiastic about the potential power of Cathy's recommendations in enabling the group to change and perform, he did something he'd never done before. He canceled the monthly operations review and insisted that Cathy use that time to present this performance management process to his staff. He wanted everyone to get rolling the next day.

After Cathy presented how performance management would address many of the incessant problems that they constantly complained about, Jacque's staff shared his excitement and the performance management process was begun within CPSTG.

A short two weeks later, Harley Sanders, chief of CPSTG's worldwide manufacturing arm, asked Pete and Cathy to come to his staff meeting in Guadalajara to train his staff and develop an appropriate plan to cascade the process throughout the Mexico, Korea, and Malaysia plants. Harley, an experienced veteran of CPSTG who had served at one time or another as a manager in each of the three facilities, was convinced that, despite language differences and the need to translate training, there would be no culture impediment to cascading the performance management system, as Cathy had described it, to each of the management teams in the international locations. His Malaysian and Mexican GM's immediately and enthusiastically agreed. His Korean GM was less sure. He thoughtfully pondered the way in which five thousand years of Korean management style would mesh with this new approach, especially with its emphasis on behavioral expectations. He immediately, however, invited Pete and Cathy to join him in Seoul to work with his training manager in developing a plan to implement performance management in Korea.

29
Merck & Company, Inc.: Having the Vision to Succeed

Stephanie Weiss
and
David Bollier

A. An Expensive Care for a Poor Market

In 1978, Dr. P. Roy Vagelos, then head of the Merck research labs, received a provocative memorandum from a senior researcher in parasitology, Dr. William C. Campbell. Dr. Campbell had made an intriguing observation while working with ivermectin, a new antiparasitic compound under investigation for use in animals.

Campbell thought that ivermectin might be the answer to a disease called river blindness that plagued millions in the Third World. But to find out if Campbell's hypothesis had merit, Merck would have to spend millions of dollars to develop the right formulation for human use and to conduct the field trials in the most remote parts of the world. Even if these efforts produced an effective and safe drug, virtually none of those afflicted with river blindness could afford to buy it. Vagelos, originally a university researcher but by then a Merck executive, had to decide whether to invest in research for a drug that, even if successful, might never pay for itself.

River Blindness

River blindness, formally known as onchocerciasis, was a disease labeled by the World Health Organization (WHO) as a public health and socioeconomic problem

---

This case was prepared as the basis for class discussion rather than to illustrate either effective or ineffective handling of an administrative situation.

of considerable magnitude in over 35 developing countries throughout the Third World. Some 85 million people in thousands of tiny settlements throughout Africa and parts of the Middle East and Latin America were thought to be at risk. The cause: a parasitic worm carried by a tiny black fly that bred along fast-moving rivers. When the flies bit humans—a single person could be bitten thousands of times a day—the larvae of a parasitic worm, *Onchocerca volvulus,* entered the body.

These worms grew to more than two feet in length, causing grotesque but relatively innocuous nodules in the skin. The real harm began when the adult worms reproduced, releasing millions of microscopic offspring, known as microfilariae, which swarmed through body tissue. A terrible itching resulted, so bad that some victims committed suicide. After several years, the microfilariae caused lesions and depigmentation of the skin. Eventually they invaded the eyes, often causing blindness.

The World Health Organization estimated in 1978 that some 340,000 people were blind because of onchocerciasis, and that a million more suffered from varying degrees of visual impairment. At that time, 18 million or more people were infected with the parasite, though half did not yet have serious symptoms. In some villages close to fly-breeding sites, nearly all residents were infected and a majority of those over age 45 were blind. In such places, it was said, children believed that severe itching, skin infections, and blindness were simply part of growing up.

In desperate efforts to escape the flies, entire villages abandoned fertile areas near rivers, and moved to poorer land. As a result, food shortages were frequent. Community life disintegrated as new burdens arose for already impoverished families.

The disease was first identified in 1893 by scientists and in 1926 was found to be related to the black flies. But by the 1970s, there was still no cure that could safely be used for community-wide treatment. Two drugs, diethylcarbamazine (DEC) and Suramin, were useful in killing the parasite, but both had severe side effects in infected individuals, needed close monitoring, and had even caused deaths. In 1974, the Onchocerciasis Control Program was created to be administered by the World Health Organization, in the hope that the flies could be killed through spraying of larvacides at breeding sites, but success was slow and uncertain. The flies in many areas developed resistance to the treatment, and were also known to disappear and then reinfest areas.

Merck & Co., Inc.—A Summary of Operations

Merck & Co., Inc. was, in 1978, one of the largest producers of prescription drugs in the world. Headquartered in Rahway, New Jersey, Merck traced its origins to Germany in 1668 when Friedrich Jacob Merck purchased an apothecary in the city of Darmstadt. Over three hundred years later, Merck, having become an American firm, employed over 28,000 people and had operations all over the world.

In the late 1970s, Merck was coming off a 10-year drought in terms of new products. For nearly a decade, the company had relied on two prescription drugs for a significant percentage of its approximately $2 billion in annual sales: Indocin, a treatment for rheumatoid arthritis, and Aldomet, a treatment for high blood pressure. Henry W. Gadsden, Merck's chief executive from 1965 to 1976, along with his successor, John J. Horan, were concerned that the 17-year patent protection on Merck's two big moneymakers would soon expire, and began investing an enormous amount in research.

Merck management spent a great deal of money on research because it knew that its success ten and twenty years in the future critically depended upon present investments. The company deliberately fashioned a corporate culture to nurture the most creative, fruitful research. Merck scientists were among the best-paid in the industry, and were given great latitude to pursue intriguing leads. Moreover, they were inspired to think of their work as a quest to alleviate human disease and suffering world-wide. Within certain proprietary constraints, researchers were encouraged to publish in academic journals and to share ideas with their scientific peers. Nearly a billion dollars was spent between 1975 and 1978, and the investment paid off. In that period, under the direction of head of research, Dr. P. Roy Vagelos, Merck introduced Clinoril, a painkiller for arthritis; a general antibiotic called Mefoxin; a drug for glaucoma named Timoptic; and Ivomec (ivermectin, MSD), an antiparasitic for cattle.

In 1978, Merck had sales of $1.98 billion and net income of $307 million. Sales had risen steadily between 1969 and 1978 from $691 million to almost $2 billion. Income during the same period rose from $106 million to over $300 million.

At that time, Merck employed 28,700 people, up from 22,200 ten years earlier. Human and animal health products constituted 84% of the company's sales, with environmental health products and services representing an additional 14% of sales. Merck's foreign sales had grown more rapidly during the 1970s than had domestic sales, and in 1978 represented 47% of total sales. Much of the company's research operations were organized separately as the Merck Sharp & Dohme Research Laboratories, headed by Vagelos. Other Merck operations included the Merck Sharp & Dohme Division, the Merck Sharp & Dohme International Division, Kelco Division, Merck Chemical Manufacturing Division, Merck Animal Health Division, Calgon Corporation, Baltimore Aircoil Company, and Hubbard Farms.

The company had 24 plants in the United States, including one in Puerto Rico, and 44 in other countries. Six research laboratories were located in the United States and four abroad.

While Merck executives sometimes squirmed when they quoted the "unbusinesslike language" of George W. Merck, son of the company's founder and its former chairman, there could be no doubt that Merck employees found the words inspirational. "We try never to forget that medicine is for the people," Merck said. "It is not for the profits. The profits follow, and if we have remembered that, they have never failed to appear. The better we have remembered it, the larger they have been." These words formed the basis of Merck's overall corporate philosophy.

The Drug Investment Decision

Merck invested hundreds of millions of dollars each year in research. Allocating those funds among various projects, however, was a rather involved and inexact process. At a company as large as Merck, there was never a single method by which projects were approved or money distributed.

Studies showed that, on the average, it took 12 years and $200 million to bring a new drug to market. Thousands of scientists were continually working on new ideas and following new leads. Drug development was always a matter of trial and error; with each new iteration, scientists would close some doors and open others. When a Merck researcher came across an apparent breakthrough—either in an unexpected direction, or as a derivative of the original lead—he or she would conduct preliminary research. If the idea proved promising, it was brought to the attention of the department heads.

Every year, Merck's research division held a large review meeting at which all research programs were examined. Projects were coordinated and consolidated, established programs were reviewed and new possibilities were considered. Final approval on research was not made, however, until the head of research met later with a committee of scientific advisors. Each potential program was extensively reviewed, analyzed on the basis of the likelihood of success, the existing market, competition, potential safety problems, manufacturing feasibility, and patent status before the decision was made whether to allocate funds for continued experimentation.

The Problem of Rare Diseases and Poor Customers

Many potential drugs offered little chance of financial return. Some diseases were so rare that treatments developed could never be priced high enough to recoup the investment in research, while other diseases afflicted only the poor in rural and remote areas of the Third World. These victims had limited ability to pay even a small amount for drugs or treatment.

In the United States, Congress sought to encourage drug companies to conduct research on rare diseases. In 1978, legislation had been proposed that would grant drug companies tax benefits and seven-year exclusive marketing rights if they would manufacture drugs for diseases afflicting fewer than 200,000 Americans. It was expected that this "orphan drug program" would eventually be passed into law.

There was, however, no U.S. or international program that would create incentives for companies to develop drugs for diseases like river blindness, which afflicted millions of the poor in the Third World. The only hope was that some Third World government, foundation, or international aid organization might step in and partially fund the distribution of a drug that had already been developed.

The Discovery of Ivermectin

The process of investigating promising drug compounds was always long, laborious, and fraught with failure. For every pharmaceutical compound that became a "product candidate," thousands of others failed to meet the most rudimentary preclinical tests for safety and efficacy. With so much room for failure, it became especially important for drug companies to have sophisticated research managers who could identify the most productive research strategies.

Merck had long been a pioneer in developing major new antibiotic compounds, beginning with penicillin and streptomycin in the 1940s. In the 1970s, Merck Sharp & Dohme Research Laboratories were continuing this tradition. To help investigate for new microbial agents of potential therapeutic value, Merck researchers obtained 54 soil samples from the Kitasato Institute of Japan in 1974. These samples seemed novel and the researchers hoped they might disclose some naturally occurring antibiotics.

As Merck researchers methodically put the soil through hundreds of tests, Merck scientists were pleasantly surprised to detect strong antiparasitic activity in Sample No. OS3153, a scoop of soil dug up at a golf course near Ito, Japan. The Merck labs quickly brought together an interdisciplinary team to try to isolate a pure active ingredient from the microbial culture. The compound eventually isolated —avermectin—proved to have an astonishing potency and effectiveness against a wide range of parasites in cattle, swine, horses, and other animals. Within a year, the Merck team also began to suspect that a group of related compounds discovered in the same soil sample could be effective against many other intestinal worms, mites, ticks, and insects.

After toxicological tests suggested that ivermectin would be safer than related compounds, Merck decided to develop the substance for the animal health market. In 1978, the first ivermectin-based animal drug, Ivomec, was nearing approval by the U.S. Department of Agriculture and foreign regulatory bodies. Many variations would likely follow: drugs for sheep and pigs, horses, dogs, and others. Ivomec had the potential to become a major advance in animal health treatment.

As clinical testing of ivermectin progressed in the late 1970s, Dr. William Campbell's ongoing research brought him face-to-face with an intriguing hypothesis. Ivermectin, when tested in horses, was effective against the microfilariae of an exotic, fairly unimportant gastrointestinal parasite, *Onchocerca cervicalis*. This particular worm, while harmless in horses, had characteristics similar to the insidious human parasite that causes river blindness, *Onchocerca volvulus*.

Dr. Campbell wondered, could ivermectin be formulated to work against the human parasite? Could a safe, effective drug suitable for community-wide treatment of river blindness be developed? Both Campbell and Vagelos knew that it was very much a gamble that it would succeed. Furthermore, both knew that even if success were attained, the economic viability of such a project would be nil. On the other hand, because such a significant amount of money had already been invested in the development of the animal drug, the cost of developing a human formulation would be much less than that for developing a new compound. It was also widely believed at this point that ivermectin, though still in its final development stages, was likely to be very successful.

A decision to proceed would not be without risks. If a new derivative proved to have any adverse health effects when used on humans, its reputation as a veterinary drug could be tainted and sales negatively affected, no matter how irrelevant the experience with humans. In early tests, ivermectin had had some negative side effects on some specific species of mammals. Dr. Brian Duke of the Armed Forces Institute of Pathology in Washington, D.C. said the cross-species effectiveness of antiparasitic drugs are unpredictable, and there is "always a worry that some race or sub-section of the human population might be adversely affected."

Isolated instances of harm to humans or improper use in Third World settings might also raise some unsettling questions: Could drug residues turn up in meat eaten by humans? Would any human version of ivermectin distributed to the Third World be diverted into the black market, undercutting sales of the veterinary drug? Could the drug harm certain animals in unknown ways?

Despite these risks, Vagelos wondered what the impact might be of turning down Campbell's proposal. Merck had built a research team dedicated to alleviating human suffering. What would a refusal to pursue a possible treatment for river blindness do to morale? Ultimately, it was Dr. Vagelos who had to make the decision whether or not to fund research toward a treatment for river blindness.

* * * * * * * *

The Merck case is continued and developed more fully in the *Instructor's Guide* where cases B, C and D can be found.

30
Selling Development to Somalia: The Food Monetization Program

John D. Irons
and
Anne-Lise Quinn

A letter from Tom, the IRC Food Monetization manager, to his brother:

Two weeks ago we were involved in a fire-fight when the Ethiopian army tried to kill rebel forces who had taken sanctuary in the Kenyan Police compound. We were forced to cower next to a pile of bricks while tracers lit up the sky above.

In Somalia there is no central authority, not to mention trustworthy people. The government is non-existent and the traditional authorities have been replaced by anarchists with automatic weapons. Every Somali we talk to says that he has it under control and that he or his group is the authority. As far as I can see, everyone just sits around with their guns chewing *mira* (stimulant from Kenya) and preying upon aid workers and their programs. I just heard today that a UNICEF worker was shot in the head in Kismayo as he left the office. It seems like these incidents are increasing as the U.S. army pushes to occupy many of the cities in southern Somalia. And talking about *mira,* did you know that the sons-in-law of Generals Barre and Aideed (leaders of the two military factions in the country) are both brothers-in-arms (excuse the pun!) in trading this lucrative market commodity. The politics and economics of war, eh?

I thought that I would be able to apply my international business skills to this project. It should be the best of both worlds; the satisfaction of helping others while also honing business skills that would be transferable. It is a fantastic opportunity, working with the U.S. Agency for International Development (USAID) and the United Nations High Commissioner for Refugees (UNHCR), and to be able to use market systems and market-oriented solutions instead of the traditional response of just giving away food. Actually, the refugees at the camp aren't getting any food at the moment. Until recent-

315

ly, the UNHCR was distributing food for some 80,000 refugees, but according to non-governmental organizations working there the refugee population is around 30,000. The food is being hoarded by clan elders and sold on the open market. The World Food Program official here is refusing to give out more food (except to those who are obviously malnourished) until the UNHCR registers the refugees and gets a more accurate estimate of numbers in the camp. That's easier said than done. The last time they tried to register the refugees they had big problems: UNHCR enlisted the help of the International Relief Committee in the chore and told them to mark with a dye the little finger of each refugee's left hand. Well, did no-one tell them that the left hand in Islamic culture is only used for wiping one's bottom?! After five hours of almost riotous registering UNHCR called the event to a halt: the refugees were not being cooperative. So now the elders are up in arms—they want food and they want to do the registering their way, which effectively means the elders will tell UNHCR how many members of their clan are in the camp. Well, that's just not good enough—we know they double or triple the figures and so we'll be back to square one. But there's another problem—the elders are conspiring to do an exclusive interview with CNN to tell the world how UNHCR and World Food Programme are refusing to feed the starving thousands in Mandera refugee camp. They've done it before. They round up some of the most malnourished children they can find (most of whom are usually not related to them) and say, "Look at my starving child. Please help me. I just want to feed my child." That they themselves are almost fat on the wealth they have acquired from the sale of aid food is not the point. That they have been theoretically "over-fed" for the last year is also not the point. In short, beware of news stories which only give one side of the refugee problem!

It takes forever to do anything here: either you do it yourself or it doesn't get done. I have been trying to start this program for two months and have made very little progress. It is not how I thought it would be. The non-governmental organizations are backed by huge budgets and pressured into quickly showing some accomplishment to donors. This pressure has been further exacerbated by the closing of the border because of "car"-jackings. Now aid agencies are competing with each other—marking off specific areas and vying for qualified labor and high-profile projects. Money doesn't seem to be an issue.

I am still optimistic and hope everything goes well. That Ayn Rand book you sent out was great, has she written anything else? Also send some more film (there are great photo opportunities here), some mosquito spray, and possibly a bullet proof vest.

Background to Somalia

Somalia is located on the Horn of Africa and shares formal boundaries with Kenya, Ethiopia, and Djibouti. It consists of approximately 400,000 square miles of arid savanna grasslands that form the habitat of Somalia's largely nomadic population. The livestock raised by these nomads—camels, sheep, goats, cattle—are sold almost exclusively to Saudi Arabia and comprise Somalia's biggest foreign exchange earner at 60–70% of GNP. The long shoreline, which runs along the Gulf of Aden and down into the Indian Ocean, provides another lucrative livelihood for Somalis: fishing.

Somalia as a nation came into existence in 1960 and has a population of approximately four million Somalis; another two million Somalis live in neighboring Ethiopia and Kenya. Almost all Somalis belong to a family of African peoples generally referred to as Cushites or Hamites; a small proportion of Somalis, however, are Bantu peoples who live in dispersed communities along the Juba and Shabele Rivers. As a nation, Somalia can be described as one of the most ethnically homogeneous in Africa: they share a common culture (though there are variations pertaining to the different lifestyles of the nomads and agriculturalists), a common language (Somali), and a common religion (Islam). The Somali language, first written down in the early 1970s, has a rich oral history; poems, debates, metaphors, analogies, and proverbs figure importantly in everyday discussions. Somalis also share other definitive cultural traits, such as a severe form of female circumcision.

Prior to the outbreak of civil war in December 1990, Somalia was described as a "nation of constituent, segmented clans in which political forces are carefully balanced to share power."[1] There are six main clan families in Somalia: the Darood, Hawiye, Isaaq, Dir, Gigil, and Rahanwayn. These clan families are divided into patrilineal sub-clans, which are further sub-divided into lineages. With regard to the political organization and ethos of the Somalis, Lewis[2] has written:

> Like many pastoral nomads who range far and wide with their herds or camels and flocks, the Somalis have no indigenous centralized government. And this lack of formal government and instituted authority is strongly reflected in their extreme independence and individualism. Few writers have failed to notice the formidable pride of the Somali nomad, his extraordinary sense of superiority as an individual, and his firm conviction that he is sole master of his actions and subject to no authority except that of God. If they have perceived it, however, they have been for the most part baffled by the shifting character of the nomad's political allegiance and puzzled by the fact that the political and jural unit with which he acts on one occasion he opposes on another.

Despite the stress that Somalis put on their individuality, there is nevertheless a strong concept of community in certain situations, especially with regard to privilege and obligation. Under the institution of *heer* (social contract), for example, individual culpability is overridden by the concept of collective guilt: that is, when a person commits a crime the guilt is not directed solely upon the perpetrator but rather transmitted to all members of his or her kin. Members of the aggrieved will seek revenge not just on the perpetrator but on any members of his lineage. Debts of blood money are paid collectively; traditionally a man is worth 100 camels, while a woman is worth 50.[3]

The outbreak of civil war in Somalia, which left many thousands of Somalis dead, injured, displaced, or seeking refuge, exposed the harsh nature of the fundamental

---

[1]*Somalia: A Nation in Turmoil,* A Minority Rights Group Report, 1991, p. 6.
[2]Lewis, I. M., *A Pastoral Democracy,* London: Oxford University Press, 1961, p. 1.
[3]Ibid p. 26.

clan schisms. It also revealed the problems the country had trying to establish a centralized government in the aftermath of the colonial era—clearly evident in the poorly developed infrastructure. These problems have been further exacerbated by a region-wide drought that has caused massive population movements, widespread starvation, and decimated livestock herds.

The Ghedo Region of Somalia has experienced all the ravages of the war and more. The former president of the country, Siad Barre (Darood clan), who was ousted from office by General Aideed (Hawiye clan), came from Garba-Harrey in the center of Ghedo Region. Aideed brought the war to Ghedo but after a few months of indiscriminate bombing and looting, the dominant sub-clan of Ghedo, the Maryhans, regrouped and took back the area. Most non-governmental organizations like the International Relief Committee (IRC) who have been involved in cross border relief and development work in Somalia, operate out of Mandera and El Wak. The main security problem at the moment for non-governmental organizations working on either side of the border is with the small groups of Somali bandits who continue to hijack UN or Kenyan-registered vehicles from time to time. Mandera lies in the northeastern corner of Kenya and is located just across from the Somali border town of Bula Howa. Bula Howa is typical of most towns in Somalia and can be likened to an old west border town, or, more appropriately, ghost town. Strewn with garbage, spent cartridges, bleached bones, and shot-up, stripped-down vehicles, Bula Howa is home to wandering camels, goats, sheep, and humans alike, searching for shade from the scorching sun and the heat of the war.

Major Players

Tom. The International Relief Committee's food monetization manager who is responsible for implementing the program. His background is in international business management and finance.

Jane. Jane is the assistant food monetization manager. Her major responsibility is the funding and monitoring of labor-intensive projects financed by the proceeds received from the sale of food commodities. Her background is in social anthropology. Jane and Tom have been married for 2 years.

International Relief Committee. The IRC is a small non-governmental organization (NGO) based in New York that deals with emergency relief and development in war-torn countries. The organization traditionally focuses on health, water, sanitation, and rehabilitation projects, but has recently branched out into new ventures in aid work such as food monetization. For the purpose of their work in Somalia, IRC has agreed to a partnership with the United Nations High Commissioner for Refugees (UNHCR) in a bid to rehabilitate areas in the Ghedo Region for repatriated refugees: UNHCR provides much of the funding for the IRC, which implements the projects.

The United Nations High Commissioner for Refugees. The UNHCR is the United Nations body responsible for protecting refugees and peoples displaced as a result of war or persecution. The organization tends to be very hierarchical, political, and bureaucratic. Where it operates with NGOs, the UNHCR usually takes on a coordinating role.

The Fundamentalists. The members of the Islamic Organization, most commonly referred to as Fundamentalists, are extremely conservative Sunni Muslims who uphold a very strict moral code that prohibits smoking tobacco, drinking alcohol, and the chewing of *mira,* a leafy plant that is commonly chewed in Somalia as a stimulant. Together with the Somali National Front (SNF) they managed to defend the Ghedo Region from Aideed's army. Today they remain a strong military force and essentially control Bula Howa, Dollo, and Luq Ganana, which is their stronghold. The Fundamentalists are in the process of teaching the people of Luq and Bula Howa about their beliefs—specifically their strict observance of *Shari'a* law. They say that they do not discriminate against any Somali with respect to clan because they are all Muslim; they are offering an alternative socio-political system to the current one, based on factionalism, which is devastating Somalia. The Fundamentalists have an NGO liaison officer, Abdikadir, who is very personable and speaks excellent English.

The Elders. These are the traditional authority figures in the various communities, villages, and cities of Somalia. They are senior clan members who are responsible for representing the community, and are often recognizable by their hair and beards died red with henna to hide the gray. They are also responsible for advising the various chiefs. In the Mandera refugee camp the elders have been known to reject food because it was not in sufficient quantities or to their liking. Food aid distributed across the border routinely finds its way back into the Mandera marketplace.

The Chiefs and the Chief of the Chiefs. Despite the acephalous nature of the clan system in Somalia, there are nevertheless men who have emerged as chiefs and chief of chiefs. It would appear that they are the senior elected representatives of lineages and assume their title over territorial settlements, such as the "Chief of Bula Howa" or the "Chief of Chiefs of Gedo Region." Though they are not military figures, they appear to have some political clout and often approach aid organizations as representatives of their communities.

The Somali National Front (SNF). The Somali National Front, under the national leadership of General Morgan (author of the "Letter of Death" in the mid 1980s that called for the extermination of the Isaaq clan) is militarily in control of most of the Ghedo Region. It is unclear what the relationship is between the SNF and the Fundamentalists who control the northern towns; but when three SNF "technicals"—Toyota Land-cruisers with .50 caliber machine guns mounted in their beds—came for service to Bula Howa they were warned by the Fundamentalists to leave in three days. Leave they did.

Description of the Program

The Food Monetization Program is funded by the U.S. Agency for International Development (USAID) and the United High Commissioner for Refugees, and is being implemented by the International Relief Committee (IRC). The goal of food monetization is to sell food that has been donated. Generally, the food, donated by the U.S. under the PL 480 law, is sold at a minimal price with the proceeds being used to cover the transportation and distribution costs of the food. In this particular case the program involves selling commodities at favorable prices to Somali traders in the Ghedo Region and then using the proceeds to fund labor intensive development activities. Projects will be initiated in the same general area as the food sales so as not to deplete the community's money supply.

The goals of the program are as follows:

1. To increase the amount and to reduce the price of food in Somalia.
2. To reduce the negative consequences such as dependency, low self esteem, and displacement that result from free food distributions.
3. To create funds that can be used for development programs in the area. These programs will help to rehabilitate critical infrastructure, and support livestock and agricultural recovery.
4. To provide jobs so that the Somali poor will be able to purchase food.
5. To help to revive the market mechanisms that have traditionally existed both between Somalia and Kenya and within Somalia itself. Besides the obvious benefits, it is felt that the revival of market mechanisms will contribute to stabilizing the region.

Much of the food destined for free distributions in Somalia has been looted. It is felt that by selling the commodities to Somali traders and by extension, their clan, they will be less of a target to looters as they have the clan and political associations that international organizations do not.

Originally, IRC was given a grant to cover the operating expenses incurred in facilitating a monetization program that CARE was initiating. IRC's responsibilities were to identify Somali traders, monitor sales, and identify development projects to fund with the proceeds. For several reasons the grant was expanded and the relationship with CARE severed so that IRC could initiate its own monetization program and be fully responsible for its implementation and operations. IRC's field of operations is the Kenya-Somalia border area extending from Kenya to the Juba River in

Somalia. CARE is to handle operations from the coast and in the north where they have had a program running for some time.

Program Set-up

Tom's first task was to locate a site where he could set up his operations. Because IRC had not yet moved into Somalia, Tom had to choose a cross-border location on the Kenyan side: Liboi, El Wak, or Mandera. He chose Mandera as an initial starting point for the program because (a) in the light of the American invasion into Somalia it appeared to be more secure, (b) Mandera has always played a key role in trade between Kenya and Somalia, and (c) the traders in Bula Howa were more enthusiastic about the program than those in El Wak and Liboi. Once Mandera had been targeted as a center for monetization, the process of setting up the program began.

Tom was well aware of the friction that the program might cause with Kenyan wholesalers, after all a large percentage of their business was in catering to Somali traders from across the border. Tom thought that by using a Kenyan wholesaler as his agent he would be able to deflect some of the problems that might occur if he purchased, transported, warehoused, and sold the goods himself. Another factor he had to consider was the risk involved in sending trucks north to Mandera, which meant four days of travel though bandit country.

In late December, and with this idea in mind, Tom went into what looked like a prosperous shop, owned by Mohammed Hussein. After greeting Mohammed and his nephew, Tom began explaining what the monetization program was all about. Tom was cut short by Hussein who said that now was the time for serving his customers, not for talking business. Tom was slightly taken aback, but was interested in talking more with him because he seemed to be serious about his business. Tom suggested having lunch or dinner together: Hussein said to come back at 4:30.

When they next met, Tom further outlined the program. Hussein repeatedly asked what commodities Tom was going to sell. He told Tom that the Kenyan Grain and Cereals Board also wanted to set up an office in Mandera for the sale of subsidized grain. Hussein explained that the traders got together with officials from the board and worked out an agreement as to what grains they could sell and at what price they could sell them. He further explained that the government agreed to only use Mandera traders as the transporters of the commodities.

Tom had the feeling that Hussein didn't appreciate what this program would do in helping to revive trade between the two countries. Nor did he think that the trader realized that he would make a lot of money through an agency. Before the discussion could be concluded, Hussein announced that it was time for prayers and that he would discuss the situation with the other traders of Mandera. Tom couldn't understand why he didn't jump at the chance of becoming an agent for the program; he was, after all, a businessman. Tom was further worried that the whole project was becoming too complicated, too political, and very time consuming.

Two days later a man came to see Tom to tell him that the biggest trader in town, known simply as Yunis, was interested in his project. Tom met with Yunis and after a short discussion they came to an agreement: Yunis would purchase in-transit commodities in Mombasa and have them transported to Mandera where he would store them for two weeks; Tom would put down half the total cost of commodities, transportation, and storage costs now, and half when the goods arrived. Following the meeting, a Somali colleague cautioned Tom that if the other traders discovered that he had made a deal with one without giving the others an equal chance he would have "trouble." What that "trouble" would consist of Tom didn't know, but to avert it he decided to distribute a letter to all traders, including Yunis, asking them to submit bids for listed commodities. He received four responses, none of which could beat that of Yunis' bid. It then dawned on Tom that had he received a better deal from elsewhere, he would nevertheless have been committed to dealing with Yunis.

Tom's next problem was to identify those commodities that he would most successfully be able to monetize. Informal discussions with Somali traders in their stores in Bula Howa gave Tom a strong indication of what commodities they wanted to buy, but he needed to check the markets further afield. For that he required help. To hire his first employees, Tom spread the word among the local staff who were already employed by IRC in Mandera. When he had chosen from among several applicants with varying levels of education and work experience, he sent them out to monitor the prices of goods at local town markets and also to record the local Kenyan/Somali exchange rate. From these reports he discovered two things: (1) there were few high value commodities available (sugar, tea, pasta, salt); and (2) many of the widely available commodities, such as wheat and rice, had originated from free food distributions—either marketed by recipients or the looters of distribution convoys.

Assessment Trips

To let Somali traders know about the program and encourage local elders to identify labor-intensive projects that could be funded by the proceeds, Tom arranged two trips to principal towns in Ghedo Region: Luuq-Ganana and Garba-Harrey. Outlines of the criteria for use of the monetization proceeds were translated into Somali and distributed among the traders and elders; their response was largely enthusiastic.

The Goods Arrive

Yunis placed the order for food commodities with his brother in Mombasa, and told Tom that it would take the trucks four or five days to reach Mandera. The goods, however, didn't arrive until four weeks later due to the collapse of a bridge at Habaswein. Tom was particularly concerned about his goods being stuck anywhere on the road up north because there had been a spate of armed attacks on trucks recently; the *shiftas* or bandits were coming across the border from Somalia and looting towns and vehicles. When the goods arrived, Tom happily declared the news at a cross-border nongovernmental organization meeting.

The next day the UNHCR team leader recommended that Tom not begin selling his goods: the UN had to put the refugees at the camp[4] on quarter rations because they had run out of food for them, and he was concerned that if Tom started "selling" food, albeit high value commodities sold to Somali traders, they might have a riot on their hands. Tom was puzzled as to why the UNHCR hadn't done something about the food before they were forced to reduce distributions to quarter rations. Because Tom had traders at his door asking for the commodities, and also because the UNHCR had poached one of his employees who had recently renewed his contract with Tom, he decided to just go ahead and start selling the goods anyway.

Dealing with Customs

Selling commodities to Somali traders from within Kenyan was to produce more problems for Tom than he had originally anticipated. Initially, Tom had assumed that the Somali traders would simply take the goods across the border as they always did. However, he soon learned that the traditional method employed by the traders was illegal; they didn't formally deal with customs procedures and regulations. This method also increased the price of the goods, which was one of the things that the program was trying to combat. Another problem was the temporary closing of the Kenyan border with Somalia: the civil war increased incidences of banditry and the anticipation that Somalis might attack border towns in Kenya if the UN peace-keeping forces headed into Ghedo Region were enough of an incentive for the border police to clamp down on cross-border traffic.

Tom met with the head of customs and the officer in charge of the police division (OCPD) to discuss whether Somali traders could come to Mandera to buy goods. Tom tried to explain that the sooner the local Somali economy was set back in motion the sooner the Somali refugees would want to leave Mandera and head home. (Tom was more than aware of the national and local political problems that the refugees were posing for the Kenyan authorities.) The officials agreed to let traders come through *only* if they presented a letter written by Tom on IRC letterhead addressed to the customs police. Tom thought that would be simple enough: he would use his monitors to take letters down to the border to prospective traders.

But the traders had several complaints about the system. First, even with a letter of authorization they were being hassled by the police and detained for hours until the traders agreed to hand over bribes; that they were carrying large sums of money with them meant that they were expected to give even more than was usually expected. Second, due to strict Kenyan insurance laws, no Somali vehicles could cross into Kenya without having appropriate insurance papers; these could be bought from customs police but at a high price. Tom was unsure about what he should do: Should

---

[4]Because the UN has not officially registered the refugees at the camp, it is referred to as a site.

he stay down at customs and walk each trader through (he assumed the police wouldn't ask for bribes in front of him)? Should he hire a truck so that he could deliver the merchants' goods to the border so they didn't have to worry about taking their trucks across?

These weren't his only dilemmas. As Tom's goods were "in transit" he legally needed to store the goods in a bonded warehouse. This meant that every time he wanted to take goods from the warehouse, he had to have a customs official open it for him. On top of this, Tom was about to run over his contract with Yunis and would either have to extend it or look for another warehouse.

Trouble with the Kenyan Traders

The price of the commodities Tom was selling to the Somali traders was slightly above cost price and approximately 20% below the wholesale price in Mandera. Tom was happy that the Kenyan traders had put up so little opposition to his program and assumed it was because the non-governmental organization presence in Mandera made up for the loss of trade from Somali traders. Furthermore, the program didn't impinge on the trade they did with Ethiopians.

Tom varied the price of commodities to Somali traders depending on where they came from in the Ghedo Region: those who came from farther away paid less for the commodities because they had to also pay for transport costs. Tom also hoped that by doing this he would encourage traders to take the goods into Somalia. Providing transportation was not a risk Tom was willing to take. To appease both the Kenyan and Somali traders, Tom sent monitors out with every Somali trader to make sure that they did indeed take their goods to the stated destination. He even marked the goods with spray paint to distinguish them from goods bought and sold on the Mandera market. Nevertheless, within a few weeks some commodities started showing up at the Mandera marketplace. The Kenyan traders called Tom to a meeting in which they expressed their annoyance at what had happened: unless Tom did something, they would hold a demonstration and protest to the district commissioner.

Tom set up a meeting with Somali traders in Bula-Howa. He was feeling very annoyed that they had not maintained their side of the bargain; he realized that it might not have been them, but he vented his frustrations on them anyhow. Using his interpreter, Tom told them he was going to have to raise the prices of the commodities. He didn't need an interpreter to understand the traders response to that announcement; for five minutes the traders made angry exclamations and argued loudly among themselves while the interpreter obviously didn't know what exactly he should translate back to Tom. Tom realized that his approach had been wrong. He asked the interpreter what he had said to the traders. Rather puzzled the interpreter repeated what Tom had told him to say. Tom exclaimed that was not what he had meant—he wanted to ask the traders what he should do about the prices! The interpreter excused his inability to understand what Tom had really meant to say, and passed the last message on. Obviously relieved, the traders calmed down and discussed the matter among themselves. They announced that they should all meet the next day in the presence of the chief of Bula-Howa.

At the meeting the next day Tom decided to take a more humble approach. He offered all his guests chairs to sit on and he sat on a packing crate. Tom explained that the Food Monetization Program was developed to help the people and the economy of Somalia; if the donors of the program found out that goods were returning to Kenya and were not benefitting the intended recipients then they would close down the program. What ideas did the chief and the traders have to solve this problem? The traders eventually came to the conclusion that the only viable way to stop the goods from returning to Kenya was to increase the price of the goods.

Problem. Some of the traders buy commodities, saying they are taking them to Bardera (and therefore getting the commodities at a cheaper price), but then store them in a warehouse in Bula Howa with the excuse that there's no transportation available. Some Bula Howa traders are complaining about this because they know some of these goods are showing up in their marketplace. The monitors are also experiencing problems trying to keep up with all the traders. Should Tom standardize the prices of the commodities?

Locating the Warehouse

Tom was still left with the problem concerning customs and warehousing. At a time when Tom was contemplating this problem, Abdikadir, liaison officer of the Fundamentalists, said that if an office and warehouse were set up in Bula Howa he would be able to guarantee the safety of the commodities, the proceeds, and also Tom's personal safety. When Tom discussed the matter with Jane, she said that she would worry about the IRC appearing to support one faction over another. The Somali National Front, for example, was still a force to be reckoned with in the Ghedo Region and may not appreciate what may look like IRC siding with one faction. However, Tom felt that although the security situation across the border was still somewhat precarious, the Fundamentalists seemed to have a handle on it. Recently, for example, they had gone in hot pursuit of bandits who hijacked a vehicle from a non-governmental organization in Mandera. When they captured the bandits they handed them over to the Kenyan Police.

Problem. Tom has been working every day and is under a lot of stress. He feels like he may be losing his perspective. Should he open a warehouse in Bula Howa?

31
Managing a Culturally Diverse Work Force in a Southern African Gold Mine

Jeffrey Ovian

Environment Introduction

Few 20th century industrial enterprises can compare with a southern African gold mine. These mines have 50 to 50,000 employees on site. The mine properties often extend over 100km². Gold is extracted from underground depths below 4,000m. Men are not only employed underground but also a significant number work on the surface processing the ore and in the various repair shops. By North American standards, a surprising amount of ancillary work is done on site.

Typically, mines have several shafts. Radiating out from these shafts are underground haulages often extending several kilometers before intersecting the ore body. Small trains shuttle back and forth along these haulages bringing the gold-bearing rock to the shaft for hoisting to the surface. The gold is found either in a gently dipping plane-type structure approximately one meter thick, or in a vein-type structure. Frequently, the ore body is broken and displaced by geologic faults. Once the haulages are in close proximity to the ore body, smaller travelling ways and ore passes are developed from the haulage to the ore body.

Primarily, all the development is in waste rock, so it is essential to minimize these excavations. Once in the ore body, excavations are best confined to the ore body itself. Excavating waste rock produces no revenue and is costly. Excavating is usually performed on a two-shift, six-day basis.

During the day shift, holes for blasting are drilled by hand-held pneumatic drills. Excavation support is situated, and water and compressed-air pipes are advanced. After the shift has left the working areas, blasting begins. To allow the ventilation system to exhaust the blast fumes, there is a several-hours break between shifts. During the night shift, the broken rock is removed from either the ore body or the advancing haulages and brought to the shaft for hoisting.

Although considerable mechanization has occurred in the last 50 years, underground labor is strenuous and dangerous. Working quarters are hot, cramped, soaking wet, and noisy. The pneumatic drills are heavy. They require considerable muscle power to carry, let alone operate. The timber packs to support the surrounding rock are installed by hand. In hard-to-reach areas, hand shoveling is common. Most of the broken ore, however, is dragged by a scraper that is pulled by an electric winch. If the ore body is primarily horizontal, small winches will be arranged in a dendritic pattern to clean an area. The central winch will draw rock from several tributary winches to an ore pass where it will fall to a waiting train.

Most mine activity is focused on the day shift. During this time, miners are accompanied underground with electricians, samplers, surveyors, and mechanics. The night shift crews total less than 20% of the day shift. The difference underground is palpable and stark. Only the trains, winches, and hoists are operative at night.

Organizationally, the superintendent is responsible for the entire mine. Reporting to the superintendent is the resident engineer, mine manager, metallurgical manager responsible for ore processing and the administrative manager. On smaller mines these posts are combined. The resident engineer and the mine manager have various hierarchical levels beneath them based on geographic areas of the mine. For instance, there may be east and west sections for two different managers or engineers, which are divided into specific levels and sublevels. The engineering staff's job is to provide electricity, water, machinery, and compressed air to the miners in the haulages and ore body. Each area and subarea of the mine is given a monthly production and development target. The mine itself is assigned an annual target by the corporate office.

The mine management structure is vertical, and the larger mines include at least eight formal levels. Selective information percolates up, and only instructions pour down. Although there are significant differences, the mine management structure has many similarities with a regimental structure.

The key motivation for mine employees primarily is linking production targets to remuneration. The closer the employee is to direct production responsibility, the greater the proportion of bonus pay in the total remuneration. There is, however, an incongruity in that the mine is assigned a target of so many kilograms of gold by the corporate office, while specific sections of the mine are assigned a target of so many tons of ore. In fact, many sections are assigned a target of cubic meters to extract each month.

Primarily, the superintendent is left to reconcile how this is to be achieved. A balance must be struck between easily accessible ore that has a low gold content, and difficult-to-obtain high gold content ore. If development is not done in conjunction with ore removal, access to the ore body soon diminishes. By the same token, because development is primarily done in waste rock, if only haulages were excavated, no gold would be produced and no revenue could be generated from gold sales.

A consequence of the autocratic management style that manifests itself in the assignment of targets and, subsequently, the earning of bonuses, is that one's superior determines one's target. Often, even reality will not alter a production target. The only performance restraint to achieving a production target is injury. An intense amount of pressure is applied at every level to achieve production targets.

Cultural Diversity

Company towns, especially mining communities, have several special attributes. The mine becomes the landlord, town planner, and social chairman. Staff are allotted housing based on their position in the company. An accommodation problem is often brought to the attention of one's immediate superior if the housing department is slow or unwilling to act. It is hard to escape the extensive reach of this corporate paternalism.

Houses are described not by their size, quality, or location, but by the company position of the intended occupant. For instance, a certain size house is a manager's residence, a smaller house is for artisans. Within the same remuneration band, all houses are as identical as possible. Because occupants change every few years, the interiors and exteriors take on a bland appearance that is designed to offend no one. Typically, in the center of the community will be the company swimming pool, several tennis courts, sporting fields, and the social hall.

Although it is often said that in a small community there are no secrets, in a mine town the degree of familiarity among the inhabitants is exceptional. People see each other as co-workers, neighbors, and club members. If one is successful in the mine, one is successful in the community.

This relationship manifests itself in many ways. It is common for the superintendent's wife to be the chairperson of the ladies' or social club. If employees in a certain area of the mine are not meeting their production targets, an element of alienation or even ostracism, is created in the community. A newcomer to the community is judged by his company credentials. The higher the position the greater the respect and trepidation that is warranted.

Community life in southern Africa is a product of the region's various ethnic groups. After the Boer War, an identifiable southern African culture slowly began to emerge. Today, especially in the major centers, it is difficult to find separate cultural components in their original form, let alone vestiges of the country's colonial past. The southern African economy has been the driving force, forging an integrated culture from the region's ethnic groups.

Mining has played a significant role in the economy. It has also brought south Africa's diverse ethnic groups in closer contact. A dichotomy arose despite the various groups' proximity on the mine. The region's colonial past would produce a strict class society in the mine community. Artisans would socialize with artisans and supervisors with supervisors.

Earlier in this century, as Afrikaners began displacing the immigrant English miners, the scene was set for cross-cultural tension. With growing economic empowerment, the differences among Xhosa, Tswana, Shona, Ndebele, Shangaan, Basotho, and Zulu workers, who would often find themselves on the same mine, became more apparent. This tension has continued to the present as former laborers have been promoted to supervisory positions leaping what was perceived to be a cultural and racial divide. Class and cultural differences are highly pronounced in the country. Southern Africa's racial problems have exacerbated both the tension between ethnic groups and the violence often associated with mine disputes.

Case Introduction

The Jordan shaft at the northern border of the Occidental mine was nearly 30 years old. To say that the shaft had seen its best days would be an understatement—the Jordan shaft was on borrowed time. In its prime 4,000 people toiled in this subterranean recess. When Seth Wilson arrived, there were barely 300. Occidental was somewhat farther from the nearest city than his last posting, but it was closer to a tourist area. Seth was looking forward to an occasional trip to a game park.

The Jordan shaft was now expected to increase Occidental mine's life. Although the shaft had three working levels, high hopes were held for the extension of haulages on 18-level (an underground level where production was underway). Corporate staff were convinced the decade-long decline of Occidental mine could be arrested. They were hopeful that in less than a year these haulages could be extended to what was a large portion of overlooked ore between two faults. Previous geologic interpretations had not identified this ore. As for the existing production on 18-level, some new ground was exposed by the only new development to take place on this shaft in twelve months.

Most of the existing production on Jordan came from 15-level. At the fringes of older worked-out areas, various remnants of ore were found, although little development had occurred. Enough ore was found to carry the shaft for the last several months. The problem here was the dispersion of the working areas; the areas were so spread out that it was difficult to equip these areas for efficient mining. No sooner was all the equipment in place when the ore was exhausted. Several days would be spent moving the winches and pipes to a new area.

A critical situation was apparent on 13-level, the last and uppermost working area of the Jordan shaft. This level of the shaft had not achieved its budgeted target for nearly one year. The few identified remaining ore remnants were soon to be exhausted, and all the production resources were to be shifted to 18-level.

The superintendent presented the Jordan shaft as a turnaround-in-the-making to Seth Wilson. Of course, it would not be easy. Of course, there were two or three presently viable shafts on the mine, but for a young man with several years' production experience Jordan was the place to begin.

Seth raised his concern that Jordan had only met its production target one month out of the last 12. These concerns fell on unsympathetic ears. The superintendent was convinced the ore was there and that fresh perspective and youthful ambition were all that were needed to coax the gold from the earth. The ore production target shortfalls for the past year averaged only about 10–20% each month; certainly Seth had it in him to create this marginal improvement. Had Seth more experience, the lack of development over the past year on Jordan shaft would have figured much more prominently in the discussion. Even so, a much more pressing problem was soon apparent.

Jordan shaft had been a problem to Occidental mine long before Seth Wilson's arrival. It was not only a matter of often failing to produce 150kg of gold a month, but also Jordan shaft was Mr. Kile's private fiefdom. Jan Kile was an Occidental institution. He had spent years placing his relatives throughout the section and was now able to offer senior management a multitude of incontestable reasons why objectives could not be met. And if this were not enough, he had on occasion influenced the surveyors to measure his section's production favourably. Jan Kile was comfortable. He used the system to his benefit. If outside suppliers were willing to court him, he would order their products. With Occidental's own resources Mr. Kile could be quite generous. Frequently, several of the 300 laborers in the section could be found working off the mine property during the shift. This lapse was discreetly tolerated by Mr. Kile. The few mine supplies that could be used elsewhere were always over-ordered.

Jan's comfortable situation persisted for some time, but as it became more difficult to meet production targets, and as costs throughout the southern African mining industry rose considerably, Jan's methods became untenable. He had on occasion attempted to influence the surveyors to measure his section's production favorably. Shortly before Seth's arrival, Jan resigned and Seth replaced him.

During Seth's first month on the mine, before he became responsible for Jordan shaft, there were glimpses and whispers of its chequered past. Most people were sympathetic but not forthcoming with vital information. Seth often suspected that anyone contemptuous was Jan's relative or ally. His suspicions were nearly always correct. Seth would soon become aware that although the chief was gone, his lieutenants remained.

As if the section's physical and staff problems were not enough, the superintendent was due to retire within two years. The mine manager had been passed over for promotion many times.

He expected to retire later, too, but this was his last opportunity to create a sense of trepidation in his subordinates by asserting the superintendent's authority. The underground manager, Mr. Bauer, was competent, energetic, and knowledgeable, presenting the image of a modern rational manager, and it was surprising that he had not advanced further. However, his life's most impressionable experience was fighting as a soldier in one of the continent's older conflicts.

How had Seth found himself in this position? The divisional manager in the corporate office met briefly twice a year with all the young, high-potential staff in his region. Over the last eighteen months the relationship that developed between Seth and the divisional manager was businesslike but detached. Occidental was the weakest performer of the many mines in his division. It was also the one most under the spotlight of corporate attention. When a position became available for reasons that Seth may never entirely know, a transfer was initiated. The divisional manager in all likelihood had some knowledge of the shortage of available ore and of the difficult personnel problems on the Jordan shaft.

As Seth took over the Jordan shaft in May, the superintendent's words from the previous week were ringing in his ears, "You have to play with the cards you are dealt." When asked if he agreed with this statement, Seth wholeheartedly replied, "That is absolutely right." Seth spent dozens of evenings in the antiquated planning department's files reviewing Jordan's ore body extraction and development over the years. He had enjoyed deciphering the very old plans, and was pleased, when after several hours' effort, he found an out-of-sequence or misplaced plan. If the mining was anything like the planning, hard work in terms of effort and perseverance would pay off. These cards were bad, but they could be played. What Seth did not know that first day in May was that these bad cards were the best he had.

Seth calculated that development would have to increase nearly 400% to sustain the production of 150kg of gold a month. This was possible. However, the real problem was determining where to develop. If the wrong area was accessed, the gold content of the rock might not support the required level of gold production. There was little room for error because they were exhausting the ore body daily. This was the primary focus of his first meeting with his shift supervisors who appeared to be typical of mine staff. One of the four could have actually worked elsewhere in the mine, while the other three had been selected by Mr. Kile for other reasons.

Mr. de Bruyn, in charge of 13-level, had Mr. Kile's brother working for him as his most senior foreman. On 15-level Mr. Van Bil, who often achieved his production targets, was the anchor for section's production. Mr. Whyte on 18-level had overstepped his abilities. The rigors of a section and the responsibility for 60 people left him overextended. The night shift supervisor was Mr. Riley, married to Mr. Kile's sister. Other relationships with Mr. Kile became apparent with the passage of time.

June

Once again the Jordan shaft had underperformed by 15% in May. Seth had emphasized the importance of development and began daily to traipse through various parts of the shaft, with special emphasis on 18-level where his superiors felt the future was. He began to have doubts. One newly opened portion was found to have sub-economic ore; the cost of mining would exceed the revenue. Another of the working areas was very difficult to keep open. In effect, the roof kept coming down.

Mr. Bauer was adversarial every morning, offering no solutions, only management rhetoric, during his morning meetings. During their joint underground visits, the focus was constantly on details. As soon as Seth mentioned the lack of payable or accessible ore, Mr. Bauer would focus on track alignment or inadequately supported ventilation piping. They were not communicating. Seth felt that Mr. Bauer's bombastic tone was insincere, and Mr. Bauer felt that if details were adhered to the gold would appear.

When Seth was not the subject of Mr. Bauer's verbal abuse, he was coaxing and cajoling his shift supervisors to perform. Already, he had decided that somehow or some way Mr. Whyte had to be replaced and Mr. Riley had to leave the section.

Seth also was appalled at the daily attendance figures among the laborers and even some of the junior foremen. To combat absenteeism Seth began using the harshest response permissible by the company; three unexcused absences within a year warranted a dismissal. Once a week, Seth, together with the personnel staff, would complete the dismissal paperwork, and as a result, often three or four men were fired.

To advance the 18-level haulages to the portion of ore that was nearly one year away, a small obstacle had to be overcome. Over the past 20 years, a loading gate connecting 18-level to another disused shaft system had rusted through, allowing the broken rock to pour onto the rails of the haulage, blocking passage to its end, 100 meters ahead. As no one had worked in this part of the mine for at least 10 years the obstacle had never been a concern. Now that 18-level was in the spotlight, this had to change. Extending the haulage would not be possible until the broken rock was removed. Every day as a train load of rock would be loaded and hauled away, more rock would pour through the gate. No one seemed to know how much rock remained above.

Mr. Van Bil was close to meeting his targets for 15-level, and had a reasonable projection for the next two months. Many of the working places on 13-level were sub-economic or near the margin. Mr. de Bruyn and Kile's brother were not concerned about the payability nor the lack of ore in six weeks' time. Their joint approach to Seth was to agree with everything and do nothing.

Seth's monthly review with the mine's top management appeared to go well. He tried to be upbeat and Mr. Bauer was noticeably quiet. They went through the plans level by level. Every time he tried to raise the issue of payability or where, based on their many years' of experience on Occidental, to investigate, either the subject changed or an insubstantial palliative was offered. The superintendent, in pronouncing the review over, said he was hearing good things about Seth through his various sources, however, the results of the Jordan shaft were expected to improve over the next few months. The mine manager remained distant from the entire review.

July

Two pressing concerns confronted Seth at the beginning of July; the superintendent's underground inspection and who would replace Mr. Whyte on 18-level. Seth convinced his superior of the need for a replacement, however, he was not permitted to influence the selection of the new supervisor and, even if he could, he did not know individuals on other shafts. Mr. Bauer would draw the replacement from another shaft.

As for the Superintendent's inspection, tradition dictated that this be a highly orchestrated affair. Usually, one or two of the other shafts would lend a crew for two or three days to help tidy the workings. Although this temporary allocation occurred, it was never acknowledged, although it was highly probable that the superintendent was aware of his staff's behavior, he never broached the subject. Sometimes the inspections were announced months in advance, while at other times less than a week's notice was given. As this was to be Seth's first inspection on Occidental, he was anxious to inspire confidence and make a favorable impression.

Regarding the ore-pass problem on 18-level, either Mr. Bauer and the mine manager were uninformed on the situation or were withholding information from him. This ore pass led to an old shaft system that was abandoned while both of them worked on the mine. As for his staff, Seth was frustrated that they could not solve this problem; yet he did not expect them to do something dangerous. No sooner would they report that all the ore was removed than the following day the timber crew would telephone to say more rock had fallen onto the tracks. After spending several late hours at the planning office reviewing diagrams of the area, Seth concluded that between shifts he and one of the laborers would clear the ore pass from its top in the abandoned shaft system.

Seth felt that by doing a challenging job that had defeated others, he would lead by example, and also that clever methods would inspire confidence in his staff. Explosives would be lowered into the ore pass and then detonated from a considerable distance. Seth explained to his shift supervisors the details, and made arrangements to pick up the explosives underground. It was important, Seth felt, that his staff knew what he was doing and that the origin of this idea was his. With the exception of unanticipated time spent walking underground to the old shaft system, the plan to clear the ore pass worked flawlessly. But his success had little effect on the attitude of his staff. The following morning he concealed his anger when Mr. Bauer did not even offer grudging acknowledgment.

Seth's nightly efforts in the planning office began to pay off. On 13-level he found seven or eight weeks of ore in two separate blocks. This ground was confirmed on one of his weekly inspections, and was found to be high grade. At the time he wondered why De Bruyn and Kile's brother showed so little interest.

Sometime, also, he had mentioned to Mr. Bauer that, overall the Jordan shaft was under manned. Mr. Bauer admitted that several shafts on Occidental were short of labor. Seth pointed out that his production targets were based on having enough men to do the job. Finally, Mr. Bauer said a mine-wide reallocation would occur and that the four shafts under him would be able to increase their crews from about 50 men that had been transferred. On Wednesday morning, one supervisor would go from each shaft to select men.

Seth had some experience with reallocations. Typically, management shed their worse people, and with 50 men this would be more of a circus than normal. Seth decided to send his most competent supervisor, Mr. Van Bil, and his night shift supervisor. He expected them there one hour before time. Because they had arrived so early, the Jordan shaft got its allocation, and some of the men had good records. Seth arrived on the shaft that morning to find his colleagues on the other shafts howling mad. Their men had arrived only 30 minutes early! When his colleagues complained to Mr. Bauer, Seth was mildly surprised that no changes were made.

The superintendent's visit near the end of the month was unsatisfactory. Seth and Mr. Bauer both anticipated that 18-level would be the focus of attention. Several days before, extra effort was made to clean the expected route and making sure that all equipment was in order. Seth had reasonable answers to all the superintendent's questions, although he felt that some questions should have been directed to Mr. Bauer or the mine manager, who were also part of the entourage.

When they entered the 18-level haulage extension, the superintendent was upset that no one knew why an escapeway to the disused shaft system above was made so large. This excavation had been planned several months before Seth's arrival and everyone of his superiors had approved of it weeks before he was responsible for its excavation. By then, no one was interested in seeing the success they had in plugging the old ore pass problem and the superintendent stormed out.

In retrospect, Seth felt that although he did not design or approve the excavation, if he had not been so busy with other matters he could have got the paperwork rolling to change the dimensions. He knew that both Mr. Bauer and the mine manager were the first and the second line of defense in preventing specifying larger-than-necessary dimensions, yet he did not attempt to shift the blame.

July's review somehow overcame the visit failure. The Jordan shaft had managed to hold its shortfall at previous levels and development actually increased. His superiors seemed to be in a hurry to meet other appointments. Seth did note that the mine manager had a lot more to say, however, it was just a milder version of the daily cacophony that Mr. Bauer provided every morning. He was disappointed that none of these three men provided any advice that could be translated into direct action. Seth realized how alone he was.

August

Seth believed the solution was to work harder. He had a new man on 18-level and he was intent on other changes. Seth's plan was for Mr. De Bruyn and Kile's brother to spend the afternoon redirecting the railway tracks to a more convenient haulage to access the two new blocks on 13-level. With their supervision it would take eight men about five hours. Working in the haulages after the shift's blast is usually difficult because it takes several hours for the fumes to clear. This area of the 13-level haulage was a fresh air intake and would not be affected by blasting fumes. Weekend haulage work would be a good opportunity to show everyone in the section that extra effort was required. It was also very efficient planning.

Earlier in the week, he had gotten approval from Mr. Bauer for his plan, and had instructed Mr. De Bruyn to select eight men for the overtime work. Normally, one shift supervisor stayed on until the shift was cleared from underground. Seth anticipated that Kile's brother or Mr. De Bruyn would, in some way, thwart his plans so it was his intention to spend time in his office reading and catching up on paperwork.

Early that morning, Kile's brother called in sick. Within three hours, Mr. De Bruyn was complaining from 13-level via the mine telephone that he was having difficulties finalizing the arrangements for the between-shift period. Seth was livid but undeterred. He shouted that at the shift's end he would personally review Mr. De Bruyn's progress, and if only he and Seth were left to complete the work, so be it. They would work through the night to Monday morning to finish.

When Seth arrived, the situation was a shambles, only three laborers remained and Mr. De Bruyn was full of excuses. All Seth could think of was that after 20 years De Bruyn should know how to organize overtime weekend work despite his senior foreman's absence. This failure was deliberate. Yet no matter how well he presented it to Mr. Bauer, Seth knew that Mr. Bauer would not support De Bruyn's dismissal. Seth felt that under the circumstance if the five of them spent 10 hours completing the work, not only would his weekend be ruined but De Bruyn's as well. Because De Bruyn was in no shape for arduous labor and would be exhausted and angry, perhaps some of his anger would percolate down to Kile's brother, the man who initiated this problem. The hours wore on but they finally cleared the shaft at 8:30 p.m. The trains would be taking a new route on Monday, and have full access to develop the new blocks on 13-level.

Two positive developments occurred in August that heartened Seth. The first was that the new blocks on 13-level were marginally larger, and the grade of the ore was significantly better than expected. The second positive development was his efforts at improving attendance. When he started, at its worst, sometimes 30 laborers were absent. Presently, only five to eight workers were absent daily. This was tangible. Unfortunately, he was surrounded on all fronts by other difficulties, severely restraining any feelings of optimism. At best, all he could conclude was that he could, after an inordinate amount of time identify some areas of promise. His policy of discharging laborers for work-practice violations did have some effect. However, he was responsible for several hundred people and several square kilometers of the mine. The obstacle was motivating his shift supervisors and their senior foremen to act.

Shortly before the month's end Mr. Bauer declared that he had been reviewing the amount of ore hoisted from the shaft and that it was noticeably below the amount calculated from blasting.

Seth was aware of this discrepancy and although he felt there were more pressing problems like finding gold rather than moving unpayable rock, he had no choice but to join the mine manager and Mr. Bauer on a midnight tour to review cleaning procedures on 18-level. Seth was somewhat surprised that the mine manager's first visit would be at night. Where had he been for the last three months?

Most items underground were in order, and the topic of conversation was general mine matters. For some reason Seth did not raise his litany of problems, nor were they especially inquisitive. When they arrived in the working area, they stopped near one of the intermediary scrapers that dragged the ore out to the trains. The three men watched a wire rope drag a partially full scraper out and bring the same one back empty every 40 seconds. Little was said. Seth mentioned that the support problems remained unsolved in this area and that by next month additional winches from elsewhere would be in place.

The mine manager motioned that it was time to leave, and they scrambled out to the haulage. The mine manager told Seth and Mr. Bauer that he had observed worn scrapers, and from his own budget he would allocate four new scrapers to Seth's section. Typically, scrapers, depending on use, only lasted a few months. Although Seth was grateful for new scrapers, the ones observed were only a few weeks old, and the overall effect of new ones would be negligible. Seth had trouble accepting that he was getting the best from the mine manager's 30 years of experience.

During the monthly planning meeting, Seth stared in disbelief as Mr. Bauer increased his budget figures by nearly 10%. There was not enough ore to meet his previous target, let alone this new one. And then Mr. Bauer had the audacity to say he would try to get him some of the winches he had been requesting for months.

Surely this was convincing proof that his superior had a fundamental lack of understanding about the underground situation? Those words about playing with the cards you are dealt with came back to haunt him. Could it be that he failed to convey the severity of the problem to Mr. Bauer? Mr. Bauer had nearly 20 years' experience in the mines. Mr. Bauer could compare the ratio of winches, drills, men, etc., to the amount of monthly production with the other shafts under his responsibility. Seth long wondered if Mr. Bauer was not allocating his resources equitably. The fact that Mr. Bauer would refuse to answer questions on the subject added to his suspicion.

August's review passed without serious incident. The superintendent noted the development on 13-level but quickly focused on the poor results on 18. Seth went through his litany of reasons, the new shift supervisor had only been there for a month, and Mr. Riley, the night shift Supervisor, had been replaced the day before. The mine manager shed his quiet stance and cited some head office or management text theories about applying men and material to the task at hand. Seth now thought that the mine manager really did not understand the underground situation. He knew that whatever initial goodwill bestowed upon him by the superintendent was now gone. Seth just felt it and saw it on the superintendent's face. He knew either that Occidental's production targets would be met or his days were numbered.

September

With grim resolve, Seth confronted another month. He was spending in excess of 12 hours a day, Monday through Friday, on the mine and somewhat less on the weekend. Few, if anyone on the mine could offer consolation, let alone advice, with a semblance of impartiality. The few times he met people in the community considerable tension was evident. He had spent such long hours on the mine that he had been unable to weave himself into the social fabric of the community.

During the first week of the month, Kile's brother did not come to work and was not contactable. Seth began to draw up the discharge paperwork. After three days passed without hearing from him, Seth felt that at a bare minimum he could have Kile's brother transferred if not fired. Even Mr. Bauer would have to support a transfer. Kile's brother had many allies and was well-placed with the union. His wife brought a letter from a doctor to one of the shift supervisor's home explaining that her husband could not come to work for seven more days. Seth had completed all the disciplinary paperwork, and had found a younger, more energetic, replacement. Although he had recommended dismissal, Seth knew despite Mr. Bauer's military demeanor, he would not have the stomach to dismiss someone who had ten years' service with the company. An unsatisfactory production record for over a year, calling in sick the day the haulages were rerouted, and now, not informing a shift supervisor of his absence for three days should more than warrant a dismissal. Seth had no choice but to accept Mr. Bauer's recommendation to transfer Kile's brother to a lower paying position and not dismiss him.

The promise of the newly opened areas on 18-level never materialized. The area had been fully assayed and the values were not close to being economic. During one of the planning meetings, Seth finally thought he had framed the problem in such a way that Mr. Bauer had to provide a well-considered rationale for such unrealistic targets with no ore to mine. In response Mr. Bauer simply pointed to the subeconomic areas on 18 and said, "Mine here. What else are you going to do?"

In their minds Seth and Mr. Bauer knew that delivering below grade ore to the concentrator was expensive, and it robbed, through dilution, some of the gold in the ore coming from other shafts. The net result would be to increase costs and decrease revenue. Seth now realized that the management pressure for tons of rock far outweighed commercial sanity. Mr. Bauer was prepared to sacrifice profit in order to quench his superiors' thirst for tons. Seth was not. To him, what was suggested was wrong, and Seth would be responsible, not Mr. Bauer. Seth was capable of compromise, but not under these conditions. Seth did not plan to mine the subeconomic areas. As he left the plans with Mr. Bauer, he wondered what would be the greater problem, lack of payable ore next month or the lack of production this month.

September ended decisively. The Jordan shaft's ore production was nearly 30% below the planned target. Seth had anticipated 13-level's weak performance. Little had changed on 18-level; however, 15-level's results were truly unanticipated. Rather than coming in somewhat high, 15-level had slightly under-achieved. With all Jordan's other problems, the additional shortfall had not been apparent. Seth wondered if he would last the month. Mr. Bauer and he had a loud argument shortly after the results were known. Mr. Bauer did not consider the Jordan's true situation. During this acrimonious outburst, Seth emphasized that development had improved by more than 200%, and that absenteeism had been reduced to nearly zero.

On the third morning of the month, Mr. Bauer informed Seth that within the next few weeks Seth would leave Occidental. In the meantime, he would fill in on another shaft. One of the last points that Mr. Bauer made was that the motivation for the transfer had come from the superintendent and mine manager. Mr. Bauer said that he had tried to give Seth another month. Several days later when the superintendent was discussing future plans with Seth, Seth could not help but remember Mr. Bauer's comment when the superintendent said "he had no choice but to accept the mine manager's and Mr. Bauer's recommendation for Seth's transfer." Seth wondered if the mine manager would also deny responsibility for the transfer.

Post September

Initially, after Seth's departure from the Jordan, ore production improved somewhat. However, within four months, after extraordinary shortfalls exceeding previous figures, the Jordan's target was reduced by 60%. During this time, Seth was promoted to a new position on another mine.

Seth's replacement on the Jordan had to contend with grave problems in addition to production, and ultimately was transferred to a technical position far away from Occidental. By the end of the year, the Jordan shaft's production had been merged with another shaft. Somewhat later a major shake-up occurred at the corporate offices that coincided approximately with the superintendent's retirement. Fundamental reductions were initiated mine-wide to optimize results.

A few years passed before traditional underground activity ceased.

32
Managing a Diverse Work Force in Indonesia

John E. Walsh, Jr.

Indonesian Enterprises

Paul Korsvald, the general manager of a large Norwegian paper company's subsidiary, Indonesian Enterprises, had several decisions to make before the day was over. His first decision was whether to build a small mosque next to his corrugated carton plant near Jakarta, Java. Among the Indonesian Enterprise workers, 34 were Chinese and were primarily Confucians and Buddists, 4 were Javanese Christians, and 2 of Indian extraction were Hindus. The other 352 plant workers and supervisors and the 48 office managers, and workers under him said they were Muslims (see Appendix). Many, however, were not strict followers. They practiced an Islam that had been blended with Hindu, Buddhist, and other beliefs. Jim Sterba (*Wall Street Journal*, September 29, 1987) observes:

> Islam is different in the world's largest Moslem nation, Indonesia. It has a sense of humor. It doesn't seem so stern and insistent. It is more tolerant than Islam elsewhere.

This toleration was attributed by scholars to Indonesia's vast diverse land and population. The country, comprising 13,677 islands of which 6,000 are populated and covering 3,200 miles, has a population of more than 180 million people of 366 different ethnic groups. Although 250 different languages are spoken, Bhasa Indonesia is the official language taught in the schools. Half of the population was Javanese and two thirds of all Indonesians lived in Java, which constituted 7% of the land mass.

Friday is the holiest day of the week for Muslims, and the company was required by custom to permit workers, especially the men, to attend noon prayers and collective recitals of the Koran. Although government offices closed at 11:00 a.m. on

Fridays, Indonesian Enterprises' policy was to close the plant and offices from 11:30 a.m. until 2:30 p.m. only. Paul Korsvald observed that typically fewer than 20 Muslim factory and office workers returned to work on Friday. Many excuses were given by the others such as it was impossible to catch a bus or services were longer than expected.

Actually, after services was a time for workers to visit with friends to gossip and learn what had taken place during the week. It was also a time to bargain, barter, and buy a variety of goods and food sold near the mosque.

What bothered Paul Korsvald most was the loss in production output and paying people for not working. The average monthly salary for factory workers was approximately US $100; for office workers, it was US $150 for a six-day work week. The day began at 7:00 a.m. and ended at 3:30 p.m. including an hour-and-a-half for lunch.

How could he meet the religious needs of the Muslims and non-Muslims without losing production output and keeping costs down? To build a mosque would cost about US $30,000. Four thousand dollars of this would be spent to purchase and transport sacred stones from Mecca. If Korsvald decided to buy the mosque, he would then have to obtain the services of the local hadji (one who had made the pilgrimage to Mecca) for US $15 to bless the ground before construction began. In addition, he would be required to purchase a goat for sacrifice for about US$ 20. The goat's head would be buried near the mosque; the remainder given to the workers for a feast. He would also have to provide onions and green peppers to be placed on a stick to keep the rains away on the opening day of the mosque.

If he decided not to build the mosque, Paul Korsvald could also continue the current practice or he could rent seven buses for three hours, at a cost of US $50 per bus. While the buses would probably arrive on time to take the employees to the mosque, Korsvald was unsure if employees would return to the factory on the buses.

The Possible Purchase of Call or Prayer Call Clocks

Korsvald was faced with another dilemma as well: whether to buy from Maruem Murakemi and Company, Ltd. either ten semi-automatic prayer call clocks or fully automatic prayer call clocks, or some combination of the two. Good Muslims are required to pray five times a day, first in the morning when they arise, before lunch, mid-afternoon, after sunset and before retiring. This schedule did not have to be followed to the letter, for according to the Koran, "When ye journey about the earth, it is no crime to you that you come short in prayer if you fear that those that disbelieve will set upon you." Typically, employees would pray whenever they had spare time. However, by not praying at the prescribed times, some of the reward was lost. According to Muslim tradition, every corner of Allah's universe was equally pure, so the employees would spread their prayer rugs wherever they were when they decided to pray. Standing erect with their hands on either side of their face and their thumbs touching the lobes of their ears, they would begin, "God is most great." Still standing, they would continue with the opening Ayat (passage from the holy Koran):

Praise belongs to God, Lord of the Worlds,
The Compassionate, the Merciful.
King of the day of Judgment.
Tis thee we worship and thee we ask for help.
Guide us in the straight path.
The path of those whom thou hast favored.
Not the path of those who incur thine anger
Nor of those who go astray.

Unfortunately for Paul Korsvald, the prayers continued from noon to afternoon, because each Muslim employee would wait until he or she had spare time. If Paul Korsvald bought the semi-automatic clocks for US $30 and the fully automatic for $35 and placed them in prominent locations throughout the plant and office, the clocks could be synchronized to proclaim an Azan (prayer call) ten minutes before noon and at 2:40 in the afternoon.

Another option existed. He could eliminate the lunch hour, the practice of the Dutch-owned companies, and end the working day at 2:00 p.m. Rather than buy the clocks, he would make it known through supervisors that plant operations would cease ten minutes before noon for prayers.

The Need to Increase Productivity During Ramadan

A third decision confronting Korsvald dealt with solving the problem of low productivity of employees during Ramadan, the holy month of fasting and the ninth month in the Arabian calendar. In this month, Muhammed, according to Muslim tradition, received the holy Koran from God as guidance for his people and made his hyiria from Mecca to Medina. From dawn to dusk, during this period Muslims abstain from food and drink. Among those automatically exempted were the sick, the very old, very young, pregnant and nursing women, soldiers in war, and persons on long trips. Although no one in Indonesia is legally compelled to fast, many Muslim employees did.

When Ramadan fell during the hottest season, fasting took its toll. Employees, observing tradition, were noticeably nervous, excitable, and prone to flare-ups of temper. Korsvald estimated that productivity in the plant and office declined 20–30%. Korsvald had identified three options to address this issue and suspected there were others. First, he could start the plant at 3:30 in the afternoon and end at midnight. Second, he could close the plant for two weeks and require employees to take their vacations during this time. Third, he could require only those Muslim employees who were fasting to take vacations.

Selecting the Manager of the Accounting Department

A fourth decision had nothing to do with religion. He had to decide whether Mr. Abukar, a native Javan, or Mr. James Lee, an Indonesian of Chinese nationality, should be appointed to the position of manager of the accounting department. In Norway, promotion decisions were primarily based upon employee's prior work performance. However, discussions with other Western general managers operating in Java and researchers from *Business International* revealed a consensus that decisions on promotions in Indonesia placed more importance on ethnic background, personalities, and individual circumstances. Thus, managers in Indonesia had to consider whether a prospective manager was Javanese, an outer islander, Chinese, or Indian. Although Indonesia's motto is "Unity in Diversity," it made a difference for instance if a prospective manager was Javanese, Sumatran, or Moluccan.

The Javanese are considered an agrarian-based conservative people proud of their traditions and strong family ties. They value harmony and sensitivity to others, characteristics that historians attribute to feudal influences. Additionally, they are reluctant to convey information that could displease business associations or cause conflicts.

The outer Islanders, the Bataks of Sumatra and the Moluccans, are more prone to say what they think. The Dutch set up large tobacco, rubber, and palm oil estates in Northern Sumatra, so modern agricultural developments were concentrated there. Because these products were produced primarily for export in contrast to rice production in Java, which is consumed locally, natives possessed greater experience in international trade. The straightforwardness of the outer islanders complemented the style of Western managers, resulting in a disproportionate number of outer islanders holding key positions in foreign companies in Java.

While the Chinese accounted for less than 2% of the population, they played a key role in business and owned, according to reliable sources, more than 50% of the nation's private capital. Despite high levels of education and administrative experience, they were excluded from the bureaucracy and the military, which was dominated by the Javanese.

The official ideology of the Indonesian government was Pancasila, which consisted of five principles affirming belief in one God, humanitarianism, national unity, democracy, and social justice. A balance between national unity and social justice proved difficult. Any foreign company having too many Chinese executives would be vulnerable to resentment from indigenous Indonesians (pribumi) workers, and the Indonesian government might intervene and press for social justice. While Indians were also vulnerable to resentment they were too small a group to constitute a threat.

Paul Korsvald had many issues to consider. James Lee was older, and age was important to Indonesians. He was unquestionably the best qualified of the two, technically and in managerial experience. He had more years of work experience with the company. Lee, fearing a backlash from the pribumi staff, might fail to give them firm orders to take disciplinary actions when needed.

On the other hand, Mr. Abukar was reasonably competent technically, pleasant to all employees and well-liked by the Indonesian accounting staff. He came from a respectable family, with several relatives working as lower level executives in the government. Further, the promotion would help him financially, because he had a large family to support. In the past, he had been extremely loyal to the company. He had been reluctant, however, to assume authority, make decisions, and work over-time. Due to a dearth of pribumi managers, it would not be difficult for Mr. Abukar to find another job at a higher salary.

Korsvald could seek a consensus (mufakat) of his key executives through tedious consultation (muskawarah). Whatever choice this consensus brought about, he risked shaming the candidate (malu) in front of others if he did not handle the pro-motion well. Under no circumstances did he want to create malu.

The Need to Formulate Policies

His last decision was how to formulate a policy covering responsibilities of his employees to achieve results, to reduce kickbacks, and to determine under what cir-cumstances loans would be made to employees.

The frequent cases of stomach ulcers and heart attacks among European and American managers in Indonesia, he thought, resulted from their failure to counter-act djamkeret ("dj" pronounced like "j") or rubber time. He observed that Indonesians could not be rushed and would leave an employer who tried to make them move faster or work harder. When asked, "When will the job be finished," adherents to djamkeret would simply reply, "sometime during the next few days." Modern plants with international commitments could not operate this way. So, he needed a policy that could dampen the excuses of djamkeret.

European companies operating in Asia have been offering bribes and kickbacks since the 1600s when the British East India Company won duty-free treatment for its exports by giving Mongol rulers expensive gifts including rare paintings and carvings. Korsvald, however, had difficulty adjusting to the succession of kickbacks and payoffs necessary to conduct business in Indonesia. On one occasion, his sales manager had to send twelve bottles of scotch for a party given by a purchasing agent of a large corporate customer. On another, he had to give U.S. $10,000 to the large corporate customer's local director. In the latter case, he was surprised to receive a silver tray as a gift from the local director. Last year on Christmas morning, he awoke to find a Christmas tree brightly lit and heavy with gleaming ornaments. On it was a card from another company's director to whom he had been forced to make kickbacks for years. "Muslim economics require that the wealth of her people be widely shared," he mused, "it insists that acquisitions and competitiveness be bal-anced by fair play and compassion."

In addition to kickbacks to customers, many foreign businessmen in Indonesia felt it was necessary to place someone in power in the Indonesian government associat-ed with their company. It was rumored the family of the president of Indonesia owned shares in 15 companies including a hotel, a flour mill, and two cement factories. The president's brother strongly denied any favoritism and added that several charitable foundations were set up with business earnings.

Trading on influence was not considered corrupt unless it involved excesses. To maintain a low profile, distant relatives of top military and government officials were placed as heads or directors of companies rather than members of their immediate families.

Korsvald observed that the Chinese were adaptable. If they had to give gifts to generals or make deposits to an official's Singapore bank account and become friends for life, they did so. According to Barry Newman in (*Wall Street Journal,* April 14, 1978):

> The strategy of gift giving has been perfected by Cukongs of Indonesia, about 30 moneyed Chinese who have made fortunes for themselves and, as it happens, for the country's ruling elite. "We don't worry," says a manager in one of their many companies. "We have information first hand. We know what's going on." Occasionally, when there is money to be made, a Cukong will take a fellow Chinese for a ride on his coattails.

Korsvald wondered if kickbacks and payoffs to high officials known as the "untouchables" should be continued by his company. Frequently, he had trouble determining whether middlemen who received bribes from the company to give to his ranking officials still had influence. He was never sure how much to pay or if he was paying the right person. His experience in Indonesia convinced him that establishing good personal relations and trust did not always entail a payoff.

Lower-level civil servants continually practiced the ancient Indonesian form of social commerce called the "sticky handshake." Traditionally, funds acquired through extortion were called "smooth money," "lubricating money" or "rule 2000" (it will cost you 2,000 rupiahs). More recently, they have been labeled "illegal levies" and were required for everything from processing a passport to exporting corrugated boxes. It would be almost impossible to stop "illegal levies," because low-level civil servants needed them to live. Nevertheless, the National Command for the Restoration of Security and Order, a government body, was, at present, trying to ban illegal levies. The response was a combination of outrage and jealousy from civil servants who believed that the higher-ups were taking more and not spreading it around. Although Indonesian Enterprises' workers were better paid than civil servants, they, too, sought ways to increase their incomes. Any items the company had in stock that could be sold easily, like glue and starch, had to be closely monitored and physically secured, or they would be stolen.

Korsvald knew compassion was necessary and could produce practical results each morning. He provided free bottles of "vitasoy," soy bean milk processed in Indonesia by the Hong Kong Soy Bean Products Company of Hong Kong, to mitigate the effects on his employees of malnutrition and tuberculosis, both common aliments in Indonesia. The result was an increase in worker productivity.

Sometimes, though, his compassion created problems. He gave 25 corrugated boxes to one employee who said he wanted the boxes for moving to a new home. Later, he discovered that the boxes were sold to a woman going to Pakistan. When Korsvald confronted the employee, the employee became nervous and started to cry. "My wife was sick and I needed the money," the employee sobbed, "I'm not a criminal." Korsvald knew it would be difficult to fire the employee because of strict Indonesian labor laws, so he returned the money to the woman and treated the payment as an advance loan to the employee. Later, the employee sent flowers to Korsvald.

He wondered about what other policies he should prepare for purchasing and advancing loans. Should his purchasing agent be responsible for all purchases up to a certain amount, say $300 in Indonesian rupiahs? Should the purchasing agent be able to further delegate authority to other departments? Should he let a policy on advance loans be made by the comptroller? Weren't there inherent dangers?

In one Western company in Jakarta, when loan policies were delegated to a pribumi comptroller, salary advances had more than quadrupled. The chief executive called in the comptroller to find out if the report was in error. It was not.

The comptroller said that, rather than follow the policy blindly, cases were judged individually. The company's new chief engineer needed a large sum of money to pay three years' rent advance for the house he had just leased and such advances were normal in Jakarta. A one-year advance in pay was made to an older employee who was making his pilgrimage to Mecca (Haj), which every devout Muslim was required to do at least once in his or her life. While the comptroller gave explanations for each advance in salary, the chief executive noticed a loan of four months' salary to a recently hired factory worker. When the comptroller was questioned about this advance he said, "The man is my brother-in-law, and my wife would be embarrassed if I didn't grant him this favor."

Korsvald wanted policies that would prevent such a problem from occurring in Indonesian Enterprises.

Appendix: Islam and the Koran

The word *Islam* literally means submission to the will of anybody, but in a religious sense it is properly defined as acceptance of what has been ordered or commanded by God via a man named Muhammed. The principles that regulate the life of Muslims in their relationship with God are called the Five Pillars of Islam. The first pillar is Islam's creed, "There is no God but Allah and Muhammed is his prophet." The second pillar is prayer and Muslims are required to be constant in prayer which under normal conditions means praying five times a day. The third pillar of Islam is charity. Those with money should help those who are less fortunate. The fourth pillar is the observance of Ramadan the ninth month of the Arabian Calendar. Ramadan commemorates God's making Muhammed a prophet and ten years later Muhammed's Hijiah flight from a Mecca to Medina. The fifth pillar of Islam is pilgrimage. Once during a lifetime a Muslim is expected to visit Mecca.

The word *Koran* literally means "that which is read," but to Muslims it is the sacred book that contains the word of God as revealed to Muhammed. The book consists of 114 chapters, of 6,000 verses, and over 80,000 words. There is no specific order except the shorter chapters are at the beginning. It contains information pertaining to prophets and the people to whom they were sent. It also contains laws, dogmas, and ethical ideas. In addition, it is considered by Muslims as a first-rate piece of literature. Many Muslim writers copy its style which they consider a miracle of eloquence. In many parts it is rhymed and unlike ordinary prose, it is chanted rather than read. During daily prayers Muslims usually recite the opening chapter of the Koran and any other part they like.

33
Banking on Diversity: Familiarity Breeds Contempt at Security First Bank

David O. Braaten

Introduction

Tossing the report summary she had just read for the third time onto her desk, Susan Respess leaned back in her chair and squeezed the small nerf basketball. It was difficult to believe an employee could write about Security First Bank, "I hate this place. I wish to God that I could win the lottery and walk away from this hell hole."

But someone had. The evidence was staring her in the face in the text of this preliminary report on communication in the organization. Whatever the other communication issues may have been, what caught her attention and focus was the harshness of many of the comments made about fellow workers, supervisors, and managers from different cultures. The existence of problems with the working relationships of the nonexempt workers, as well as their reactions to management, was a shock to the system.

Disappointing Results

It was clear that Susan's previous efforts at improving morale and team building in the operations group (OG) of Security First Bank were not as successful as she

This case has been prepared as a basis for discussion rather than to illustrate either effective or ineffective handling of an administrative situation. Names of the company and people have been disguised to preserve confidentiality. The author would like to acknowledge the assistance of Joseph Lombardo and Wendy Connelly in the preparation of this case.

had expected. In fact, informal indicators pointed to a steady decline over the past few months. As vice-president and manager of personnel, Susan was responsible for benefits, affirmative action, and training, which, by default, put her in charge of company morale. This also gave her the unpleasant task of going into the office of her boss, Chester Blanchard, executive vice-president for operations (EVP), with a set of reasons why her department's past efforts had not brought about the anticipated results. In addition, she needed some significant insights into the current problems among the nonexempt workers, as well as ideas for rebuilding morale.

Susan looked across her office and glared through the wall at the EVP's office. Chester had been EVP here at "3rd Street" for only six months and had become fascinated by the cultural diversity in the organization. He had encouraged the project that led to the report she had just finished. He believed that the employees in the group should be "one, big, happy SFB family" and expected her to make sure that happened.

Slowly shaking her head, Susan asked herself how you maintain, let alone improve, morale in an organization with 2,200 people, in two locations, who speak 64 different languages and dialects, many of whom are first generation immigrants? Things were a lot easier when her expected focus had been the white collar folks on the top eight floors. She threw the nerf ball at the backboard on her wall and hurried out the door to her third affirmative action complaint meeting this week. Chester will have to wait until tomorrow; in the meantime, she had better come up with something good—and soon.

Operations Group, Security First Bank

The Operations Group (OG) of SFB was the operational service facility for the hundreds of branches of SFB throughout the state of California. The OG ran on three shifts, 24 hours a day, though the night shift was a skeleton crew. Its personnel handled customer accounting, counted the daily cash transactions, moved the mail for the bank, and did all the electronic and paper handling. A semi-independent company of the bank, the OG was expected to run at a profit, providing income into the overall banking organization.

Of the total work force of 2,200 employees at two locations, about 1,700 people worked at the major facility located near downtown Los Angeles, and approximately 500 worked at the northern California facility near San Jose. Operations for the main facility in L.A. were organized into six divisions: commercial market services (CMS), retail market services (RMS), check processing services (CPS), electronic product division, management service division, and personal financial management. The San Jose facility housed departments from RMS, CPS, and CMS only. All the divisions are structured around the needs of the OG, branch customers, and individual financial customers.

Personal financial management was the smallest division and consisted of white collar professionals who sold financial products to individual and corporate clients. Management service division personnel included exempt (salaried) employees responsible for the overall management of the group, plan and control, as well as administrative project support. Offices for these two divisions were on the floors two through eight of the 3rd Street facility. Also above ground were interbank compensation, product support, product management, daylight overdraft, branch control, automated clearing house, money transfer operations, and cash management departments of the CMS. The RMS departments of duplicating and consumer credit are above ground as well.

The remaining two divisions were below ground, as were the rest of the departments of the CMS (customer services, lockbox, and overdrafts) and RMS divisions (returned items, adjustments, microfilm, branch services production support, statements, cash vault and publications). The electronic product division handled telephone banking. CPS was responsible for mail and distribution, proofing, reconcilement, batching, sorting, high-speed processing, and receiving and dispatching.

OG Employees

The operations group of SFB was a culturally diverse work environment, though this diversity was reflected in particular divisions of the organization rather than the OG as a whole. This diversity was pointed to with some pride by the OG management as an indication of the fair hiring practices of SFB. The concentration of cultural groups was not noticed by upper management.

The personnel of the management service and personal finance management divisions were primarily of European descent. For clerical and support staff positions, a high school education was important. Middle and upper managers were college educated, many holding business degrees. Managerial positions were usually filled through recruiting or transfer from bank branches. Promotions were often from within the management personnel.

Lower level managers were often promoted from supervisory personnel. Those workers who followed directions and worked hard were promoted from the "line" to be supervisors over the areas in which they worked. A high school education was helpful for earning promotion to these levels in the company, but not essential if other extenuating circumstances existed. These positions were filled mostly by Anglos, African Americans, and Filipinos, depending upon department. (Filipino supervisors were especially prevalent at the San Jose facility.)

The cultural diversity of the work force was seen in the labor intensive services of the departments of the CPS, RMS, and CMS, such as cash vault, batching, reconcilement, statements, etc. Because these jobs involved machine loading, counting, matching, sorting, and other manual skills, employees were able perform adequately without much formal education nor a command of English. In fact, in several areas, such as the cash vault where the cash is counted, most workers had minimal English ability, if any. In areas such as the mailroom, where knowledge of English was essential, most of the workers were Anglo or Chicano.

Major cultures present in the departments on the lower levels were Filipino, Mexican, Salvadoran, Chicano, African American, Anglo, Chinese, Korean, Japanese, Armenian, Eastern European, Indian, Vietnamese, Thai, and Middle Eastern. Most of these were immigrants.

Operational Structure of the OG

The OG was structured hierarchically. Upper management was headed by the executive vice-president, and reporting to him were division vice-presidents and managers, area directors and some special project assistant vice-presidents. Middle management included assistant vice-presidents, assistant managers, and some area managers depending on division and program. Lower management consisted of line managers and supervisors.

Upper and middle managers were expected to attend management training programs. Lower management was encouraged to go, except for supervisors, who were kept on the line when promoted, and were given basically punitive responsibilities over their workers.

OG Customers

The several hundred local branches of the SFB made up the primary customer base for the OG. To serve most effectively the needs of the branches, a goal of twenty-four-hour turn-around of all paper work and cash transactions was considered essential. Also crucial was the accuracy of the information flowing through the OG departments to and from the bank branches.

The individuals and companies who banked at SFB branch offices only dealt with local branch personnel; the OG operated, unknown and unseen, behind the scenes. Bank customers assumed that any problems they had with their banking transactions was the responsibility of the branch itself, even those services provided to the branches by the OG. Therefore, the accuracy, efficiency and effectiveness of the operations group were important to the branch managers. As a result, the branches put significant pressure on the OG management for timely and accurate service.

OG Physical Environment

At both facilities, the physical plant and layout were similar except for size. The Los Angeles facility had eight floors above ground and three levels below ground; San Jose had four floors above ground and three levels below.

The offices of most of management and exempt support staffing, with the exception of the training department, were housed on the upper floors. Basically, white collar and clerical support personnel were housed above ground, menial and blue collar jobs were performed on the lower levels. As with most hierarchical institutions, the more significant positions, such as upper management, essential support services and financial customer services, had offices on the higher floors.

Most "floor" work stations consisted of five-foot-high movable cubical walls within large open department areas. Most department managers had individual offices with large windows for easy eye contact with the floor. All the floor areas and offices were carpeted. Elevators were convenient, as were drinking fountains and restrooms. Windows brightened the work areas, and offices had windows as well. Interaction among employees was encouraged.

Lower "levels" flooring, with a few exceptions, was exposed cement. Access to the levels via elevators was limited, for security reasons. Restrooms and drinking fountains were inconveniently placed and their use was limited outside of break periods. Fluorescent ceiling lamps were the sole source of light in this windowless environment. Most work areas were open, broken-up by heavy machinery, or rows of work tables or desks. The noise from the operation of much of the mechanical equipment, such as check sorters, was extremely loud. Managers had private offices with one or two glass walls for observation of work areas. Supervisors had separate desk areas, but remained on the floor.

Morale and the VP

In the late night silence of the empty eighth floor, Susan heard only the buzz of her fluorescent lamp as she turned from the window where she often reflected on the events of the day while enjoying the lights of L.A. Her eyes searched for the cover of the report she had tossed on her desk earlier. Carefully sipping the scalding black coffee she had just brewed, she thought back to the implications of the report. Somehow she was missing the boat in her current morale/team building program.

HR Morale Boosters

Susan slowly sat down in the chair at her desk and a wry smile crossed her face as she mentally listed some of her previous efforts at morale and team building. These had been fairly well-received by all the employees, or so it had seemed. The morale boosters she used were tried and true, not only in this organization, but every other she could think of.

1. Interdepartmental competition, with a traveling departmental trophy as the prize, had created a lot of enthusiasm. Most departments really pulled together to try to win.

2. The two Fridays a month designated as causal clothes days seemed to break down barriers among the suits and between suits, clerical and exempt personnel, making people feel more comfortable with each other.

3. It had taken many hours to gather the birthday dates of all the employees so that they could be recognized. People always enjoyed seeing their names in the newsletter. This allowed fellow workers to get involved in the lives of their peers.

4. The various theme months she instituted got people thinking about their relationship to one another and the bank. Coming up with themes that were both fun and encouraged the growth of the "SFB Team" usually was very rewarding, especially when she saw how people got enthused about the theme and began really incorporating it into their work.

5. Maybe the latest morale booster had been a little much, creating a SFB Team Mascot, a rabbit, and sending it around to push the latest theme and lighten the mood around the various offices. But, people seemed to get a kick out of it as it broke up their day a bit. Many times she had heard comments from folks wondering if the rabbit would show up today.

6. She had even talked the food service into starting ethnic food days, twice a month, so that everyone could try eating some of the foods from the different cultures in the company. She was sure this would help people get to know a little about the culture of the people they work next to. She hoped it led to conversations in the cafeteria about various cultures.

7. One of the best ideas had been to have upper management, starting with the EVP, eat in the cafeteria for lunch one day a week to demonstrate their availability and ownership in the idea that all of the employees were part of the SFB Team.

But, it was clear to Susan that these were not doing the trick, at least among the employees in the lower levels of the building.

Employee Perspectives on Cultural Differences

Leafing through the report for a fourth time, Susan saw a world of frustration, anger, and pain enfleshed in the comments of the folks from the lower levels of the OG. Frustration and anger were aimed at supervisory and lower level managers. Pain was expressed in the distrust and hostility people felt for one another. Sure, many positive comments were given about one culture for another, and it would be easier to focus on those, but taken as a whole, people did not get along, and it was clear it would get worse.

Susan skimmed the lists of negative comments to get a picture of how the people of the OG SFB world saw one another. In so doing, she tried to summarize the negative perceptions she had read about the major cultural groups and about worker perceptions of management. She wondered how much of these observations were the result of stereotypes, how much personal experience, and how much the work environment.

Perceptions of Management

Susan was amazed at the anger directed towards management. Described as hostile, unconcerned, accusatory, intolerant, too task-oriented, condescending, and superior, to name a few, it was clear that people did not see management as any sort of supportive group. This did not sound like the group of managers she knew and worked with. If these comments were a true reflection of how management treated the workers, Susan was surprised anyone was down in the lower levels at all. The general comments she received about "good" versus "poor" management styles were as follows:

"Good" Management Styles

- Listen/fair
- Not accusing
- Show respect and not make person feel small
- Supportive
- Accepting of mistakes
- State appreciation
- Polite
- Give reasons
- Calm and private
- Supportive, explain mistake, why it happened, and what should happen
- Seek facts and ask questions before judging
- Made inquiries privately
- Willing to apologize when wrong

"Poor" Management Styles

- Powertrip
- Won't listen and intolerant
- Favoritism
- Don't hear both sides and takes sides quickly
- Lack of understanding and compassion
- No one to complain to without jeopardizing job
- Public questioning and humiliating others
- Supervisors takes sides
- Unorganized
- Lack of common skills
- Don't show concern for problems, nor offer solutions
- Accuse and discuss in private
- Assume the negative instead of checking it out
- Too strict with procedures
- Unfair
- Manipulative

- Stop listening when don't like what is said and marked as trouble maker
- Won't let me explain
- Don't question performance in public, do it in private
- Abuse of power; humiliating
- Inability to say when wrong, put blame on others
- Condescending
- Commanding
- Third party comments; indiscretions
- Inconsistent
- We are forced to work with groups or races not qualified to do job; they work at lower pay; all pay goes down
- Our management doesn't listen to a "clerk" because we're not important; fail to see we have feelings, not fortunate enough to go to college; we "employees" make managers shine; hearing "you're doing a good job" would be a miracle
- Managers and assistants talking bad about employee mistakes
- Don't check things out
- Maintaining first impressions
- Threats
- Yelling vs. requesting information
- Jump to conclusions, unwilling to work together
- Lack of trust in worker given authority
- If you disagree with superiors, they say you don't understand
- Expect extra time
- Make people feel guilty without checking on it
- Misuse and abuse; long hours expected; no respect for individual needs
- Don't listen to employees
- Check out, don't assume

Perceptions of Anglos

Overall, Anglos treated their counterparts in a way that was overbearing, arrogant, superior, unfair, and disrespectful of most groups of people. But, how many of these comments were actually about management?

Anglos' Perceptions of Anglos

- We speak English
- Don't always feel superior because we're white
- Others should learn our language; many managers unfair and stop listening
- I'm an individual
- All basically equal
- Speak English during work
- Should treat people with respect
- Make our decisions; agreements made when company policy differs from cultures

- Judge myself, not my culture
- All people should be treated fairly indifferent, apathetic
- Knowing other cultures more important than knowing one's own
- Everyone's an individual
- Speak English; my opinion of all, if in superior position polite and considerate
- They are just like everyone else, hate, discriminate
- Individuals are more important than cultures; too much emphasis placed on cultures
- Don't always think alike or react like minority
- Diverse people
- No opinion on their culture
- We are all equal; white is not better
- They should speak English; it's America
- Some things said and done are part of culture and not to be taken personally
- American culture should be first in America
- Not superior to other cultures
- Evaluate by work, not culture
- Good values, hard working
- Honest, helpful, respectful
- Have adverse feelings about them
- Traditional, value on family and ethics

Afro Americans' Perceptions of Anglos

- Majority good
- Feel superior
- Oppressive
- Professionally deceiving
- Are ok, I guess
- Get away with more
- Rude, insensitive, unjust
- Feel better than others

Filipinos' Perceptions of Anglos

- Eager
- Curious
- Aggressive
- Don't keep grudges
- Prejudiced
- Hypocritical; don't mean what they say; don't like outspoken humor
- Nice and friendly
- Tough, have no feelings; too business-like
- Inconsiderate
- Frank, straightforward, overlooks human side of employment

Hispanics' Perceptions of Anglos

- Think they are superior
- Fair, if fair with them
- Prejudiced
- Professional
- Overconfident, cocky, disrespectful, except to other whites, lazy and manipulative
- Given best opportunities to succeed
- Domineering and discriminating
- Give more merit to Anglo than to Hispanic ideas

Perceptions of Filipinos

Susan noted that the Filipinos were perceived in a very negative light. Their co-workers were suspicious of them, their clannishness and ambitiousness. They were seen as taking advantage of their work positions and did not treat others fairly or with respect. People very much resented their use of their native language, Tagalog.

Filipinos Perceptions of Filipinos

- Friendly
- Proud
- Honest
- Industrious
- Helpful
- Religious
- Sympathetic
- Conservative, closed minded
- Competitive
- Courteous
- Nosey
- Good manners
- Educated (more than others)
- Very sensitive
- Respectful
- Loyal
- Fun
- Need more respect for superiors
- Value politeness, consideration
- Patient
- Insecure; afraid of losing jobs to others
- Easily offended
- Welcome constructive criticism
- Stubborn

- Bad tempered
- Willing to learn
- Bright
- Open minded
- Witty
- Have diverse culture
- Can get to top, if work hard
- Treat us as equals
- We are no different than any other culture
- Want more understanding
- Should be allowed to speak Tagalog at work
- Should be given same opportunities
- Use Tagalog to express selves and show respect
- Culture teaches not to offend
- High boundary of Filipino, but only if you speak the language
- Bring old attitudes; don't change old behaviors

Afro Americans' Perceptions of Filipinos

- Untrustworthy
- They need to speak English in work area
- Pushy, greedy for power
- Some nice
- Talk too much in their language

Anglos' Perceptions of Filipinos

- Outwardly open, proud, men are flirts
- Intelligent, hardworking try too hard when in authority
- Clean, easy going
- Can't take constructive criticism; see you as threat, get defensive, accused of prejudice
- Petty; play favorites
- Very rude; try to get away with as much as they can
- Abuse power; treat other races unfairly when in majority
- Favoritism; give each other best work
- Close knit, insular, unwilling to confront problems; talk about you in Tagalog
- Try to get away with as much as they can
- Don't speak English around others

Hispanics' Perceptions of Filipinos

- Nice people
- Friendly, cooperative
- Proud, brag, ambitious, hurt others
- OK
- Considerate; mind own business

- Arrogant
- Friendly
- Good workers
- Kind people
- Get mad easily

Perceptions of Hispanics

To Susan, the comments about Hispanics seemed to display more of a reliance on stereotypes than interaction, as they were viewed as either fun-loving, hardworking, or pushy by nature.

Hispanics' Perceptions of Hispanics

- Want respect for customs
- Timid, easily embarrassed
- We aren't different; we are equal; treat us equal
- Have feelings, educated, sensitive, knowledgeable about job
- Not as bad as media claims
- We are a people, not a minority
- We have rights
- Good workers; good leaders; trustworthy, sincere, people-oriented
- Friendly
- Smart (I can do anything others can do)
- Have more knowledge than given credit for
- Not lazy and dishonest
- Not thieves
- Value respect and professionalism
- Not second-rate citizens; have feelings, ideas have values
- Proud
- Sincere

Afro-Americans' Perceptions of Hispanics

- Cocky and pushy

Anglos' Perceptions of Hispanics

- Very fine
- Need consideration and respect
- Friendly and fun loving
- Same as others
- They are different from anyone else
- People same as others; we're different and same as non-Hispanic

Filipinos' Perceptions of Hispanics

- Helpful
- Understanding
- Lack of intellect
- Similar in culture
- Hardworking

Vietnamese Perceptions of Hispanics

- Friendly and open minded

Perceptions of African Americans

Susan was surprised by the comments on African Americans, because there were not that many in the OG. But again, certain stereotypes were expressed such as lazy, distrustful, and used race as a weapon to manipulate the race issue.

African Americans' Perceptions of Afro Americans

- Equal or better than other
- Like everyone else
- Have dreams and ambitions
- Very intelligent
- We are all human
- If qualified, should get job, we speak English and are not inconsiderate
- No different than any other group; good and bad people
- Our history
- Want respect; don't favor others; don't look down on us
- All people created the same; people with money the same as those without it
- Pride in ourselves, give people second chance
- Responsible and trustworthy
- Just as competent as next; give us same chance as next
- Other races hate us; words not said in right manner can upset us
- Are ok, I guess
- We hate being stereotypes
- Need more recognition for contribution to organization

Anglos' Perceptions of African Americans

- As American as I
- Very prejudiced
- Positive opinion
- Lazy, dishonest
- Exploit race, emphasize their color; hide behind color, use as weapon or excuse
- No different from rest of us

Filipinos' Perceptions of African Americans

- Educated are good and friendly
- Uneducated are rude and mean
- Not different
- Professional managers
- Easy to get along with
- Talk too much; talk too loud
- Get envious; don't repay when borrowing anything
- Hardworking

Hispanics' Perceptions of African Americans

- Don't trust others
- Competitive
- Good and bad

Perceptions of Asians

The various Asian cultures were quite a mixed bag. She let the comments speak for themselves. Koreans proud; Chinese not friendly, defensive, nosey, polite, shrewd, hard working; Japanese angry-sounding; Thais rude.

Anglos' Perceptions of Chinese

- Positive
- Polite shrewd, intelligent, accurate

Anglos' Perceptions of Thais

- Very rude

Anglos' Perceptions of Japanese

- Efficient

Chinese Perceptions of Chinese

- Hard working and dedicated
- Friendly and easy to talk to
- We are not lazy, are intelligent and hard workers
- We are not all shy and good at math

Filipinos' Perceptions of Chinese

- Strange, not friendly, no consideration, defensive

Filipinos' Perceptions of Vietnamese

- Have English problems

Filipinos' Perceptions of Japanese

* Sad except with Japanese
* Sounds like they're mad, even when not

Hispanics' Perceptions of Chinese

* Don't understand, not clean, don't listen, nosey

Vietnamese Perceptions of Vietnamese

* Keep feelings inside

Perceptions of Other Cultures

Opinions by and about many of the other, less represented groups, were quite mixed. There was either respect or animosity. It was hard to tell whether any groups really liked, accepted, or even tolerated each other. Susan chuckled at one observation that jumped off the pages. People certainly saw themselves quite differently from the way others saw them. It was like two different people with the same name. She wondered why. A second observation made her feel sad as she noted how many of the comments asked for respect and acceptance.

Armenians' Perceptions of Armenians

* Intelligent and educated; have old culture
* Know my tradition to know how to treat me
* We are very nice people

Afghans' Perceptions of Afghans

* Love freedom, proud of country

Afghans' Perceptions of Chinese

* They do not care to know about others

Chinese Perceptions of African Americans

* Bad

Eastern Europeans' Perceptions of Eastern Europeans

* Aristocratic
* Hot blooded, don't hold tempers well
* All stuck up

Eastern Europeans' Perceptions of Filipinos

* Very sensitive

West Indians' Perceptions of West Indians

- Proud, hard workers
- We're just like everyone else

West Indians' Perceptions of African Americans

- Well behaved, willing to help
- Friendly

Koreans' Perceptions of Filipinos

- Not professional

Koreans' Perceptions of Koreans

- Respect others; respect elders and superiors
- Proud of who they are
- Very honest, hardworkers, hate making mistakes, sensitive to criticism

Middle Easterners' Perceptions of Filipinos

- Have to show and prove their power; don't care if you're hurt

Middle Easterners' Perceptions of Anglos

- Literate
- Are phoney and insincere
- They discriminate against foreigners

Middle Easterners' Perceptions of Middle Easterners

- Don't stereotype us
- We are friendly
- Normal people; high sense of morality; honest
- Male chauvinist; don't treat women with respect
- Treated fairly by our performance
- Respectful, treat foreigners with respect; don't shout and scream like Americans do
- Honest, respect others

Middle Easterners' Perceptions of Armenians

- Industrious, hardworking, mutual respect

Conclusion

People were not getting along, that was clear. Susan felt frustrated and angry. "You can't force people to like one another," she thought. "It isn't my job to overcome centuries of hostilities. After all, these people chose to work here, so they better start working together." But even as she thought this, she knew that something would have to be done. But what? She did not relish the idea of going into Chester's office and telling him that his dream of one big, happy SFB family was just that—a dream.

Chester's aspiration of having "Individuals from diverse cultural backgrounds working together to produce a common objective," sounded like a great goal. But, it appeared to Susan that the productivity and morale on the upper floors demonstrated the utility of a more homogeneous work force. The supervisory task on the lower levels seemed more to be one of controlling the problems caused by differences and opinions than managing behavior to reinforce similarity of action; but this didn't feel right either.

Susan looked over at her daily calendar and was reminded of the appointment the EVP had set for tomorrow afternoon to talk about the report. She had a handle on the problem, however vague, so she could go home tonight. But, now her task was to determine the best way to deal with it. She made a note for her secretary to clear the morning calendar. Tomorrow she would develop a preliminary, but clear framework to analyze the morale problem, its causes, and how to relieve them.

34

The Maquiladora Industry and Mexican Unions: The New National Political Strategy

John Passé-Smith
and
Edward J. Williams

Introduction

Normally, Bob Williams' morning work routine started with a ten-mile drive from the suburbs of McAllen, Texas across the international frontier into Mexico and then on to the business park. Often he would leave home early so that he could stop at a local cafe and have a cup of coffee with friends. On a normal day his plant was alive with the sounds of fan motors being assembled, but this was not a normal day. On this hot, July morning the plant lay silent beneath red and black banners signaling the wrath of the Mexican labor movement in the form of a strike. In all, sixteen plants were affected by the work stoppage.

Since the strike, Elvira's Cafe had become an informal meeting place for some of the members of the McAllen-Reynosa maquiladora association, an organization founded to represent the interests of the U.S.-owned assembly plants operating in Mexico. Not only were they responsible for crafting responses to local labor problems, but by 1989 they had also begun an effective national lobby.

Tonight the association was to decide upon a unified response to the strike. The din of the cafe faded away as Bob contemplated the situation. The strike itself was a bit unusual in that conditions in the plants affected were neither the cause nor the focus of the strike. In recent weeks Abel Hernández, a local labor official, had begun talking to workers in several plants around Reynosa about labor representation;

however, the workers were already represented by Rafael Morales de la Cruz. Bob knew that Morales was not very popular among the workers in Reynosa. If Morales did not act quickly, he may find himself with no workers and no plants to represent. Rafael Morales responded quickly by closing the fifteen plants around town. While the circumstances surrounding the strike were unusual, the outcome remained the same; nothing was being produced and money was being lost.

"Coffee, black," Bob called to the waitress as he slid into the naugahyde booth. A truck rumbled by outside and Bob looked out, but not in time. His eyes focused instead on the four buildings down the street. Four American-owned assembly plants imprisoned by chain-link fencing. The fence was a permanent feature of the assembly plants, but since the strike it seemed particularly appropriate. Inside several of the striking plants' workers defiantly occupied the buildings and demand that they be allowed to work. Many of them also wanted new labor representation.

That evening there was to be a meeting of the maquiladora association. They were supposed to arrive at a response to the strike. Disagreement between his colleagues over what to do about the strike increased the normal din at the cafe. Three distinct opinions emerged: (1) strike a deal with the least offensive of the two labor leads; (2) relocate operations to the more western states along the border where unions were weak or nonexistent; or (3) try to rid the maquiladora plants of unions altogether. That evening the managers representing the various plants belonging to the association would choose among these options.

Bob was increasingly aware that his plant was losing some of its autonomy by adhering to association decisions, but there was a growing consensus among the managers from the various assembly plants around Reynosa that solidarity among the plant managers was of vital importance. While Bob understood the power of numbers, he also realized that tonight's association vote may compel him to adopt a strategy with which he disagreed.

Three options—cooptation and cooperation, relocation, or bust the unions. Bob's company had chosen to locate in the state of Tamaulipas primarily because they preferred its relatively cooperative labor-management relations. The Tamaulipan unions had been instrumental in cutting the unbelievably high worker turnover rates—a chronic problem to assembly plant managers—to some of the lowest levels in Mexico. They had also helped the plants avoid the costly pay and benefits wars waged in other areas of the country. Besides, if organized labor became hostile in Mexico, it could become very complicated, if not dangerous, for the maquiladoras because labor is part of the governing system.

Listening to the conversations around him, Bob came to realize that his position, that of cooperation with the unions, would be acceptable to the other managers, and the association as well, only if they put their weight behind the union leader who was challenging the present representative, Rafael Morales de la Cruz. Morales, however, was clearly despised by managers and workers alike. And while this strategy may have been salable to the association, it would, in essence, be asking the Tamaulipan Board of Conciliation and Arbitration (*Junta de Conciliación y Arbitraje*) to consent to a management-supported union coup, a violation of Mexican labor law. It would also require the board to overturn its previous approval of the strike called by Morales.

Nor was Bob at all confident that the other managers were in an accommodating mood. The second option being discussed was to get the Mexican president to go along with the removal of the labor unions in the maquiladora plants. Since the election of U.S.-educated and conservative Carlos Salinas de Gortari to the presidency, Mexican economic policy favored business interests over those of labor more than ever before. For the first time since the inception of the Border Industrialization Program—since the 1910 Revolution, in fact—the Mexican government just might be amenable to the dismantling of the unions. This was the time to be aggressive, to lash out. The dogs had the scent, Bob thought, as some of the other managers loudly argued that this was the time to break the unions altogether. "With Mexico City behind us, we could rid the plants of the corrupt unions and get a tighter grip on labor costs," bellowed one of the managers.

The union-busters did not seem to recall, Bob thought, that the unions had helped stabilize wages and that the wages paid in the state of Tamaulipas were not all that high by Mexican standards. Non-union plants in both Guadalajara and Ciudad Juárez paid higher wages than the unionized plants of Reynosa. Perhaps, Bob reasoned, they wanted Mexican wages to undercut Asian labor costs. U.S. international competitiveness had certainly been hurt by the high wages paid to workers in the U.S., but could labor in the U.S. survive in their own country on the Asian wage of 50 cents per hour? If American workers couldn't be forced to accept such wages, perhaps Mexican workers could. A strategic concern of the union-busting managers was that a weak or divided association response to the strike would embolden the unions to fight for a restoration of the purchasing power lost to inflation.

The final option, Bob thought, was to relocate to the western-most states of Mexico. He knew that as one moved farther to the west union activity diminished. Some of the managers had already typified the strike and the very existence of unions as a mortal threat to the entire maquiladora industry in Mexico. They reasoned that the only options would be to relocate to areas where union representation was low or non-existent, or to leave Mexico altogether. It wasn't real clear to Bob if the doomsday predictions about unions killing the maquiladora program had any base in reality or were merely a tactic to scare the unions into a more submissive stance.

As the afternoon wore on, it became apparent that whatever their decision, the association would look to the Mexican president to protect their interests. As Bob got up and walked toward the door, another member of the association made his case for the abolition of the unions, arguing that labor-management cooptation was a policy of the past when the president of Mexico could not be counted on to defend their position.

Outside, cars raced their engines and belched clouds of black exhaust in anticipation of the traffic signal and a shopkeeper shouted "Junk for sale . . . we have the best junk in here" as tourists wandered by. Bob paused in front of the cafe and watched a swarm of kids rush from car to car cleaning windshields for whatever change they could get from the drivers. Across the street, an old woman sold home-made candy from a wax-paper covered tray. An old man extended his withered, watch-covered arm toward Bob. The children deftly located another car driven by a foreigner and swarmed, their rags and squeegees flailing.

Just last year Bob had taken his family on a tour of his fan-motor assembly plant. Bob watched his family absorb the surroundings. It was then that he realized that his world was much farther away from that of his family than the 2,000 miles between McAllen, Texas and Seattle, Washington. Nothing had prepared him for the extremes of poverty and wealth he saw in Mexico. Any perceived understanding of Mexico or Mexicans he may have thought he acquired from "learning the language" faded shortly after moving to the border. The language barrier, Bob thought, masked much deeper differences in the two cultures. He drove back toward the frontier to prepare for that night's meeting of the maquiladora association, which would determine the strategy the border assembly plants would use to try to end the strike.

The Evolution of Labor's Role in the Mexican Government

Understanding of the ramifications of the strike and its resolution is complicated by the fact that, unlike the United States, labor and government cannot be separated in Mexico because organized labor is an official part of the political party that has ruled Mexico since the 1920s. In fact it is impossible to distinguish between Mexico's official party, the PRI (*Partido Revolucionario Institucional*), and the government. The legitimacy of the Mexican government and labor's place in the party both evolve from the revolution.

For about three decades prior to the 1910 revolution Mexico was ruled by a modernizing authoritarian regime under Porfirio Díaz, which forced labor to endure extraordinary hardships not only in pay but also in very poor working conditions. The impetus to modernization came from foreign companies that invested and developed the country, but at the expense of Mexican business people. In addition, land reform laws had also been implemented that allowed peasants' plots to be taken away and consolidated into expansive landholdings. As the revolutionary response crystallized in Mexico, the call was for democracy, no reelection, higher wages, humane working conditions, land (re)distribution, and carving out a place for Mexicans in the economy. The constitution that emerged in 1917 was a progressive document that addressed each of these concerns. Because Mexico remained a relatively poor country, the constitution came to be viewed as a set of goals rather than a check to be cashed in immediately. The legitimacy of the government came to reside in the government's attempt to achieve the goals of the revolution. So, even though the political system in Mexico remains authoritarian, legitimacy obtains from their alleged attempts to democratize.

A second product of the revolutionary period was the ruling party. The revolutionary conflict in Mexico certainly had its share of losers, but it did not end in a military victory for any one side. Although the revolution is said to have ended in 1920, assassinations and political turmoil continued throughout the 1920s until Plutarco

Elías Calles called the revolutionary factions together to form the political party that has controlled Mexican politics ever since. Labor's membership in the resulting political party came about due to their role in the struggle to oust the dictatorship of Porfirio Díaz.

Government Control of Organized Labor

Since that time, the government and organized labor in Mexico have shared an asymmetrical symbiotic system characterized by a dominant government and a dependent labor section. The *sindicalista* movement reaps benefits from its intimate relationship with government, but it also pays a price. On the positive side of the ledger, the government suppresses challenges to the dominance of the labor sector of the party—organized into a labor confederation called the *Confederación de Trabajadores Mexicanos* (CTM)—or other favored unions; it rewards loyal s*indicalistas* with political and/or administrative posts; it supports the *sindicalistas* through legal and illegal subventions; and it extends social services to union members through the Mexican Social Security Institute (*Instituto Mexicano del Seguro Social,* IMSS) and other social agencies.[1]

Mexico's Federal Labor Law (*Ley Federal del Trabajo,* LFT) bestows upon labor several powerful instruments to strengthen its position; the rights of exclusivity and exclusion are the most notable. The exclusivity provision establishes a union shop and gives the *sindicato* a significant role in hiring procedures. Not many unions exercise that right. The exclusion provision compels management to dismiss workers who transgress union rules and regulations. Again, the right of exclusion is not frequently used, but, along with exclusivity, it offers Mexican labor union leaders powerful leverage in their dealings with management.[2]

But what the federal government gives, it can also take away—or, at least, manipulate. The Mexico City government does that in spades and, in the process, has molded a highly political union movement controlled by the national elites and formally directed by a frequently timid and often corrupt cadre of leaders. Mexican labor union chiefs pursue political power through political strategies. Such strategies prompted one management consultant in the maquiladora industry to compare Mexican unions with "the Daley machine in Chicago, Tammany Hall in New York, and the Irish machine in Boston, for the Mexican union functions in the same way."[3] This is not to say, however, that this political bent is misguided; given the realities of the system, political strategies may well be more effective in improving the lot of the workers than more traditional, plant-oriented activities.

These political strategies, however, frequently prove ineffective because organized labor does not operate independently in an open, responsive system. Rather, its political activities are dictated by the governing elite of a highly centralized, semi-authoritarian system. In short, Mexican unions are controlled: they are not independent, but rather form part of the government.[4] The Board of Conciliation and Arbitration (*Junta de Conciliación y Arbitraje*) is the most pervasive institution of governmental control in labor-management relations. A federal *junta* reigns in Mexico City and state boards operate in the capital cities of the several states, with branches in many of the border cities. The boards apply and interpret the LFT. They hear petitions from unions and/or individual workers, grant official recognition to aspiring union organizations, and, most significantly, rule on the legitimacy of strikes. The *juntas* are composed of three members representing industry, labor and the government. The government uses its vote to tip the balance in favor of either labor or management.[5]

Extrapolating from its political bent and its subservience to government, the Mexican labor union movement is almost always timid, frequently shot through with ideological and personal corruption, and usually non-democratic. *Sindicatos* in the assembly plants have produced their share of leaders worthy of the title "*charro*," the sold out, ostentatious, vulgar union boss. One commentator dryly observed that a union leader in Ciudad Juárez was flaunting "fine clothes and jewelry not usually accessible to a man in his official income bracket." To add final insult, the overwhelming majority of Mexican *sindicato jefes* rule their unions dictatorially, perpetuating themselves through manipulation, intimidation and outright fraud.[6]

Thus, organized labor in Mexico derives its position in government from Mexico's revolution. In effect, it represents the revolutionary goal of providing a better life for workers than existed under the prior dictatorship, a goal that constitutes a healthy part of the very legitimacy of the government. For labor to bolt from the party would mean far more to the present governing system than the mere loss of a large number of labor votes. But what is the likelihood of labor exiting PRI and what is the role of the maquiladora industry and the strike in all of this? To answer these questions Bob had to examine the changing relationships between the state, labor, and industry.

The Border Industrialization Program

Relations with the Mexican Government

Traditionally, the Mexican government viewed the assembly plants as evidence of their dependence upon the United States, not an integral part of their strategy of economic development. The Border Industrialization Program (BIP) along the U.S.-Mexican border was in part created to stem the flow of illegal migrants from Mexico into the United States. The maquiladora industry was to provide jobs for Mexicans *in* Mexico as well as allow U.S. industry to take advantage of inexpensive Mexican labor. The BIP clearly has not suppressed migration, but as a relatively low-labor-cost outlet for U.S. business, it is a success. The initiative evolved from modest beginnings to the massive industry of today. Twelve plants operated on the border in 1965; by 1990, the assembly plants numbered approximately 1700 and employed about a half million workers. To be sure, many Mexican policy elites continue to see the assembly plants as U.S. intrusions into their territory, but on the whole that attitude has given way to a more sympathetic posture.

In 1982, as a response to Mexico's debt problems, then-President Miguel de la Madrid declared the maquiladora industry a "priority sector" of the economy. Indeed, the maquiladora industry is more highly prized in Mexico in the 1990s than at any other time in its history. Mexico increasingly welcomes private foreign investment of all types. The de la Madrid administration initiated a policy of flexibility in overriding legal norms requiring 51% Mexican ownership in Mexican industry. The Salinas government went a significant step further in administratively redefining the norms, abrogating the 51% requirement in many areas. In addition, the industry and its suppliers enjoy an exemption from Mexico's IVA tax, the federal government's most important impost. The industry also successfully fought back attempts to tax the maquiladora plants to finance infrastructural improvements in the border cities. Indeed, Mexico's development bank, Nafinsa, finances industrial parks and other improvements designed to lure the industry to Mexico. The 1988 legislation on private foreign investment facilitated more sales in the Mexican market for the maquiladoras and permitted them to change their legal status to that of a 100% foreign-owned company.[7]

Industry Relations with Organized Labor

In 1986, the assembly plants along the U.S.-Mexican border organized the Border Trade Alliance (BTA). The tactics of the BTA demonstrate the industry's growing political sophistication as it crafts a binational lobbying strategy to push its position in both Mexico City and Washington, D.C. But its Mexico City presence and its intervention in labor affairs carries the most cogency for this discussion. Indeed, it is useful to note that the BTA owes its existence to the industry's reaction to an AFL-CIO-led campaign in 1986 that forced the U.S. Commerce Department to revoke its sponsorship of a maquiladora trade show in Acapulco. The AFL-CIO's victory triggered fear and foreboding along the border and in the industry. The BTA formed and has emerged as the most influential voice of the industry in articulating a coherent and successful political strategy in Mexico City (and in Washington). The maquiladora industry also continues to interact with the Mexican federal government through the Maquiladora Advisory Council of the American Chamber of Commerce of Mexico (AMCHAM); and it has intensified its commitment to operating through the Maquiladora Industry Council (CNIME).[8]

In its direct relations with organized labor, the maquiladora industry usually attempts to avoid unionization and puts together a bewildering concoction of defensive strategies in the process. In a "how to" article entitled "Union Avoidance in the Twin Plants," an industry consultant sets out the disadvantages of unions for the industry: escalating wages, sharing policymaking authority with union leaders, dealing with workers through a third party rather than directly, and the threat of strikes. A fair number of companies, however, prove exceptions to the general rule. Many in the industry celebrate the advantages of unionization. Union leaders can discipline problem workers, manage sports and cultural programs, assist in the distribution of benefits, recruit workers, and maintain labor peace.[9] Many of these exceptions locate in Tamaulipas.

The anti-union strategy followed by most companies range from cooptation and cooperation to intimidation in worker relations and include general corporate policies concerning the location of plants, several gradations of "sweetheart" arrangements, and sensitivity to the local and national political environments. In the area of cooptation, the company's goal is to seduce the worker into choosing not to be unionized. For example, some consultants advise management "to anticipate the union" by offering several fringe benefits including such things as daycare, personal leave, and flextime. One such company, Motorola in Guadalajara, boasts a well-earned reputation for its good working conditions and relatively high wages.[10]

Evidence suggests that some companies have eschewed reason for more aggressive strategies. Ortiz described the actions of managers in the Solidev strike in Tijuana, stating that the managers' "policy [was] to recruit to their side those members without a strong commitment to the union"; at the same time, "the company attempted to remove the solidly committed union members from their current positions and place them in less strategic ones." In truth, the Solidev management appeared less vindictive than many managers who simply fire union organizers and workers aligned with them. Even more brutal, charges circulate about company-sponsored (and government-sponsored) goon squads intimidating organizers and sympathetic workers.[11]

Decisions on site location afford companies another strategy to work against the unionization of their assembly plants. Companies strongly opposed to *sindicatos* generally choose not to locate in the state of Tamaulipas. Instead, their plants are placed in Nogales or farther west, in the interior, or even outside of Mexico, as in the case of the Crescent Company, which moved from Mexico to Puerto Rico and, finally, to Taiwan. Numerous companies over the years have closed shop, claiming that militant labor unions had driven them from Mexico, a charge that might in fact veil other factors contributing to company failure. Some of the *causes celebres* include Solidev in Tijuana, Mattel in Mexicali, Acapulco Fashion in Ciudad Juárez, and more than half the industry in Nuevo Laredo.[12]

Some companies in the industry reject conflict with and/or repudiation of Mexican *sindicatos.* They embrace a policy emphasizing accommodation of Mexican labor unions. Depending upon time, place, and the dispositions of the several actors involved, accommodation can imply strategies ranging from collusion with corrupt labor *caciques,* the negotiation of sweetheart arrangements, to something resembling collective bargaining agreements hammered out by approximate equals. Bribery of union officials exemplifies one extreme of the accommodation policy. Although no cases of outright bribery surfaced during the research for this study, whispers, rumors, charges and countercharges about union leaders on the take abound. To be fair, reports and rumors of corruption often ignore whether it is the management offering money to the union official to get what they want or the union bosses or *caciques* assuming the initiative to wring money, special gifts, or a high salary from the assembly plant management. Indeed, both actions are known to the industry. At a few companies in Nogales, the local CTM *jefe* and a company representative prepared a contract without the knowledge of the workers, that was used to block bids to organize the plant by other unions. The contract documents that the maquiladora is already unionized. According to one source, the contract might also be used to turn away a worker's complaint or petition by demonstrating that the contract prohibits the disputed activity.[13]

The establishment of company unions (*sindicatos blancos*) forms yet another gradation of assembly plant companies adapting to Mexican norms. Independent company unions are to be found in almost every maquiladora city in Mexico. In some instances they have a diffuse relationship with one of the national confederations; in other cases, they are completely independent. They range from fairly effective representatives of the workers to the complete captives of the management.

A customary accommodation between labor and management also can involve an implicit (and sometimes explicit) understanding emphasizing mutual tolerance between the two contestants. To be sure, such arrangements do not allow for the aggressive representation of labor, but they are not uncommon because they mirror the Mexican culture, which is hierarchical, corporativistic, paternalistic, and authoritarian. An overview of Mexico reveals a corporativistic economy, paternalistic norms in the reigning sociocultural value system, and a political arena defined by an omnipresent governmental authority. In the Mexican context, the industry-labor relationship is dominated by the more powerful partner, industry, but union leaders enjoy the fruits of their position.

Future presidents in Mexico may seek to strengthen their relationship with labor once again and thus strengthen labor's hand, but in the meantime, the industry grows ever more experienced at lobbying in the Mexican political arena. The industry's experience and new closeness with the government has emboldened them to act more aggressively against organized labor. Industry leaders are enjoying a sense of Mexico City's growing friendship toward and support of the maquiladora program. Even in Tamaulipas, where the industry had evolved a fruitful accommodation with the CTM and maintains the lowest worker turnover rate in the entire maquiladora industry, the maquiladora association grows more militant in its ambition to weaken the position of labor.

Mexican Organized Labor

Labor's Maquiladora Strategy

Mexican organized labor emphasizes political goals and methods that seek to influence Mexico City's policymakers. Strikes, for example, frequently look to pressure political decision-makers rather than assembly plant managers. The movement places less priority on organizing and representing workers in the local assembly plant than on their national political lobbying strategy. A profound and debilitating ambivalence afflicts Mexican labor's stance on union organization of the Border Industrialization Program, an attitude that weakens organized labor's commitment to unionize the industry.

Fidel Velázquez is the embodiment of the ambivalence that plagues Mexico's union leadership. Velázquez sees himself as a Mexican nationalist first and a union leader second. As a nationalist dedicated to Mexico's development, he assumes the posture of labor statesman in facilitating the foundation and growth of foreign participation in the maquiladora industry. Velázquez and other syndical leaders are eager to help Mexico's economy. Battling for decent wages (or at least maintaining the status quo), for safe working conditions, etc. while still a duty of the unions, is secondary.

While there is absolutely nothing wrong with Mexicans supporting the job-creating assembly plant industry, Fidel Velázquez's job is to represent labor. He is, after all, the head of the largest labor confederation in Mexico, the Labor Confederation of Mexico (CTM). Yet, as early as 1966, Fidel pledged that "the CTM would not pressure without cause the industrialists who come to this area of the country (the border). On the contrary, in every occasion, it would support those investments, avoiding unjustified labor-management conflicts." More than 20 years later, in the context of the 1989 strike at Reynosa, Velázquez is reported to have promised visiting U.S. congressmen no more labor problems on the border.[14]

It must be noted that Mexican *sindicatos* sometimes go beyond collaboration in economic development to pursue conventional union goals like better wages and working conditions. But after 1982 the Mexican government shifted its policy output to a more pro-business stance. Since the labor-government relationship went sour, organized labor has been unable or unwilling to reestablish its position with respect to the government. Fiery calls to action emanate from Mexico's labor leaders, but they have produced precious little.

Labor's Changing Relationship with the Government

The austerity programs begun under the de la Madrid administration sharpened worker discontent and the union leadership's dissatisfaction with the *técnico*-dominated government. Privatization policies doubled the tension between labor and government. Labor opposed such measures on principle, and to make matters worse, union-busting frequently accompanied privatization, as the transfer of companies to private ownership voided previously negotiated contracts.[15]

Labor also fared badly in the events of 1987–88 when Salinas was nominated as the PRI candidate and subsequently "elected" president. In the first instance, the labor *jefes* opposed the selection of Salinas as the PRI standard bearer; Fidel Velázquez then compounded the error by petulantly refusing to acknowledge the Salinas victory. In an outrageous transgression of acceptable political behavior, another labor leader, Joaquín Hernández Galicia ("La Quina"), followed by publicly questioning whether union people should support Salinas. Operating under the orders of the new president, La Quina was literally blasted out of his home in 1989 by federal troops.[16] Labor union *jefes* had strayed from accepted practices in their relationship with recognized political leaders.

Fidel Velázquez, who turned 90 in April 1990, and the rest of Mexico's aging and ineffectual union leadership are no match for the president and his associates. Mirroring the attitudes of their generation, many of the union leaders believe in what Jesús Reyes Heroles termed "*México bronco*," an ungovernable Mexico constantly on the precipice of chaos. The fear that Mexico could slide back into the violence and destruction of the revolutionary period causes labor to give priority status to the nationalistic goal of providing a docile labor force in hopes of enhancing the prospects of growth. The looming specter of the *Mexican bronco* and the political culture itself also results in a labor leadership imbued with authoritarian values.[17]

Those several factors matured during the 1980s to contribute to the initiation of a series of new labor policies and programs by the government. When Federal District *transportistas* (transportation workers) called a strike in the late-1980s, the government summarily fired all 23,000 and reorganized forthwith the district's bus system. Reflecting a similar ham-fisted attitude, the government-controlled Federal Conciliation and Arbitration Board declared illegal in early 1990 a strike by workers at Mexico City's Modelo Brewery that produces Corona beer, a significant earner of U.S. dollars. The government called in police to disperse pickets.[18]

Privatization programs neutralized airline workers, miners, and *telefonistas*. The government privatized *AeroMexico* and *Mexicana* airlines, in whole or in part, during 1988 and 1989, and the Cananea copper mine and state-owned telephone monopoly in 1989 and 1990. In every case, part of the privatization program canceled union contracts, reduced the size of the work force, and diminished the influence of the union in the industry. Union busting may not have been the primary goal in the privatization process, but it certainly evolved as a significant part of the program.[19]

In response to its declining influence, Mexico's organized labor movement has done little more than fume, but a hint of a new policy featuring a more independent posture has appeared on the political horizon.[20] Speculation abounds that the official CTM may repudiate the official PRI, shattering the coalition that has reigned and ruled in Mexico since the mid-1920s. Organized labor charges that the Salinas *técnicos* are clearly unwilling and probably unable to fathom the plight of Mexico's masses and certainly exhibit no appreciation of labor's contribution to Mexico's growth and stability since the horrors of the Revolution. In a more specific instance, the union stalwarts have been outraged with the PRI's coalescing with the rightist National Action Party (PAN), particularly in the deal that reprivatized the banking system, a move that labor opposed at the outset.[21]

Within and without the official family, some see organized labor as forming its own political party. Well-placed political and labor *jefes* have discussed the options. In response to the PRI's "stupidity" in having "handed over power" to the PAN in the Baja California gubernatorial elections in mid 1989, the CTM secretary for political action set out the argument for a separate political party at an official conclave of the CTM. While declaring the time for the split inopportune, Rigoberto Ochoa Zaragosa declared that "the constitution of a party of the working class is urgent and there ought to be a gradual process toward that objective."[22]

Organized labor's affiliation with the Democratic Revolutionary Party (PRD) forms the second hypothetical outcome of a split with the official party. A move to join the nationalistic opposition PRD implies shaking the system to its foundations. Cuauhtémoc Cárdenas, the PRD standard bearer, certainly appeals to proletarian groups and the dispossessed in general. He drew a significant portion of the vote in the 1988 elections and some even claim that he won. Cárdenas routinely rallies striking workers, personally showing up at many of the sites of worker-management (or governmental) confrontation including the Cananea mine in Sonora, the Modelo brewery in Mexico City, and the Sicartsa steel works in his home state of Michoacán. Despite documented support among labor's rank and file and some lower level *jefes,* the top tier of Mexico's labor leadership has run from cold to lukewarm on Cárdenas and the PRD. Some change may be afoot, however, while the initial response tended to repudiation, a softer tone began to surface in late 1989. Choosing a national meeting of the PRI as his context, Fidel Velázquez announced that the CTM would pursue a "dialogue" with the PRD, although he was quick to dampen optimistic expectations of substantial agreement between the two.[23]

As of 1993, there has been no labor revolt in PRI and Mexican organized labor is running scared; a bunker mentality pervades the movement. And well it should; a perceptive analysis of the post-1982 period correctly concludes that "organized labor has suffered an irreversible loss of negotiating leverage vis-à-vis the state."[24] To the point of this discussion, the labor movement's loss of political punch undermines its ability to unionize the maquiladora industry and to maintain or improve sound wages and good conditions in the assembly plants.

Conclusion

In mid-1989, Reynosa exploded in turmoil as union leader competition catalyzed a strike in the maquiladora industry. The strike broke out in mid-July 1989 and dragged on for nearly a month.

Competition for turf between two union *jefes* served as the immediate cause of the strike. One of the *jefes,* Rafael Morales de la Cruz, carried a well-earned reputation for arbitrary authoritarianism and corruption in union affairs and in his relationships with the assembly plant management. The maquiladora management clearly despised him; a fair number of the workers evidently shared that sentiment. The 1989 strike at Reynosa symbolized the evolving balance of power between organized labor and business.

For the maquiladora association, three distinct options emerged: reach an accommodation with labor leaders; relocate operations; or rid the maquiladoras of unions altogether. The first option, accommodation, has a relatively long history in the state of Tamaulipas. Here the unions have participated to varying degrees in the hiring and firing of workers. In doing so they have reduced the worker turnover to one of the lower rates in the country. Unions have also stabilized the wages and benefits paid to workers allowing the assembly plants to cooperate with each other rather than becoming embroiled in wage and benefit wars to attract the best workers.

While this accommodation provided a relative degree of harmony, some managers and companies believe that wages could be lowered if not for the unions and many benefits could be withdrawn. These companies pursued a policy of union busting; lobbying to remove union organization from the plants altogether. This approach is not uncommon for the business community in Mexico and elsewhere. In Mexico, it could result in a labor force hostile to business interests. It could also mean that labor would renounce its traditional ties with the Mexican ruling party. It is not clear what that would mean for Mexico, but the possibilities certainly include violence.

The final option that emerged in 1989 was to avoid the battle by relocating assembly plants to one of the western states where the unions are weaker. For the plants already established in Tamaulipas this would entail a costly move of equipment and management personnel. Whereas the plant could be union-free, the management would then have to deal with worker turnover rates that sometimes reach 10 to 15% per month rather than 2 to 3%.

References

1. For an extended discussion, see George W. Grayson, editor, *Prospects for Mexico* (Washington: Foreign Service Institute, U.S. Department of State, 1988), pp. 130–140.

2. Alberto Trueba Urbina and Jorge Trueba Barrera, *Ley Federal del Trabajo, Comentarios . . . ,* 60a edición, (Mexico, D.F.: Editorial Porrúa, S.A., 1989), p. 187. See Carillo y Hernández, *Mujeres . . . ,* pp. 156–158, for additional commentary. See below for an analysis of a forthcoming major revision of the LFT, pp. 94–95.

3. For the quotations, see Susan V. Lowery, "A Time of Transition: Union Activity in Chihuahua," *Twin Plant News,* IV, No. 4, November 1988, p. 66; and Kevin J. Middlebrook, "The Sounds of Silence: Organized Labor's Response to Economic Crisis in Mexico," *Journal of Latin American Studies,* XXI, Part 2, 1989, p. 213.

4. For an example of Mexican opinion in a border city, see "No hay Sindicalismo Independiente," *El Mañana* (Nuevo Laredo), 21 de Agosto, 1989, p. 3.

5. See Carrillo y Hernández, *Mujeres . . . ,* pp. 169–171; and Ian Roxborough, *Unions and Politics in Mexico* (London: Cambridge University Press, 1984), Chapter 8, "The Labour Courts," pp. 145–175.

6. Van Waas, *The Multinationals' Strategy . . . ,* p. 291. See below for a more specific discussion of the unions in the assembly industry.

7. For description, commentary and analysis, see "No hay deficiencia ni saturación en la Aduana local," *El Informador* 22 de Julio, 1989, p. C1; "Otorgará Nafinsa créditos a maquiladoras," *El Mañana* 23 de Agosto, 1989, p. A4; and Charles Thurston, "Softer rules may bring new face to maquilas," *Arizona Daily Star* June 11, 1989, p. C1.

8. This discussion is informed by Leslie Sklair, *Assembling for Development: The Maquila Industry in Mexico and the United States* (Boston: Unwin Hyman, 1989), pp. 64–65, 180–190.

9. Lois Elias, *Twin Plant News,* III, No. 12, July 1988, p. 64. See also Susan V. Lowery, "A Time of Transition: Union Activity in Chihuahua," *Twin Plant News,* IV, No. 4, November, 1988, p. 19.

10. Elias, *ibid.;* Lowery; *ibid.* Van Waas, *The Multinationals' Strategy . . . ,* pp. 258, 274.

11. See Carrillo y Hernández, *Mujeres . . . ,* p. 176; Ortiz, *Labor Conflicts . . . ,* pp. 160–161; Peña, "Las Maquiladoras . . . ," *Atzlan,* II, No. 1, Fall, 1980, p. 189; and Van Waas, *The Multinationals' Strategy . . . ,* p. 288.

12. See Carrillo, *Conflictos . . . ,* p. 16–18; Carrillo y Hernández, *Mujeres . . . ,* pp. 150–158, 160; Carolyn Howe, "Multinationals and Labor Unity: Both Sides of the Border," *Southwest Economy and Society,* IV, No. 1, Fall, 1978, p. 52; Ortiz, *Labor Conflicts . . . ,* p. 12; and Van Waas, *The Multinationals' Strategy . . . ,* p. 379.

13. Interviews in Hermosillo and Nogales, October and November, 1989.

14. For the quotation, see Van Waas, *The Multinationals' Strategy . . . ,* p. 321; for the 1989 statement, see "Border Row Ends With Pro-Management Accord," *Mexican Update,* September 1, 1989; on the same theme, see also Harry Bernstein, "U.S.-Mexican Unionists Teaming Up on Border Dilemma," *Los Angeles Times,* February 9, 1989, Section 4, p. 1. The quotation below is from Juanita Darling, "Era of Limits for Mexico's Mighty Unions," *Los Angeles Times,* March 4, 1990, ISLA, 1238.

15. For the general analysis, see "Bad Day in Tampico," *The Economist,* January 14, 1989; Marjorie Miller, "Labor Bosses' Power Declining in Mexico," *Los Angeles Times,* January 21, 1989, Information Services on Latin America (ISLA) 19; and Larry Rohter, "Mexican Labor Chiefs Are Now Feeling the Heat," *New York Times,* February 27, 1989, ISLA 605.

16. Guy Gugliotta, "Election Weakens Mexican Labor," *Miami Herald,* July 7, 1988, ISLA 64; and Middlebrook, "Sounds of Silence . . . ," p. 201.

17. See Middlebrook, "Sounds of Silence . . . ," for the quotation and further analysis.

18. For representative reporting, commentary and analysis, see "Army tames battling petroleum worker groups in Mexico, 78 hurt," *Arizona Daily Star,* May 19, 1989, p. A11; Hector Cruz López "Exculpa un juez a Venus Rey y Wallace; deben declarar: PGJDF," *Uno Más Uno,* 1 de Agosto de 1989, p. 11; "Government Gets Tough With Dissident Labor," *Mexico Update* VII, No. 9, May 15, 1989, pp. 1–2; Richard Johns "Charges brought against Mexican musicians' leader," *Financial Times* January 18, 1989, ISLA 20; Larry Rohter, "Strikes pose problems for ruling party leaders," *Arizona Daily Star* (Tucson), April 8, 1990, p. C2; Rohter, "Battleground in Mexico: Union Power," *New York Times,* January 12, 1989, ISLA 5; and Ben Ross Scheider, "Partly for Sale: Privatization and State Strength in Brazil and Mexico," *Journal of Inter-American Studies,* XXX, No. 4, Winter, 1988, pp. 100–105.

19. For representative reporting, commentary and analysis, see "Cananea seguirá funcionando," *El Mañana,* 23 de Agosto, 1989, p. 1; "Cárdenas llega hoy a Cananea, *El Diario* (Nuevo Laredo), 27 de Agosto, 1989, p. A3; David Gardner, "Unpopular unions lose Aeromexico battle" *Financial Times,* June 2, 1988, ISLA 3735; "Inquieta a trabajadores la venta de Mexciana," *El Mañana* 23 de Agosto, 1989, p. A4; Adrian Lajous, "Teléfonos de Mexico," *El Informador* (Guadalajara), 11 de Julio, 1989, p. A4; Keith Rosemblum, "Mexico nullifies labor contract with copper miners in Cananea," *Arizona Daily Star,* September 13, 1989, p. A14; and "Officials Reviewing Plans to Privatize Communications," *Mexico Update,* VII, No. 5, March 15, 1989, pp. 4–5.

20. For some discussion, see "La CTM formaría su propio partido," *El Informador,* 6 de Julio, 1989, p. A15; "CTM no permitirá afiliados del PRD: Hernández Juárez," *El Diario,* 27 de Agosto, 1989, p. A6; Renato Dávalos, "Provocaría Mayores Diferencias un Diálogo Fingido con el PRD," *Excelsior,* 26 de Noviembre, 1989, p. A1; "Formaría la CTM su propio partido," *El Norte,* 6 de Julio, 1989, p. A1; Middlebrook, "Sounds of Silence . . .," p. 202; and "Sin la CTM se liquidaría el sistema," *El Mañana,* 27 de Agosto, 1989, p. A1.
21. For the analysis, see "Follow-up need on political front," *Latin American Weekly Report,* November 9, 1989, p. 3; and Middlebrook, "Sounds . . .," p. 201.
22. The quotation is from "La CTM formaría 'su propio' partido," *El Informador,* 6 de Julio de 1989, p. 15. See also "Formaría la CTM su propio partido," *El Norte,* p. AI; 6 de Julio de 1989; and "Sin la CTM se liquidaría el systema," *El Mañana,* 27 de Agosto de 1989, p. A1.
23. See Renato Dávalos, et al., "Provocaría Mayores Diferencias un Diálogo Fingido con el PRD," *Excelsio,* 26 de Noviembre de 1989, p. A1; "'CTM no permitiría afiliados del PRD': Hernández Juárez," *El Diario,* 27 de Agosto de 1989, p. A6; and "Salinas Swats a Rebellious Union," *Latin American Weekly Report,* March 29, 1990, p. 8.
24. Middlebrook, "The Sounds of Silence . . .," p. 209.

35
A Quality Implementation Case: *Kaizen* at Firestone New Zealand

Jason S. Schweizer
and
Suresh Balan

Introduction

"That's a pretty broad objective we've set for ourselves," Harry McMillan thought to himself. As manufacturing director of Firestone New Zealand, he would be largely responsible for implementing the following strategic goals developed in a series of top-level management meetings:

1. Ensure the survival of manufacturing in New Zealand.
2. Provide customers with the best performing tire in the New Zealand market.
3. Continuously improve on all key factory indices of quality, cost, and productivity.
4. Focus the factory on passenger and light truck steel belted production, while providing the sales department with the sizes, types, and quantities of products that can be economically produced.

Ensuring the survival of manufacturing in New Zealand was not exactly what he had anticipated he would be doing when he arrived from Akron eight years ago. On the other hand, providing customers with the best performing tire in the New Zealand market, was just exactly what he intended to do.

After 27 years working for Firestone in the U.S., Kenya, Brazil, and Thana, Harry was all too familiar with how a domestic manufacturer could fall prey to foreign competitors that offered lower prices and better quality. Hadn't Firestone U.S. in fact been bought out by Bridgestone of Japan because it had failed to adapt quickly enough to global competition?

He was well aware that *survival* was at stake for tire manufacturing in Firestone New Zealand. He intended to ensure that the company would both survive and be profitable well into the future. In his long career in tire manufacturing, he had visited Japanese tire factories and studied numerous advanced manufacturing techniques such as JIT, KANBAN, and TQC, but none was as comprehensive and seemingly as critical to quality and price issues as *Kaizen*. He was convinced that this cultural philosophy of "thinking" continuous improvement was how Firestone NZ would meet its strategic goals. But how could he make this happen in the New Zealand subsidiary of an American corporation owned by a Japanese company? He would need a lot of help from his managers and the "rubber workers" if such a program was to succeed.

The Bridgestone/Firestone "Marriage"

As was the case with most American tire manufacturers during the 1980s, Firestone had faced substantial competition from overseas tire manufacturers, particularly Japanese, who had become increasingly efficient in producing high quality at lower cost. In the early 1980s Firestone struggled with high labor costs and poor sales. Although substantial cuts in personnel during the decade returned the company to profitability, little money for investment in new technology and more efficient manufacturing methods had been allocated.

Recognizing the need for improved methods, techniques, and particularly technology, Firestone needed to find a way to provide the necessary investment. To do so, then-CEO John Nevins made several efforts to sell or partner with Bridgestone in 1984 and 1986. Finally, in 1987, after competitive bidding from Pirelli, Bridgestone's chief executive, Mr. Akira Yeiri, decided to buy Firestone. The American company became Bridgestone/Firestone, Inc., a subsidiary of Bridgestone in Japan.

However, given the long-term perspective on profit and market share characteristic of large Japanese companies, and the growing resentment of Americans towards large, visible purchases of American assets by Japanese companies, Mr. Yeiri decided to pursue a slow, and deliberate approach to changing the culture of the new Bridgestone/Firestone, Inc. organization.

Bridgestone sent many Japanese managers to "pair" with European counterparts to teach them the Bridgestone way of "thinking" and operating in the company's European divisions. At Bridgestone/Firestone, Inc. however, few "pairings" were initiated, and previous managers and organizational structures were retained. Additionally, aggressive application of "Japanese management" practices such as just in time, total quality management, theory Z style, and "consensus decision making," which had been the essence of the Bridgestone organization's competitive successes, were not implemented.

Instead, the strategy of the U.S. company, following the $2.6 billion Firestone purchase, consisted of providing another $2.9 billion in capital improvements and equipment upgrades to meet Japanese operations standards. Up to 1991, however, Bridgestone had yet to reap the increases it expected would put it at, or near, the efficiencies in its own plants. In fact, by late 1991, average efficiency in the Firestone operations was still only 60% of Japanese levels. Almost four years passed without the significant improvements in quality, efficiency, and profitability that Bridgestone had expected.

Because the efforts made by Bridgestone to avoid major cultural clash with the American system had not worked sufficiently, Bridgestone installed a Japanese chairman and chief executive named Yoichiro Kaizaki to bring Japanese methods and attitudes to the Firestone operations. Also at that time, the Bridgestone/Firestone mission was revised to reflect the following perspectives:

Philosophy/Mission. Bridgestone/Firestone, Inc., as a member of the global Bridgestone family, is an organization dedicated to serving its diverse customer base by engineering, manufacturing, and marketing the highest quality products and providing superior customer service.

Values. To integrate a diverse cultural base, carry out our mission, and achieve our objectives, Bridgestone/Firestone, Inc. will operate consistently with the following values: quality, integrity, and social responsibility.

Quality. Bridgestone/Firestone, Inc. emphasizes quality in all aspects of its business operations. The importance of attaining 100% quality and reliability in all of the products and services provided to our customers and to those within our own company is paramount. Total quality control (TQC) will be a common direction for all employees and the guideline for day-to-day behavior.

Integrity. Bridgestone/Firestone, Inc. requires that all management decisions be legal and ethical.

Social Responsibility. Bridgestone/Firestone, Inc. will be a socially responsible member of the worldwide communities in which it conducts business, respecting the values, traditions, and cultures of all host communities. Bridgestone/Firestone, Inc. seeks to contribute to the common good of those communities by making any management decisions affecting our natural resources on an environmentally sound basis.

Firestone New Zealand

Firestone New Zealand, Ltd. was registered in 1928 as an importer of tires and started manufacturing tires in 1948. Given Bridgestone's strategy to "go slow" following its purchase of Firestone, Bridgestone continued to use the previous U.S.

organizational structure. Firestone's manufacturing operations were spread over 18 countries worldwide; Firestone New Zealand was a subsidiary of Firestone's Latin America/Pacific Rim division. The New Zealand operation headquartered in Auckland, New Zealand employs about 800 people, 298 work in the factory; the others are employed in the finance, administrative, and marketing areas.

Although Firestone was an efficient producer of tires in New Zealand by New Zealand standards, the company was increasingly faced with cheaper imports from overseas in the replacement market. As New Zealand dismantled much of the protection afforded manufacturers by way of licensing and import tariffs, increased pressure was created for local manufacturers to compete with cheaper and often better quality products from overseas. This was particularly true for Firestone New Zealand. The company faced stiff competition from overseas manufacturers that could sell their products in NZ more cheaply than domestic producers because of:

1. Economies of scale; New Zealand companies are unlikely to ever become high-volume producers on the scale of companies in South East Asia and Far East.
2. Lower factor costs of production, especially labor.
3. Ability to sell over-runs to New Zealand at marginal cost.

Specifically, according to the Tire Industry Plan implemented by the New Zealand government, removal of licensing of imports began on July 1, 1985 and a progressive reduction of tariffs on imports was also initiated from 40% to 20% over the period 1986 to 1994. The ultimate objective was to reduce import duties on all goods to 10%. Firestone NZ would have very little protection left from the protective tariffs.

Firestone NZ also faced other problems including a slow growth general economic environment, problematic interest rates, and the closing of several of its Original Equipment Manufacturer (OEM) motor vehicle assembly customers in New Zealand. Thus, the company not only had to maintain and expand its replacement market share in New Zealand, but also to look for overseas markets, especially Australia, for sales. The company needed to cultivate its ability to compete on price and quality in local and overseas markets.

When he became plant manager in 1984, Harry McMillan was well aware of the substantial challenges facing Firestone New Zealand. During his first visit to Firestone New Zealand in 1983, it became apparent that dramatic improvements in productivity and quality would be necessary to survive. Six months later, his "evaluation" visit became a permanent position. His recommendation for a more experienced manager to improve quality and productivity was given to *him*.

Although he would have liked to have initiated implementation of an overall program of continuous improvement at the time, two "critical issues" needed immediate attention: union relations and standards of performance. Therefore, his attention in late 1984, 1985, and 1986 was focused on improving performance standards and getting union cooperation in these areas. While this required a great deal of effort and was difficult for both the company and the union, the process resulted in new relationships, standards, and performance that greatly improved the situation and allowed Harry to plan for the initiation of *kaizen* (a continuous improvement process) in 1987.

The purchase of Firestone by Bridgestone in 1987 looked like it would further McMillan's improvement efforts at Firestone NZ. The purchase appeared to create an ideal opportunity for reestablishing Firestone's leadership in quality and performance, and *kaizen* would be at the core of such an effort. However, besides the deregulation of the industry, Bridgestone's "go slow, hands off" strategy for Firestone did not generate much contact with the Japanese parent company. The few visits from Bridgestone's Australia group provided little "Japanese" influence at Firestone New Zealand.

Firestone NZ needed to do something to ensure they would be able to lower costs while continuing to provide a high-quality product. Harry recognized that improving methods and techniques would help, but a change in people's attitudes and behaviors would be essential in accomplishing these goals.

As early as 1985 and 1986, members of union leadership had been sent to Japan to visit tire plants and see first-hand how Japanese plants operated. In addition, they attended Deming seminars held in New Zealand, taught by Deming *himself.* Along with his managers, Harry saw the people on the shop floor as the key resource needed to initiate and sustain a "continuous improvement process" called *kaizen.* He was committed that each employee would understand and accept the cultural change required for future success.

Kaizen: **Process and Culture**

In 1989, Masaaki Imai, the prime exponent of *K aizen* wrote: *Kaizen* means continuing improvement in personal life, home life, social life and working life." Thus, in this sense, *kaizen* is a way of life that often has been characterized as the "Japanese worker's way of thinking." It, therefore, is part of, and inseparable from, the culture that is learned through years of socialization in Japan. Growing up with school six days a week, highly competitive college entrance exams, and a constant reinforcement of continuous improvement behavior in the work place has "grown" the *kaizen* philosophy in most Japanese employees.

Particularly in Western organizations then, this "philosophy of life" must be *translated* into a process that will develop the same attitudes and behaviors characteristic of those that have grown up in such an environment. Applying the *kaizen* strategy means that management must constantly strive for improvement in *all* aspects of doing business. In particular, the fundamental emphasis must be placed on "improvement together" and total involvement. Thus, when this process is applied to the work place, *kaizen* means continuous improvement involving everyone— managers and workers alike. For Firestone NZ, *kaizen* was the answer, providing both a short-term solution as well as a long-term perspective for growth. The driving mechanism behind *kaizen* is simple and straightforward: improvement. The starting point for improvement is recognition of the need. *Kaizen* emphasizes problem awareness and provides tools for identifying and solving problems. The best way to implement this generic process of improvement at Firestone NZ was to apply *kaizen* to every aspect of every employee's activities throughout manufacturing process.

Manufacturing Strategy

An old system of management and production methods had been in place at Firestone NZ through the years. Due to the company's small operation with a comparatively small volume of production, much of the design of new products and the research and development for new tires was conducted at the parent company's research laboratories in Rome, Italy or Akron, Ohio. At Firestone NZ, there was considerable development work to make sure that guide specifications were adapted to New Zealand driving conditions. Additionally, the small size of production operations prohibited expensive manufacturing technologies such as flexible manufacturing systems, computer-aided manufacturing, and robotics.

Even so, as a result of import protection up until 1985, Firestone had enjoyed a good market share, averaging 35% throughout the '80s, and high profit margins in New Zealand. During the same period, very little capital investment was made to upgrade process technology. Also, employees were not trained in new management and production methods. Thus, the company had a disadvantageous cost structure vis-a-vis overseas manufacturers. Firestone NZ needed a system to improve its manufacturing performance that did not require much capital investment, and at the same time, retained its present infrastructure to the greatest extent possible.

Thus, the new *kaizen* program would be directed toward streamlining manufacturing operations. The implementation of modern technology, process, and thinking in Firestone was rooted in a desire to expand market share by reducing production costs, improving quality, and meeting delivery times. Improving manufacturing and refocusing on both New Zealand and overseas customers, was counted upon to generate the competitive advantage the company needed to survive, improve market share, and increase profitability over importers and other manufacturers.

In 1987, Harry McMillan viewed *kaizen* as a fundamental catalyst for the design, implementation, and growth of such a manufacturing strategy. He saw the added potential of boosting manufacturing operations to competitive heights by coupling the philosophy of *kaizen* with the manufacturing planning and control techniques of advanced manufacturing technology (AMT).

Implementing Change in Manufacturing

McMillan, therefore, initiated a series of activities aimed at generating and sustaining change in culture. This process started with a management retreat at which goals and strategies to attain the objectives were set. This was followed by development of

Table 35-1
The Changing Nature of Management

Old: Supervisor	New: Team Leader
Scheduler of work	Coach of self managed work team
Rule enforcer, manager of union contract on management behalf	Facilitator, getting experts to help the team as needed
Lots of planning	Lots of problem solving
Focused (down or up) the organization	Focused horizontally, working with other functions to speed action taking
Transmitting middle/top management needs "down"	Selling teams ideas and needs "up"
Providing new ideas for workers	Helping workers/teams develop their own ideas, providing ideas for cross functional systems improvement

Role of New Team Leaders	
* Facilitators	* Area housekeeping
* Conduct team briefing	* Total preventive maintenance
* Organize employee involvement groups	* Problem solvers

an "in house" training program to teach all employees about *kaizen* and how it was going to help improve operations (see Table 35-1 for examples of training materials).

Heavy emphasis was placed on teams and the concept of participative management. Supervisors were now identified as "team leaders," "coaches," and "facilitators." Employees were empowered to stop the line to address quality problems.

Harry began regularly meeting with his "team leaders" and briefing them on the *kaizen* process. They, in turn, were required to meet once a week with employees to identify and solve problems leading to improvements in quality and waste reduction. Harry also began regular meetings with union leadership.

To compete effectively in this "new" environment, Firestone NZ also had to redefine its manufacturing strategy. Especially important was the incorporation of advanced technological issues with strategic decision making in manufacturing. McMillan believed that surviving the onslaught of competitive pressure would require emphasis in the following areas:

1. Competitive production costs for reduced run lengths and increased product mix
2. Superior, reliable, consistent quality
3. Ability to introduce new products quickly
4. Ability to change over products without delay

5. Adequate return on investment
6. Competitively short production cycles
7. Competitively short delivery delays

To accomplish these objectives, Firestone NZ required a powerful manufacturing strategy that was simple, logical, and visible to obtain widespread support of all of its constituencies, including management, labor, suppliers, and customers. The strategy needed to be easily implemented without much capital investment and capable of being improved upon gradually. In tire manufacturing, quality is of paramount importance. Thus, cost cutting with no regard to its effect on quality was out of the question. Embracing the *kaizen* philosophy offered the possibility of increases in both quality and profitability.

Using the training and the regular meetings as the beginning, small work teams were formed to focus on problem solving. This provided a framework that allowed people to work effectively with others and build team spirit. The performance objectives for each work team were created to reflect small incremental improvements rather than sweeping generalizations or complete solutions. Above all, the work teams were assured of the complete support and commitment of management.

Using these work teams as quality improvement teams, three major areas of manufacturing strategy were targeted for immediate action using the *kaizen* philosophy and the work teams:

1. Productivity improvement
2. Just in time/*kanban*
3. Total quality control

Productivity Improvement

Firestone NZ produces up to 80 different sizes of tires per month, so the factory works as a batch process. This results in frequent changes in machine settings, stock cutting, and preparation to cater to the frequent change-over in sizes. The major objectives of the productivity improvement program were to minimize movement of material from one work station to another and to reduce cycle time for each of the work stations/machines.

Although productivity improvement methods had been introduced in the past, the regular *kaizen* meetings, emphasis on empowerment, and communication with management began to have the desired effect.

One such improvement was the switch to a "production cell layout," where groups of material and processes were completed together. It became more like an assembly operation, where the operators finished a whole operation at one work station before feeding it directly to the next work station. This was coupled with a change in how parts were stored and provided to the work stations. Previously, parts produced were kept in a storage area and operators requiring them had to walk to the storage area to collect and bring them back to their respective work stations for further processing. Now, parts were directly placed onto movable skids and carted to the next work station. These changes reduced material handling time and work-in-process storage area.

The new philosophy also resulted in new technology being introduced where appropriate. For example, installation of programmable logic controls (PLC) units on old curing presses reduced cycle time of curing each tire from 1.8 minutes to 1.3 minutes. This increased the curing output by 120 tires per day. The cost of installing the PLC units was negligible compared to the capital expenditure that would have been necessary to increase curing output by installing new presses.

Just in Time (JIT)/*Kanban*

Kaizen was also used in the area of material flows where most of the operations were repetitive in nature and parts produced were usually small in volume. Given the production of the almost 80 different sizes in batches, many operations had to be changed each time to produce the varied tire sizes. Thus, synchronizing material flows with production operations and machine set up was a difficult problem.

Again, with the input and involvement of all employees, this process was changed from a "push" *kanban* to a "pull" *kanban*. In this way, materials are delivered or used just when needed (JIT), not pushed through the system based on available inventory. Thus, the attention is focused on customer demand or desire rather than preset expectations of production.

Now, much of the production scheduling is handled by the operators. The number of scheduling staff was reduced from 6 to 2 people, and the average time for "green tires" (tires awaiting final vulcanization in the presses) from 3 *days* of production to 2 *shifts* or 16 hours. The ultimate aim is to operate only 1 shift of green tires.

Total Quality Control

Lastly, according to *kaizen* philosophy, *quality* management was seen as the key to success in manufacturing. Although tools such as statistical process control (SPC) had been used since 1984, total quality control (TQC) was to establish a fundamental relationship between the organization, its functional departments, and the customers it served.

Under the *kaizen* banner then, Firestone NZ initiated a company-wide quality improvement (CWQI) program that included top management, managers, team leaders, and workers in all areas of corporate activities such as marketing, sales, manufacturing, administration, finance, purchasing, training, and education. The CWQI program became a comprehensive system of corporate problem solving and improvement activity in Firestone NZ.

Firestone NZ's commitment was to provide complete satisfaction by the provision of products and services, delivered on time, within budgeted costs and to the users' requirements. This commitment was to be realized through a steadfast, long-term and continuous business philosophy that:

1. Acknowledged the customer above all else, whether that customer was the consumer of tires, the next department in the production process, or the recipient of a departmental project.
2. Insisted that seeing the problem for one's self in the place it happened was essential to knowledgeable decision making.
3. Relied on teamwork.
4. Respected people and recognized that their contributions determined the company's success.
5. Encouraged the ceaseless and untiring efforts of all employees in reducing defective product, in eliminating waste, and in improving all functions performed in the company.
6. Made provisions for people to improve their individual performance through training and education.

Implementation of CWQI was also supported by Bridgestone/Firestone Inc.'s own quality efforts and a growing involvement on the part of all employees in ensuring a high quality product was delivered to the customer.

The implementation of TQC focused specifically on the statistical application of quality control concepts, including the use and analysis of statistical data. Situations and problems under study by the quality teams had to be quantified as much as possible. This required much training, time, and effort on the part of all employees to develop the skills and knowledge to effectively apply the concepts. Team meetings regularly used statistical data to support both analysis and improvement suggestions, and ongoing use developed a growing confidence in operators.

Thus, it was not surprising to find that now, if the quality was considered unacceptable, operators took action. Operators were in a position to make decisions based on Statistical Process Control (SPC) data and could call the maintenance staff as required. If problems with a machine were imminent, they did not continue production until failures occurred. Instead, they stopped the machine and took proper action to rectify the problems. Quality was maintained and machine downtime also reduced as the SPC system gave operators more responsibility in their jobs, and the positions of line inspectors were eliminated. With SPC, the working relationships between operators, maintenance staff, "team leaders," and management has improved.

Human Resource Strategy

Many companies in competitive manufacturing emphasize improving performance through modern equipment and process technology rather than people. In addition to the improved manufacturing techniques, Harry also recognized the need for emphasizing the "soft" side or the "human resource side" of advanced manufacturing technology. This focus on instilling the *kaizen* "thinking" in people as part of the process, required no capital investment and appeared to provide a "long-term solution" in an uncertain environment.

However, Harry also saw that the "participative management" required for effective implementation of *kaizen* would be difficult to bring into the Firestone culture. Participative management, quite literally, resulted in "cultural shock," as it was not the traditional management style to which successful managers at Firestone had been accustomed. The traditional style, which was allowed to continue for several years after the purchase by Bridgestone, was quite autocratic and cost focused. Thus, management-derived methods given to supervisors to increase efficiency through manufacturing techniques did not encounter a great deal of resistance. However, getting managers to accept worker participation in decisions, was quite different. Participative management required managers to give up power; even workers found it difficult to adapt to new behaviors that required them to assume responsibility.

It was not easy to adopt because it required a conscious shift away from managing tasks and toward leading people. This meant involvement of those who were responsible for day-to-day execution of tasks in problem solving and decision making. Management had to believe that employees were the company's most valuable assets and that people would respond positively if given a reason and an opportunity. Harry himself developed the comparative statements seen in Table 35-1 to expose managers to ideas about change in organizational style and roles and to more clearly communicate the differences that would be necessary in each employee's behavior.

Previously, employees had been encouraged to suggest improvements in operations and were individually rewarded for doing so. They were now additionally being prompted to do so directly in weekly meetings with team leader and in the problem solving and improvement teams that had been created. Department managers were required to provide a timely evaluation of ideas and, if the suggestion was not accepted, department managers had to explain why.

Through the in-house training program developed by the human resource department, employees were also given the opportunity to participate in education and training programs that emphasized the value and processes associated with *kaizen.* Outside literature was also supplied that provided the ideas and practices of total quality advocates such as Crosby's *Quality is Free,* Peters' *Thriving on Chaos,* and Imai's, *Kaizen.* Key staff were also sent to tire plants in Japan and Europe to see first-hand how the philosophy was applied.

Lastly, Harry knew that involvement and close cooperation with the union would be vital to success. But, he did not expect it to be as difficult as it might have been in the U.S. Fortunately, the emphasis placed on improving union relations through 1985 and 1986, had facilitated cooperation between the union and company. Also, he had found the New Zealand workers to be easy-going, mellow individuals. They had always appeared adaptable and much less resistant than U.S. workers to foreign products, practices, and behaviors. New Zealand relied heavily on imports of electronic products, cars, household goods, etc. from Asia, and "foreigners" to New Zealand were typically well-received and welcomed.

Unions members appeared to recognize the need for change to ensure survival, and Firestone NZ was thus able to negotiate a new, progressive, three-year agreement in November of 1988. It tied wage increases to after-tax profits. One part of the wage increase is guaranteed at 2.7% in the first year and 1.3% in the subsequent two years. The other part of the wage increase was linked to net profits, so that as the company prospered in the future, the workers would also benefit. Payment of accumulated sick days as wages upon retirement, resignation or redundancy was also approved. Since the agreement, a 50% reduction in absenteeism, and no major stoppages have occurred, indicating worker satisfaction.

Results

In the next five years, continuous improvements became the norm. Following the review of methods, layout, materials and the introduction of new standards and incentives, productivity gains were achieved ranging from 3% to 50% depending on the operation. Improvements in waste reduction were equally impressive. In fact, since the beginning of *kaizen*'s implementation in 1987, overall waste has been cut in half.

Using the *kanban* "pull" process has dropped total work in process from 8.5 days of production in 1985 to 4.7 days in 1992; and the goal is to reduce it further to 4.0 days by 1993. Floor space has now been released for expansion and installation of new equipment. Approximately 80% of the plant is now covered by *kanban* systems and efforts continue to increase its use.

As of late 1992, Firestone U.S.A.'s $15 million investment in Firestone New Zealand, although small by world standards, seems to have yielded the benefits that eluded Bridgestone following their initial purchase of Firestone U.S.A. Production of 2,719 tires per day in 1984 with 435 employees, grew to 3,531 tires per day with 298 employees in 1992; a substantial improvement in output while at the same time, accompanied by a decrease in the number of personnel. The investment in modernization of operations coupled with Harry's belief and use of *kaizen,* has resulted in a 120% overall improvement in productivity.

The Future

"So," Harry thought to himself, "What now? We have had good results in a number of areas. Productivity is improved, we've reduced work force and labor costs, and we've maintained or improved the overall quality of our product. In fact, our improvement in quality has earned us Ford's Q-1 award, which is awarded to Ford's high quality supplier and should yield additional business in Australia and other Pacific Basin countries."

"It even seems we have changed the attitudes of our people. As a result of managers giving out more information and making decisions with workers, the workers seem more enthusiastic, happier, and more *kaizen*-driven. Whereas before, an employee finding a defect or quality problem often would let it go and create much waste before the problem was caught later in the line, more immediate action is now being taken to stop the line, fix the problem, and then restart."

In fact, Harry had seen numerous examples of "teamwork" between workers, electricians, mechanics, and "team leaders." Previously, if a machine was producing a poor product, the operator would likely call the supervisor; and, when the machine was stopped, would leave until the mechanic or electrician had fixed it. Now, it was common to see operators stopping the machines, calling the "fitters" (electrician/mechanics) themselves directly, and *staying* and working with them until the repairs were completed.

Even relations with the union had improved. Strikes, common prior to *kaizen* improvement efforts, had not happened. In fact, there had been none in the last few years and recent interactions with union representatives had been much more cooperative.

"But can we still improve? Can we continue to get better and not only survive but prosper? Under *kaizen* thinking, we can and must always improve. But these improvements have been hard and not without pain. Can we continue to do so? Will employees continue to challenge themselves and us to do better? Have we managed to instill kaizen thinking in all of us? How long will it take to reach our new goal of achieving ISO9002 certification?"

These were the questions that filled Harry McMillan's thoughts as the future of Firestone New Zealand loomed ahead!

36
Service Excellence in the Travel Industry: Singapore Airlines

Robert T. Moran
and
Georgi Vicari

Singapore Airlines

Mark Lee, president of Singapore Airlines (SIA), sat at his desk early Monday morning reflecting upon the intense competition within his industry, a factor driving the need to continuously improve service excellence. SIA had for years been the leader in service excellence—the walls of his office were covered with awards to prove it. Most recently, Euromoney's 1990 Business Travel Survey listed the company, along with Swiss Air and British Airways, as one of the top three airlines in the world. He knew, however, that getting to the top was the easy part, staying there was another story.

He asked his secretary to hold his calls for the next hour, leaned back in his chair and contemplated a statement made at a recent "Evening Talks." The SIA Management Development Center sponsored this series of presentations by international speakers on various topics, ranging from social and political issues to global management. The statement was:

> I think we all know that service excellence is not something that is static. One cannot take it for granted; it has to be continuously nurtured and improved upon. . . . When we talk about service excellence, what we are talking about is consistently high-quality ser-

The case study is designed for educational purposes and classroom use. Assistance in critiquing the case was provided by Pamela Unternaehrer. Thanks also to Sim Kay Wee of Singapore Airlines and Jacki Bowers of Bowers Worldwide Travel Management Company.

vice. It is not being satisfied with the average, it is offering high-quality service and delivering that service all the time.

"Delivering that service all the time," he repeated to himself, "that was the challenge." Each time he had flown SIA he was pleased with the service, but he could not help wondering whether the service was exaggerated because he was on board. And, if this was the case, how was the average person treated? What did excellent service really mean for the typical SIA passenger?

Why not take a trip and not let anyone know who he was? It was a worthwhile idea and might answer his questions about the service on SIA flights. Normally, his secretary coordinated his travel plans, but he decided to handle the arrangements personally this time, starting with booking the flight through a travel agency.

Travel Agency

The travel agent that Lee located in the telephone directory and visited was incredibly helpful. She took the time to find the best route possible and asked several questions about his travel preferences. She inquired about his seating preference, favored type of rental car, and kinds of hotel amenities he required. He was pleasantly surprised by the amount of interest she took in him. He was even more pleased to hear that, as far as she was concerned, SIA was, without a doubt, an excellent airline. Lee wondered if all clients received the same level of service.

He noticed that a bud vase and flower rested on each agent's desk and inquired as to the reason for this. With a smile, she responded that this helped reinforce the feeling that all employees were part of the agency "family." The "bud" vase helped remind them that they were all a Bower's buddy. She further spoke of the growth of the agency from one to many locations and the involvement of employees in the decision-making process. Most of the employees had been with the company 10 or more years and had watched and helped the agency grow. She indicated that no amount of money could buy the loyalty that respect from the owners engendered.

The agent was highly enthusiastic about the environment in which she worked, and Lee noted that this kind of enthusiasm was truly infectious. He found himself feeling increasingly comfortable and confident that the agent would make the best possible arrangements for his trip. As she continued telling him about the continued training and seminars offered to agency employees to learn new ways of providing outstanding service to clients, he knew he would be in good hands.

His trip would start in Singapore with a flight to Los Angeles via Hong Kong on SIA. Next, he would take American Airlines to Chicago, spend the night, and then fly British Airways to England, where he would spend another night. Finally, he planned to return to Singapore, flying business class on SIA's latest airplane, the 747-400 megatop.

He intended to depart Wednesday morning and return Monday morning, thereby losing just three working days. Due to the short notice, the agent experienced some difficulty locating the seats Lee preferred; thus, he was forced to settle for middle seats during several legs of the trip. However, the agent explained that the Seat-Finder service would scan his flights, look for available seats closer to his request, and reserve such seats if located.

The booking process had taken longer than he had anticipated, so the agent offered to have his tickets delivered that evening. As he left the agent's office, he felt satisfied that, even on short notice and with several legs to his trip, he could not have received better or more helpful service. The agent had clearly taken a personal interest in his needs and had tried to match them to the available services. To his pleasant surprise, she had shown understanding and empathy for the rigors of long distance travel.

History of SIA

Lee was excited about the prospect of flying SIA's new megatop as it represented the culmination of many years of hard work, dedication, and trial and error—to think that it was only 44 years ago that SIA embarked upon its maiden voyage. On May 1, 1947, a twin-engine Airspeed Consul, flying under Malayan Airways, took off from Singapore to Penang, carrying five passengers, a radio operator, and the pilot.

Since those days SIA had grown considerably. As of 1987, it owned fourteen B747-300s, nine B747-200s, four 757s, six A310s, and transported passengers to 52 destinations in 34 countries around the world. Lee smiled; they had come a long way indeed!

The Journey—Singapore to Los Angeles

The check-in procedure proceeded smoothly. Upon presenting his ticket, he was relieved to learn that his seat assignment had been changed to meet his preference for the flight to Los Angeles and then to Chicago. He had especially dreaded occupying a middle seat during the Singapore to L.A. segment.

Lee was also impressed with the way an SIA employee handled an emotional incident that occurred in the short line at the counter. From what Lee could gather, a mother was sending her nine-year-old daughter to visit her father in the U.S. Crying bitterly, the young girl was quite emotional. The SIA counter clerk handled the situation well, taking time to talk with the young girl and reassure her that the trip would be fun. The girl's sobs subsided as the clerk leaned over the counter, gave her something, and promised her that she could see the cockpit during the flight. Lee could see the relief on the mother's face and was pleased with the way the clerk handled the incident. He thought to himself that this was an excellent example of one of SIA's hallmarks: care and genuine concern for the customer.

Lee saw the young girl from the ticket counter again later, this time alone at the departure gate sitting quietly in a chair. Her crying had stopped, but he could tell by the look in her eyes that she was still frightened.

About fifteen minutes passed before boarding commenced, and Lee noticed that not one person during that time had approached the child. The SIA representative announced the boarding of first-class passengers and those needing extra time to get settled. Usually, this was the time that unaccompanied children were supposed to enter the plane, but no one appeared to assist the child.

As was his usual manner, Lee waited until everyone had boarded. Still, the little girl waited. Annoyed, he made his way to the counter and mentioned his concern about the lack of attention toward the young girl. The representative thanked him with a smile and responded that the girl would be taken care of in just a moment. She herself would accompany the child on board the plane.

The flight itself was pleasant; although it was difficult acclimating to economy class after becoming accustomed to first class. The seats were closer together, and leg room was scarce. Lee, however, recognized that little improvement could be achieved in this area given the limitations imposed by space constraints and cost efficiency.

Flight Attendants

At first, afraid of being recognized, Lee refrained from asking for service from the flight attendant. After some time, when it seemed that he had successfully escaped notice, the requests Lee made were met with pleasant and prompt responses. Analyzing the quality of service, however, was difficult for Lee, because he was accustomed to the individualized attention of first class.

The quality of SIA's flight attendants is critical to the provision of the level of service for which SIA has become known. The Singapore woman in her sarong Kebaya has traditionally served as the "logo" for the company, and passengers expect the same Oriental charm and friendliness from each SIA attendant. Thus, significant financial resources are allocated toward the recruiting and training of flight attendants.

Moreover, SIA's recruitment and training programs are the most rigorous in the industry. A series of three interviews culminating in formal tea is followed by a three-month training program once an attendant is hired. Attendants must possess and convey confidence in their ability to provide outstanding service to the customer, while at the same time imparting a sense of humility. A difficult quality to describe, Lee knew, but an important part of SIA's philosophy.

Training in all functions, not only for flight attendants, within SIA is highly valued. The company expends $30 million annually on staff training programs, one reason that SIA was awarded the National Training Award for the service sector in 1990.

Lee noticed an older hostess, Gao Xiarong, who would seen be forced to retire at the age of 35. Stewards, however, were allowed to work until they were 40; and, if promoted to chief steward, they remained eligible to continue working until age 55.

However, careers as flight attendants for women were short-lived. In fact, a tenure of more than ten years was considered long, because SIA only hired women between the ages of 18 and 25. The argument to extend the retirement age for women and men was a sensitive and often-debated issue at SIA. Many in support of extending the age limits argued that an older crew offered several advantages, including more experience and greater respect. Extending the retirement age would also lower turnover and, therefore, reduce costs.

The Wait

Lee arrived at the Los Angeles Airport on time, with more than 40 minutes to catch his connecting flight. Upon reaching the departure gate, he still had nearly a half-hour, so he bought some coffee and sat down near the windows overlooking the runway. He decided against finding a telephone to make some necessary calls, because the time to board was fast approaching. In fact, a glance at his watch revealed that the plane should have already commenced boarding—this meant that it would be running late.

Every few minutes, Lee glanced at his watch, becoming more frustrated as time passed. It was not so much the fact that the flight would depart late that annoyed him; it was the absence of an announcement about the situation. As far as he knew, the plane could depart in five minutes or five hours. Once again, he reflected upon another comment made during an Evening Talk: "The person who is annoyed will be satisfied if you apologize." How true, Lee mused. All he wanted to hear was some kind of apology and explanation about the cause of the delay and the expected departure time.

No sooner had he finished this thought when an announcement was made apologizing for the delay. Apparently, the pilot had fallen ill and was unable to fly, and a replacement would arrive in forty-five minutes to an hour. Although this was disappointing news, nothing could be done. In any case, at least now he knew how long he could expect to wait and could plan accordingly. A glance at other passengers' faces revealed that they, too, had reached the same conclusion.

After an hour passed and no new announcement concerning the situation was forthcoming, Lee could feel the frustration of the passengers rising again. During this time, several passengers approached the counter to ask for an update, and a group of business people congregating near the water fountain could be heard criticizing the delay and the company. Any announcement, thought Lee, even the same news, would be preferable to the silence.

Satisfying customers, even under unexpected circumstances, was an airline's greatest challenge. Expecting the worst to happen and being adequately prepared to handle crises as they arose resulted in loyal customers. Lee recalled how SAS rebounded from near failure and huge losses to earning millions of dollars in just one year by setting three nonnegotiable standards: technology, operations, and service. SIA's goal was to meet and, if possible, surpass customer expectations in these three areas. Service excellence, noted Lee, was an effective strategy to differentiate an airline in this highly competitive industry.

Nearly two hours after the original departure time, Lee finally boarded. Tired, like the rest of the passengers, he just wanted to get to Chicago as soon as possible.

Understanding that the delay was attributable to circumstances beyond the airline's control, Lee sympathized with its dilemma. However, he was aggravated with the way the airline handled the situation. Not only did they fail to inform the passengers promptly and periodically about the situation, the counter clerks were rude and unapologetic. If only the employees realized the damage that their mishandling of the situation inflicted on corporate goodwill, thought Lee. Satisfying customers is important in all industries, acknowledged Lee, but it is absolutely crucial in the airline industry.

Studies have shown that an individual pleased with a product or service will tell at least five others. Alternately, a dissatisfied customer will usually relate a negative experience to twenty people. Thus, based on this assumption, 2,000 people could possibly, directly or indirectly, receive a negative image of the airline as a result of this one delay. Multiply this figure by the number of times a company makes a similar mistake without apologizing, and the figures could be quite alarming, thought Lee. If every employee understood the importance of their actions in shaping a customer's overall impression, who knew how successful a company could become based on the power of word of mouth?

The Journey—Los Angeles to Chicago

As Lee settled into his seat, he noticed that the carpet on the wall was peeling, and the interior looked shabby. In addition to the ragged carpet, an occasional drop of water fell from the ceiling. While Lee knew that these drops, which originated from accumulated condensation, were nothing to worry about, he was aware that this did little to enhance passengers' confidence in the safety of the airplane.

Because the average person lacks the ability to accurately assess the importance an airline places on technical thoroughness and safety, they search for surrogate signs. Lee was well-aware of this "surrogate" issue, and hence the importance of maintaining a well-kept, functional and aesthetically-pleasing airplane. Subconsciously, customers analyze the cabin to judge the overall condition of the plane. Peeling carpet and drops of condensation will cause a passenger to question the safety of the plane.

Overall, thought Lee, the service could not be described as poor, but a striking difference between the Singaporean and the American hostesses existed. Perhaps this was due to culture—the SIA flight attendant appeared more willing to serve. Although friendly and efficient, the American hostess seemed somewhat insincere to Lee. She tended to be perfunctory in performing her duties, rather than showing genuine concern for each passenger. The SIA flight attendant, on the other hand, appeared more compassionate and willing to help an individual have a more comfortable flight. As far as Lee was concerned, this difference is what established SIA as a leader in service.

The plane finally landed in Chicago after a two-hour delay. As Lee waited for his luggage, he again saw the young girl from Singapore, standing alone waiting for her bags. It was the first time he had seen her since the departure gate, and he had almost forgotten about her. No flight attendant accompanied her, and Lee could not believe she had been left alone. He made his way toward her and asked if a flight attendant was helping her. The young girl replied that one had accompanied her here and instructed her to retrieve her luggage and meet her at the end of the baggage claim area.

Lee helped her get her bags and carried them down to the door. The flight attendant, sitting in the room drinking coffee, thanked Lee for his assistance. Lee refrained from commenting on the attendant's misconduct at the time. Instead, he asked for her name, intending to report her negligent behavior upon returning to Singapore.

SIA adhered to a strict policy regarding complaints, and compliments, for that matter. All passenger comments and evaluations are analyzed and receive responses. Samples of both positive and negative submissions are published each month in *Outlook,* the in-house newspaper of the SIA group.

The incident brought to mind a report he had recently read about a Delta Airline employee's interview with a researcher. The employee was helpful and enthusiastic and provided a great deal of useful information. Upon leaving, the researcher thanked the employee and apologized for taking so much of his time away from work. "Oh," replied the employee, "I'm on vacation this week. I just flew in from Miami for this interview with you. I enjoy talking about our airline. All of the Delta family feels the same way." There existed an amazing contrast between this Delta employee and the American flight attendant who could not be troubled to leave her coffee to help a young girl alone on a flight half-way around the world. It was yet another example of service excellence, and an additional reference to the feeling of "family" in the work environment, for Lee to ponder.

The Last Leg

Lee had chosen to travel business class from England to Singapore to experience the new facilities offered by the megatop. In 1981, SIA introduced a business-class option, but encountered some difficulty marketing it to customers. The minimal difference between the services in SIA's economy class and those offered by other airline's business class was a primary reason. Also, care had to be taken to avoid confusing passengers about the difference between this class and first class. Renowned for its outstanding first-class travel accommodations, SIA was wary of the possibility that the business-class option could detract from its first-class service. However, SIA was unable to ignore the benefits that business class conferred. Thus, changes were made—the new megatop represented the latest.

Once again, Lee was one of the last to board despite the fact that passengers flying business class, along with those in first class, are allowed to board first. He made his way upstairs to a room that held 80 seats, gave his jacket to the flight attendant, sat down, and proceeded to slip on a pair of complimentary slippers. The seats were extremely comfortable and almost fully reclinable—a great luxury considering the eleven-hour flight ahead.

The service was spectacular and easily comparable to that of first class. The four flight attendants assigned to this section allowed for superior personalized attention, although not quite meeting the level provided in first class. Each attendant was courteous, willing to please, and friendly.

Now that Lee had come to the last leg of his travels, it was time to draw some conclusions. He reflected upon the four essentials of service excellence set forth by experts in the airline industry:

1. Consistency: reliability, getting it right the first time.
2. Attentiveness: paying attention and knowing what the customer needs.
3. Recoverability: handling unexpected situations well.
4. Evaluation: continuously assessing and improving performance.

Lee reclined in his seat. Did SIA possess these attributes? What other factors contribute significantly to service excellence? Did the airline industry as a whole possess the qualities necessary for service excellence? Lee had much to think about, but he also had more than ten hours of relaxing, uninterrupted flying to do it.

About the Contributors

Julian H. Allen served as senior international business executives for many years with two different companies, and as a professor at Elmira College. He worked for Corning Glass Works for over forty years, including senior positions with responsibility for production, marketing, personnel and purchasing, and a fourteen-year period where he was responsible for six separate European subsidiaries during Corning's international expansion. He came to Elmira College in 1981 as Executive in Residence and Corning Glass Chair of Business. After his retirement in 1985, he served as a member of the Grace Commission Private Sector Survey on Cost Control. During his time at Elmira College, Allen helped set the framework for a new bachelor's degree in International Business.

Suresh Balan, Ph.D., is assistant professor of operations management, EIPM, France. He started his industrial experience with General Motors-Isuzu Motors and while working in Japan was trained in all aspects of Japanese manufacturing and management systems. Later, he worked for the truck and car divisions of the company in India. He then joined Bridgestone-Firestone in the Asia-Pacific and worked in their manufacturing plants in Indonesia, Australia, and New Zealand. As process control manager, he was involved in production control systems and quality aspects in tire manufacture. He has published several articles in production/operations management areas in various journals and international conference proceedings and is currently lecturing in MBA programs in France.

Arvind Bhambri, Ph.D., is an associate professor of management and organization in the Graduate School of Business Administration at the University of Southern California. He consults widely in strategic planning. He has written and co-written several articles and cases dealing with strategic issues. His Ph.D. is from the Harvard Business School. He is a member of the editorial board of the *Strategic Management Journal.*

David Bollier is a journalist and consultant with extensive expertise in business affairs, public policy and law. A former contributing editor for *Channels* Magazine, Mr. Bollier has been an independent writer based in New Haven, Connecticut since 1985, consulting with nonprofit organizations and contributing to many magazines. He is the author of four books. Mr. Bollier has previously worked as a congressional aide; as research director for People for the American Way; and as editor of *Public Citizen* magazine.

David O. Braaten, Ph.D., is an associate professor at Thunderbird, The American Graduate School of International Management, where he specializes in cross-cultural communication. Previously, he was on the faculty of the International Business Education and Research (IBEAR) MBA program in the Graduate School of Business Administration at the University of Southern California. David has consulted with managers and executives from international companies enhancing cross-cultural perspectives for a global marketplace. He has worked in Mexico and lectured in Taipei, Taiwan. His Ph.D. in communication arts and sciences is from the University of Southern California. David has written in the area of social explanations of behavior in relational and managerial contexts. He is on the Editorial Advisory Board of the *International Directory of Intercultural Resources.*

William Coon was a founder and officer of a company that manufactured and marketed electronic telephone systems in China and Hong Kong. He spent seventeen years in international sales and marketing positions, most of them as international sales manager for a global company in the bottling industry. During this time he established sales offices in 13 countries. Mr. Coon received undergraduate degrees in electrical engineering and romance languages from the University of California. Later, he obtained graduate degrees in business and international affairs from Washington University in St. Louis, Missouri.

John Davis, Ph.D., is the executive director of the Owner-Managed Business Institute in Santa Barbara, California, which specializes in consulting with family-owned businesses in the areas of executive succession, strategy development, and change. He formerly was on the faculty of the Graduate School of Business Administration at the University of Southern California. He is a frequent lecturer for the Young President's Organization. His Ph.D. is from the Harvard Business School.

C. Roe Goddard, Ph.D., is currently an assistant professor in the Department of International Studies at Thunderbird—The American Graduate School of International Management, Glendale, Arizona. He has written numerous articles on the political/economic context of international business and in 1993 authored a book titled *U.S. Foreign Economic Policy and the Latin American Debt Issue.* Dr. Goddard is the managing editor of *International Studies Notes.* He holds a Ph.D.

from the University of South Carolina and an M.B.A. in International Business from the University of Denver. Formerly with The Upjohn Company, Dr. Goddard has consulted with numerous international firms.

Alan Goldman, Ph.D., is president of Goldman and Associates, Scottsdale, Arizona, a group providing training and consulting services to international organizations. Dr. Goldman is the author of six books on communication, business, and management, his most recent for SUNY Press, *Doing Business With The Japanese: A Guide to Successful Communication, Management, and Diplomacy.* He is widely published in management and communication journals, and has served as chief trade writer for the Bush Administration's and U.S. Congress's international publication, *Five Hundred.* The author lived and worked in Tokyo, where he has been an intercultural and managerial consultant and trainer for a variety of Japanese corporations. Goldman is also editor of *The Arizona Communication Journal,* a publication highlighting intercultural and international business and management studies.

Kirk O. Hanson is senior lecturer in business administration at the Stanford University Graduate School of Business where he has taught since 1978 in the MBA and Executive programs. Mr. Hanson also serves as president of The Business Enterprise Trust, a national business responsibility organization headquartered on the Stanford Campus. Mr. Hanson has been a national leader in the development of teaching and research on business responsibility and business ethics. He was the founder and chairman of The Hanson Group, Inc., through which he conducted corporate values and ethics workshops for over thirty companies during the 1980s. Mr. Hanson is a graduate of Stanford University and the Stanford Graduate School of Business and has held graduate fellowships and research appointments at the Yale Divinity School and the Harvard Business School.

C. Thomas Howard, Ph.D., is an associate professor at Denver University in the Finance Department where he is responsible for teaching investment management and international finance courses. He is an instructor at DU's nationally ranked Executive MBA program. In addition, he has been a guest lecturer at SDA Bocconi, Italy's leading business school and at Handelshojshole Syd in Denmark. Howard presents seminars throughout the U.S. for the American Association of Individual Investors.

Dr. Howard has published both articles and monographs dealing with a range of topics including economic forecasting, housing investment and futures markets. His articles have appeared in academic journals as well as more popular publications such as *Barron's.* In 1985 he received the Faculty Research award as the top faculty researcher within the Business School, and in 1992 was designated a Willemssen Professor. After receiving his BS in Mechanical Engineering at the University of Idaho, Howard worked for Proctor & Gamble as a production and warehouse manager for three years. He then entered Oregon State University where he received an MS in management science after which he received a Ph.D. in finance from the University of Washington in 1978.

John Irons was raised in Hawaii. After receiving a BA from Hanover College where he majored in business administration and international studies, John returned to Hawaii where he established Gourmet Yard Service, a landscaping company. John joined the Peace Corps in 1988 as a Training Officer for the Malawi Union of Savings and Credit Cooperatives. Upon completion of his service John attended the American Graduate School of International Management from which he graduated in 1992. Currently, John is employed by the International Rescue Committee as their monetization manager for the Horn of Africa Program.

Cheryl Johnson graduated from Stanford University in 1981 with a degree in English/American literature and creative writing. Participation in an earlier Semester at Sea program prompted a decision to teach English in mainland China after graduation through Volunteers in Asia. Following two years in Wuhan, Hubei Province and an additional year and a half in Shenyang, Liaoning, Ms. Johnson returned to California, where she helped coordinate an International Management Development program for Japanese managers at IRI International, Inc. In 1985, she began another assignment in Changchun, Jilin, married a Chinese national, and returned to California in 1987. She attended the American Graduate School of International Management and received a Master of International Management in 1991. She now resides in northern California working for Syntex Laboratories, Inc.

John R. Kerschen received his B.A. at Wichita State University and his Master of International Management at the American Graduate School of International Management. His cross-cultural experiences include six years of work at the Intensive English Language Center of Wichita State University and a year of travel in Latin America. Mr. Kerschen is now International Market Manager for Central America and the Andean Region at Hach Company, a manufacturer of systems for water analysis.

Ralph Krueger has a Master of International Management (MIM) from the American Graduate School in International Management, Glendale, AZ (USA). He also has a German Diplom-Betriebswirt (FH) degree from the Fachhochschule Reutlingen, Europäisches Studienprogram für Betriebswirtschaft (ESB) and an English B.A. (Hons.) degree from the Middlesex University, London. He has emphasized strategic management, international marketing, international finance and cross-cultural management in his studies.

Yuen Ching Karen Lee is currently working in Taiwan after obtaining a Master of International Management from the American Graduate School of International Management, Glendale, Arizona.

Joseph N. Lombardo is a graduate of The American Graduate School of International Management, Thunderbird Campus, Glendale, Arizona; with a Master of International Management (MIM) degree. He earned his B.A. in Honors Business Administration from the Richard G. Ivey School of Business Administration at the University of Western Ontario, London, Canada. Mr. Lombardo has lived in the former Soviet Union and has consulted for American firms wishing to establish operations in the newly independent states. He has lectured on joint venture initiation, effective negotiating, marketing and general management to students and senior executives in Belarus and Ukraine.

Robert P. McGowan is associate professor of Management in the College of Business, University of Denver where he specializes in public policy and business and corporate strategy. He has previously published in such journals as *Policy Studies Journal, Policy Studies Review,* and *Public Administration Review* and is currently researching in the area of international strategic alliances.

John P. Millikin, Ph.D., is the vice president and director of Human Resources for Motorola, Inc., CPSTG in Phoenix, AZ. He is a former national vice-president for the Society for Human Resource Management and is on the Editorial Review Board for *Employment Relations Today.* His fields of interest are self leadership and team empowerment. He holds an MBA from the University of Southern California. His Ph.D. is from the College of Business Administration at Arizona State University.

Robert T. Moran, Ph.D., is an organizational and management consultant with specialties in cross-cultural training, organizational development, and international human resource management. At present, he is the director of the Program in Cross-Cultural Communication and Professor of International Studies at the American Graduate School of International Management. During the academic year 1987-88, he was Visiting Professor at Ecole Superieure Des Sciences Economique Et Commerciales in France.

He has co-authored *Managing Cultural Differences,* Third Edition, (seven printings), *Successful International Business Negotiations,* and *Developing Global Organizations: Strategies for Human Resource Professionals.* He is the author of *Getting Your Yen's Worth: How to Negotiate with Japan, Inc., Venturing Abroad in Asia, Cultural Guide to Doing Business in Europe* and is the senior editor of *Global Business Management in the 1990s.*

Jeffrey Ovian in the late seventies left Vermont to study at the Colorado School of Mines. He earned a mining engineering degree and a place in the McBride Program in Public Affairs. Ovian has worked in various capacities in African and North American base and precious metal mines. Over the years since his first international posting in 1981, finance and marketing responsibilities have become part of his work. He graduated from the American Graduate School of International Management in 1989. Presently, he has a finance assignment in London with the subsidiary of a large transnational natural resource group.

Gerald Parkhouse's career with Mobil Oil Corporation and various of its subsidiaries started in the U.K. In the course of a career spanning thirty-two years he worked and traveled extensively around the world and filled a variety of line and staff functions, mainly in marketing and general management. After retiring it was his good fortune that Elmira College was looking for its first Corning Glass Professor of International Business. He has degrees from Boston, Harvard, Oxford and Tufts Universities.

John T Passé-Smith, Ph.D., is an assistant professor of political science at the University of Central Arkansas. He teaches political and economic development in Latin America and Third World Politics. His research and teaching focus on the politics of Latin America, the political economy of development, and international political economy.

Corinne Pfund has a Master of International Management (MIM) from the American Graduate School in International Management, Glendale, AZ (USA). She also has a German Diplom-Betriebswirt (FH) degree from the Fachhochschule Reutlingen, Europäisches Studienprogram für Betriebswirtschaft (ESB) and a French Diplôme d'Etudes Supérieures Européennes de Management (DESEM) degree from the Ecole Supérieure de Commerce (ESC) de Reims, Centre d'Etudes Supérieures Européennes de Management (CESEM). She has emphasized cross-cultural management, strategic management, and international finance in her studies. She has lived in seven different countries including France, Germany, England, The United States, French Guyana, Djibouti, and Senegal.

Anne-Lise Quinn lived in Northern Ireland until she graduated from Queen's University, Belfast with a BA in Social Anthropology. She enrolled in the doctoral program in the Department of Social Anthropology at Cambridge University, England, and subsequently conducted long-term research in Malawi, her interests lying in the fields of religion and politics. She has recently submitted her dissertation and is currently employed, along with her husband, John Irons, by the International Rescue Committee.

Kathleen K. Reardon, Ph.D., associate professor of management and organization in the University of Southern California Business School and core faculty member in the MBA and International Business MBA programs is a leading authority on persuasion, negotiation, and interpersonal communication. She is the author of four books the latest of which is *Persuasion in Practice* (Sage Publications). Dr. Reardon has published numerous articles in communication and business journals, including *The Harvard Business Review.* She has been a speaker and consultant for numerous organizations. Her current research and lectures focus on methods of persuasion to manage and motivate employees, negotiation within the U.S. and across cultures, communication challenges of a diverse workplace, and persuasion methods for changing health-related behaviors.

Geke Rosier obtained her Master of International Management from the American Graduate School of International Management in Glendale, Arizona and is working in Switzerland.

Hendrick Serrie is professor and chairman of the anthropology and international business programs at Eckerd College in St. Petersburg, Florida, and holds degrees from the University of Wisconsin, Cornell University, and Northwestern University. He has worked in Mexico, Syria, Taiwan, China, Cayman Islands, The Netherlands, Kenya, Southeast Asia, England, and Brazil. He is the director of two documentary films on solar energy (with James Silverberg, 1963 and 1964), and the editor of *Family, Kinship, and Ethnic Identity among the Overseas Chinese* (with Francis L.K. Hse, 1985) *Anthropology and International Business* (1986), and *What Can Multinationals Do For Peasants?* (with Brian S. Burkhalter, 1993, in press).

Jason Schweizer, Ph.D., has 20 years of experience specifically on the development of the World Class manager. His work, research, and teaching are in the areas of strategic management of the multinational and internationalizing company, skills needed for the international manager, the management of international human resources, and the development of World Class/*Kaizen* driven international organization. He has lived and worked both as a professor and manager in the United States, Japan, Mexico, Finland, France, England, and the Czech Republic. He is a professor of world business at the American Graduate School of International Management (Thunderbird) in the U.S.A. and is currently one of the initial professors at the school's new campus in Archamps, France.

Mitja I. Tavcar, Ph.D., holds degrees in electrotechnical and electronic engineering and industrial marketing from Ljubljana University. He earned his Ph.D. in international corporate industrial strategy from Maribor University. Dr. Tavcar held several managerial positions in Iskra Group, a large manufacturer of electronics, before retiring as a vice-president of strategic planning. He is also a professor of corporate policy and international management, Faculty of Economics and Business Administration, Maribor University. He has extensive consulting experience and is a member of Expert Committee, ITEO Consulting Ljubljana; member of Expert Listing, Slovenian Management Institute; expert of the Association of Slovenian Economists. He is on several boards of directors of Slovenian corporations. His current interests include corporate restructuring, crisis management, reprivatization of Slovenian companies, and change management.

Mary B. Teagarden, Ph.D., is an associate professor of management at San Diego State University where she teaches global strategic management, comparative management, and business strategy. Her research interest include strategic human resource management, off-shore manufacturing and technology transfer with regional emphasis on the Mexican *maquiladora* industry, business dynamics in the Asian Pacific Rim, and centrally planned economies. She has published articles in *Human Resource Management, Organizational Dynamics* and numerous other journals and has edited and co-authored three books. Currently she is completing an *International Management* textbook and finishing a three-year research project on "best practices in international human resource management."

Bertram K. Tsutakawa is presently an associate manager with Arbitron Ratings, Phoenix, Arizona. He received a Master of International Management from Thunderbird-American Graduate School of International Management. Mr. Tsutakawa holds an engineering degree from the University of Missouri, where he was an Honors Scholar. He came to Thunderbird after a significant experience in Japan as a business consultant. This followed a successful technical career with General Dynamics where he was involved with the testing and development of printed circuit boards for F-16 and F-111 aircraft avionics. He was also involved in the development of a computer-driven logistics system for the General Dynamics Systems Integration Laboratory.

Georgi Vacari holds a Master of International Management from the American Graduate School of International Management in Glendale, Arizona. She is currently working with a global company in Italy.

Mary Ann Von Glinow, Ph.D., is a professor at Florida International University in the Department of Management and International Business. She was on the faculty of the University of Southern California's Graduate School of Business Administration from 1977–1993, studying problems related to "best practices" of international HRM, international technology transfer, and managing diversity. She has a Ph.D. in management and an MBA and MPA from Ohio State University. In the last five years she has authored numerous journal articles and six books, as well as received several grants, including *U.S.—China Technology Transfer,* and *International Technology Transfer and Management.* She consults widely to both domestic and multinational enterprises and serves as a Mayoral appointee to the Shanghai Institute of Human Resources in China.

Jacqueline Karin Wagner came to the United States from Switzerland in 1979 as a high school student for one year, which then turned into a prolonged stay of 12 years. She graduated from the University of Texas, Austin with a Bachelor of Arts in French in 1985 and subsequently worked for several foreign multinationals in Texas and Georgia before attending the American Graduate School of International Management in 1989. After graduating from Thunderbird with a Master of International Management degree, she returned to Switzerland and is now working in the marketing department of a large American software firm.

John E. Walsh, Jr., D.B.A., is professor of management at the John M. Olin School of Business, Washington University, St. Louis, Missouri. He received his doctorate degree of business administration from the Harvard Business School where he was the recipient of the first Zurn Foundation Fellowship. He has taught at Stanford University; the European Institute of Management in Fountainebleau, France; Korean and Yonsei Universities in Seoul, Korea; the Tatung Institute of Management in Taipei, Taiwan; and ESAN in Lima, Peru. He has been a consultant to the Agency for International Development, the Asian Productivity Organization, the Asian Sources Media Group, the Cupples Products Company, the Dae Woo Company, the Ford Foundation, the J.M. Huber Corporation, the Monsanto Company, the Seven-Up Company, the Tatung Company, and the United Nations. He is the administrative director of the Kearny Foundation and is on the executive committee of the Economic Strategy Institute. His books include: *Preparing Feasibility Studies in Asia, Guidelines for Management Consultants in Asia, Planning New Ventures in International Business, Strategies in Business,* and *Management Tactics.*

Su-ging Wang is a professor at the University of International Business and Economics in Beijing, China. She received her Masters of International Management from the American Graduate School of International Management, Glendale, Arizona.

Stephanie L. Weiss has been a research associate with The Business Enterprise Trust. She has conducted much of the background research on nominees for the Business Enterprise Awards, and has been involved in the writing of cases and monographs for dissemination of these stories to business schools and the press. Stephanie is a graduate of Stanford University. While at Stanford, she worked as the administrative assistant in Tresidder Memorial Union's business office. In addition, she completed a summer internship at Yves Saint Laurent of America, Inc., in New York, where she was the administrative assistant in the executive offices.

Victoria R. Whiting is a doctoral student in the Department of Management and Organization at the University of Southern California. She has been selected as a Sample Fellow by the Leadership Institute. Prior to pursuing her Ph.D., Victoria was director of Technical Services at Digital Systems International.

Victoria received her bachelor's degree from the University of Colorado and her MBA degree from Seattle University. Her current research focuses on leadership and motivation issues impacted by diversity within the workforce.

Edward J. Williams, Ph.D., is a professor of political science at the University of Arizona. He teaches, researches, and writes on Latin American, Mexican, and U.S.-Mexican border public policy and politics.

Youming Ye is a graduate student at American Graduate School of International Management. Born and raised in Beijing, China, Mr. Ye attended Xiamen University in the southern part of China and earned a BA degree in British Literature. After graduation, Mr. Ye joined CITIC and worked for the firm for about six years both in Beijing and overseas assignments in Kuwait, United Arab Emirate and Hong Kong. Mr. Ye immigrated to US in 1989 and worked for an Option Trading firm at Chicago Mercantile Exchange for two and a half years.

Carolyn Scott Younker received a Master of International Management degree from the American Graduate School of International Management in 1991. Before attending Thunderbird, Carolyn was the co-founding partner at Orion Pay Phones in San Diego, California. Born and raised in San Diego, she graduated from San Diego State University with a Bachelor of Science in Business Administration/Management and a minor in French. Her professional experience includes small business start-up, telecommunications, finance and real estate.

John M. Zerio, Ph.D., is an associate professor of international marketing in the World Business Department of the American Graduate School of International Management in Glendale, Arizona since 1986. He came to Thunderbird from Syracuse University where he received his Ph.D. in export marketing after having received his M.A. from The Johns Hopkins University of Advanced International Studies in 1982. In Brazil he earned an M.B.A. in marketing from Fundacao Getulio Vargas. At Thunderbird Dr. Zerio's major areas of teaching and research are: international business-to-business marketing, export strategy, and the corporate consulting program. He has consulted with domestic and foreign multinational corporations in Brazil, Japan and Mexico, and taught at universities in Brazil. Dr. Zerio has been a Distinguished Visiting Professor of Marketing at the Instituto Technologico de Monterrey, Mexico.

Index